Flyfisher's Guide to™
MICHIGAN

Titles Available in This Series

Flyfisher's Guide to™

MICHIGAN

Jim Bedford

Wilderness
Adventures
Press™

Belgrade, Montana

This book was made with an easy opening, lay flat binding.

© 1999 Jim Bedford

Cover Photograph © 1999 Jim Bedford
Photographs contained herein © 1999 Jim Bedford or as noted
Photos pages 450 and 451 © 2001 Chris Suydam
Fish description artwork © 1999

Maps, book design and cover design © 1999 Wilderness Adventures Press, Inc.
Flyfisher's Guide to™

Published by Wilderness Adventures Press
45 Buckskin Road
Belgrade, MT 59714
800-925-3339
Website: www.wildadv.com
email: books@wildadv.com

Printed in the United States of America

Library of Congress Cataloging-in-Publication Data

Bedford, Jim.
    Flyfisher's guide to Michigan / Jim Bedford.
        p. cm.
    Includes index.
    ISBN 1-885106-76-9
    1. Fly Fishing—Michigan—Guidebooks.   2. Michigan—Guidebooks.   I. Title.

SH509.B44 2000
799.1'24'09774—dc21

                                                                                99-088741

Table of Contents

Acknowledgments

Many, many people have helped me with this book. I am not going to try to name them all as I would probably leave some out. Two groups of people were especially helpful.

First were the personnel in the Fisheries Division of Michigan's Department of Natural Resources. This is a very professional group of biologists and others who sincerely want to help you enjoy fishing in Michigan and enhance your success. Dell Siler from the Upper Peninsula, Tom Rozich from the northern Lower Peninsula, Jim Dexter from southwest Michigan, and Todd Grischke of the Lansing office were especially helpful.

Fly shop owners, guides, and tackle representatives were all very helpful and patient with my questions. They also want you to be successful and will help you in any way they can so that you have a fine experience on Michigan waters. Tony Paglei, a warmwater fishing guide and professional fly tier, Dennis Dann, a manufacturer's representative, and Pete Schantz, a shop owner, helped me with my flyfishing questions and frequently fished with me over the past year.

To all others that helped and answered questions, I am no less grateful to you. Finally, I really appreciate the opportunity that Chuck and Blanche Johnson gave me and the help and guidance that Darren Brown of their staff provided as I put this large volume together. Thanks also to those who will read this book—don't forget to release most of your catch.

Jim Bedford

Introduction

I have probably been a river rat since I was 10 years old. My love for river fishing was really reinforced in college when I started wading streams in earnest. First it was for smallmouth bass and northern pike but soon the trout and steelhead bug bit me. When I finished my schooling, I found it hard to look for a job away from Michigan and luckily found employment in what had become my home state.

Many fishing trips have taken me to the Pacific Northwest, British Columbia, Alaska, and Montana. Spectacular fishing for trout and/or salmon and steelhead is present in each of these locales. However, I believe it is hard to beat Michigan for year-round fishing for both anadromous and resident salmonids. Add the great opportunities for bass, pike, walleyes, and panfish to this excellent coldwater fishing and you can see why it's not easy to top Michigan as a venue for wetting a line.

Some of my first trout were caught fishing the brown drake hatch in southern Michigan. A parachute Adams probably did not match the hatch very well but the fly was easy to see and enough brown trout inhaled it to keep it my first choice. Most of the trout creeks close to my home in southern Michigan are way too brushy to flyfish. Thus, much of my trout fishing has been with ultralight spinning tackle and spinners and other small lures. A fly reel was packed in my vest so I could switch when a good hatch started, but my casting with a rod that was not well matched left something to be desired.

Since much of my "angling background" is with spinning tackle, you're probably wondering how I came to write this book. Well, a flyfishing friend, Eric Palo, and his friend, Kelly Galloup, owner of the Troutsman in Traverse City, convinced Chuck and Blanche to talk to me about the project. Apparently they were impressed enough with my knowledge of the waters, the fish and fishing in Michigan, and the fact that I spent close to 1,000 hours a year in my waders to give me the go ahead.

This project coincided with my retirement from my "day job" and was the perfect excuse to do a lot more flyfishing. I've really enjoyed traveling the state and finding out what was around a whole bunch of new bends.

Michigan Major Roads and Rivers

© Wilderness Adventures Press

Michigan Facts

Nickname	Wolverine State
Flower	Apple blossom
Bird	Robin
Mammal	White-tailed deer
Fishes	Trout, brook trout
Gem	Isle Royal Greenstone (Chlorastrolite)
Stone	Petoskey stone
Tree	White pine
Reptile	Painted turtle
Wildflower	Dwarf Lake iris
Name Origin	From the Indian word meaning great or large lake
Area	56,809 sq. mi.
Rank	8
Highest point	Mount Arvon, 1979 feet
Lowest point	Lake Erie, 571 feet
Capital	Lansing
Counties	83
Population	9,594,350
State Parks	96 (265,000 acres)
State Forests	6
State Game Lands	61

Tips on Using This Book

Luckily for anglers, Michigan is a very wet state. Surrounded by the Great Lakes, it has more coastline than any state except Alaska. There are more than 38,000 miles of streams, all of which eventually send their water to the Great Lakes. Trout live in about one-third of these stream miles, and 868 miles are considered premier quality trout waters and classified as Blue Ribbon Trout Streams. The following criteria must be met to be a Blue Ribbon Trout Stream: It must be one of Michigan's best trout streams; be able to support excellent stocks of wild resident trout; have the physical characteristics to permit fly casting but be shallow enough to wade; produce diverse insect life and good fly hatches; have earned a reputation for providing an excellent (quality) trout fishing experience; and have excellent water quality.

Thus, by definition, Blue Ribbon streams are flyfishable. Rather arbitrarily, I've tried to note the approximate upstream limit for "comfortable" flycasting throughout this guide. Such a determination is very subjective to each angler, and even some of the Blue Ribbon water may not be roomy enough for everyone. Conversely, smaller, brushier water may be fine for other anglers, and while the stream reach may not often be flyfishable throughout, there will be sections that open up in meadows or mature forests. There is seldom a problem with casting room in warmwater rivers. However, no matter how big the river, you will need to keep the roll cast in your repertoire because fish are often near the well-vegetated banks.

Michigan has over 11,000 inland lakes for anglers who prefer stillwaters. The vast majority of these contain warmwater fish, but there are also plenty that are home to trout. Emphasis is given to trout lakes because bass and bluegill lakes are so ubiquitous. While it is hard to think of the Great Lakes as stillwaters, their shorelines also offer many flyfishing opportunities.

In listing information on restaurants and motels for the hub cities, national chains were, for the most part, not included. This is because most of the larger towns and cities have a good selection of them. In addition, many of the chains have 800 numbers, so you can find out if the ones you are looking for are located near the rivers or lakes you will be fishing.

Insect populations are fairly similar in the various rivers of Michigan. Hatch times vary pretty much by latitude, as you will note in the hatch charts. Weather can play a big role, and it is important to check ahead to find out if the hatches are on schedule or how much they have been altered. The rivers in the Upper Peninsula seem to be more affected by weather than in the Lower Peninsula, and thus, hatches can "catch up" to the northern Lower Peninsula when summer temperatures are warm. Likewise, they'll fall further behind when it is cold. Whenever there is no apparent hatch, crayfish pattern streamers are great "searching flies," and attractor patterns work on fish other than brook trout.

Michigan is divided into six sections for this guide. The Upper Peninsula is split into western and eastern divisions. The Lower Peninsula is split north and south as well as east and west, creating four areas that are approximately equal in size.

The goal of this guide is to give you an idea of what the bodies of water are like and what fish will probably be present. It will not tell you exactly where to fish or what rock or log to cast to; nor is every river or reach described. Rather, it is designed to help you in your exploration of Michigan's bountiful fishing waters. Enjoy.

Michigan Fishing Regulations

The Michigan Department of Natural Resources publishes the "Michigan Fishing Guide" each year. This guide is provided to everyone who purchases a fishing license. While its primary purpose is to provide a summary of Michigan's fishing regulations, it also has a lot of additional information about our fish and fishing.

As this book is being written, Michigan is in the process of developing new regulations for coldwater species. The new regulations will be in place for the 2000 angling year, starting April 1. Classifying all of Michigan's trout streams and lakes is a major part of the revision. Regulations will be tailored to productivity, water quality, and the trout growth potential of each body of water. In general, the new regulations are being implemented to provide better quality fishing through higher size limits and reduced harvest.

Streams and lakes with special regulations are noted in this book. New special regulations will also take effect on April 1, 2000. There is a chance that some of the regulations may be modified slightly by the time this is published or in future years. Because of this, it is very important to consult the "Michigan Fishing Guide" when fishing in the Great Lake State.

Michigan is also trying to introduce legislation that will allow management of more streams with special quality regulations, such as "fly only," "no kill," etc. Currently, there is a 100-mile limit for streams having special regulations, and this quota is full. If legislation is successful, many more streams will be designated for special regulations, and this should improve the already fine fishing the state has to offer.

To obtain more information via the internet, go to the Michigan Department of Natural Resources site: www.dnr.state.mi.us. There is a wealth of information available, including a listing of all the designated trout streams (listed under the Fishing heading at the left of the screen by going to Fishing Publications and then selecting DFI 101—Designated Trout Streams). Information can also be requested by writing to the Fisheries Division, MDNR, Box 30446, Lansing, MI 48909.

Western Upper Peninsula

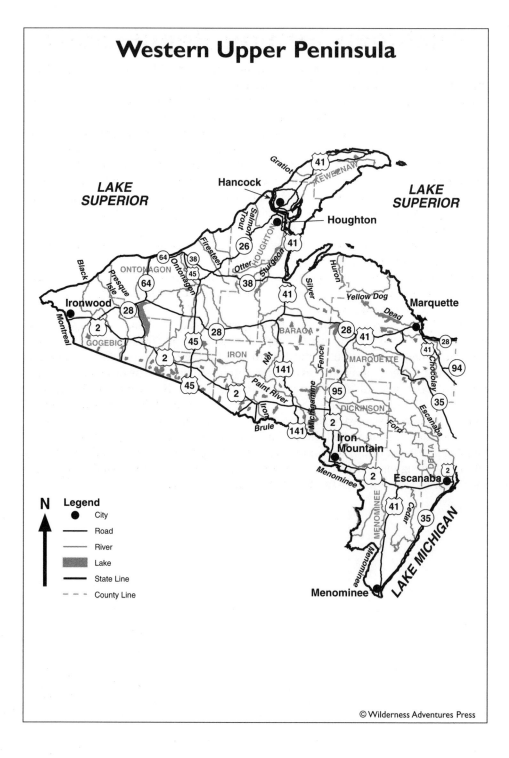

LAKE
SUPERIOR

LAKE
SUPERIOR

Hancock

Houghton

Marquette

Ironwood

Iron
Mountain

Escanaba

Menominee

N

Legend
● City
— Road
— River
▧ Lake
— State Line
- - - County Line

© Wilderness Adventures Press

Western Upper Peninsula

If there is a last frontier for fly anglers in the eastern United States, Michigan's Upper Peninsula is probably it. In the western part, streams flow north in to Lake Superior and south in to Lake Michigan. Their banks are relatively undeveloped, and on some you can fish all day without seeing any sign of people.

Brook trout are found in most of these rivers and creeks, but there are good fisheries for brown trout, steelhead, and warmwater species as well. Compared to Lower Peninsula rivers, these streams are lightly fished, especially after the trout season has been open for awhile. The majority of the streams are freestones, and many are highly stained with tannins. Most of the Lake Superior tributaries have high gradients, and waterfalls and bedrock rapids abound. Despite the northern latitude, many trout waters can become too warm for trout during hot, dry periods, forcing fish to move to and concentrate in cooler reaches and small springfed tributaries.

MONTREAL RIVER

The East Fork and the mainstream of the Montreal River divide Michigan from Wisconsin in the far western Upper Peninsula. The East Fork becomes the border where Layman's Creek joins it about 10 miles south of Ironwood. Upstream from Ironwood, the river is kind of tight for flyfishing, but there are open areas and good access at Norrie Park and upstream along an abandoned railway that parallels the river on the Wisconsin side. Both browns and brookies are present but tend to run on the small side in this freestone stream.

Downstream from Ironwood, the river increases in size and so do the trout, especially below Peterson Falls. The reach between these falls and the confluence with the West Fork provides some of the best trout fishing. Because the West Fork is impounded in Wisconsin, it is a warmwater stream when it joins the East Fork. This makes the mainstream marginal for trout, and you are likely to find some northern pike and smallmouth bass mixed in with the browns and brookies.

There are two waterfalls on the mainstream with a dam just above each of them. The impoundment of Saxon Falls warms the river further, resulting in mostly a warmwater fishery below it. In addition to the usual bass, pike, and panfish mix, muskies are sometimes encountered in the river.

Anyone who thinks Michigan is a flat state should visit the lower Montreal. In addition to its three falls, the river has cut a 200-foot-deep gorge in the Lake Superior Escarpment that continues for about 2 miles and is called the Montreal Canyon. Below Superior Falls, a drop of 45 feet, a modest run of steelhead provides a spring fishery. The peak of the run is usually in early May, and a few lake-run browns and brook trout might also be encountered as they chase spawning smelt.

A very nice brown trout.

Montreal River

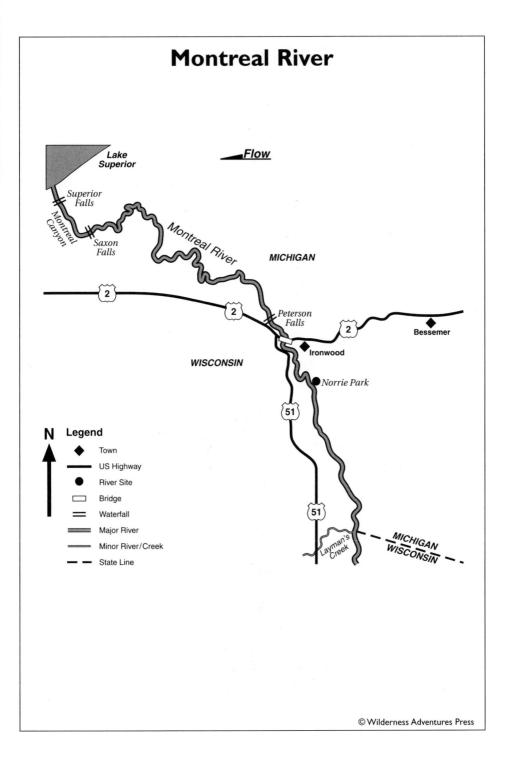

Lake Superior

Flow

Superior Falls

Montreal Canyon

Saxon Falls

Montreal River

MICHIGAN

2

2

Peterson Falls

2

Bessemer

Ironwood

WISCONSIN

51

Norrie Park

N

Legend

◆ Town
— US Highway
● River Site
▭ Bridge
═ Waterfall
▬ Major River
▬ Minor River/Creek
‐ ‐ State Line

51

Layman's Creek

MICHIGAN

WISCONSIN

© Wilderness Adventures Press

Black River

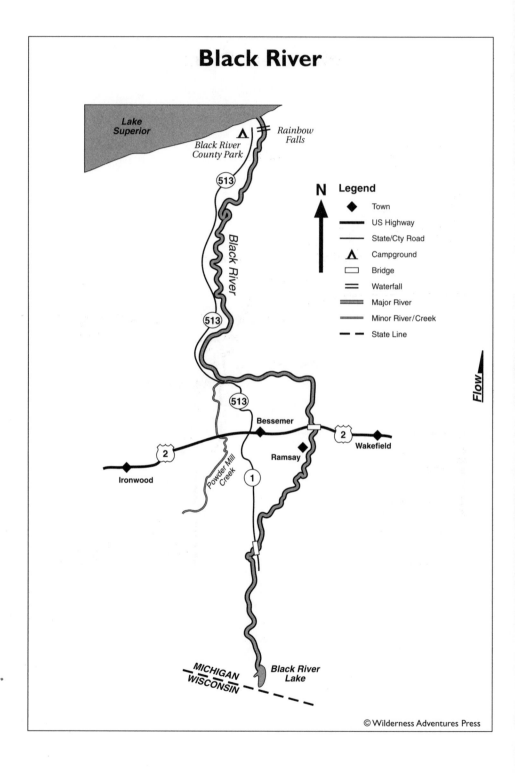

Lake Superior

Black River County Park

Rainbow Falls

513

Black River

N

Legend

◆ Town

─── US Highway

─── State/Cty Road

Λ Campground

▱ Bridge

═ Waterfall

▬ Major River

─── Minor River/Creek

─ ─ State Line

513

Flow

513

Bessemer

2

2

Wakefield

Ironwood

Ramsay

Powder Mill Creek

1

MICHIGAN
WISCONSIN

Black River Lake

© Wilderness Adventures Press

Water flows are a key to success on the Montreal throughout the year. High water in the spring can hinder fishing, and summer dry spells can really shrink the river and make fishing difficult. Timing your trip well after snowmelt occurs in the spring and when rainfall has been plentiful in the summer will pay dividends.

BLACK RIVER

Michigan's Lake Superior Black River begins near the headwaters of the East Fork of the Montreal. Like the East Fork, it starts in Wisconsin and is soon dammed to form Black River Lake. Because of this impoundment and the swampy, flat nature of this area, the Black begins as a warmwater stream. As the river increases in size, the water slowly gets cooler and the gradient increases.

You can gain access to the Black River from two bridges in the town of Ramsay and along US 2. Downstream from Ramsay, the fishing improves, with both browns and brookies present. But, the now rocky substrate requires careful wading, and a wading staff is recommended. About 7 miles downstream from Ramsay, Powder Mill Creek flows into the Black, further cooling the mainstream. This creek has a good brook trout population, and its lower reaches can be flyfished.

Below Powder Mill Creek, the Black really starts to tumble down to Lake Superior. There are seven named waterfalls between here and the big lake. County Road 513 parallels the river and provides access to those who want to hike in and view the various falls and fish the pools.

Rainbow Falls is the last cascade, and below it the river soon reaches the level of Lake Superior, resulting in a slow, deep channel. Some large resident rainbows can be caught here, and in the spring, the river gets a run of steelhead. In the fall, there is a run of chinook, as well as a few steelhead and coho. A county park and a national forest campground provide good access to the lower river and Lake Superior.

PRESQUE ISLE RIVER

The Presque Isle River begins as three branches, all originating near the Michigan/Wisconsin line. While each begins as a warmwater stream, the East Branch soon cools enough to support a good population of brook trout. The fishing is best in the spring between the juncture with the other two branches and County Road 525, west of Pomeroy Lake. Most of the brookies are in the 8- to 10-inch range, but some large trout are possible. The East Branch brook trout share the stream with creek chubs, and streamers imitating chubs will entice the larger brookies in the deep holes.

Springs downstream from Marenisco cool the river enough that good numbers of brook trout are present. In fact, in the heat of the summer, brook trout actually migrate downstream to this reach. While the migration of brook trout to cooler waters is a common phenomenon in the western Upper Peninsula, trout usually move upstream, not down, to find colder environs. Because trout in the relatively sterile mainstream grow slowly, this migration actually moves larger trout into this reach from the East Branch.

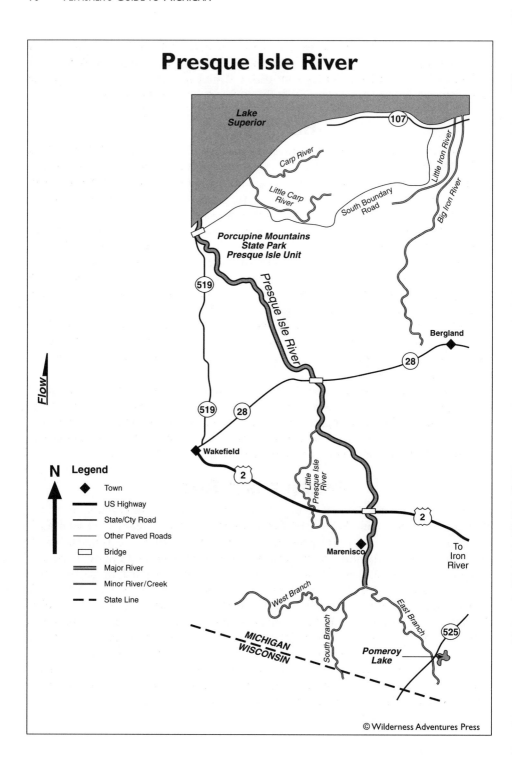

Presque Isle River

Lake Superior

Carp River

Little Carp River

South Boundary Road

Little Iron River

Big Iron River

107

Porcupine Mountains State Park Presque Isle Unit

519

Presque Isle River

Bergland

28

Flow

519

28

Wakefield

2

Little Presque Isle River

2

To Iron River

N

Legend

◆ Town

▬ US Highway

— State/Cty Road

— Other Paved Roads

▭ Bridge

▬ Major River

▬ Minor River/Creek

- - - State Line

Marenisco

West Branch

East Branch

525

MICHIGAN
WISCONSIN

South Branch

Pomeroy Lake

© Wilderness Adventures Press

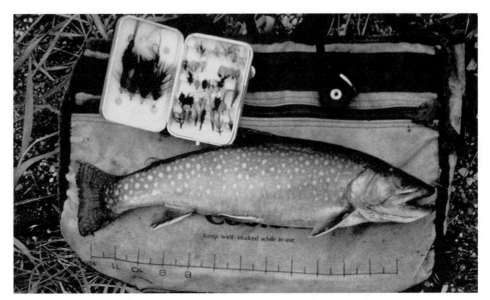

This brook trout is a nice size at 14 inches.

Brook trout continue to be present in the lower Presque Isle. The river really drops fast below M-28, and there are lots of falls and rapids, making it difficult to wade or navigate with a drift boat or raft. It is generally considered too dangerous for canoes, although some try at certain water levels. In addition, the hike in is tough. In short, the river demands a lot of work to catch trout on the small side, but the scenery is fantastic.

The last 5 miles or so of the Presque Isle flow through the Porcupine Mountain Wilderness State Park, where there is a campground at its mouth. Anadromous fish are stymied by falls within sight of Lake Superior, but you can still catch steelhead and the occasional salmon in this short stretch. Nonmigratory rainbows are also planted at the mouth and provide a good fishery.

A number of relatively small rivers flow into Lake Superior in and on the north side of the Porcupine Mountains State Park. The Little and Big Carp Rivers are within the park and offer wilderness fishing for small brook trout and steelhead up to the first barrier falls. The Little Carp is more accessible, but fishing both streams will mean some exercise. Hiking trails parallel most of this small river, and when the trail does leave the stream, you can fish these loops until the trail comes back near the river. North of the park, the slightly larger Big Iron and Little Iron offer similar angling opportunities to those who want to get away from it all.

Chinook salmon are planted in the Big Iron and run the lower river in the fall, and some steelhead run both the Big and Little Iron. Most of the Big Iron and its West Branch are open during the extended season from April 1 to December 31, while the Little Iron is open up to Nonesuch Falls.

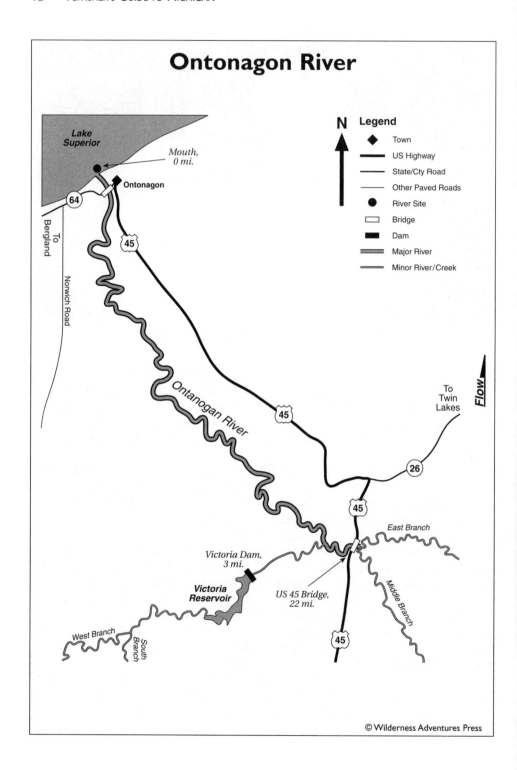

Ontonagon River

Lake
Superior

Mouth,
0 mi.

Ontonagon

To
Bergland

Norwich Road

64

45

Ontanogan River

45

Victoria Dam,
3 mi.

Victoria
Reservoir

US 45 Bridge,
22 mi.

West Branch

South
Branch

45

N

Legend

◆ Town
━━ US Highway
── State/Cty Road
── Other Paved Roads
● River Site
▭ Bridge
■ Dam
━━ Major River
━━ Minor River/Creek

To
Twin
Lakes

Flow

26

45

East Branch

Middle Branch

© Wilderness Adventures Press

ONTONAGON RIVER

The Ontonagon River is the Au Sable of the western Upper Peninsula. While the mainstream is relatively short and too turbid for flyfishing as it nears Lake Superior, its four major branches provide a wide variety of flyfishing opportunities. Natural red clay is the culprit, but the steelhead and chinook salmon seem to have no problem navigating the nearly opaque water.

The West Branch of the Ontonagon is the outlet of the very large Lake Gogebic, a popular walleye and perch fishery. It remains a warmwater stream all the way to its confluence with the East Branch to form the mainstream. Cascade Creek, a major tributary, contains brook trout, and in the spring, you might find some brookies in the West Branch near the confluence. Otherwise, this branch is home to a mixed bag of smallmouth bass, northern pike, and walleyes. Lake Gogebic is one of the Upper Peninsula's best walleye lakes and can contribute some marble eyes to the river. Streamers in flashy patterns are good bets for all three predator species. Access is somewhat limited, with only two road crossings at Norwich and M-28 just below Lake Gogebic.

The South Branch of the Ontonagon, which joins the West Branch at the head of the Victoria Dam backwater, is also a warmwater stream for most of its length. Upstream from its tributary, Ten Mile Creek, the South Branch is called the Cisco Branch, and it is

*A brookie caught
at Bond Falls.*

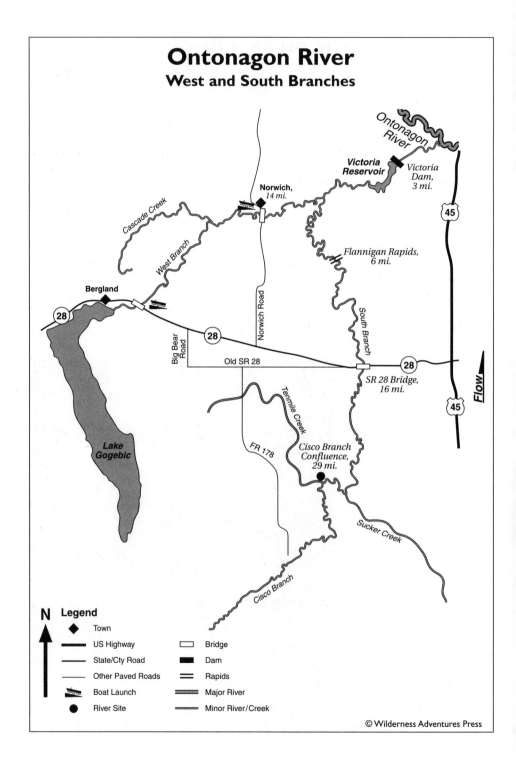

Ontonagon River
West and South Branches

*The East Branch
of the Ontonagon
after moisture has caused
it to become muddy.*

here that you can catch some brook trout in the spring. Bridges on US Forest Service Roads 178 and 182 provide access on the upper part of this branch. In July and August, brookies move into cold tributaries. Smallmouth bass are the primary game fish species in the South Branch downstream from the 18 Mile Rapids. Brookies from small tributary creeks may surprise you at any time when fishing in the spring.

Beginning as the outlet of Crooked Lake in eastern Gogebic County, the Middle Branch of the Ontonagon soon cools to become a fine trout stream. About 3 miles upstream from Watersmeet, the river becomes classified as a blue Ribbon trout stream, retaining this status down to the Ontonagon County Line. Browns, brookies, and rainbows are found in this reach, offering the angler a chance at an Upper Peninsula "triple double," or three species of trout greater than 10 inches in length. Tag alders can limit casting room at times, but you can both float and wade this water.

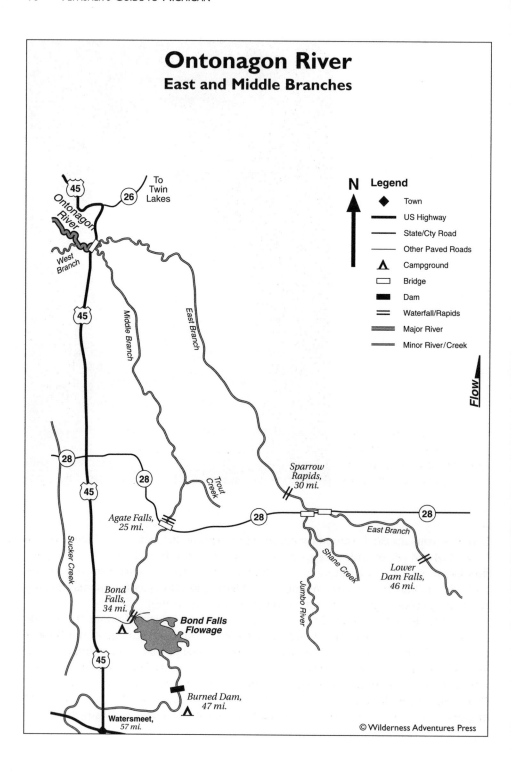

Ontonagon River
East and Middle Branches

N

Legend

◆ Town

▬ US Highway

── State/Cty Road

── Other Paved Roads

Λ Campground

▭ Bridge

▬ Dam

☰ Waterfall/Rapids

▬ Major River

── Minor River/Creek

45

26 To Twin Lakes

Ontonagon River

West Branch

45

Middle Branch

East Branch

Flow

28

28

Trout Creek

Sparrow Rapids, 30 mi.

Agate Falls, 25 mi.

45

28

East Branch

28

Shane Creek

Lower Dam Falls, 46 mi.

Sucker Creek

Jumbo River

Bond Falls, 34 mi.

Bond Falls Flowage

Λ

45

Burned Dam, 47 mi.

Λ

Watersmeet, 57 mi.

© Wilderness Adventures Press

Bond Falls, located on the Middle Branch of the Ontonagon, in the rain.

Excellent access is provided by County Road 208 and an old railroad grade. Both parallel the river. This allows you to fish as long a stretch as you want and then have a very easy walk back to your vehicle. Because of the fine trout population and accessibility, this stretch of the Middle Branch is popular with anglers. Nymphs and small streamers in a wide variety of patterns will tempt the trout here. Because of the fishing pressure, a stealthy upstream approach and a fly drifted close to the cover will pay off in lots of hookups. There is a campground (Burned Dam) just below a falls at the lower end of the blue ribbon water. As the river nears Bond Falls Flowage, it starts to warm, and smallmouth bass intermingle with trout. Walleyes and northern pike might also move from the impoundment up into the river.

A deepwater draw out of the Bond Falls Flowage results in a cooler river and another stretch of prime trout water down to M-28. While the cold water helps trout fishing, there have been problems getting an adequate release of water below this dam. About half of the river is diverted to Sucker Creek, which flows to the South Branch. There is no doubt in my mind that this water's fishing would improve if allowed to stay with the Middle Branch. While we have run-of-the-river flow out of many dams in Michigan, some still have release schedules that result in daily or seasonal cycles of drought flows and floods.

There is excellent access at Bond Falls, where there is a very scenic vista. Brook trout crowd the base of the falls and hit Royal Trudes and Coachmen with abandon. You can work your way downstream hopping rocks as far as your ambition will take

Middle Branch of the Ontonagon River.

you. I like to go far enough that I can fish my way back to brookies that have forgotten I've already passed through.

Just below M-28, Agate Falls blocks the upstream migration of steelhead and salmon. The best flyfishing for the anadromous fish occurs in the first few miles below the falls as the river slowly picks up more turbidity, especially below the incoming Trout Creek. The best steelheading occurs in the spring, with early May the peak time. There is also a fall run along with brown trout and a few chinook salmon. Resident brook trout continue to be present in the steelhead water.

Beaver dams and small lake outlets keep the East Branch's headwaters a bit warm for good brook trout numbers. But good trout fishing begins below Lower Dam Falls and continues to Sparrow Rapids. In fact, the trout are above the average size for most trout in western Upper Peninsula streams, with browns approaching 20 inches and brookies in the low teens. Some juvenile steelhead that have reverted to being resident rainbows make this a stream also capable of producing a triple double for you. Tag alders keep the casting room a bit tight, but lots of woody cover and deep bend holes provide good habitat.

While there is a campground at each end of this prime trout reach, access is a bit spotty with only two road crossings. There is walk-in access on National Forest land from USFS Road 207, downstream from M-28. A plus is that the tougher access results in less fishing pressure. The ambitious streamer angler can fish the reach from the campground at Sparrow Rapids up to the confluence with Jumbo River and really have a good time with sizable browns and brookies. Trout continue to be present downstream from Sparrow Rapids, but it becomes even harder to reach the river. This means that for those willing to hike, some unmolested browns and brookies can be found. Eventually the East Branch becomes turbid due to natural clay in its drainage.

Steelhead run the East Branch in the spring, and the river is open up to M-28 from April 1 until December 31. A tributary, the Jumbo River, which joins the East Branch just downstream of M-28, is also open during the extended season and hosts a good steelhead run. The Jumbo's upstream limit is a falls located about 3 miles south of M-28. Having the Jumbo close at hand provides an alternative when fish aren't found in the East Branch or it is too high and turbid for fishing. The lower Jumbo also offers good trout fishing in the summer for brookies and juvenile steelhead. It is easy to read, and wade and attractor patterns work well. Up until early June of most years, there will still be steelhead lingering in both the East Branch and Jumbo. Hooking a Lake Superior rainbow on trout gear will provide a thrill you won't soon forget. The same bright colored streamers that get the big brook trout's attention will also entice a take from a steelhead.

Stream Facts: Ontonagon River

Seasons
- Mainstream open all year.
- East, Middle, and West Branches open all year to designated upstream limits.
- Bass must be released between January 1 and the Saturday before Memorial Day.
- Walleyes and northern pike must be released between March 15 and the last Saturday in April.

Special Regulations
- Size limit for all trout and salmon between October 1 and last Saturday in April is 16 inches.

Fish
- Smallmouth bass, walleyes, panfish, brown trout, brook trout, rainbow trout, and steelhead.

River Miles
- Lake Superior—0
- West and East Branch Confluence—22
- West Branch: Mouth—0
- Victoria Dam—3
- Norwich—14

South Branch
- West Branch—0
- Flannigan Rapids—6
- M-28—16
- Cisco Branch—29

Middle Branch
- East Branch—0
- M-28—25
- Bond Falls—34
- Burned Dam—47
- Watersmeet—57

East Branch
- Mouth—0
- Sparrow Rapids—30
- M-28—36
- Lower Dam—46

River Characteristics
- Wide range of habitat in the four branches of the Ontonagon.
- In most cases the upper reaches provide a mixture of bedrock rapids, gravel riffles, and meandering sandy reaches with deep bends and log holes.
- The lower river becomes too turbid for flyfishing most of the time due to natural red clay in the system.

River Access
- Access is available at each landmark except Flannigan Rapids (noted above with river miles).
- Much of the river is relatively remote—you can hike in or use two tracks on national forest land.

ONTONAGON RIVER MAJOR HATCHES

Insect	Jan	Feb	Mar	Apr	May	Jun	July	Aug	Sep	Oct	Nov	Dec	Time	Fly Patterns
Hendrickson					X								M/A	Hendrickson #12–14; Quill Gordon; Red Quill; Adams
Blue-winged Olive					X	X	X	X					A	Blue-winged Olive #18–20; Sparkle Dun Baetis; Iron Dun; Olive CDC Mayfly Dun
Little Black Caddis				X	X	X	X	X					A	Little Black Caddis #16–18; Griffith's Gnat; CDC Emerging Caddis Brown; Black Ant
Grannom				X	X	X	X						M/A	Grannom #14–16; Medium Brown Sedge; Elk Caddis Brown-olive
Net-building Caddis					X	X	X	X	X	X			M/A	Spotted Sedge #16–18; Eastern Elk Wing Caddis; Goddard Caddis
Sulphur Dun							X						A/E	Sulphur Dun #16; Pale Morning Dun; CDC Comparadun Yellow; Pale Evening Dun
March Brown						X	X						M/A	March Brown #12–14; Dark Cahill; Gray Fox; Ginger Quill
Gray Drake						X	X						E	Gray Drake #12–14; Gray Adams
Brown Drake						X	X						E	Brown Drake #10–12; Adams; CDC Brown Drake
Hexagenia						X	X						E	Hex #4–8; Great Olive-winged Drake; Spring's Wiggler; Hare's Ear
Trico							X	X	X	X			M	Tiny White Wing Black #24–28; Parachute Adams; CDC Trico; Spent Wing Trico
White Fly									X				E	White Fly #12–14; White Miller
Streamers	X	X	X	X	X	X	X	X	X	X	X	X	M/A/E	Woolly Buggers #6–12; Clouser's Minnow; Muddler Minnows; BC Craw; Matukas
Terrestrials						X	X	X	X				M/A/E	Woolly Worm #8–12; BC Spider; Letort Cricket; Joe's Hopper #6–10; Dave's Hopper; Dropper Hopper

HATCH TIME CODE: M = morning; A = afternoon; E = evening.

Firesteel River

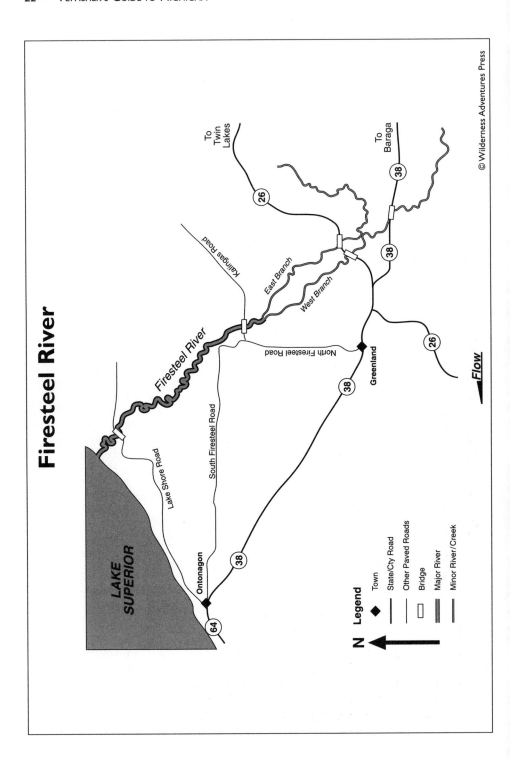

LAKE SUPERIOR

Firesteel River

Lake Shore Road

South Firesteel Road

North Firesteel Road

Kalingas Road

East Branch

West Branch

Ontonagon

Greenland

To Twin Lakes

To Baraga

64

38

38

38

38

26

26

Flow

© Wilderness Adventures Press

Legend

N

◆ Town

State/Cty Road

Other Paved Roads

☐ Bridge

Major River

Minor River/Creek

Firesteel River

The Firesteel River quickly flows through forested hills to Lake Superior about 8 miles northeast of Ontonagon. It is home to brook trout and hosts a spring run of wild steelhead. The Firesteel begins as two branches that parallel each other only a mile or two apart until they join north of M-26. Both branches can be navigated with a fly rod below M-26, and parts of each can be fished upstream from these bridges. But be prepared to do lots of roll casting. Despite the proximity of the two branches, the West Branch has more clay and can run muddy after a rain, while the East Branch can still be fishable. The Kalingas Road Bridge provides access to the mainstream about a mile downstream from the confluence of the two branches. There is a public easement along the river downstream for about half a mile, where it is possible to wade upstream to the confluence and then sample both branches before retreating to the bridge. North Firesteel and Lake Shore Roads provide additional access to the lower river.

While much of the steelhead fishing takes place in the mainstream, both branches up to M-26 are open during the extended season. Brown trout are planted at the mouth of the river, and some move into the river to spawn in the fall. Some steelhead and chinook and coho salmon may join them. Waiting until most of the snow has melted in the spring is the best plan for steelhead, as the river really rages at the peak of the runoff. Though it varies year to year, lots of bare ground is usually seen by early May. Conversely, good rains bring the steelhead, browns, and salmon into the river in the fall.

Salmon Trout River

It is probably stretching it a bit to call the Salmon Trout a river, but this diminutive stream has a good population of brook trout and hosts a spring steelhead run. It is open enough to cast with a fly rod below Obenoff Creek, and access is available where Obenoff Road deadends at the river. Two tracks offer additional access, and if 7- to 10-inch brook trout in a wild setting turn you on, this is the place.

Steelhead can only run the river to the Redridge Dam, less than a mile from Lake Superior. For this reason the DNR plants steelhead smolts here because there is little river available for natural reproduction. Because of the small size of this river and the settling effect of the impoundment, the Salmon Trout is likely to be in shape when nearby rivers are high and muddy. Spring is the best time for fishing, with the peak usually occurring in early to mid-May. Similar fishing is found in nearby Misery River and a number of other short streams that flow quickly to Lake Superior.

Gratiot River

Farther north in the Keweenaw Peninsula, the Gratiot River tumbles down to Lake Superior. It is home to wild brook trout with some hatchery supplementation of yearling trout. If you like pocket water where the trout have to make a quick decision, you will enjoy this stream. It is very fast, and a wading staff is recommended. It has a diverse population of aquatic insects, but attractor patterns in sizes 10 and 12 often work better than trying to match smaller naturals.

Salmon Trout River

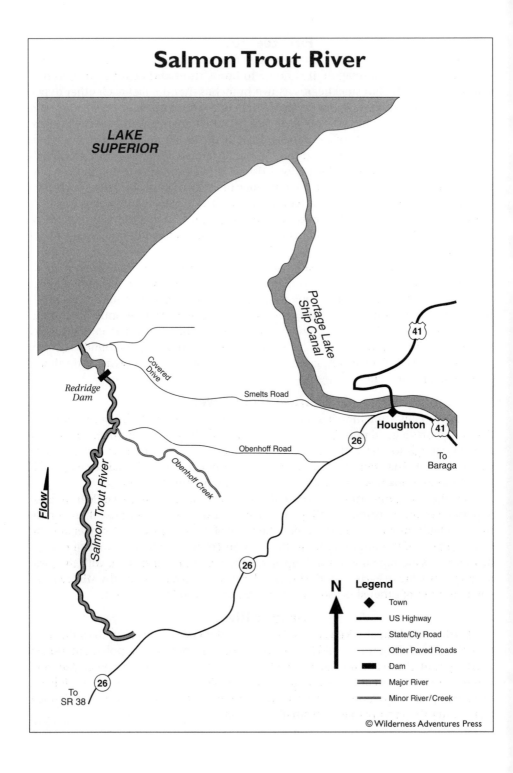

LAKE
SUPERIOR

Portage Lake
Ship Canal

41

Covered
Drive

Redridge
Dam

Smelts Road

Houghton   41

26

Obenhoff Road

To
Baraga

Obenhoff Creek

Salmon Trout River

Flow

26

26

To
SR 38

N

Legend

◆   Town

US Highway

State/Cty Road

Other Paved Roads

■   Dam

Major River

Minor River/Creek

© Wilderness Adventures Press

There is an extended season for steelhead on the Gratiot. It is open to the first bridge, but the steelhead are stopped by two falls near the mouth. Thus, the best fishing for steelhead is between Lake Superior and the first falls. There is an access road on the south side of the river that leads to the mouth. Just to the east, the Trap Rock River, which flows south into Torch Lake, offers fishing for resident brook trout. It also has a steelhead run.

Sturgeon River

Michigan's Lake Superior Sturgeon River begins as a brook trout stream in central Baraga County and flows west and then north into Keweenaw Bay via the Portage River. Wading the upper river is difficult because much of it is slow and deep. This fact, plus the relative lack of access sites, makes floating a good option. Brook trout fishing is best after spring runoff but before the heat of summer. The Sturgeon

Sturgeon River.

Sturgeon River
West Branch Confluence to Keweenaw Bay

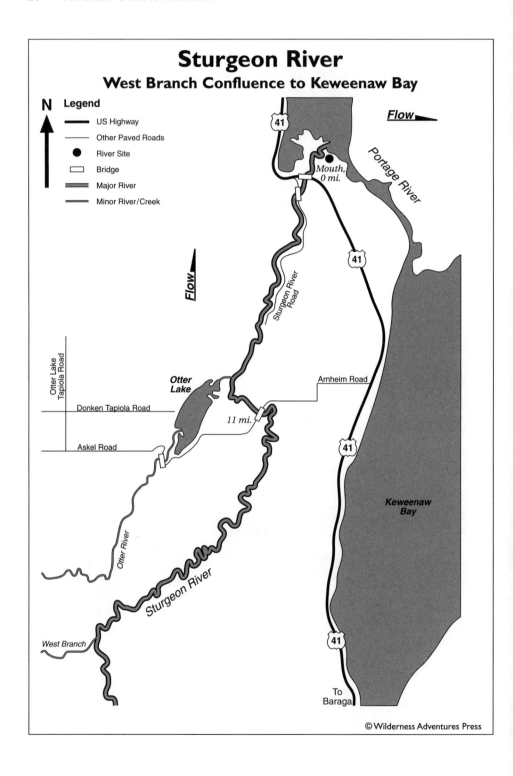

N

Legend

▬▬▬	US Highway
───	Other Paved Roads
●	River Site
▭	Bridge
▬▬	Major River
━━	Minor River/Creek

Flow

41

Flow

Portage River

Mouth, 0 mi.

41

Sturgeon River Road

Otter Lake Tapiola Road

Otter Lake

Arnheim Road

Donken Tapiola Road

11 mi.

Askel Road

41

Otter River

Keweenaw Bay

Sturgeon River

West Branch

41

To Baraga

© Wilderness Adventures Press

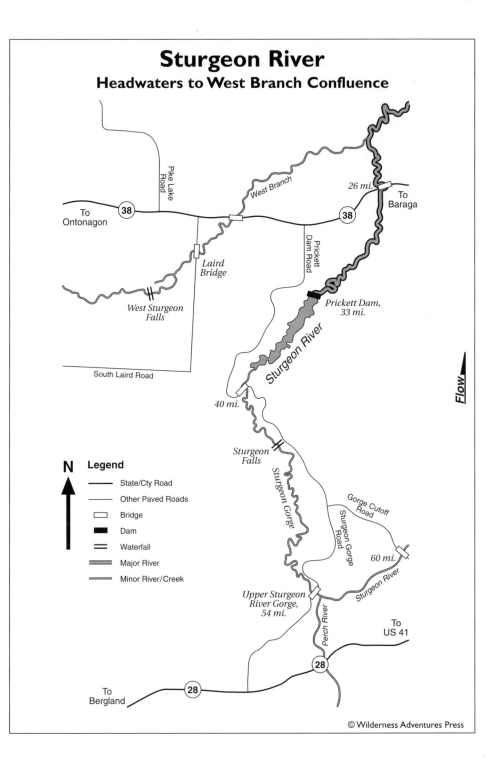

Sturgeon River
Headwaters to West Branch Confluence

Pike Lake Road

West Branch

26 mi.

To Baraga

To Ontonagon

38

38

Prickett Dam Road

Laird Bridge

West Sturgeon Falls

Prickett Dam, 33 mi.

Sturgeon River

South Laird Road

Flow

40 mi.

Sturgeon Falls

Legend

N

— State/Cty Road

— Other Paved Roads

☐ Bridge

■ Dam

= Waterfall

━ Major River

━ Minor River/Creek

Sturgeon Gorge

Gorge Cutoff Road

Sturgeon Gorge Road

60 mi.

Sturgeon River

Upper Sturgeon River Gorge, 54 mi.

Perch River

To US 41

28

28

To Bergland

© Wilderness Adventures Press

A smallmouth bass can create a lot of excitement for a fly angler.

becomes quite warm during hot spells, and brookies then migrate to colder water tributaries and springs.

Continuing downstream, the river continues to warm, and the predominant species become smallmouth and rock bass, walleye, and northern pike. While floating is still the best option, there are a number of falls that must be portaged. The water is quite stained so streamers with lots of white or bright colors help get the attention of the fish. The float between the two bridges on Sturgeon Gorge Road is a good one, but a portage is necessary around the gorge and falls. There will be a few brown and brook trout intermingled with the warmwater fish, but smallmouth bass are the primary catch. The Perch River joins the Sturgeon in this reach and has a reasonably good population of small brook trout. It is less likely to become muddy after a rain, so it can be a backup stream when the Sturgeon is out of shape.

Prickett Dam is the upstream barrier for steelhead and other anadromous fish. Brown trout are planted as yearlings at M-38, about 6 miles downstream from the dam, and some of these carry over. In addition to steelhead, some walleyes run the river in the spring, and brown trout and coho salmon enter the river in the fall. Good fall rains also put some steelhead in the river in October and November.

West Branch of the Sturgeon

The West Branch of the Sturgeon is easier to wade than the mainstream and offers better trout fishing. The best angling is found upstream from M-38, and the 5-mile reach between the West Sturgeon Falls and the highway is classified as blue ribbon trout water. Laird and Old Rink Road Bridges provide additional access in this reach.

Otter River

A fairly pristine river and the largest tributary of the Sturgeon, the Otter is home to a good population of brook trout. Most of the Otter is split into two main branches. The upper North Branch is quite brushy but opens up at Donken-Tapiola Road, where the gradient is good and gravel is the predominant substrate. Wild brook trout are augmented with plants of fingerling brookies. The fishing remains good down to the junction with the West Branch of the Otter River.

There is ample room for flyfishing beginning at Pike Lake Road on the West Branch. Brook trout are the main draw in this branch as well, but occasionally the offspring of steelhead and lake-run browns can be caught. The mainstream down to Otter Lake continues to hold brook trout, but they are not as numerous as in the branches. Wild steelhead provide a good spring fishery, and the mainstream is open during the extended season from April 1 to December 31. Below Otter Lake the river splits and flows into the Sturgeon in less than a mile.

Otter River

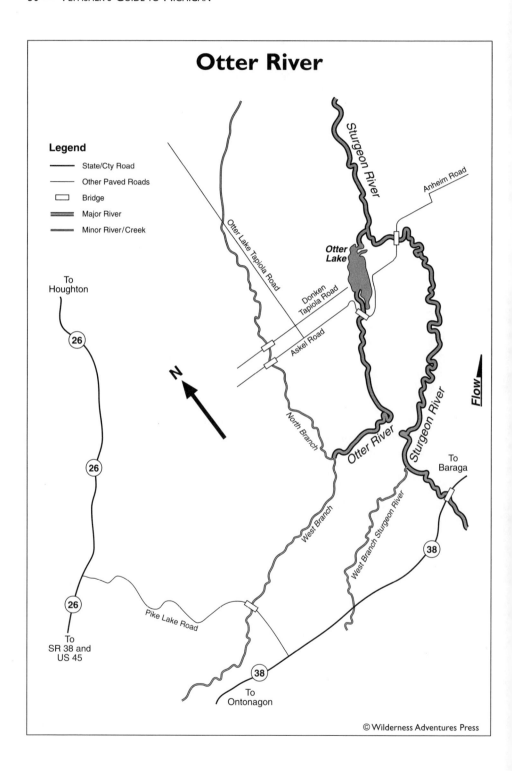

Legend

— State/Cty Road
— Other Paved Roads
▭ Bridge
━ Major River
━ Minor River/Creek

Sturgeon River

Anheim Road

Otter Lake

Otter Lake Tapiola Road

To Houghton

Donken Tapiola Road

Askel Road

N

North Branch

Otter River

Sturgeon River

Flow

To Baraga

West Branch

West Branch Sturgeon River

26

26

26

To SR 38 and US 45

Pike Lake Road

38

38

To Ontonagon

© Wilderness Adventures Press

Stream Facts: Sturgeon River

Seasons
- Open all year below Prickett Dam.
- Bass must be released between January 1 and the Saturday before Memorial Day. Walleyes and northern pike must be released between March 15 and last Saturday in April.

Special Regulations
- Size limit for trout and salmon below Prickett Dam between October 1 and last Saturday in April is 15 inches.

Fish
- Resident brook and brown trout, smallmouth and rock bass, walleye, and northern pike.
- Anadromous brown trout, steelhead, and salmon.

River Miles
- Portage River/Canal—0
- Arnheim Road—11
- M-38—26
- Prickett Dam—33
- Lower Sturgeon Gorge Road—40
- Upper Sturgeon Gorge Road—54
- Gorge Cutoff Road—60
- US 41—69

River Characteristics
- A river highly stained with tannins and quite variable in gradient.
- It ranges from slow, deep water to bedrock rapids and falls.

River Access
- Access is available at each landmark noted above with river miles.
- Additional road crossings provide access, but much of river is accessible only by trails and primitive roads that are seasonally impassable.

Silver River

The Silver River tumbles over a number of small waterfalls on its way to Huron Bay in Lake Superior. The last set of cascades is called Silver Falls, and unless there is exceptionally high water, it blocks the migration of steelhead and salmon. Despite the relatively limited amount of river available to anadromous fish, the Silver gets a modest run of steelhead each spring. Some coho and pink salmon enter this river in the fall.

Small brook trout are present in the upper river. Even though they only measure in the single digits because of fast water, they are fun to catch. They don't have much time to see a fly, so use bright, bushy attractor patterns.

On either side of the Silver, there are three other small tributaries to Lake Superior. To the west, the Falls River enters the lake at the town of L'Anse, and true to its name, has a barrier falls close to its mouth. On the other side, the Slate and Ravine Rivers also add their water to Huron Bay. All three rivers have resident brook trout and runs of wild steelhead. The Slate also has a barrier falls less than a mile from its mouth. Logically, these falls also serve as upstream limits for an extended season fishing. On the Ravine River, Sicotte Road is the upstream limit for the October through last Saturday in April extended season. You can easily try all four of these rivers in one day and only put 20 miles on your odometer. This is especially helpful in the spring when chasing steelhead, both for water conditions and the presence of fish.

A pretty stretch of the Silver River.

Silver River

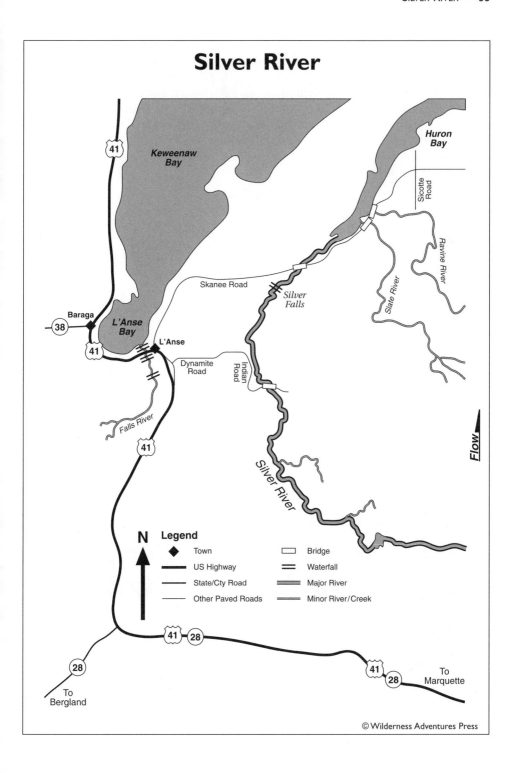

Huron Bay

Keweenaw Bay

41

Sicotte Road

Ravine River

Skanee Road

Slate River

Silver Falls

Baraga

38

L'Anse Bay

41

L'Anse

Dynamite Road

Indian Road

Flow

Falls River

41

Silver River

N

Legend

◆ Town

▬ US Highway

— State/Cty Road

— Other Paved Roads

▭ Bridge

▬ Waterfall

▬ Major River

▬ Minor River/Creek

41 — 28

28

To Bergland

41

28

To Marquette

Steve Koski of Indian Country Sports in L'Anse highly recommends the brookie fishing in these rivers, and he and his family chase them hard themselves. He related that when the area was trying to entice a flyfishing doctor from Montana to relocate in upper Michigan, it was his job to "hook her." At first she was disappointed that his store was not exclusively a fly shop. Steve explained that with the small Upper Peninsula population base, a sporting goods store had to cater to all anglers and hunters. Once he got her on a river that tumbled down to Lake Superior like the mountain streams she was used to and where there were no other anglers, she decided to take the job.

Huron River

Most of the Huron River flows along the eastern edge of Baraga County, but it tumbles into Lake Superior in Marquette County. The river is also called the Big Huron, although it is much smaller than its Lower Peninsula counterpart. The Huron begins as two branches that flow north, 2 to 3 miles apart, until they merge just upstream from Eric Road. There are barrier falls on each branch that halt the upstream migration of steelhead and salmon. Above the falls of both branches, brook trout are present but are relatively small in number and size. Although the West Branch probably has better numbers, both branches are fast, flashy, and relatively sterile.

Below the falls and in the mainstream, juvenile steelhead join the brook trout. Their presence signals the main fishery for the Huron, and that is steelhead. Wild steelhead are supplemented with annual plants of smolts, and the river is open all year below the Eric Road Bridge. While the main steelhead runs are in the spring, fall rains cause steelhead to move into the lower river. Modest runs of wild pink and coho salmon also occur, with the pinks running in September and the silvers in October. Egg flies and gaudy streamers get the attention of all three species. There is a campground at the Eric Road Bridge and additional access at the Huron Road Bridge. On the west side of the river, off of Huron Road, there is an unimproved road that runs to the river's mouth.

A steelhead that was hooked by a green butt skunk.

Huron River

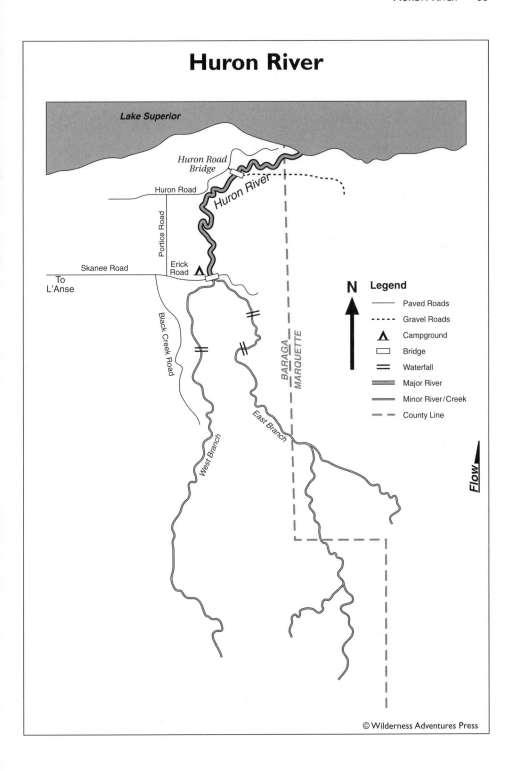

Lake Superior

Huron Road
Bridge

Huron Road

Huron River

Portice Road

Skanee Road

Erick
Road

To
L'Anse

Black Creek Road

BARAGA

MARQUETTE

West Branch

East Branch

N

Legend

——— Paved Roads

- - - - Gravel Roads

Λ Campground

☐ Bridge

≡ Waterfall

━━ Major River

─── Minor River/Creek

- - - County Line

Flow

© Wilderness Adventures Press

Yellow Dog River

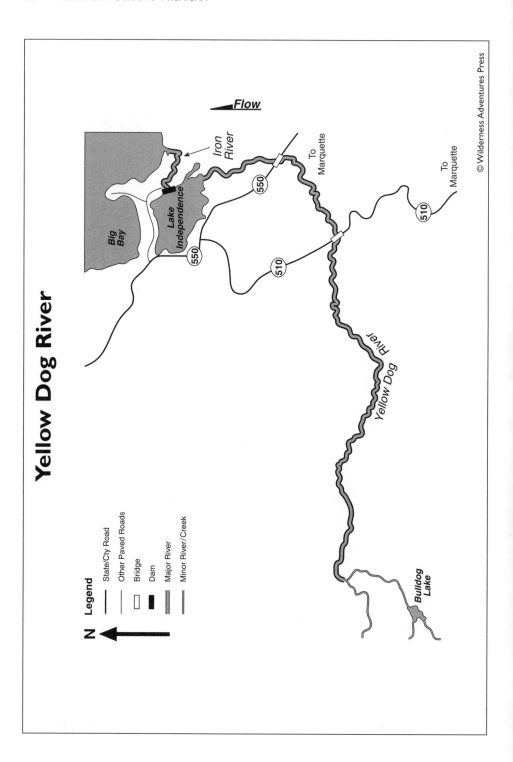

Thick cover crowds the banks of the Yellow Dog River.

Yellow Dog River

All three species of trout are found in the Yellow Dog River. It begins as the outlet of Bulldog Lake, and within a few miles the West Branch of the Yellow Dog adds its flow. Even though the stream is relatively small, there is room to cast a fly rod. Plan on making lots of roll casts because of the river's many nooks and crannies.

The upper river flows through a relatively flat area called Yellow Dog Plains; the upper river is deeper and slower than downstream. It is also one of the better reaches for larger fish. Overall, the river has a high gradient and a number of falls. While in general the trout are on the small side, 20-inch browns and double figure brookies are present. The entire stream is wadeable, and this is the preferred means of fishing it. Because of the logjams, falls, and other obstacles, floating would be more trouble than it is worth.

While some natural reproduction of all three species occurs, yearling trout are planted—brookies in the upper river and browns and rainbows in the lower half.

Wild brookies are present throughout the river. Access is somewhat limited because there are only three bridges over the stream. Several relatively primitive roads parallel the river in spots, and others deadend close to it.

The Yellow Dog River flows into Lake Independence, which has a dam at its outflow to Lake Superior, and thus there is no run of anadromous fish. The outlet stream is called the Iron River, and there was an attempt to establish a run of coastal brook trout in it. Occasional steelhead and coho salmon also run the river. Because of Lake Independence, the Iron is almost always fishable, so keep that in mind if rains cloud the Yellow Dog or other area streams.

Dead River

The Dead River approximately parallels the Yellow Dog and flows into Lake Superior just north of Marquette. When free flowing, the river has a high gradient, but dam builders have worked overtime on this small river causing almost half of it to be impounded. In spite of the power dams, the Dead River remains cool enough for trout along most of its length.

Silver Lake Basin is the uppermost impoundment on the Dead and gathers the waters of the mainstream, its south branch, and several creeks. It is heavily stocked with splake and is fishable from shore as well as from small boats and float tubes. Below the dam the Dead River is large enough to fish with fly rods, and while browns

An angler plies the waters of the Dead River.

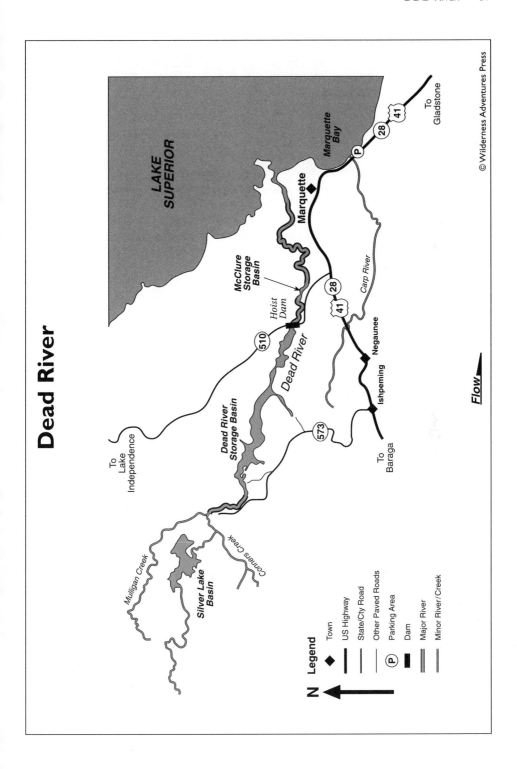

are found, brook trout is the principal species present. Two high quality tributaries, Mulligan and Connors Creeks, join the Dead and supply both cold water and some wild brookies. Gentle riffles alternate with pools for about 9 miles until the river enters the next impoundment.

The Hoist or Dead River Storage Basin is about 10 miles long and is home to mostly warmwater fish, such as walleyes and yellow perch, but there are some browns and brookies. A coldwater draw from the Hoist Dam results in a mini-tailwater fishery until the river becomes impounded again in the McClure Storage Basin. This short reach was damaged by a heavy load of sand when the dam partially collapsed, but much stream improvement has been done since the failure, and the river is heavily stocked with brown trout.

Some brown trout continue to be present in the lower Dead River even though the river's flow is interrupted two more times by dams. Below the Tourist Park Basin Dam, there is a fishery for coho and chinook salmon in the fall, with the last half of September usually the prime time.

On the southern edge of the city of Marquette, the diminutive Carp River flows into Lake Superior. This tumbling stream is principally home to brook trout and steelhead fingerlings. The last mile or so before the Big Lake is open enough for flyfishing, and you can roll cast your way for another 10 miles upstream. On the east side of the river, a parking area is provided at the mouth on the north side of M-28. There is a good steelhead run in the spring and chinook salmon in the fall from both stocked fish and natural reproduction. The mouth is protected from prevailing westerly winds, and you can reach staging salmonids while standing thigh deep in Lake Superior.

CHOCOLAY RIVER

With more groundwater input than most Upper Peninsula streams, the Chocolay River provides fine fishing for resident brook and brown trout. along with anadromous runs of steelhead, coho, chinook and pink salmon. The river begins as two branches in central Marquette County and flows mostly north to Lake Superior.

The best flyfishing reach is between the juncture of the East and West Branches and Mangum Road. The gradient is good with lots of gravel and cobble on the bottom. This section of river is wadeable and can also be floated. There is enough room for some flyfishing in the branches as well, especially the lower West Branch. While the trout are not large, with most brookies under 10 inches and relatively few browns reaching the mid-teens, their numbers are good. There are also good numbers of juvenile steelhead, ensuring lots of action.

When the river turns and parallels the Lake Superior shore for its last 7 or 8 miles, it slows and deepens. Even though the bottom is mostly sand, the water depth and logjams can make wading difficult. This is the prime reach for intercepting anadromous fish. There are runs of wild pink, chinook and coho salmon, as well as steelhead. Steelhead and coho salmon were planted in the past, but currently the river receives no hatchery fish.

Chocolay River

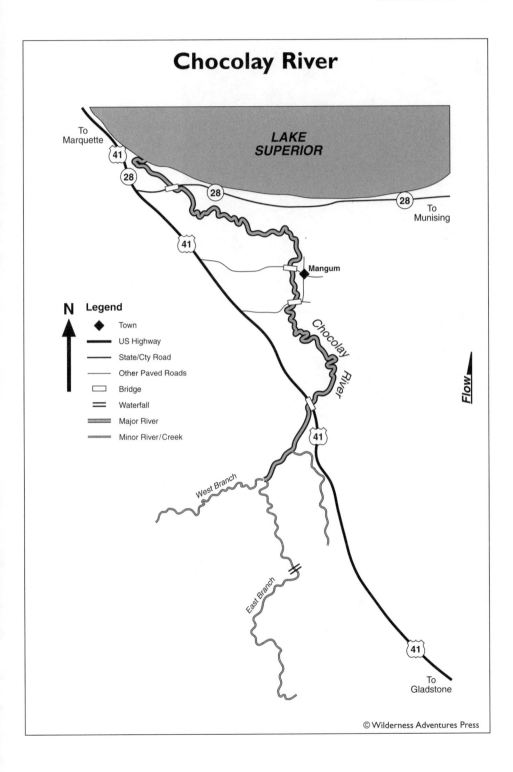

Chocolay River.

September is prime time for pink and chinook salmon, with a modest coho run following late in the month and continuing into October. With good rainfall there can be a fall fishery for steelhead, and the Chocolay is one of relatively few Upper Peninsula rivers that offer the possibility of winter steelheading. Spring is, of course, the prime time for steelhead, with the run usually peaking in early May. A mild winter and warm spring can result in an earlier spawning migration. The upstream limit for year-round steelhead and salmon fishing is the US-41 Bridge.

MENOMINEE RIVER

The Michigamme and Brule Rivers join together to form the Menominee, the largest Upper Peninsula river flowing into Lake Michigan. The Menominee forms the border of Michigan and Wisconsin throughout its length, and much of the river is impounded by a string of dams. However, when the river is free flowing, it offers the

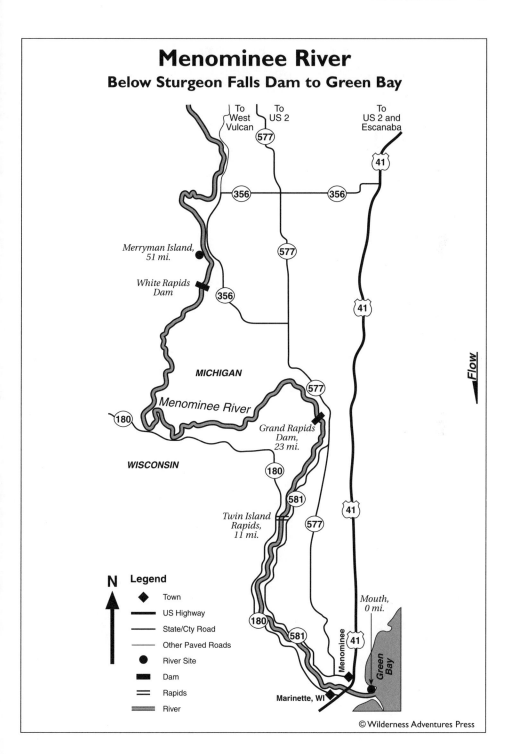

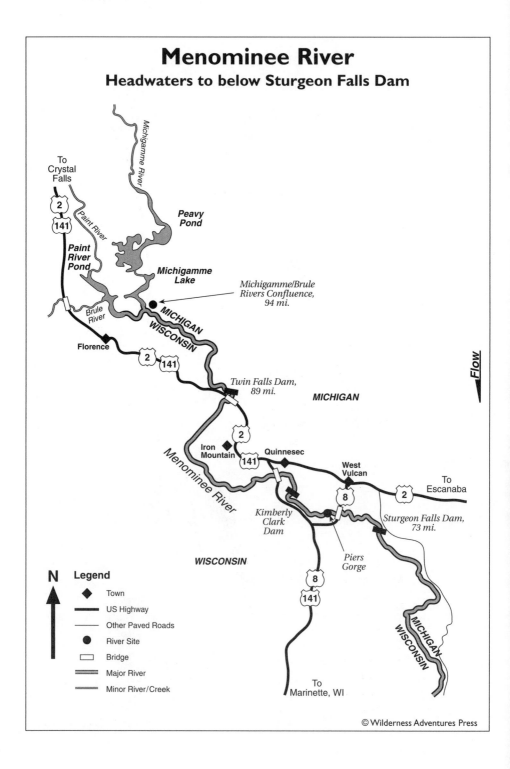

Menominee River
Headwaters to below Sturgeon Falls Dam

Michigamme River

To Crystal Falls

Paint River

Peavy Pond

Paint River Pond

Michigamme Lake

Michigamme/Brule Rivers Confluence, 94 mi.

Brule River

Florence

MICHIGAN
WISCONSIN

Twin Falls Dam, 89 mi.

MICHIGAN

Flow

Iron Mountain

Quinnesec

West Vulcan

To Escanaba

Menominee River

Kimberly Clark Dam

Sturgeon Falls Dam, 73 mi.

Piers Gorge

WISCONSIN

To Marinette, WI

N

Legend

◆ Town
▬ US Highway
— Other Paved Roads
● River Site
▭ Bridge
▬ Major River
▬ Minor River/Creek

© Wilderness Adventures Press

Menominee River.

fly rod angler some excellent fishing for smallmouth bass. In some reaches and in cold months, brook trout can be found, but overall the river is home to warmwater species.

Long, narrow flowages are created in the upper Menominee by a series of four dams in the first 20 miles. Short reaches of flowing water occur below the dams and offer fishing for smallmouth bass, northern pike, walleye, and muskellunge. The water has a pretty good tannin level, so the river is stained a copper color. Clarity is good, and the stain can help keep fish from being spooky when the sun is bright. Floating into the upper parts of the impoundments and swinging and then retrieving streamers can be effective for fish-eating predators.

A somewhat longer free-flowing stretch occurs below the Kimberly Clark Dam south of Quinnesec. The whitewater rapids at Piers Gorge are a special feature of this reach. The flyfishing is challenging here, and when you hook a good-sized smallmouth and it surges into the fast water, you will be in for a good tussle. Kayakers and rafters frequent this area, and if you hook one of them, you will have an even tougher battle.

The river's prime smallmouth fishing is found between the Sturgeon Falls Dam and the Chalk Hill Flowage. In summer, the Menominee is wadeable, and smallmouth are numerous with 50-fish days possible. There is good access to the best water at Sturgeon Bend and Welling Parks, and County Road 356 parallels much of this part of the river. Hellgrammites and crayfish are plentiful in the rocky habitat, and your favorite imitations of them are sure to interest the smallies. Occasional walleyes and pike, along with rock bass, spice up the action. Some brook trout might also find your streamer or nymph in the early summer before the water temperature rises to the 70-degree mark.

Another long stretch of free-flowing water occurs below the White Rapids Dam. The river can be waded at low flows for several miles below the dam, and there are good populations of smallmouth bass, walleyes, and northern pike. Once Wisconsin's Pike River adds its flow, wading gets tougher, and some kind of floating craft will help you get to the fish. Channel catfish start to join the mix, and if you hook something on a nymph that just moves off slowly and refuses to stop, you've probably encountered one of the Menominee's resident sturgeon.

Below the Grand Rapids Dam, a small boat helps to get to the numerous smallmouth bass, walleyes, and channel catfish that inhabit the lower river. Below the lowest dam, just a couple of miles from the mouth, there is a run of steelhead. Brown trout and splake are also planted at the river mouth, and some move into the river in the fall. It's possible to fish from the shore or piers, but a boat is better. Expect a few stray chinook in the fall. When there is good rainfall, some steelhead will join the salmon and brown trout. This is big, stained water, so large, highly visible streamers help to get the attention of trout and salmon.

Stream Facts: Menominee River

Seasons
- Open all year. Bass must be released between January 1 and June 19 and the month of December.
- Northern pike must be released between March 1 and May 1, and muskellunge must be released from January 1 to May 15 and the month of December.
- Lake sturgeon may only be kept between September 4 and November 1, and the limit is one fish per season.

Special Regulations
- Size limit for trout and salmon between the mouth and the first dam is 10 inches.
- Only one walleye may be kept between March 2 and April 30.

Fish
- Resident smallmouth and largemouth bass, northern pike, walleye, muskellunge, lake sturgeon, channel catfish, carp, and panfish.
- Brook and brown trout are present in tributaries.
- Anadromous rainbow and brown trout, splake, chinook salmon are present from fall through spring.

River Miles
- Lake Michigan—0
- Menominee Dam—2
- Twin Island Rapids—11
- Grand Rapids Dam—23
- White Rapids Dam—51
- Pemene Falls—57
- Sturgeon Falls Dam—73
- Twin Falls Dam—89
- Brule/Michigamme confluence—94

River Characteristics
- Large, highly stained (tannins) river with a rocky bottom except where impounded.
- Periodic falls and rapids punctuate the free-flowing parts of the river.
- It is surprisingly wadeable in the summer.

River Access
- Access is available at each landmark noted above with river miles.
- Additional access sites are noted on the maps, as well as several roadways that closely parallel the river.

MENOMINEE RIVER MAJOR HATCHES

Insect	Jan	Feb	Mar	Apr	May	Jun	July	Aug	Sep	Oct	Nov	Dec	Time	Fly Patterns
Hendrickson					▓								M/A	Hendrickson #12–14; Quill Gordon; Red Quill; Adams
Blue-winged Olive					▓	▓	▓	▓					A	Blue-winged Olive #18–20; Sparkle Dun Baetis; Iron Dun; Olive CDC Mayfly Dun
Net Building Caddis					▓	▓	▓	▓	▓	▓			M/A	Spotted Sedge #16–18; Eastern Elk Wing Caddis; Goddard Caddis
Sulphur Dun						▓	▓						A/E	Sulphur Dun #16; Pale Morning Dun; CDC Comparadun Yellow; Pale Evening Dun
Gray Drake					▓	▓							E	Gray Drake #12–14; Gray Adams
Brown Drake						▓							E	Brown Drake #10–12; Adams; CDC Brown Drake
Hexagenia						▓	▓						E	Hex #4–8; Great Olive-winged Drake; Spring's Wiggler; Hare's Ear
Trico							▓	▓	▓	▓			M	Tiny White Wing Black #24–28; Parachute Adams; CDC Trico; Spent Wing Trico
White Fly									▓				E	White Fly #12–14; White Miller
Streamers	▓	▓	▓	▓	▓	▓	▓	▓	▓	▓	▓	▓	M/A/E	Woolly Buggers #6–12; Clouser's Minnow; Muddler Minnows; BC Craw; Matukas; Zonkers; Hellgrammites
Terrestrials						▓	▓	▓	▓	▓			M/A/E	Woolly Worm #8–12; BC Spider; Letort Cricket; Joe's Hopper #6–10; Dave's Hopper; Dropper Hopper

HATCH TIME CODE: M = morning; A = afternoon; E = evening.

BRULE RIVER

Like the Menominee, the river it flows into, the Brule forms the boundary between Michigan and Wisconsin. Unlike the Menominee, however, the Brule is mostly free-flowing with only a few abandoned low-head logging dams slowing its flow.

Like many Michigan trout streams, the Brule begins as the outlet of a lake and is initially too warm for trout. But in a very short distance, Wisconsin's Elvoy Creek helps the Brule cool down to trout-loving temperatures. The M-73 Bridge marks the beginning of the blue ribbon water and provides access to the river. This highway becomes W-55 on the Wisconsin side and running to the small town of Nelma. The Brule continues to carry the blue ribbon designation down to the M-189 bridge, a river distance of about 12 miles. State highway M-189 runs straight south of the town of Iron River. The river holds a mixture of both brown and brook trout, and growth is good with 20-plus-inch browns definitely possible.

Access to the blue ribbon water is somewhat limited, with only one additional bridge in the reach. Brule River Road connects to M-189 and crosses the Brule about 3 miles up from the highway. A campground on the Wisconsin side of the river downstream from M-73 also provides access. Canoes work well on the river and are a good way to get to water that receives less fishing pressure. Much of the bottom consists of

The Brule River when it turns muddy.

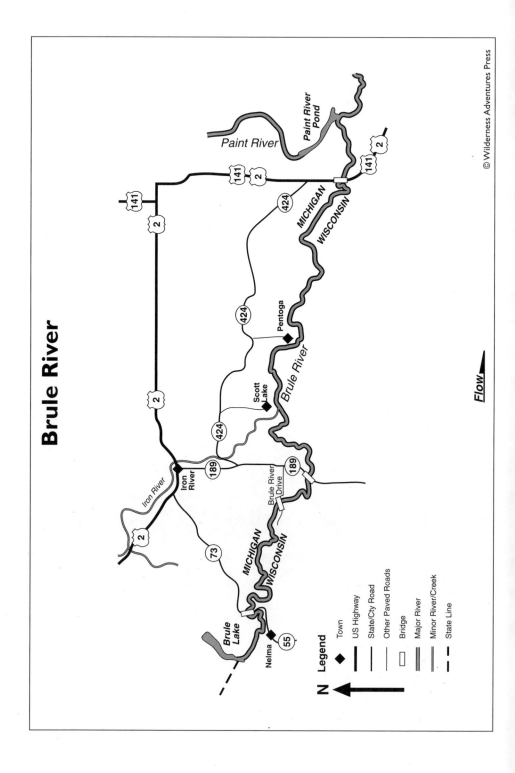

Brule River

Paint River

Paint River Pond

141
2

141
2

2

141

424

MICHIGAN

WISCONSIN

424

Pentoga

Scott Lake

Brule River

424

189

189

Iron River

Iron River

Brule River Drive

MICHIGAN

WISCONSIN

2

73

Brule Lake

Nelma

55

Flow

© Wilderness Adventures Press

Legend

◆ Town

US Highway

State/Cty Road

Other Paved Roads

Bridge

Major River

Minor River/Creek

State Line

N

cobble-sized stone, which can be quite slippery, making a wading staff and felt soles helpful. Mayflies and caddis flies are abundant, and crayfish are a staple in the diet of larger trout. Swinging muddlers, woolly buggers, and crayfish streamers under the streamside vegetation and through the deep riffles should produce some fine trout if they are actively feeding.

The Brule River is a favorite of DNR fishery biologist Dell Siler. He likes to float this river and recently tangled with a brookie in the 18- to 20-inch class, but the big char escaped at the boat.

While the Brule warms downstream, the Iron River adds its slightly cooler flow about 4 miles below M-189, helping to keep the stream in the trout comfort zone. Smallmouth bass and walleyes begin to show up in the catch as the Brule nears Pentoga, but there is still some fine fishing for large brown trout. Putting in at M-189 and taking out at Pentoga makes a full day. If you like a slower pace, you can take out at the Scott Lake Bridge. If floating the full distance, the bridge can be used as a reference point since it is slightly more than halfway. Fish the mile below the Iron River juncture with extra intensity.

Mixed species continue to be the rule downstream from Pentoga. In the summer smallmouth bass and walleye dominate the catch, but both brown and brook trout are present in the cooler months. They migrate into cold tributaries when the mainstream gets too warm. A good strategy is to check a tributary stream's temperature with a thermometer—if it is significantly colder than the main Brule, it is a good place to find fish. The Brule joins the Paint River in an impoundment before merging with the Michigamme River to form the Menominee. Warmwater species often move out of the impoundment and up into the lower Brule.

IRON RIVER

The Iron River is home to an excellent population of wild brook trout. The North Branch gets off to a good start with the addition of lots of spring water north of Raft Lake in central Iron County. In just a few miles, it is not only large enough to allow roll casting, it is a designated a blue ribbon trout stream. The Iron keeps this classification down to its namesake town.

The South Branch of the Iron joins the North Branch about a third of the way through the blue ribbon water. It is the outlet of a lake and remains too warm for trout and too small to provide a significant warmwater fishery. Some brook trout can be found in its lower reaches in the spring.

As you might expect from the name of the river, the Iron is quite stained with tannins. This makes the bright attractor patterns that brook trout like to grab even more effective. The river's bottom ranges from gravel and cobble riffles to firm sand, and the insect population is diverse.

Downstream from the town of Iron River, the number of brook trout decrease, but there is a slightly better chance of hooking one in the midteen size. The native char continue to be present all the way to the Iron's juncture with the Brule. In the

Iron River

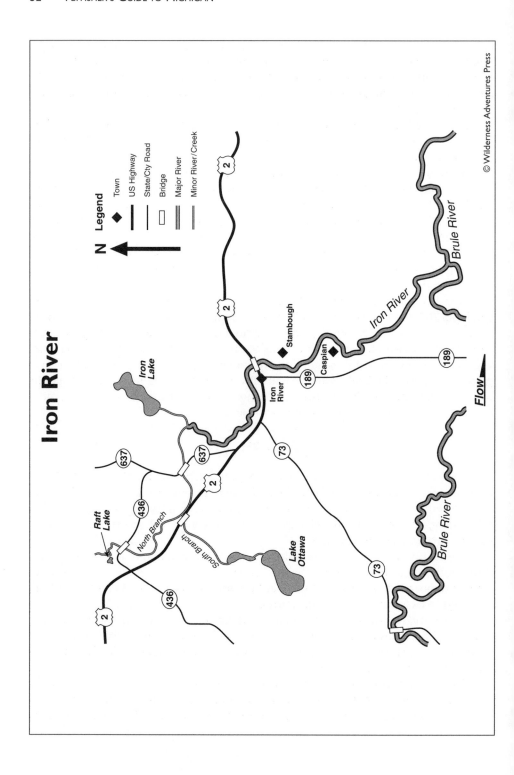

Legend

- ◆ Town
- US Highway
- State/Cty Road
- ▭ Bridge
- Major River
- Minor River/Creek

© Wilderness Adventures Press

Thick canopy over the waters of the Iron River.

lower Iron, some brown trout mix with the brookies, most likely migrants from the Brule River. There are more road crossings over the Iron than most Upper Peninsula rivers, and there is an old railroad grade that parallels and crisscrosses the river for even more access. County Road 436 crosses the upper Iron twice, and the towns of Iron River, Stambaugh, and Caspian each have several river crossings. Just remember which side of the river the railroad grade is on, as that is the way back to your vehicle after you have finished exercising the brookies.

IRON, PAINT, AND BRULE RIVERS MAJOR HATCHES

Insect	Jan	Feb	Mar	Apr	May	Jun	July	Aug	Sep	Oct	Nov	Dec	Time	Fly Patterns
Hendrickson					X								M/A	Hendrickson #12–14; Quill Gordon; Red Quill; Adams
Blue-winged Olive								X	X				A	Blue-winged Olive #18–20; Sparkle Dun Baetis; Iron Dun; Olive CDC Mayfly Dun
Little Black Caddis								X					A	Little Black Caddis #16–18; Griffith's Gnat; CDC Emerging Caddis Brown; Black Ant
Grannom							X						M/A	Grannom #14–16; Medium Brown Sedge; Elk Caddis Brown-olive
Net-building Caddis					X	X	X	X	X	X			M/A	Spotted Sedge #16–18; Eastern Elk Wing Caddis; Goddard Caddis
Sulphur Dun						X	X						A/E	Sulphur Dun #16; Pale Morning Dun; CDC Comparadun Yellow; Pale Evening Dun
March Brown						X							M/A	March Brown #12–14; Dark Cahill; Gray Fox; Ginger Quill
Gray Drake						X	X						E	Gray Drake #12–14; Gray Adams
Brown Drake						X							E	Brown Drake #10–12; Adams; CDC Brown Drake
Trico						X	X	X	X	X			M	Tiny White Wing Black #24–28; Parachute Adams; CDC Trico; Spent Wing Trico
White Fly								X	X				E	White Fly #12–14; White Miller
Streamers	X	X	X	X	X	X	X	X	X	X	X	X	M/A/E	Woolly Buggers #6–12; Clouser's Minnow; Muddler Minnows; BC Craw; Matukas
Terrestrials					X	X	X	X	X				M/A/E	Woolly Worm #8–12; BC Spider; Letort Cricket; Joe's Hopper #6–10; Dave's Hopper; CDC Ant #10–16

HATCH TIME CODE: M = morning; A = afternoon; E = evening.
Expect slight changes in hatch times as you move upstream in this system, i.e., hatches on Cook's Run will lag a few days behind those of the Brule.

PAINT RIVER

The Paint River begins as two branches, each traveling a fair distance before merging. The North Branch of the Paint is essentially a warmwater stream that does not provide a very good fishery. Some trout are present at times, but it is hard to focus on this branch when the South Branch and its tributary, Cooks Run, provide some of the best trout fishing in the Upper Peninsula.

The South Branch begins just a couple miles north of the state line and is home to trout throughout its length. At Forest Service Road 149, it simultaneously becomes a blue ribbon stream and large enough to fish with a fly rod, but there is room to roll cast and cast parallel with the current upstream from there. Both wild brown and brook trout are present in the South Branch, and although most are of modest size, a 15-inch brookie or 20-inch brown is not out of the question.

A major tributary, Cooks Run, joins the Paint about 6 miles below USFS 149, significantly increasing its size. Basswood Road crosses Cooks Run just above the South Branch, providing a good access point and providing the chance to try both rivers on the same walk. The same abandoned railroad that parallels the Iron River also runs along the upper reaches of the South Branch of the Paint. The gravel- and

A beautiful brown trout from the South Branch of the Paint River.

Paint River

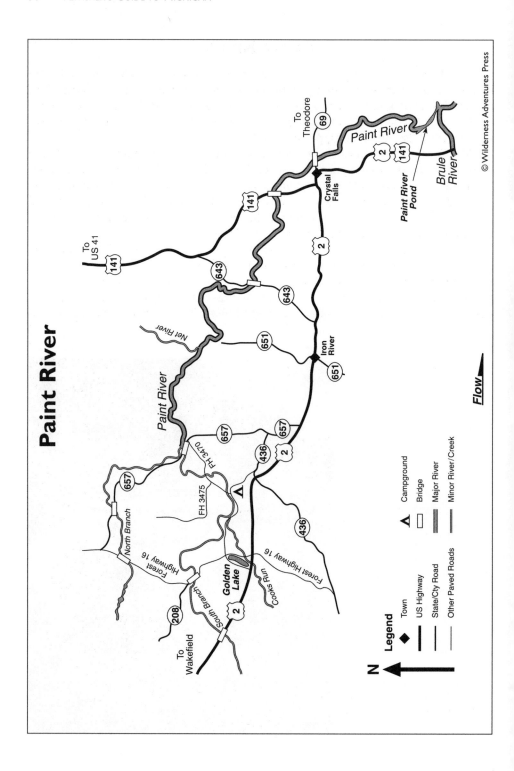

© Wilderness Adventures Press

Netting a brown trout
on the South Branch
of the Paint.

cobble-bottomed stream remains very wadeable even though there is definitely now more room to cast. The flow of the South Branch is more stable than most Upper Peninsula streams, and insects are both abundant and diverse.

The blue ribbon designation continues down to County Road 657, just below the confluence with the North Branch. A fair amount of stream improvement has been done in this reach, and with the addition of cover to go along with the excellent water quality and food supply, there is great trout habitat. US Forest Service Road 3475 crosses the river twice, providing access to the lower part of the blue ribbon water. The North Branch does not warm the stream much, nevertheless, trout numbers slowly decrease downstream. The wild trout population is augmented with stocked brown trout below CR-657. Even though the Net River further increases the flow, the Paint still remains wadeable. However, many anglers canoe this area for more mobility.

Smallmouth bass become increasingly prevalent downstream. By the time the Paint reaches the town of Crystal Falls, smallmouth bass are the principal game fish species. Some northern pike and an occasional muskie join them downstream from Crystal Falls. The Paint becomes impounded before it joins the Brule, and warmwater fish often move upstream out of the impoundment.

The confluence of Cooks Run (left) and the South Branch of the Paint.

Cooks Run

Cooks Run is one of the few "spring creeks" in the Upper Peninsula, and its stable, clear flow is home to good numbers of browns and brookies. Tag alders keep the fishing tight, but there is room for a fly rod for the last 6 to 8 miles before joining the South Branch of the Paint. In this reach, the water races over cobble riffles and slides through some sand-bottomed meadows that abound with deep holes and undercuts. From US-2 down to the South Branch, Cooks Run is very deserving of its blue ribbon designation. Additional access is provided by U.S. Forest Service Road 16, which crosses Cooks Run about a half-mile downstream from the highway.

The mayflies and caddisflies are abundant, with some type of insect activity happening throughout most of the season. But because Cooks Run is relatively small and narrow, terrestrials play an important role in the food chain as well. Undercut banks abound and provide great cover for browns and brookies. Thus, for both cover and food, trout seem to be very oriented to the bank, and well-placed casts seem to be a lot more important than the pattern. Covering lots of water will also pay dividends.

Cooks Run.

Net River

A major tributary of the Paint River, the Net begins as two branches in central Iron County. If exploring a relatively lightly fished, remote river is your goal, then the Net River would be a good choice. The East Branch offers the best fishing for brook trout, while the mainstream features a good population of smallmouth bass. Beaver dams and a small earthen dam that creates the Net River Flooding have had an impact on the West Branch. There are some brook trout in its headwaters, but the lower part of the West Branch is home mostly to northern pike and rock bass.

The mainstream of the Net is quite wide through much of its length and too warm for trout. There is a natural "lake" a few miles down from the confluence of the two branches called the Widewaters. Much of the Net is wadeable, but a canoe or other floating device is probably a better way to fish it. Rock bass and northern pike add to the fine population of smallmouth bass in the Net.

Net River

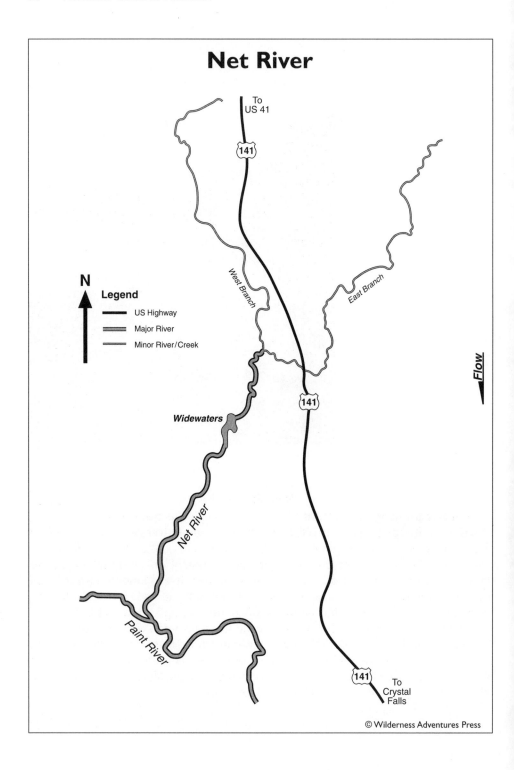

To
US 41

141

N

Legend
US Highway
Major River
Minor River/Creek

West Branch

East Branch

Flow

141

Widewaters

Net River

141

To
Crystal
Falls

Paint River

© Wilderness Adventures Press

MICHIGAMME RIVER

The Michigamme is a large, warmwater river that flows south from southwestern Marquette County to join the Brule River and form the Menominee River. Much of it is impounded, and the river begins as the outlet of Lake Michigamme, a large inland lake. Several dams keep most of the water impounded for the next 14 miles.

About 5 miles downstream from the Michigamme River Basin dam, the river becomes free-flowing for over 20 miles. Smallmouth bass and walleyes are plentiful in this reach. Wading is possible in some areas, but a canoe or small boat helps cover more water. Witbeck Rapids is a prime spot in this stretch, with smallmouth hanging around the boulders and walleyes in the slower pools. Bright streamers that are very visible in the stained water get the attention of these predators. Northern pike are also present.

The next 6 miles of river are submerged in the Michigamme Reservoir. Below Way Dam, which creates the large impoundment, there is relatively fast, shallow sec-

A good-sized northern pike brought to the net.

Michigamme River

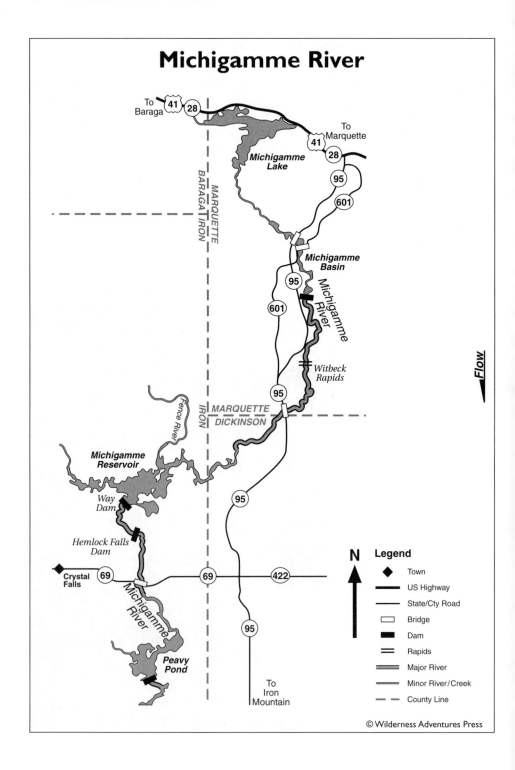

tion that harbors good-sized smallmouth bass, along with walleyes and northern pike. Hemlock Falls Dam again slows the river, but then there is another stretch of shallow, rocky water that harbors the same three species. In addition, there is the chance of having a muskie grab a streamer. Two more dams then impound the remainder of the river.

The presence of high levels of mercury in its predator fish is a black cloud hanging over the Michigamme River system. The silver lining is that the system's fish consumption warning results in less angling pressure and more released fish, which, of course, improve the fishing.

Fence River

The Fence River is the Michigamme's largest tributary and is home to a fine population of brook trout. It begins as two branches, West and East, and when they join to form the main Fence, the river is designated a blue ribbon trout stream.

The East Branch is the colder of the two branches and is open enough to flyfish in its lower reaches. If the weather has been hot prior to your arrival, you may want to investigate the East Branch, because the brookies in the system have been known to move considerable distances to cooler water. The West Branch is also open enough for flyfishing in many areas, but the lakes in its headwaters make the stream temperature marginal for brook trout. Mead Road, off of the Amasa Spur Road, crosses both

A good day for fishing the Fence River.

Fence River

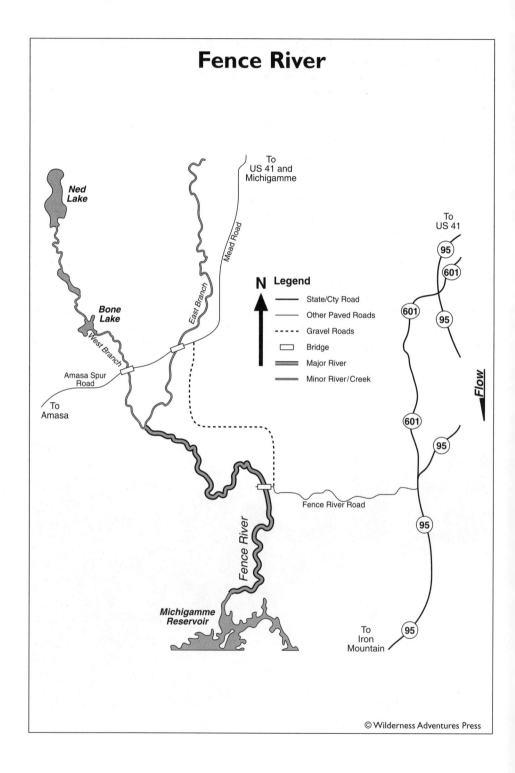

Ned Lake

To
US 41 and
Michigamme

Mead Road

East Branch

N **Legend**
State/Cty Road
Other Paved Roads
Gravel Roads
Bridge
Major River
Minor River/Creek

To
US 41

95

601

601

95

Bone Lake

West Branch

Amasa Spur Road

To Amasa

601

95

Fence River Road

95

Fence River

95

Michigamme Reservoir

To
Iron
Mountain

95

Flow

© Wilderness Adventures Press

Fence River.

branches. The Fence River Road Bridge is about 3 miles down from the confluence of the two branches.

The blue ribbon designation continues for 12 miles downstream from the confluence of the branches. Most of the brookies are between 8 and 11 inches, but trophies in the 16-inch class are possible. The remoteness of the stream keeps it lightly fished, and brookies take a wide variety of flies. Streamers that imitate creek chubs are just the ticket for seducing one of the larger brook trout out of a deep hole.

Michigan (aka Mitchigan) River is a cold tributary that holds good numbers of small- to medium-sized brook trout. It flows into the lower part of the blue ribbon water and helps to keep the mainstream cool. Accurate roll casts help extract brookies from logjam holes.

CEDAR RIVER

Even though the Cedar River is also known as the Big Cedar, it is a small- to medium-sized river that parallels the Menominee and flows directly into Green Bay. Free flowing throughout most of its length, it contains a diverse population of fish.

The upper Cedar River is home to brook and brown trout, but marginal temperatures and lack of spawning gravel limit their numbers. Because of the low numbers, trout are stocked to augment the limited numbers of natural fish. In addition, attempts have been made to improve both the cover and spawning habitat. It is important to put

Cedar River

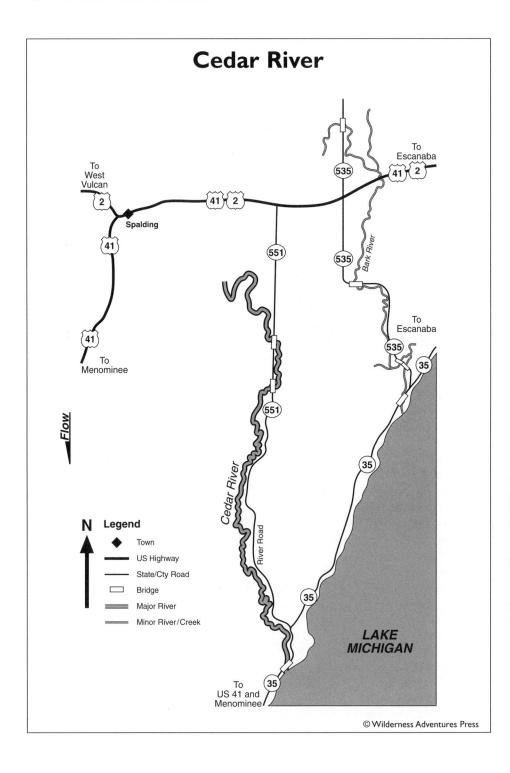

© Wilderness Adventures Press

your thermometer to use when fishing the upper river for trout. Cold tributaries really concentrate the trout during warm spells.

Smallmouth bass are the dominant game fish in the lower half of the Cedar. Walleyes and northern pike add to this mix. Most of the lower Cedar flows through the Escanaba State Forest, and this fact, coupled with River Road paralleling the stream, results in good access. Smallmouth here are not large, but their numbers provide lots of action on streamers and leech patterns.

The Cedar River receives a yearly steelhead plant, and brown trout are planted at the mouth. Some of the browns and steelhead move upriver in the fall if rainfall is ample. The main steelhead run occurs in the spring, normally peaking in late April. Finding some of the relatively scarce spawning gravel and then concentrating on the good holes and runs above and below it is a good strategy for hooking up to the silvery rainbows.

A few miles to the east of the Cedar, the smaller Bark River follows a parallel path before joining Green Bay. There are brook trout in its upper reaches, and it receives a modest run of steelhead. Following a heavy rain or snowmelt, it becomes fishable sooner than its neighbors.

FORD RIVER

Flowing through parts of four counties, the Ford River travels first to the east and then to the south into Green Bay just south of Escanaba. It offers a mixed bag of fisheries, with brook trout in the upper river and smallmouth and walleyes nearer the bay.

Wild brookies are supplemented with regular stockings in the Dickinson County portion of the Ford River. Brookies up to 18 inches are possible, but the water temperature can become marginal for brook trout when hot weather occurs. A stream thermometer helps determine if brook trout are there and are active. When it reads above 70 degrees, look for cooler water because brookies will be moving into it. There are also a few brown trout present, and smallmouth bass start to show up at the county line.

The brushy North Branch joins the mainstream just before the Ford flows into Marquette County. The river is deeper and wider here, and while trout continue to be present, smallmouth bass are also likely. The West Branch is a warmwater stream, and it joins the Ford when the mainstream cuts across the corner of Menominee County. This pretty much ends the possibility of trout, but smallmouth fishing can be very good. The bass population keeps getting better closer to Green Bay, and its appears that there is a migration of bass from the bay into the Ford River in summer. Fishing the lower river with streamers in crayfish, leech, and minnow patterns could make a hook-up with several bass that break the 4-pound barrier possible.

Due to a yearly plant, the Ford has a good run of chinook in the fall, and September is the best month to intercept these fish in the lower river. There is a good chance of hooking salmon and trophy smallmouth on the same outing. In the spring there is a modest run of steelhead.

Ford River

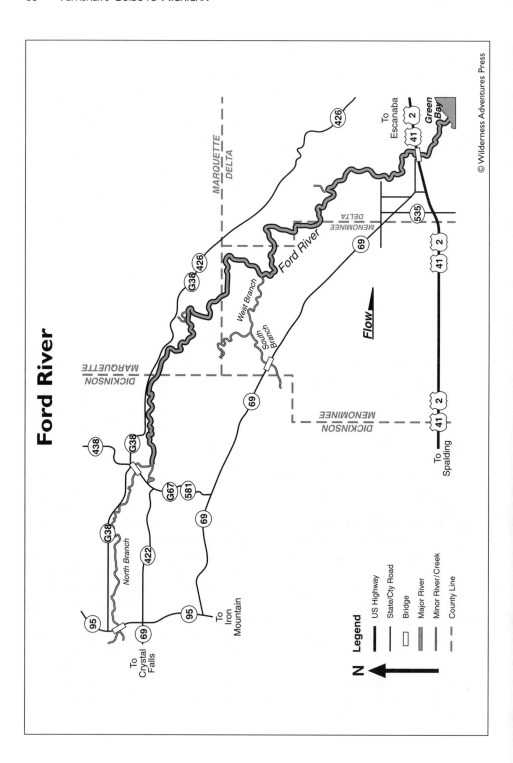

© Wilderness Adventures Press

Legend

N

— US Highway
| State/Cty Road
□ Bridge
━ Major River
━ Minor River/Creek
╌ County Line

ESCANABA RIVER

The Escanaba River drains a large area of the west central Upper Peninsula, and two of its three main branches begin a lot closer to Lake Superior than they are to their final destination, Lake Michigan. This river system offers a wide variety of fishing opportunities. Brown trout are the main draw but brook trout abound in its tributaries, and fine fishing for smallmouth bass is present in its lower reaches.

The Middle Branch begins as the outlet of Wolf Lake and is not considered the mainstream until the East Branch of the Escanaba joins it in the town of Gwinn. The upper Middle Branch above the Greenwood Reservoir is marginal for trout. In fact, it's pretty marginal for flyfishing. Some brook trout are present, especially near the mouths of tributaries like Second River, but small pike are more likely to be caught.

Below the reservoir, there is good fishing in spring and fall for native brook trout and stocked brown trout. Warm summer weather causes trout to move downstream and into colder tributaries. The gradient really picks up below County Road 581, and at White City Falls, the river drops about 12 feet and creates a very large pool. Granite boulders, stairstep rapids and rock walls will make you think you are out west. Browns and brookies are found wherever the water slows down. Though they are not large, they eagerly strike marabou leech, matuka, and muddler streamers. Because wading is difficult, a wading staff is recommended. County Road 478 crosses the river about 3 miles upstream from CR 581, and access to White City Falls can be gained from the south side off of Voelker Lake Road.

The Middle Branch continues to flow swiftly all the way to Gwinn, even though it's briefly interrupted by Cataract Basin. Below the basin, the river becomes broad and shallow. A lot more gravel is present, which enhances both the natural reproduction

Boney Falls on the Middle Branch of the Escanaba.

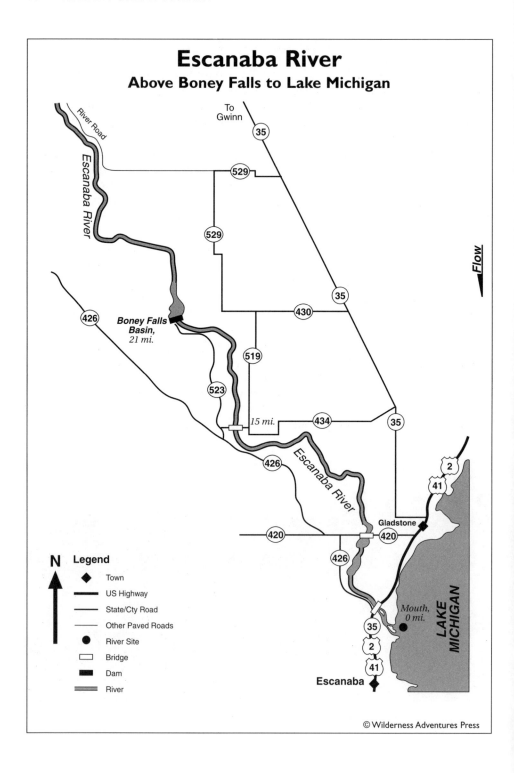

Escanaba River
Above Boney Falls to Lake Michigan

© Wilderness Adventures Press

Escanaba River

East and Middle Branches Confluence to above Boney Falls Basin

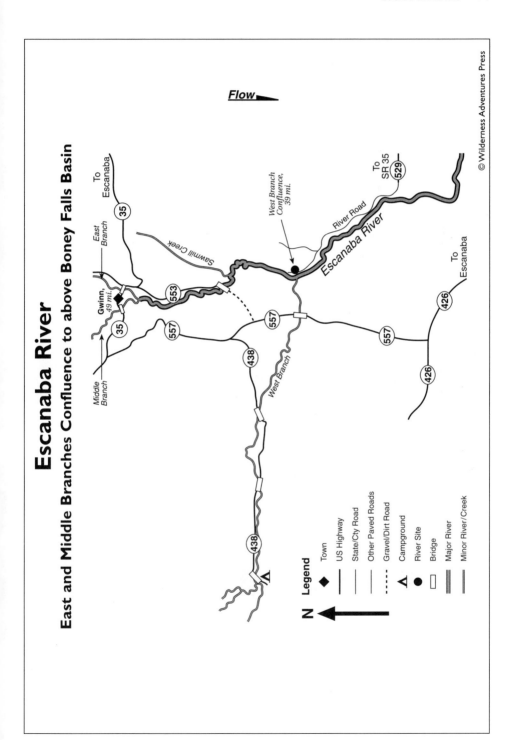

© Wilderness Adventures Press

Escanaba River
Headwaters to Middle and East Branches Confluence

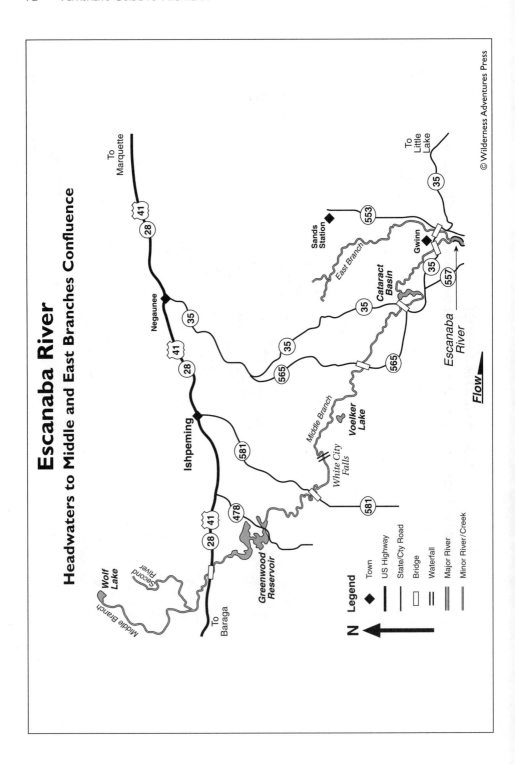

© Wilderness Adventures Press

Middle Branch of the Escanaba River.

of trout and insects. M-35 crosses the Middle Branch twice before it reaches Gwinn, and the CR 565 crossing provides another access point.

The smaller East Branch begins as the outlet of the Schweitzer Reservoir, and with the help of several cold tributaries, becomes one of Upper Peninsula's better trout streams as it nears Gwinn. Brown and brook trout are present in good numbers in the 8- to 14-inch size range, with larger browns possible. Access is via gravel and dirt roads off of County Road 553 north of Gwinn. The road to Sand Station (Mail Route NB) continues to and actually crosses the East Branch. A number of other "two tracks" deadend near the river.

East Branch is quite stained with tannins, so bright attractor patterns often work best. The trout are naturally reproduced, but you might encounter a tagged brook trout that is part of a research project on the stream. The stream is small enough to be impacted by beaver dams that could hamper your mobility in waders.

The Middle and East Branches merge just south of Gwinn to officially create the mainstream of the Escanaba River. The combined flow creates a sizable stream heavily stocked with brown trout. While there are no bridge crossings over the river below Gwinn, most of the land adjacent to the river is in the Escanaba State Forest, and Highbank Road (aka Iron Pin Trail) parallels the river. Walking in to the Escanaba from this road, you will find undeveloped stretches of a beautiful stream. At certain points you can see the river and take advantage of spots where other anglers have pulled off and hiked in.

This is wide-open, Western type water: gravel riffles alternating with sand holes and bedrock pools. There are large and diverse insect populations here, including

Hexagenia mayflies. Even with the addition of the Big West Branch, the Escanaba remains wadeable in the summer until Boney Falls Basin. Access to the mainstream continues to be on the east side of the Escanaba via the Escanaba River Road. County Road 529 connects M-35 with River Road, and there is a state forest campground at the juncture. This campground is called the Swimming Hole (named after Swimming Hole Creek, which enters the Escanaba upstream from the campground) and is a popular spot for trout anglers. River Road parallels the river for about 8 miles, and if you don't want to hike across country to the river, about 5 miles north of the campground you can fish Sawmill Creek, which flows under the road.

The Big West Branch is so named because there is a smaller tributary to the Middle Branch that is also called the West Branch. A number of creeks join to form the Big West Branch in northeastern Dickinson County. The upper part of this branch is a bit tight for flycasting, but it can be navigated with well-placed roll casts. Brookies are the main draw in this part of the river, with browns becoming more common toward its confluence with the mainstream. Access is fairly good with four county road bridge crossings and a campground on the upper Big West.

The mainstream below Boney Falls Dam is stocked with large numbers of brown trout. This reach has the potential to produce world-class fishing for large trout but is frequently handicapped by low flows and water that is too warm. In fact, several dramatic fish kills have occurred in the last 20 years due to water temperatures rising into the 80s. Because the bottom is predominantly bedrock, there is a lack of gravel, resulting in low natural reproduction. In addition, trout cover is lacking in parts of the lower Escanaba as well, and attempts to provide more have included blasting holes in the bedrock.

In spite of all these shortcomings, good fishing can be expected in the lower Escanaba when the flow is adequate and the water is cool. This is due to the fact the one thing that isn't lacking is food for trout. Crayfish, in contrast to many Upper Peninsula soft water streams, are very abundant in the lower Escanaba. Creek chubs are also numerous, so it follows that streamers imitating these two large food items are very effective, especially for larger browns. Trout can also be taken on standard dry patterns, such as Adams, elk hair caddis, Cahills, ants, and hoppers. There is very good access at the dam, access is also available via Hunter Brook on the west side of the river and the County Road 519 Bridge. I fished this area when the water was low and found wading the bedrock very easy. However, it is easy to see how stronger flows could makes felts and a wading staff necessary equipment.

The lower Escanaba is impounded by three more dams, and smallmouth bass start to predominate about 10 miles below Boney Falls. Obviously, crayfish patterns work well for them, and a large brown might just be hooked in between a series of smallmouth encounters. A floating craft is helpful in fishing the last few miles of the Escanaba. Access and a boat launch can be found where County Road 420 crosses the river. Below the first dam in the spring and fall, walleyes and the occasional steelhead and salmon migrate into the lower river, but this is not a dependable fishery.

Stream Facts: Escanaba River

Seasons
- Most of the river is open only during the regular trout season—last Saturday in April through September 30.
- Bass must be released between the last Saturday in April and the Saturday before Memorial Day.

Special Regulations
- Artificial flies and lures only from Boney Falls Dam down to the mouth of Silver Creek with a possession limit of 2 trout.
- Minimum size for brook trout is 10 inches, 12 inches for rainbows, and possession limit is 5 trout from the mouth of the West Branch downstream. No size limit on northern pike.

Fish
- Brown and brook trout, smallmouth bass, walleye, northern pike, and panfish.

River Miles
- Lake Michigan—0
- County Road 519—15
- Boney Falls Dam—21
- Big West Branch mouth—39
- Gwinn—49

River Characteristics
- This is a quick-flowing, wide, shallow, fertile bedrock river.
- Weather greatly influences fishing, as lack of rain severely reduces flow and hot weather greatly increases water temperature.

River Access
- Access is available at each landmark noted above with river miles.
* County road crossings provide additional access, and much of the upper river flows through the Escanaba State Forest.

ESCANABA RIVER MAJOR HATCHES

Insect	Jan	Feb	Mar	Apr	May	Jun	July	Aug	Sep	Oct	Nov	Dec	Time	Fly Patterns
Hendrickson					X								M/A	Hendrickson #12–14; Quill Gordon; Red Quill; Adams
Blue-winged Olive						X	X	X					A	Blue-winged Olive #18–20; Sparkle Dun Baetis; Iron Dun; Olive CDC Mayfly Dun
Little Black Caddis						X	X	X					A	Little Black Caddis #16–18; Griffith's Gnat; CDC Emerging Caddis Brown, Black Ant
Grannom						X	X						M/A	Grannom #14–16 (medium brown sedge); Elk Caddis (brown-olive)
Net-building Caddis					X	X	X	X	X	X			M/A	Spotted Sedge #16–18; Eastern Elk Wing Caddis; Goddard Caddis
Sulphur Dun							X						A/E	Sulphur Dun #16; Pale Morning Dun; CDC Comparadun Yellow; Pale Evening Dun
March Brown					X	X							M/A	March Brown #12–14; Dark Cahill; Gray Fox; Ginger Quill
Gray Drake						X							E	Gray Drake #12–14; Gray Adams
Brown Drake						X							E	Brown Drake #10–12; Adams; CDC Brown Drake
Hexagenia						X	X						E	Hex #4–8; Great Olive-winged Drake; Spring's Wiggler; Hare's Ear
Trico							X	X	X				M	Tiny White Wing Black #24–28; Parachute Adams; CDC Trico; Spent Wing Trico
White Fly								X	X				E	White Fly #12–14; White Miller
Streamers	X	X	X	X	X	X	X	X	X	X	X	X	M/A/E	Woolly Buggers #6–12; Clouser's Minnow; Muddler Minnows; BC Craw; Matukas
Terrestrials						X	X	X	X				M/A/E	Woolly Worm #8–12; BC Spider; Letort Cricket; Joe's Hopper #6–10; Dave's Hopper; Dropper Hopper

HATCH TIME CODE: M = morning; A = afternoon; E = evening.

Western Upper Peninsula Hub Cities

Marquette
Population–21,977

ACCOMMODATIONS
Birchmont Motel, 2090 US 41 South / 906-228-7538
Brentwood Motor Inn, 2603 US 41 West / 906-228-7494
Edgewater Motel, 2050 US 41 South / 906-225-1305
Imperial Motel, 2493 US 41 West / 906-228-7430
Lamplighter Motel, US 41 West / 906-228-4004
Rainbow Motel, 2603 US 41 West / 906-228-7494

CAMPGROUNDS
Gitche Gumee Campground & RV Park, 2048 28 E M / 906-249-9102
City of Marquette Parks and Recreation, 550 Cox Avenue / 906-228-0465
Craig Lake State Park, P.O. Box 88 (Champion 49814) / 906-339-4461

RESTAURANTS
Alexander's Family Restaurants, 1230 West Washington Street / 906-228-9030
Clark's Landing, US 41 West / 906-228-7011
Coachlight Restaurant, 423 West Washington Street / 906-225-0522
Garden Room Restaurant, 2050 US 41 South / 906-225-1305
Grove Restaurant, 6448 US 41 South / 906-249-1092
My Place, 1951 US 41 West / 906-225-1351

FLY SHOPS AND SPORTING GOODS
Johnson Sport Shop, 1212 North 3rd Street / 906-226-2062
Carpenter's Outdoor Outfitters, 131 West Washington Street / 906-228-6380
Linquist's Outdoor Sports, 131 W. Washington / 906-228-6380
Tom's Hunt and Fish, 2162 US 41 West / 906-228-8667

AUTO SERVICE
41 4X4 Auto Repair, 6573 US 41 South / 906-249-9252
Denny's Standard Service, 1400 Presque Isle Avenue / 906-228-7052
Formula One Auto Repair & Towing, 906 West Baraga Avenue / 906-228-3444
Marquette Automotive Inc, 730 West Washington Street / 906-228-6116
Walt's Auto Service, 2801 US 41 South / 906-249-1515

AIR SERVICE
Marquette County Airport (Negaunee 49866) / 906-475-9651

MEDICAL
Marquette General Hospital, 420 West Magnetic Street / 906-228-9440

FOR MORE INFORMATION
Marquette Area Chamber of Commerce
501 South Front Street
Marquette, MI 49855
906- 226-6591

Ironwood
Population – 6,849

ACCOMMODATIONS
Advance Motel, 663 East Cloverland Drive / 906-932-4511
Black River Lodge, North 12390 Black River Road / 906-932-3857
Coachlight Hotel, 101 North Lowell Street / 906-932-3650
Ironwood Motel, 112 West Cloverland Drive / 906-932-5520
Sandpiper Motel, 1200 East Cloverland Drive / 906-932-2000
Twilight Time Motel, 930 East Cloverland Drive / 906-932-3010

CAMPGROUNDS
Black River Harbor Camp Ground, North 15725 Black River Road / 906-932-7250
Lake Gogebic State Park, Box 139 (Marenisco 49947) / 906-842-3341

RESTAURANTS
Black River Valley Pub & Grub / 906-932-0950
J & B Cafe, 118 East Aurora Street / 906-932-2530
Joe's Pasty Shop, 116 West Aurora Street / 906-932-4412
Mike's Restaurant, 106 East Cloverland Drive / 906-932-0555
Rigonis Inn, 925 East Ayer Street / 906-932-4601
Tracy's Uptown Cafe, 518 East McLeod Avenue / 906-932-3321

FLY SHOPS AND SPORTING GOODS
Black Bear Sporting Goods, 100 West Cloverland Drive / 906-932-5253
Dunham's Discount Sports, 1440 East Cloverland Drive / 906-932-0990
Big Sno Outfitters, 309 East Lead Street (Bessemer 49911) / 906-663-4646
Trek and Trail, 1300 East Cloverland Drive / 906-932-5858

AUTO SERVICE
Geno's Service, Douglas Boulevard / 906-932-0644
Greg's Towing & Repair, 301 West McLeod Avenue / 906-932-9953
J & M's Truck and Auto Repair, 330 West Aurora Street / 906-932-4621
US 2 Service Center, 1301 East US 2 / 906-932-0700

AIR SERVICE
Gogebic County Airport, East 5560 Airport Road / 906-932-3121

MEDICAL
Grand View Hospital, North 10561 Grandview Lane / 906-932-2525

FOR MORE INFORMATION
Western Upper Peninsula Convention and Visitor Bureau
137 East Cloverland Drive
Ironwood, MI 49938
906-932-4850

Houghton / Hancock
Population – 12,045

ACCOMMODATIONS
Copper Crown Motel, 235 Hancock Street (Hancock 49930) / 906-482-6111
Ramada Inn, 99 Navy Street, Hancock, MI 49930, 482-8400
Arcadian Acres Motel, US 41 Boston Jct (Houghton 49931) / 906-482-0288
Gateway Motel, US 41 (Houghton 49931) / 906-482-3511
Portage Motel, 501 Park Avenue, Houghton, MI 482-2400

CAMPGROUNDS
F.J. McLain State Park, Box 82, M-203 (Hancock 49930) / 906-482-0278

RESTAURANTS
Armando's Restaurant, 517 Shelden Avenue (Houghton 49931) / 906-482-2003
Gemignani's, 512 Quincy Street (Hancock 49930) / 906-482-2920
Kaleva Cafe, 234 Quincy Street (Hancock 49930) / 906-482-1230
Northern Lights Restaurant, 820 Shelden Avenue (Houghton 49931) /
    906-482-4882
Nutini's Supper Club, 321 Quincy Street (Hancock 49930) / 906-482-2711
Paradise Bar & Grill, 122 Oneco Road (Hancock 49930) / 906-337-0082

FLY SHOPS AND SPORTING GOODS
Northwoods Trading Post, 120 Quincy Street (Hancock 49930) / 906-482-5210
Dick's Favorite Sports, 1700 West Memorial Drive (Houghton 49931) /
    906-482-0412
Indian Country Sports, 175 Front Street (L'Anse 49946) / 906-524-6518

AUTO SERVICE
Lakeside Auto, 16 Royce Road (Hancock 49930) / 906-482-9020
Dave's Marathon Service, Front (Hancock 49930) / 906-482-3410
Northern Auto Body Shop, 636 Quincy Street (Hancock 49930) / 906-482-3404
Ralph's Repair Service, 401 Shelden (Houghton 49931) / 906-482-4230
Torch Lake Service, 420 Calumet, Lake Linden, MI 49945, 296-3921

AIR SERVICE
Houghton County Memorial Airport (Houghton 49931) / 906-482-3970

MEDICAL
Portage Health System, 200 Michigan (Hancock 49930) / 906-487-8000

FOR MORE INFORMATION
Flat Rock Business Association
35774 Huron River North
Hancock, MI 49930
906-753-5243

Iron Mountain
Population – 8,525

ACCOMMODATIONS
Edgewater Resort Country Log Cabins, North 4128 US 2 / 906-774-6244
Moon Lake Motel, 2906 North US 2 / 906-774-3399
Pine Mountain Resort, 3332 Pine Mountain Road / 906-774-2747
Pineaire Resort Motel / 906-544-2313
Timbers Motor Lodge, 200 South Stephenson Avenue / 906-774-7600
Woodlands Motel, 3957 North US 2 / 906-774-6106
Falls Motel, 1309 US 2 (Crystal Falls 49920) / 906-875-3168
Four Seasons Motel, 1100 Crystal Avenue (Crystal Falls 49920) / 906-875-6596

CAMPGROUNDS
Frank's Campground / 906-544-2271
Iron Mountain Campgrounds / 906-774-7701
River's Bend Campground, 3905 Pine Mountain Road / 906-779-1171
Bewabic State Park, 1933 US 2 West (Crystal Falls 49920) / 906-875-3324

RESTAURANTS
Country Kitchen Iron Mountain, 900 South Stephenson Avenue / 906-774-1777
Dallas Restaurant, US 2 / 906-779-1310
Gathering Place, 427 South Stephenson Avenue / 906-774-8757
Romagnoli's / 906-774-7300
Club Felix, 2465 US 2 South (Crystal Falls 49920) / 906-875-3779
Westwood Supper Club, 1640 US 2 (Crystal Falls 49920) / 906-875-6617

FLY SHOPS AND SPORTING GOODS
DJ's Sport Shop & Marine, 31 Superior Avenue (Crystal Falls 49920) /
    906-875-3113
Jim's Sport Shop, N US Highway 2 / 906-774-4247
Northwoods Wilderness Outfitters Inc, 4088 Pine Mountain Road / 906-774-9009
Scott's Sporting Goods, 1601 North Stephenson Avenue / 906-774-8520

AUTO SERVICE
Dave's Mobil Service, 1137 South Stephenson Avenue / 906-774-7717
Hamm's Service, 301 Carpenter Avenue / 906-774-0494
Mike's Auto Repair, 701 South Stephenson Avenue / 906-774-6681
Twin City Service, 1228 Prospect Avenue / 906-774-6233
Ted's Service Center, 17 Superior Avenue (Crystal Falls 49920) / 906-875-6577

AIR SERVICE
Iron County Ford Airport, 700 South Stephenson / 906-774-4830

MEDICAL
Dickinson County Memorial Hospital, 400 Woodward Avenue / 906-779-7001

FOR MORE INFORMATION
Dickinson County Area Chamber of Commerce
600 South Stephenson Avenue
Iron Mountain, MI 49801
906-774-2002

Escanaba
Population – 13,659

ACCOMMODATIONS
Brotherton's Motel & Cottages, 4785 M 35 / 906-786-1271
Hiawatha Motel, 2400 Ludington Street / 906-786-1341
Manor Motel, 620 North Lincoln Road / 906-786-7714
Memory Lane Motel, 2415 Ludington Street / 906-786-7171
Sands Motel, 2700 Ludington Street / 906-786-9846

CAMPGROUNDS
Escanaba City Parks & Forestry, 115 North Sheridan Road / 906-786-1842
Park Place of the North, 4575 M-35 / 906-786-8453

RESTAURANTS
Alexander's Restaurant & Lounge, 1110 Ludington Street / 906-786-7211
Crispigna's, 1213 Ludington Street / 906-786-8660
Dell's Supper Club, 3765 US 2 / 906-789-9250
Drifters Restaurant, 701 North Lincoln Road / 906-789-0508
Main Street Cafe, 1301 Ludington Street / 906-786-5099
Ranch Steak & Seafood, 521 North Lincoln Road / 906-789-0630

FLY SHOPS AND SPORTING GOODS
Great Lakes Sports, 6687 US 2 / 906-789-9473
Land & Lakes Sports, 845 North Lincoln Road / 906-786-5263
Bayshore Bait & Tackle, 1323 Lakeshore Drive (Gladstone 49837) / 906-428-2950

AUTO SERVICE
Jerry's Service Center, 14 North 9th Street (Gladstone 49837) / 906-428-1512
Tom's Auto Care Center, 900 Superior Avenue (Gladstone 49837) / 906-428-3295
Dave's Auto Repair, 4379 M Road / 906-789-9355
Dunlap's Service, 800 Ludington Street / 906-789-9072
Lake Forest Auto Center, 5224 11th Road / 906-786-3072
Town & Country Motors, 2600 Ludington Street / 906-786-5531

AIR SERVICE
Delta County Airport / 906-786-2192.

MEDICAL
St. Francis Hospital, 3401 Ludington Street / 906-786-3311

FOR MORE INFORMATION
Delta County Area Chamber of Commerce
230 Ludington Street
Escanaba, MI 49829
906-786-2192

Menominee
Population – 9,398

ACCOMMODATIONS
Bay Breeze Motel, 1055 35th Avenue / 906-863-6964
Hojo Inn, 2516 10th Street / 906-863-4431
Sands Motel, Cedar River / 906-863-9897

CAMPGROUNDS
Menominee River Park, 2511 5th Avenue / 906-863-5101
J.W. Wells State Park, N7670 Hwy M-35 (Cedar River 49813) / 906-863-9747

RESTAURANTS
Dexter's, 736 10th Avenue / 906-863-1333
Harbor House, 821 1st Street / 906-863-7770
Pat & Rayleen's Restaurant, 2812 10th Street / 906-863-6241
Roadhouse Grill / 906-863-1159
Schloegel's Bay View Restaurant, 2720 10th Street / 906-863-7888

FLY SHOPS AND SPORTING GOODS
Acorns and Antlers Archery Center, 2400 13th Street / 906-863-8026
Great Lakes Sports, 2921 13th Street / 906-863-5797

AUTO SERVICE
Bay Shore Auto Service, North 1997 Range Line Drive / 906-863-6800
D & J Auto Service, 128 9th Avenue / 906-863-6400
Dugre's Auto Center, 1102 20th Avenue / 906-863-2335
Jim's Auto Repair, 4317 10th Street / 906-863-9491
Last Stop Auto Repair, 4701 10th Street / 906-864-3464
Ron's Uptown Service, 400 10th Avenue / 906-863-6649

MEDICAL
Bay Area Medical Center Bay Area Center, 3100 Shore Drive / 906-863-1251

FOR MORE INFORMATION
Chamber of Commerce
1005 10th Avenue
Menominee, MI 49858
906-863-2679

Eastern Upper Peninsula

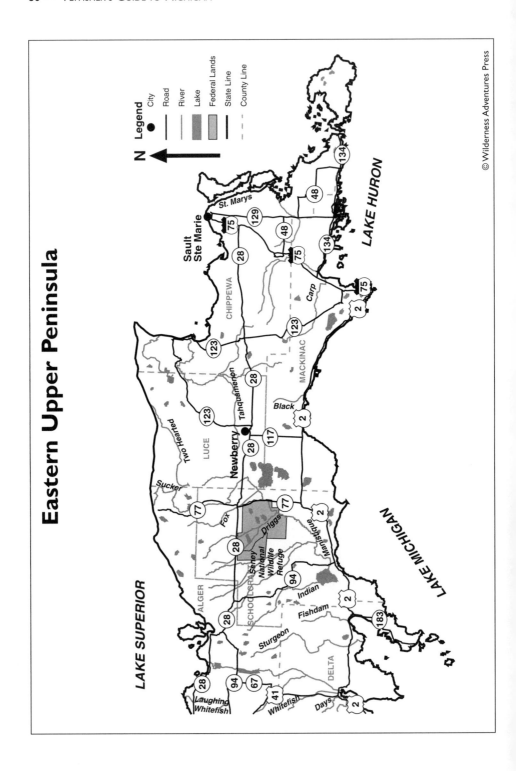

Eastern Upper Peninsula

The Eastern Upper Peninsula provides a wide range of flyfishing opportunities, from brook trout in tight, tea-stained creeks to Atlantic salmon in the awesome rapids of the St. Mary's River. Three different Great Lakes receive water from the streams and rivers of this relatively unpopulated part of Michigan. This is where Hemingway's Two-Hearted River and the Fox River, which everyone knows was really the river being described in the short story, arise close together but flow in opposite directions.

St. Mary's River

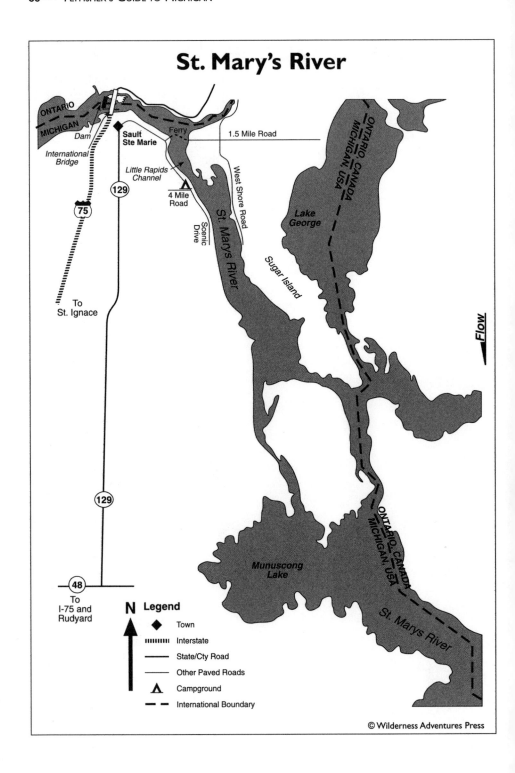

© Wilderness Adventures Press

St. Mary's River

As you would expect, the outlet of Lake Superior is a huge river. The St. Mary's separates Michigan from Ontario and flows through a series of lakes throughout most of its length. The key area of interest to fly anglers is the rapids section in Sault Ste. Marie. This is the only part of the St. Mary's that can be waded. Some flyfishing is possible from other parts of the river, but depth and current make it difficult to reach the fish. There is a *Hexagenia* hatch that brings trout and Atlantic salmon to the surface in the deep sections of the river. This is the latest Hex hatch in Michigan and generally peaks in the second half of July. A boat is needed to reach the fish in most instances.

More than half of the wadeable rapids are found on the Canadian side of the river, so I suppose technically this description should wait for a flyfisher's guide to Ontario. But since it is such a unique and special fishery with at least part of it in Michigan waters, we are going to include it here. Access to the rapids is from the Canadian side, so an Ontario license fishing license will be required. Ontario has licenses for various lengths of time, and the catch-and-release angler can save considerably by choosing the Conservation License.

Careful wading is necessary to prevent a spill in the icy water of Lake Superior. The current is strong in most of the rapids, and a wading staff is an essential piece of equipment. In addition, some kind of studded soles are highly recommended, as the rocks are slippery and depth is difficult to judge because of the extreme clarity of the

A happy angler fishing the St. Mary's River rapids.

*A beautiful, bright
steelhead caught
at St. Mary's River rapids.*

water. It should be noted that parts of the rapids near the Canadian shore can be fished without the necessity of wading the heavy current. Where a concrete berm parallels the Canadian shore, fish can be caught in the channel between the berm and shore. The wading there is somewhat easier than in the main river. Fishing from or next to the berm also helps with the wading.

Anadromous fish are the big draw at the rapids. Steelhead, Atlantic salmon, pink salmon, and chinook salmon provide a great fishery from spring until late fall. Some coho salmon and brown trout also join the mix.

The main steelhead migration begins in May and peaks around the first of June in most years, making it the latest run in the state. The reason the run lasts this late is that it takes a long time for Lake Superior to warm up in the spring. You can intercept fresh fish in the pools or try to antagonize spawning fish. Most of the spawning gravel is concentrated in the channel on the Canadian side of the concrete berm and right alongside the berm in the main rapids. Egg sucking leech, marabou spey, and woolly bugger patterns all get the steelhead's attention. Egg flies will also work well once good numbers of fish have started spawning.

St. Mary's River
rapids hen steelhead.

Atlantic salmon begin entering the rapids in June, and some of the best fishing occurs during the second half of the month. Though fishing can still be good in July, summer wears on the fish, making them tougher to entice with a fly. This is the best location to tangle with an Atlantic salmon in Michigan—being able to see one come for your fly in the crystal clear water is a special thrill. Landing them in the strong current is usually quite a bit less than an even proposition, and you must be ready to follow the fish.

In late August a large run of pink salmon enters the rapids. While most of the salmon will be less than 4 pounds, they provide great sport on light tackle—what they lack in size they make up for in numbers. During the peak of the run, you can expect to have double figure days. The runs are still a bit stronger during odd-numbered years because the accidental plant occurred in an odd-numbered year back in the 1950s. Even so, enough fish have delayed their spawning run until they were 3 years old over the years, making good runs in even years as well. Leech and woolly bugger patterns in bright pinks, purples, and reds are very effective at enticing strikes from these nonfeeding fish.

Another fine steelhead from the St. Mary's River.

The run of chinook salmon begins before the pinks are done, and this can create some problems when a 20-pound fish grabs a streamer attached to 4X tippet and a 5-weight rod. But think of the stories you can tell whether you land it or not. The kings begin entering the rapids in mid-September and peak at the end of the month. They continue to spawn well into October and provide great sport in the strong current. You will need your "track shoes," because it is important to stay close to the salmon so it doesn't wrap your line around one of the many boulders present.

About the time chinook are finishing their spawning ritual, a modest number of steelhead move into the rapids area and rest in the pools. You can fish for them until winter weather makes it impossible. This is the far north, and sometime in December single-digit temperatures and ice on equipment will make fishing too tough to endure.

There are resident rainbows and whitefish in the St. Mary's, along with some brown trout. These fish can fill in the action when anadromous fish are playing hard to get.

Stream Facts: St. Mary's River

Seasons
- Open all year.

Special Regulations
- Possession limits vary depending on the type of license purchased.

Fish
- Anadromous king, pink, and Atlantic salmon and steelhead.
- Resident rainbow and brown trout and whitefish.

River Miles
- Rapids are about 1 mile long and ¼ mile wide.

River Characteristics
- A bedrock rapids with a concrete berm separating the river into two channels.
- Spawning gravel is somewhat limited and is concentrated on the Canadian side of the berm and adjacent to the berm in the main river.
- Classic pools with tailouts, crevices in the bedrock, and whitewater rapids are intermingled.

River Access
- Access is on the Canadian side at the Canadian Lock National Historic Site.
- Fishermen gain access by following a boardwalk and hiking trails.
- Licenses and information can be obtained at the Canadian Customs/Duty Free Store just across the International Bridge.

Carp River

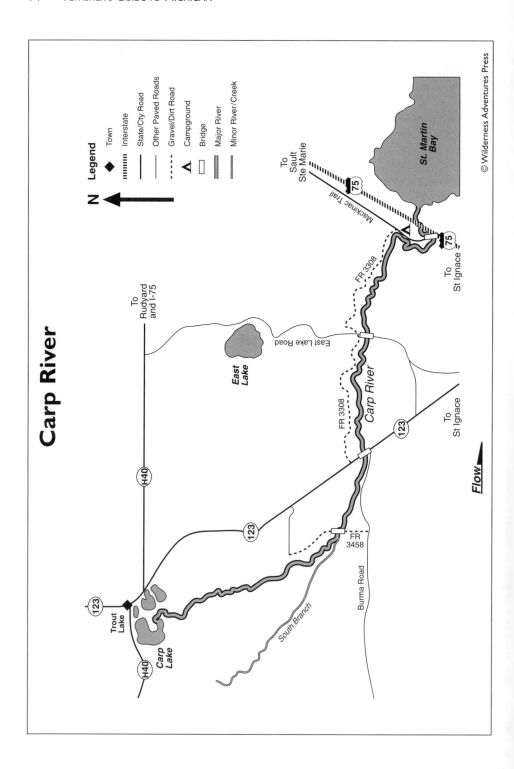

Legend

N

♦ Town
▨ Interstate
— State/Cty Road
— Other Paved Roads
--- Gravel/Dirt Road
△ Campground
☐ Bridge
Major River
Minor River/Creek

© Wilderness Adventures Press

CARP RIVER

The Upper Peninsula's other major tributary to Lake Huron is the Carp River. This small river begins as the outlet of Carp Lake, which is also known as Trout Lake, in southwestern Chippewa County. The river travels in a generally easterly direction across Mackinac County and empties into St. Martin Bay.

The Carp River is home to both brook and brown trout and becomes fishable with a fly rod when the South Branch joins the mainstream. The stream's wild brook trout are augmented with hatchery brook and brown trout. In addition, steelhead successfully reproduce in the Carp, so it's possible to catch all three species of trout on most outings. Stream improvement work, including sand traps, have been successful in exposing gravel and increasing the trout holding cover.

Most of the Carp River flows through the Hiawatha National Forest, and forest service roads cross and parallel much of the river, providing good access. USFS-3458 crosses the river just below the South Branch confluence, and you can have a good time fishing in either direction. The next road crossing (M-123) is over 4 river miles downstream, but Burma Road (USFS-3124) to the south parallels the Carp for about

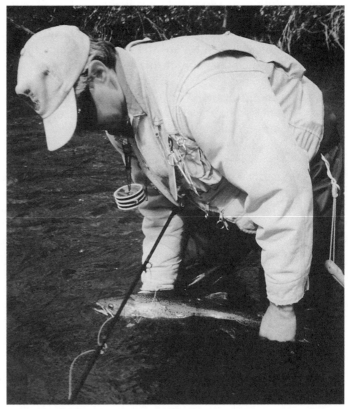

*Releasing
a steelhead.*

3 miles up from the highway. There are some two-tracks back to the river, and all of this reach is in the Hiawatha National Forest. You can hike in and out as well, with the river always less than one-half mile away. Downstream from M-123, USFS-3308 stays pretty close to the Carp for about 10 miles until the river makes a sharp turn to the south. Again, this is national forest land and East Lake Road bisects this stretch of river. You can wade as far as you like up or down from the East Lake Road Bridge and then walk back to your vehicle on USFS-3308.

Soon after the Carp leaves USFS-3308, there is a campground that is accessible from Mackinac Trail. If you are like me and like to cover lots of water, you can start at the Mackinac Trail bridge and fish up to the campground. This is a nice stretch and its advantage is that you get to cover a lot of river distance with a relatively short hike down the blacktop back to your car or truck. There is also a public access site at the Carp's confluence with Lake Huron, where you can try for anadromous fish in the lake or intercept them in the first holes upstream.

Attractor patterns fool browns as well as brookies and juvenile steelhead. This river is not as stained as many Upper Peninsula streams, and trout seem to grow to good size. Swimming woolly buggers and muddlers by the logs and undercuts is a good way to draw out the larger trout.

Anadromous runs are a big draw to anglers on the Carp. In addition to a run of wild steelhead, smolts are stocked by the DNR in the lower river. The run usually peaks in late April or early May. Because a sandy substrate is predominant on the Carp and good gravel riffles are still relatively scarce in this stream, flyfishers can really improve their chances for success with anadromous rainbows by focusing on these riffles.

Pink salmon run the Carp in good numbers each September and draw many anglers. Just below the gravel areas near the mouth, fishing bright streamers and egg flies with your normal trout tackle will result in great sport. The sooner pinks can be intercepted after they leave the lake the better.

There is also a run of wild chinook in the river, and some of the fish planted for a Native American gill net fishery in St. Martin Bay also stray into the Carp River. Trying to corral these fish in the relatively small river can be great sport. Look for them to start running in September; they continue to be present well into October. I sent a friend up to the Carp armed with tackle for pinks, but the chinook were there in numbers, and she gave me a hard time about not being geared up for these big fish. Of course, she sure loves to tell the story about landing a 23-pound king on the too-light tackle. Currently, the Carp River remains open for fishing until December 31 and has an early opener on April 1 for steelhead fishing. In the future, the stream will be open all year.

CARP RIVER MAJOR HATCHES

Insect	Jan	Feb	Mar	Apr	May	Jun	July	Aug	Sep	Oct	Nov	Dec	Time	Flies
Hendrickson					▮								M/A	Hendrickson #12–14; Quill Gordon; Red Quill; Adams
Blue-winged Olive							▮	▮					A	Blue-winged Olive #18–20; Sparkle Dun Baetis; Iron Dun; Olive CDC Mayfly Dun
Little Black Caddis								▮	▮				A	Little Black Caddis #16–18; Griffith's Gnat; CDC Emerging Caddis Brown; Black Ant
Grannom						▮	▮						M/A	Grannom #14–16; Medium Brown Sedge; Elk Caddis (brown-olive)
Net-building Caddis					▮	▮	▮	▮	▮	▮			M/A	Spotted Sedge #16–18; Eastern Elk Wing Caddis; Goddard Caddis
Sulphur Dun					▮	▮	▮						A/E	Sulphur Dun #16; Pale Morning Dun; CDC Comparadun Yellow; Pale Evening Dun
March Brown					▮	▮							M/A	March Brown #12–14; Dark Cahill; Gray Fox; Ginger Quill
Gray Drake						▮	▮						E	Gray Drake #12–14; Gray Adams
Brown Drake						▮							E	Brown Drake #10–12; Adams; CDC Brown Drake
Trico						▮	▮	▮	▮	▮			M	Tiny White Wing Black #24–28; Parachute Adams; CDC Trico; Spent Wing Trico
White Fly									▮				E	White Fly #12–14; White Miller
Streamers	▮	▮	▮	▮	▮	▮	▮	▮	▮	▮	▮	▮	M/A/E	Woolly Buggers #6–12; Clouser's Minnow; Muddler Minnows; BC Craw; Zonkers
Terrestrials					▮	▮	▮	▮	▮				M/A/E	Woolly Worm #8–12; BC Spider; Letort Cricket; Joe's Hopper #6–10; Dave's Hopper; Dropper Hopper

HATCH TIME CODE: M = morning; A = afternoon; E = evening.

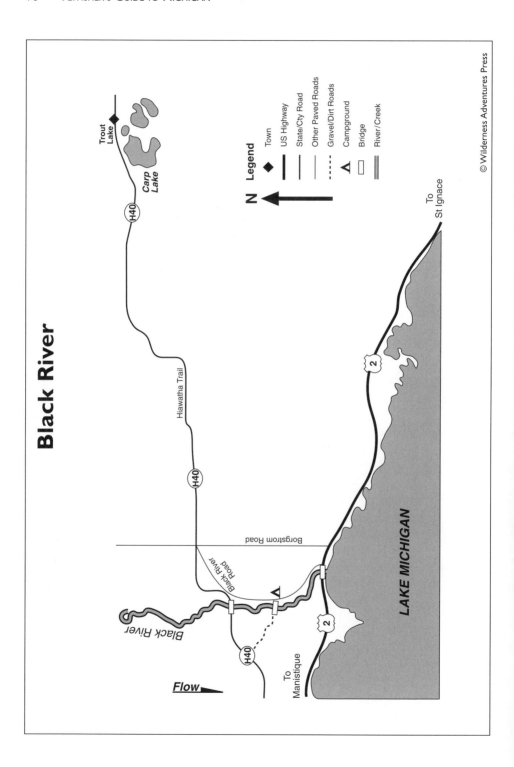

Black River

This male steelhead was caught in the spring.

Black River

This is one of Michigan's smaller Black Rivers. It flows straight south into Lake Michigan about 12 miles to the west of the Carp's headwaters. This stream is full of wild brook trout and small rainbows (juvenile steelhead), however space is tight, requiring lots of short roll casts. The river changes quickly from a slow meandering waterway near Lake Michigan into a tumbling cascade where trout have to make a quick decision. Thus, attention-getting attractor patterns work best for brookies and rainbows. Be alert and ready to lift the rod at any hesitation in the drift of your fly.

Access is found along Black River Road, which parallels the stream. There is also a campground on the river that is accessible from Black River Road via Peter's Truck Trail. Hiawatha Trail (H40) crosses the Black and offers an additional way to jump into this tumbling stream. The stream is relatively lightly fished in the summer, but steelhead attract a fair number of anglers in the spring. Up to the Peter's Truck Trail Bridge, the Black River opens early for steelhead on April 1, but in the future, this reach is scheduled to be open all year. Coho salmon also reproduce naturally in this river, and you are likely to catch juvenile cohos when trout fishing. They have larger eyes, a forked tail, and no hint of pink on their sides like steelhead parr do. Adult coho run in October, and again, can be fished up to Peter's Bridge until the end of December. With good rainfall a few steelhead also enter the Black in the fall.

MANISTIQUE RIVER

The Manistique River is a good-sized river that is probably better known for its tributaries than its own mainstream. It begins at the junction of its most famous feeder streams, the Fox and the East Branch of the Fox Rivers, about 3 miles east of Germfask. Despite the fact that both the Fox and the East Branch are fine brook trout waters, the Manistique begins as a river that is marginal for trout and contains mostly smallmouth bass, walleye, and northern pike. When you do encounter a brook trout here, though, it is likely to be a good-sized specimen.

The upper Manistique has a sand bottom for the most part and is quite deep. While parts of it can be waded, it is frequently necessary to get out and walk around deep water, which makes floating a better option. The best technique for walleyes and smallmouths is to use an actively swimming streamer. You can do a short float from Germfask down to M-77 to see how you like the river and the fishing. If the fishing is good, the reach between M-77 and the Mead Creek campground can take all day.

Smallmouth and walleye continue to be the main quarry moving downstream in the Manistique. The first big tributary is the Driggs River, a brook trout stream in its upper reaches but warms up by the time it reaches the Manistique. The Driggs comes in about a mile upstream from the Mead Creek Campground and is good landmark to check timing in the float from Germfask. Smaller creeks also add their flow to the

Manistique River.

Manistique River

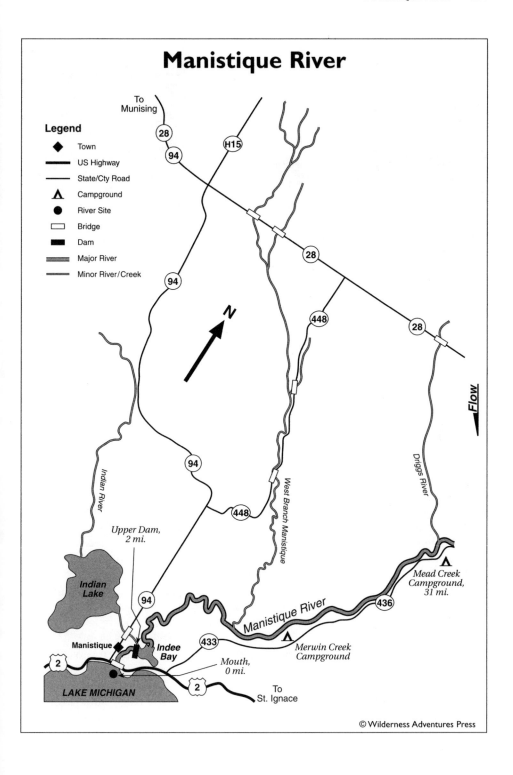

Legend

◆ Town

▬ US Highway

— State/Cty Road

Λ Campground

● River Site

▭ Bridge

■ Dam

▬ Major River

— Minor River/Creek

To Munising

28

94

H15

28

94

448

28

N

94

94

Driggs River

West Branch Manistique

448

Indian River

Flow

Upper Dam, 2 mi.

Mead Creek Campground, 31 mi.

Indian Lake

94

436

Manistique

Indee Bay

433

Manistique River

Merwin Creek Campground

2

Mouth, 0 mi.

LAKE MICHIGAN

2

To St. Ignace

© Wilderness Adventures Press

A rocky section of the Manistique River.

mainstream, and some of them could provide a chance at a big brook trout near their mouths. The Cookson Bridge and Merwin Creek Campground provide additional access to the middle part of the river.

The West Branch of the Manistique and Indian River add their water to the Manistique before it is blocked by what is called the Upper Dam. Probably the best fishing in the mainstream occurs in the 2 miles of river between the dam and Lake Michigan. Although this is urban fishing in the town of Manistique, fish are there. Access is good with several bridges and parking areas along the east side of the river near the mouth.

Smallmouth bass, channel catfish, and walleyes are present in good numbers in the lower river and are free to move back and forth from Lake Michigan. In fact, Lake Michigan resident smallmouth and walleyes move into the Manistique to spawn, providing a chance at some really outsize fish in the spring and early summer. The gradient is fairly high below the dam, and fish spawn over bedrock.

Chinook salmon and steelhead are planted in the lower Manistique and provide a good fishery in both the spring and fall. The main steelhead run usually occurs in late April, often coinciding with high water from snowmelt and spring rains. Because this is a big river that is slow to clear, calling ahead is almost mandatory. The chinook run peaks in September and continues into October, and fishing conditions are much more likely to be conducive to flyfishing in the fall. In late October and November, some steelhead might enter the river, especially if there are some good rains.

FOX RIVER

The Fox River and its East Branch are among Michigan's best brook trout streams. Surprisingly, the Fox River rises in Alger County less than 10 miles from Lake Superior but flows south, where its water eventually empties into Lake Michigan. Most of the upper river is in Lake Superior State Forest, which again seems contradictory for a Lake Michigan tributary. Soon after the West Branch of the Fox joins the mainstream, it becomes wide enough to permit flyfishing. About a mile downstream from the confluence, the Fox becomes a designated blue ribbon trout stream and keeps this classification for 18 miles down to the M-28 Highway Bridge. County Road 450 provides excellent access to the Fox above Seney. The road closely parallels the river as it flows through state forest, and there are many little pulloffs along the county road that provide river access. Above the confluence with the Little Fox River, Taylor Dam Road and two tracks off of it lead to the Fox. Downstream from Seney, access is not nearly as good, which is all right since this water is much better floated.

Narrow and fairly deep is an apt description of the upper Fox. Wading can be difficult when the water is up due to the depth of the many holes present but can be just as difficult during low to normal water levels, as well. When my partner and I fished adjacent reaches along County Road 450 north of Seney, I was able to stay in the

A beautiful piece of water on the Fox River.

Fox and Driggs Rivers

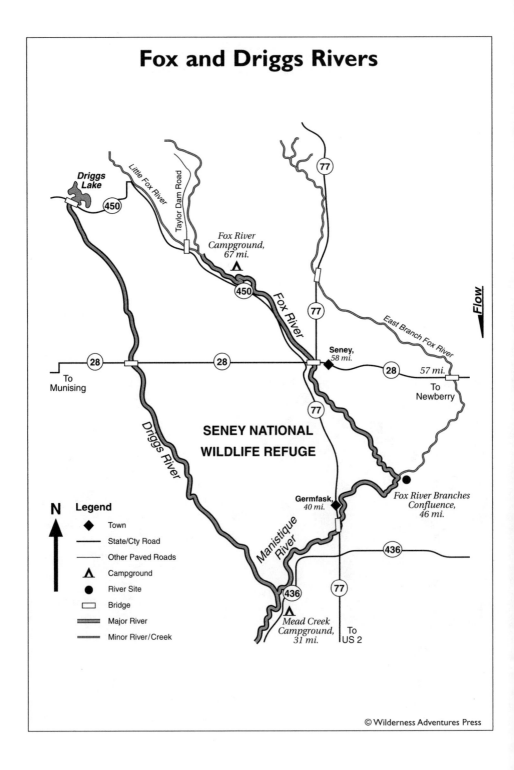

Driggs Lake

Little Fox River

Taylor Dam Road

450

Fox River Campground, 67 mi.

450

Fox River

77

77

East Branch Fox River

Flow

Seney, 58 mi.

28

To Munising

28

28

57 mi.

To Newberry

77

Driggs River

SENEY NATIONAL WILDLIFE REFUGE

Germfask, 40 mi.

Fox River Branches Confluence, 46 mi.

Manistique River

436

436

N

Legend

◆ Town
— State/Cty Road
— Other Paved Roads
Λ Campground
● River Site
⬒ Bridge
▬ Major River
▬ Minor River/Creek

77

To US 2

436

Mead Creek Campground, 31 mi.

© Wilderness Adventures Press

Fox River.

water while he had to spend most of his time on the bank. Because of the relatively gentle current, the Fox can be navigated in a belly boat. A better bet, though, would be one of the many rowable kickboats that are now available.

Even though the Fox's smaller brook trout are pretty gullible, fooling fish over 12 inches will require a stealthy approach and a good presentation. Muddlers, Clouser minnows, and black woolly buggers provide the kind of meal that larger brook trout like. Because the stream is narrow and the banks are lined with overhanging vegetation, terrestrials play an important role in the diet of brook trout as well.

Downstream from M-28 and the small town of Seney, the Fox River continues to support brook trout and the occasional brown. But because the river flows through the marshy Seney National Wildlife Refuge, some kind of floating craft is almost necessary to fish the river effectively. Many anglers make a two-day trip out of floating

An angler works the tight banks of the Driggs River.

the Fox to its juncture with the East Branch and then continue to the takeout at Germfask on what is now called the Manistique River.

The East Branch of the Fox is similar in size and length to the mainstream, and many consider it to have better numbers of large trout. In fact, because of the faster growth rate in this branch, the DNR is planning on raising the minimum size limit, which should further increase the numbers of good-sized trout. Arising from springs in northern Schoolcraft County, the East Branch parallels Highway M-77 as it gathers more water from several creeks. Once it crosses M-77, it maintains the blue ribbon trout stream designation almost to its confluence with the main stream. You can also flyfish the East Branch upstream from the highway. There is good access at the East Branch Campground and along the highway in the state forest. However, tight quarters make roll casting the main way to present a fly. It doesn't get magically wider downstream, either, so there are lots of places where a backcast won't be appropriate unless you decide to switch from trout to squirrels.

The East Branch is a bit easier to wade, but floating the lower part is still a good option. A similar float to that suggested on the mainstream can be started at the same highway, M-28, and finished at the same town, Germfask. Brookies to 3 pounds are possible in this stretch, and there are good numbers of fish 10 inches or longer. Some brown trout join brookies in the lower part of this branch.

Driggs River

The Driggs River is the unsung tributary to the upper Manistique River. And there will be some anglers unhappy to see it mentioned here. Small- to medium-sized brook trout are its attraction, and the best flyfishing water occurs for a few miles upstream from M-28 and for the first 7 or 8 miles below the highway. The Driggs starts out as the outlet of Driggs Lake, and this fact plus the frequent occurrence of beaver dams can create water temperatures that are higher than ideal for trout.

The Driggs also flows through the Seney National Wildlife Refuge, where there is good access from Driggs River Road downstream from M-28. The river widens and warms in its last half-dozen miles before it reaches the Manistique, making it more likely to catch smallmouth bass than trout.

Stream Facts: Manistique and Fox Rivers

Seasons
- The Manistique below the Upper Dam is open all year.
- The Fox and other trout containing tributaries are open from the last Saturday in April through September 30.

Special Regulations
- Size limit for all trout and salmon between October 1 and last Saturday in April is 15 inches.
- Size limits in the East Branch of the Fox are 10 inches for brookies and 12 inches for browns.

Fish
- Resident brook and brown trout, smallmouth bass, walleye, channel catfish, and northern pike.
- Anadromous rainbow trout and chinook salmon.

River Miles
- Lake Michigan—0
- Upper Dam—2
- Cookson Road Bridge—20
- Mead Creek Campground—31
- Germfask—40
- Fox/East Branch Confluence—46
- M-28-58 (M-28 on East Branch—57)
- Fox River Campground—67

River Characteristics
- Mostly sand bottomed, meandering river with lush riverside vegetation.
- Faster water below dam near mouth.
- The Fox River and the East Branch of Fox River are narrow winding streams with lots of deep holes and trout holding cover.
- Gravel riffles are present in the upper parts but there is more sand than gravel.

River Access
- Access is available at each landmark noted above with river miles except at the confluence of the Fox and its East Branch.
- Most of the river system flows through public land and one can hike in from paralleling roads.

FOX RIVER MAJOR HATCHES

Insect	Time	Fly Patterns
Hendrickson	M/A	Hendrickson #12–14; Quill Gordon; Red Quill; Adams
Blue-winged Olive	A	Blue-winged Olive #18–20; Sparkle Dun Baetis; Iron Dun; Olive CDC Mayfly Dun
Little Black Caddis	A	Little Black Caddis #16–18; Griffith's Gnat; CDC Emerging Caddis Brown; Black Ant
Grannom	M/A	Grannom #14–16; Medium Brown Sedge; Elk Caddis (brown-olive)
Net-building Caddis	M/A	Spotted Sedge #16–18; Eastern Elk Wing Caddis; Goddard Caddis
Sulphur Dun	A/E	Sulphur Dun #16; Pale Morning Dun; CDC Comparadun Yellow; Pale Evening Dun
March Brown	M/A	March Brown #12–14; Dark Cahill; Gray Fox; Ginger Quill
Gray Drake	E	Gray Drake #12–14; Gray Adams
Brown Drake	E	Brown Drake #10–12; Adams; CDC Brown Drake
Hexagenia	E	Hex #4–8; Great Olive-winged Drake; Spring's Wiggler; Wiggle-Hex Nymph
Trico	M	Tiny White Wing Black #24–28; Parachute Adams; CDC Trico; Spent Wing Trico
White Fly	E	White Fly #12–14; White Miller
Streamers	M/A/E	Woolly Buggers #6–12; Clouser's Minnow; Muddler Minnows; BC Craw; Zonkers
Terrestrials	M/A/E	Woolly Worm #8–12; BC Spider; Letort Cricket; Joe's Hopper #6–10; Dave's Hopper; Dropper Hopper

HATCH TIME CODE: M = morning; A = afternoon; E = evening.

Indian River

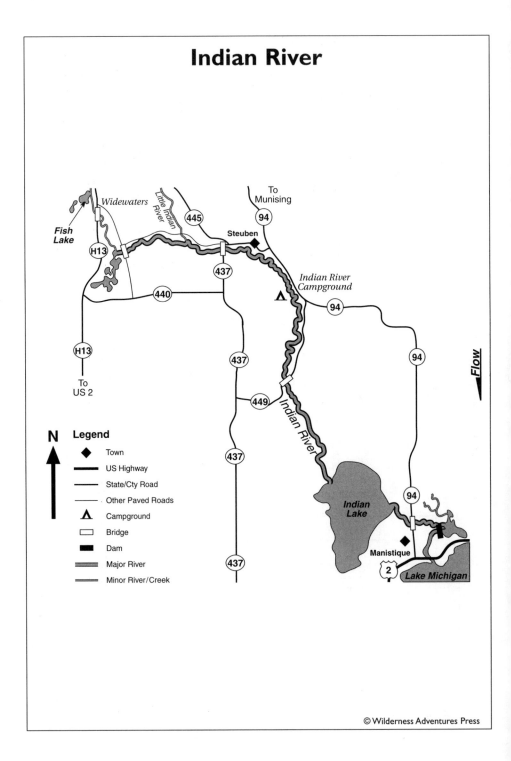

Releasing a nice fish on the Indian River.

INDIAN RIVER

Indian River begins in a chain of lakes in southeastern Alger County and flows south and east to Indian Lake. It then exits Indian Lake and flows into the Manistique River just upstream from the dam on the lower Manistique. The headwaters are fairly cool due to springs, but the reach below the Widewaters and Fish Lake becomes too warm for trout. The prime trout water begins when the Little Indian joins the main-stream and continues down to the County Road 449 crossing.

This reach begins as a gravel-bottomed, relatively shallow stream that slowly becomes sandier with much deeper holes. There is lots of wood in the water, and the jumbles of logs create great cover for large trout. And that is exactly what you will find in the Indian between the tiny town of Steuben and CR-449. Browns 24 inch and larger are present, but catching them is very difficult, as might be expected.

The Indian has one of the best *Hexagenia* hatches in the Upper Peninsula, and with proper scouting there is a chance to catch a very large brown when the big mayflies are hatching. Prime time is usually early July, but this can be altered by weather. When there isn't a good hatch, actively swimming streamers near the logs is a good tactic. There is a good population of crayfish, so use your favorite crawfish pattern. Drifting nymphs is not a very good option, because the wood will eat the flies on almost every cast.

In the reach below Steuben, there are only a few brook trout present, and small browns are not very common, either. Though this is not a river where lots of trout are caught, it is definitely a place to catch trophy-sized fish. On a recent visit, I caught and released only four trout, not counting the recently planted fingerlings, in 11 hours of fishing, but the lengths were 12, 17, 21, and 21½ inches. And I had four other encounters with fish in the 20-plus-inch range that either followed my fly or were hooked and lost, including one that almost scared me out of the river.

The Little Indian offers the chance to catch more fish, mostly brook trout. True to the system though, this river is a good one for producing large brookies. Brushy banks and beaver dams make casting a challenge, but if one of these gorgeous fish in the mid-teens grabs your fly, it is all worth the effort.

Natural reproduction is low in the Indian, but the DNR regularly plants it with sublegal brown trout. Currently, the agency is working with some new strains of trout that might survive better than the previous strains used in this put-and-grow fishery. Minimum size limits have been raised to 10 and 12 inches for brookies and browns because of their good growth potential in this river. Five bridges, parallel roads, and the Indian River Campground provide good access to this stream.

Fishdam River

It is a bit of a stretch to call the Fishdam a river, but this small stream provides some good fishing for brook trout, with a few browns and juvenile rainbows thrown into the mix. The river begins as the outlet of Stevens Lake in eastern Delta County and flows almost straight south to Lake Michigan's Big Bay de Noc. While there are a few open areas upstream, the Fishdam becomes only marginally flyfishable at USFS-2222, about 9 river miles from the mouth. The water is deeply stained with tannins, so using attractor flies in sizes that seem too large for the 8- to 12-inch brookies is a good plan.

In spring, there is a modest run of wild steelhead in the river, but you will have to wait for trout season to begin to fish for them. Summer steelhead are planted in the nearby Sturgeon River, and I recently encountered several of them that had strayed into the Fishdam. This was totally unexpected, and I was shocked, to say the least, to hook a couple of 8-pound rainbows while fishing for 8-inch brookies.

INDIAN RIVER MAJOR HATCHES

Insect	Jan	Feb	Mar	Apr	May	Jun	July	Aug	Sep	Oct	Nov	Dec	Time	Fly Patterns
Hendrickson					▓								M/A	Hendrickson #12–14; Quill Gordon; Red Quill; Adams
Blue-winged Olive					▓	▓	▓	▓					A	Blue-winged Olive #18–20; Sparkle Dun Baetis; Iron Dun; Olive CDC Mayfly Dun
Little Black Caddis					▓	▓	▓	▓					A	Little Black Caddis #16–18; Griffith's Gnat; CDC Emerging Caddis Brown; Black Ant
Net-building Caddis					▓	▓	▓	▓	▓	▓			M/A	Spotted Sedge #16–18; Eastern Elk Wing Caddis; Goddard Caddis
Sulphur Dun						▓	▓						A/E	Sulphur Dun #16; Pale Morning Dun; CDC Comparadun Yellow; Pale Evening Dun
March Brown					▓	▓							M/A	March Brown #12–14; Dark Cahill; Gray Fox; Ginger Quill
Gray Drake						▓	▓						E	Gray Drake #12–14; Gray Adams
Brown Drake						▓	▓						E	Brown Drake #10–12; Adams; CDC Brown Drake
Hexagenia							▓						E	Hex #4–8; Great Olive-winged Drake; Spring's Wiggler; Wiggle-Hex Nymph
Trico							▓	▓	▓	▓			M	Tiny White Wing Black #24–28; Parachute Adams; CDC Trico; Spent Wing Trico
White Fly									▓				E	White Fly #12–14; White Miller
Streamers	▓	▓	▓	▓	▓	▓	▓	▓	▓	▓	▓	▓	M/A/E	Woolly Buggers #6–12; Clouser's Minnow; Muddler Minnows; BC Craw; Zonkers
Terrestrials					▓	▓	▓	▓	▓				M/A/E	Woolly Worm #8–12; BC Spider; Letort Cricket; Joe's Hopper #6–10; Dave's Hopper; Dropper Hopper

HATCH TIME CODE: M = morning; A = afternoon; E = evening.

Sturgeon River

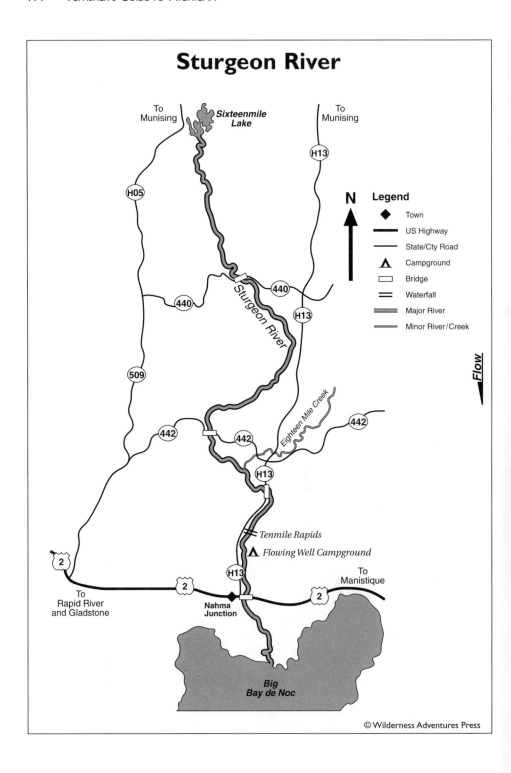

To Munising

Sixteenmile Lake

To Munising

H13

H05

N

Legend

◆ Town
— US Highway
— State/Cty Road
▲ Campground
▭ Bridge
= Waterfall
— Major River
— Minor River/Creek

440

440

H13

Sturgeon River

509

Flow

Eighteen Mile Creek

442

442

442

442

H13

Tenmile Rapids

▲ *Flowing Well Campground*

H13

2

2

2

To Manistique

To Rapid River and Gladstone

Nahma Junction

Big Bay de Noc

© Wilderness Adventures Press

STURGEON RIVER

While not as confusing as all the Black Rivers, there are certainly enough Sturgeon Rivers in Michigan. A friend of mine once tried to get the name of this tributary to northern Lake Michigan changed to the Nahma River (after the town near its mouth) but got bogged down in red tape and gave up.

At any rate, this picturesque river begins as the outlet of 16 Mile Lake in Alger County and meanders in a southerly direction to Big Bay de Noc. The Sturgeon becomes wide enough for flyfishing below Cook Lake Road. While water temperatures can become marginal for trout during hot weather, both browns and brookies must find relief somewhere, because they are present throughout the system.

One of the main attributes of the Sturgeon is that it is very lightly fished. If you want solitude on a pretty river, the Sturgeon is a good choice. Although there is plenty of cover for trout to hide in, the relative lack of gravel riffles limits insect production and spawning habitat.

This steelhead fights hard after falling for an egg fly used in conjunction with a strike indicator.

Whitefish River

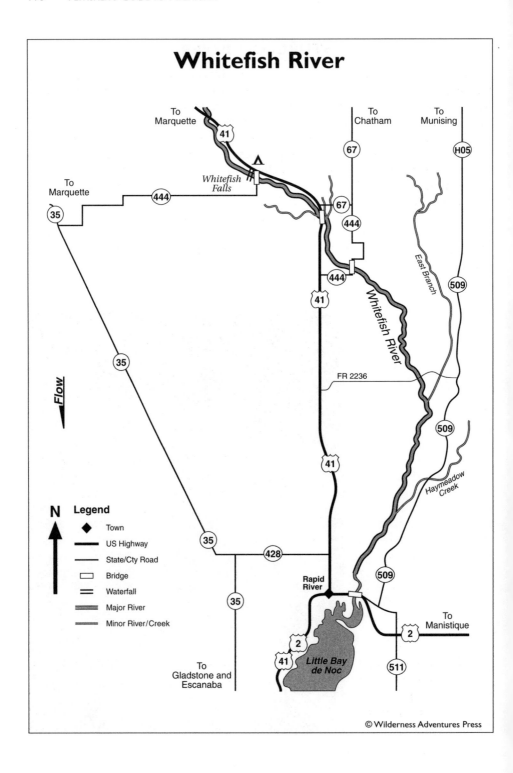

To Marquette

41

To Chatham

67

To Munising

H05

To Marquette

444

Whitefish Falls

67

444

35

444

41

East Branch

509

Whitefish River

FR 2236

509

35

Flow

Haymeadow Creek

509

N Legend

◆ Town

US Highway

State/Cty Road

▭ Bridge

Waterfall

Major River

Minor River/Creek

35

428

509

Rapid River

35

2

To Manistique

2

41

Little Bay de Noc

511

To Gladstone and Escanaba

© Wilderness Adventures Press

Eighteen Mile Creek cools the Sturgeon with its inflow, and the reach below it seems to contain higher numbers of trout than are found farther upstream. Ten Mile Rapids and the Flowing Well Campground area also seem to have above average trout numbers and are good places to check. You can start at either site, fish as far as you like, and then exit across Hiawatha National Forest land to Highway 13, which parallels the river, for an easy walk back to your vehicle. Of course, you can also reverse direction and fish back to your car. Additional access is found upstream at 14 Mile Bridge on Highway 13 and the bridges where County Roads 442 and 440 cross the river.

In addition to resident brook and brown trout, there are some rainbows present due to steelhead natural reproduction. Speaking of steelhead, both winter-run and summer-run steelhead are planted in the Sturgeon, and the river below County Road 442 is open all year. Don't be too surprised if a huge rainbow tries to destroy the 4-weight you were using for brookies and browns. A few salmon also run the Sturgeon in the fall, and October is a beautiful time to be on this river.

WHITEFISH RIVER

For most of its length, the Whitefish River is split into the East and West Branches. They come together about 12 miles upstream from the river's entry into Little Bay de Noc. The West Branch is the longer of the two and begins in eastern Marquette County. It flows mostly in a southerly direction, and within a short distance several creeks containing brookies add their waters to this branch.

By the time the West Branch of the Whitefish flows under US 41, it is plenty big enough to fish with a fly rod. Brook trout are present in reasonable numbers, both from natural reproduction in the tributary creeks and from annual stockings. Much of the river flows over bedrock here, but it is easily waded at normal summer flows. Hot weather can make the mainstream a bit uncomfortable for brookies, sending them into the tributaries.

There is good access downstream at the Whitefish Falls State Forest campground, where it's possible to encounter some juvenile rainbows due to steelhead that spawn below the falls. The river flows alongside the highway until it crosses it again. Downstream from here, the West Branch traverses some relatively remote countryside, with access limited to the crossings of County Road 444 and US Forest Service Road 2236, which is also the upstream limit for the steelhead and salmon extended season.

The smaller East Branch offers somewhat better brook trout fishing, but access is more difficult. The only road crossing it is USFS-2236, which also marks the upstream limit for the East Branch's extended season. Much of the land on the East Branch is public, so you can hike in from County Road 509.

The reach below the confluence of the two branches is almost canyonlike and definitely requires some hiking to reach. The reward for this effort is great scenery and the chance to catch a bunch of unsophisticated brookies. Haymeadow Creek flows into the lower Whitefish River and is marginally flyfishable because some of it flows through "meadow."

Admiring a fine steelhead.

On a recent July trip to the Haymeadow, I encountered an abandoned beaver dam about 100 yards below a huge active barrier. The new dam had caused much of the water to flow through the meadow and around the old dam. I caught a nice brook trout in the 12-inch range below the old dam. And on my first cast above the old dam, I hooked a huge trout that flashed its pinkish hues and then broke off. Thinking I had lost my brook trout of a lifetime, I cast some more and eventually hooked and landed another big fish. It was a spent steelhead that had been trapped above the old beaver dam It couldn't jump over or swim through the mass that had been mostly dewatered by the diversion of water around the six-foot-high dam just upstream. This was the steelhead's lucky day, since I released it below the dam so it could return to Lake Michigan.

In addition to steelhead runs in the spring, the Whitefish also receives modest runs of chinook and pink salmon in September. Later in the fall, you might also encounter a lake-run brown or a steelhead if autumn rains have brought the water level up. When trout season opens, steelhead are still likely to be in the river, so you might want to pay a visit to Whitefish Falls campground in late April and early May.

STURGEON AND WHITEFISH RIVERS MAJOR HATCHES

Insect	Jan	Feb	Mar	Apr	May	Jun	July	Aug	Sep	Oct	Nov	Dec	Time	Flies
Hendrickson					X								M/A	Hendrickson #12–14; Quill Gordon; Red Quill; Adams
Blue-winged Olive					X	X	X	X					A	Blue-winged Olive #18–20; Sparkle Dun Baetis; Iron Dun; Olive CDC Mayfly Dun
Little Black Caddis						X	X	X	X				A	Little Black Caddis #16–18; Griffith's Gnat; CDC Emerging Caddis Brown; Black Ant
Grannom							X	X					M/A	Grannom #14–16; Medium Brown Sedge; Elk Caddis (brown-olive)
Net-building Caddis					X	X	X	X	X	X			M/A	Spotted Sedge #16–18; Eastern Elk Wing Caddis; Goddard Caddis
Sulphur Dun						X	X						A/E	Sulphur Dun #16; Pale Morning Dun; CDC Comparadun Yellow; Pale Evening Dun
March Brown					X	X							M/A	March Brown #12–14; Dark Cahill; Gray Fox; Ginger Quill
Gray Drake						X							E	Gray Drake #12–14; Gray Adams
Brown Drake						X							E	Brown Drake #10–12; Adams; CDC Brown Drake
Trico							X	X	X	X			M	Tiny White Wing Black #24–28; Parachute Adams; CDC Trico; Spent Wing Trico
White Fly									X				E	White Fly #12–14; White Miller
Streamers	X	X	X	X	X	X	X	X	X	X	X	X	M/A/E	Woolly Buggers #6–12; Clouser's Minnow; Muddler Minnows; BC Craw; Zonkers
Terrestrials						X	X	X	X				M/A/E	Woolly Worm #8–12; BC Spider; Letort Cricket; Joe's Hopper #6–10; Dave's Hopper; Dropper Hopper

HATCH TIME CODE: M = morning; A = afternoon; E = evening.

Days River

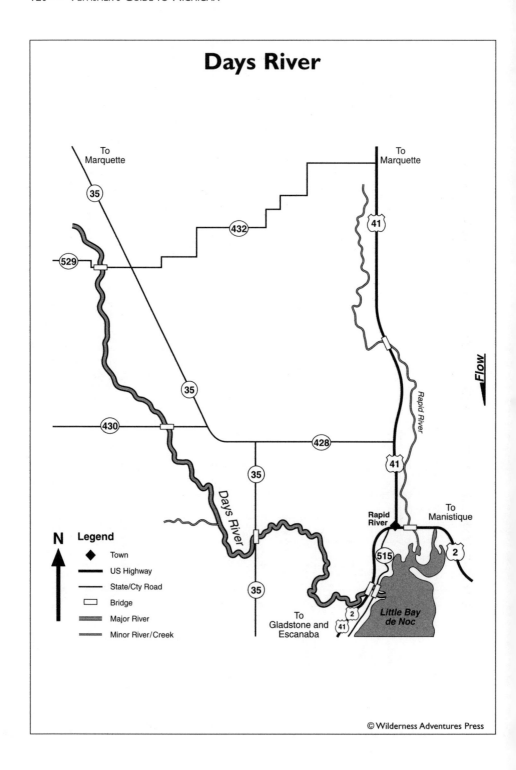

To
Marquette

To
Marquette

35

432

41

529

35

430

428

41

35

Rapid River

Flow

Days River

35

Rapid
River

To
Manistique

515

2

N Legend

◆ Town

— US Highway

— State/Cty Road

▭ Bridge

━ Major River

━ Minor River/Creek

To
Gladstone and
Escanaba

2

41

Little Bay
de Noc

© Wilderness Adventures Press

The low, swift waters of the Days River.

Days River

Days River is a small stream that flows into the west side of Little Bay de Noc. Open all year, the stream is probably best known for its spring steelhead run. It is quite often fishable when nearby larger streams are raging with snowmelt and spring rains. The lower half of the river is open enough for flyfishing, and this is where the trout are most concentrated.

The Days River flow is extremely dependent on precipitation, and it can become quite low during dry weather. A summer rain, however, seems to revive it, and brook trout and future steelhead eagerly grab attractor nymphs then. Steelhead fishing is limited to the spring and is usually concentrated in late April and early May.

Just to the east of the Days River, another flashy stream enters the tip of Little Bay de Noc. The Rapid River hosts a modest spring steelhead run, but mostly becomes too warm to support trout in the summer. It is mentioned here as a backup stream that is likely to be less crowded than the Days during the spring steelhead run.

Laughing Whitefish River

Continuing our clockwise circle around the Eastern Upper Peninsula brings us to the Laughing Whitefish River. A tributary of this small river begins within less than a mile of the West Branch of the Whitefish River, but the Laughing Whitefish heads in the other direction, north to Lake Superior. Most of the flyfishing possibilities exist

Laughing Whitefish River

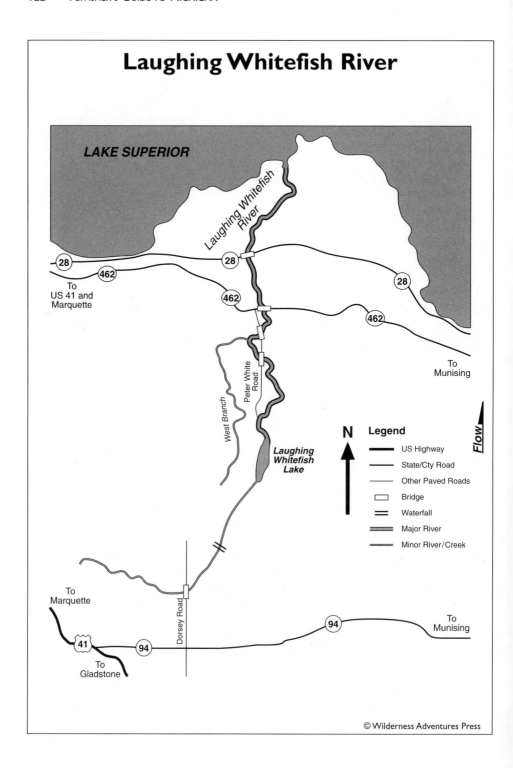

LAKE SUPERIOR

Laughing Whitefish River

28

462

To
US 41 and
Marquette

28

462

28

462

To
Munising

West Branch

Peter White Road

Laughing
Whitefish
Lake

N

Flow

Legend

━━━ US Highway

──── State/Cty Road

──── Other Paved Roads

▭ Bridge

═══ Waterfall

▬▬▬ Major River

──── Minor River/Creek

To
Marquette

Dorsey Road

41

94

94

To
Munising

To
Gladstone

© Wilderness Adventures Press

downstream from the juncture of the West Branch with the mainstream. From here until just before the river joins Lake Superior, the gradient is very high.

Small brook trout are the principal resident species and are joined by young steelhead. Most of the fishing pressure on the Laughing Whitefish is directed toward anadromous fish. The stream is open all year to fishing downstream from the West Branch. Steelhead are the main draw, with the spring run usually peaking in early May. Pink salmon run the river in September and are followed by a smaller number of cohos. Six road crossings provide excellent access to the lower river.

Anna River

The Anna River is a small Lake Superior tributary flowing into Munising Bay just east of the town of the same name. Brook trout as well as young steelhead and coho salmon inhabit the lower river's quick riffles. Competition from young anadromous fish limits brook trout production, but those that survive their early years grow to good size. Good groundwater input keeps the river running colder than most Upper Peninsula rivers in the summer, so if a hot spell occurs during your trip, you might want to seek out the Anna.

In the spring, steelhead run the Anna, and a few may even run in late fall and remain through the winter in the lower river. The river is open all year below the first railroad bridge, but the main steelhead run usually occurs after trout season has opened. In the fall there are modest runs of pink, chinook, and coho salmon.

Sucker River

Both the mainstream and the West Branch of the Sucker River begin as outlets of lakes in eastern Alger County. When they merge, the Sucker becomes a marginal flyfishing river. It varies from a meandering sand-bottomed stream to one that cascades down the escarpment to Lake Superior. It is wadeable throughout its length and is home to a fairly good population of brook trout. Some juvenile steelhead are also present.

Because natural steelhead reproduction is somewhat limited, the Sucker is planted yearly with steelhead smolts at the first bridge (Hwy 58) above the mouth. A considerable portion of the lower river is open during the extended season (April 1 through December 31), with the upstream limit at the Old Seney Road crossing. It is slated to be open all year, which may not be much of a benefit unless you have figured out how to flyfish with tip-ups. A few pink and chinook salmon enter the river in the fall, but the principal anadromous fishery is for steelhead in late April and early May.

About 8 miles to the east, the Blind Sucker River winds a short distance to Lake Superior. This river used to connect to the Sucker but was diverted directly to Lake Superior. Most of it is impounded in the Blind Sucker Flooding. This Lake Superior tributary is the steelhead angler's insurance policy in spring. When the Sucker or Two Hearted Rivers are too high and stained from runoff, the Blind Sucker is often still fishable, with the best fishing below the dam that creates the flooding. There are several campgrounds in the vicinity.

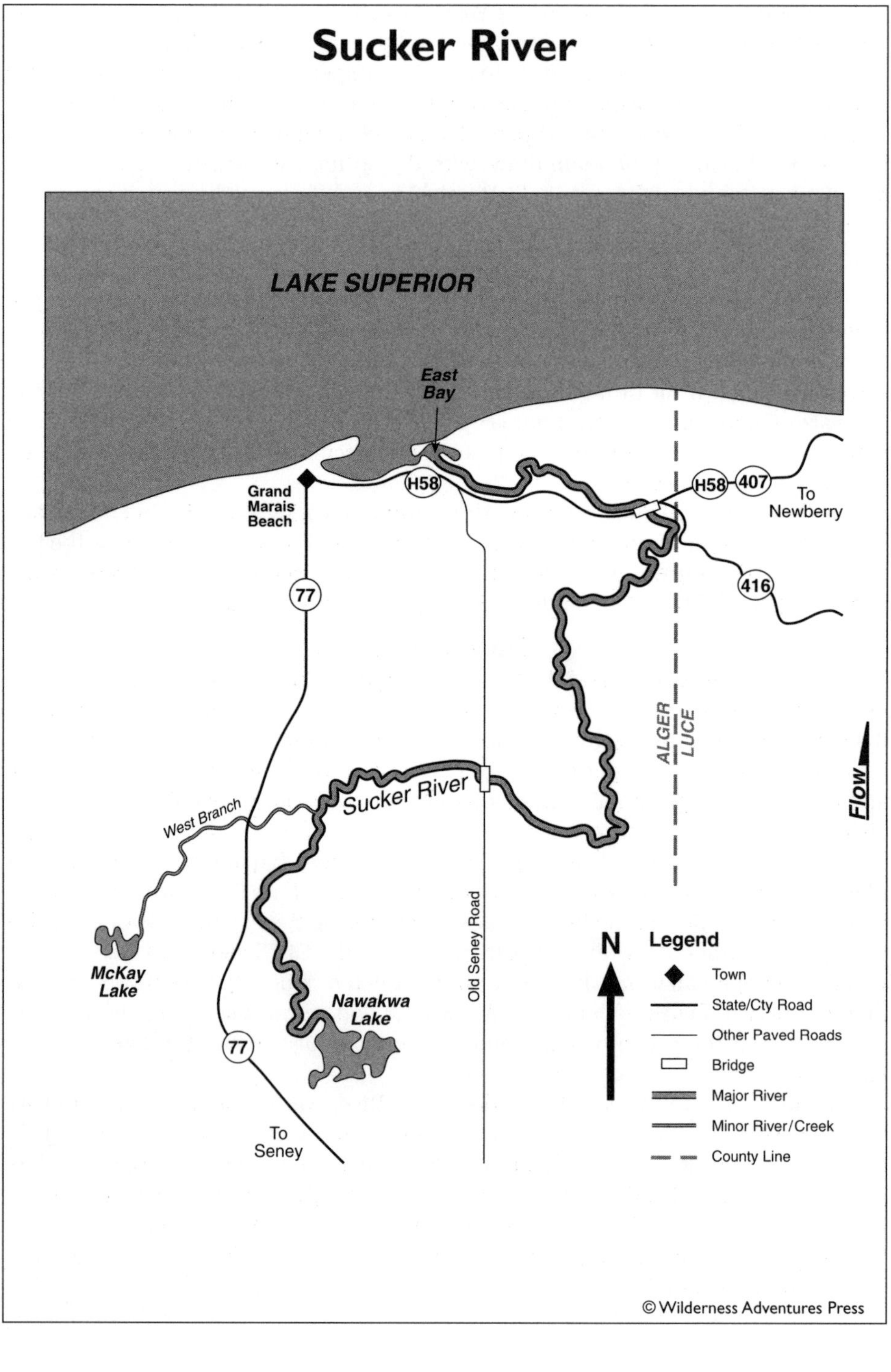

Sucker River

LAKE SUPERIOR

East Bay

Grand Marais Beach

H58

H58 407

To Newberry

77

416

ALGER
LUCE

Flow

West Branch

Sucker River

McKay Lake

Nawakwa Lake

Old Seney Road

77

To Seney

N

Legend

◆ Town
State/Cty Road
Other Paved Roads
▭ Bridge
Major River
Minor River/Creek
County Line

© Wilderness Adventures Press

Two Hearted River

The storied Two Hearted River has more miles of blue ribbon trout water than any other Upper Peninsula stream. The mainstream approximately parallels the Lake Superior shoreline in northern Luce County. Four branches eventually join the Two Hearted before it cuts through the sand to the big lake.

The West and South Branches join to form the Two Hearted, and within a short distance the North Branch adds its water. On the lower ends of these two branches, flyfishing is tight but there are plenty of eager brookies to grab a fly when you can hit the water. While there is probably a better population of brook trout in the South Branch, it is the West Branch where the blue ribbon designation, which begins on the Two Hearted.

The North Branch joins the mainstream about 7 miles below the confluence of the West and South Branches and significantly increases the size of the mainstream. Brook trout are present in the North Branch, but it probably offers the poorest fishing

Steelhead are definitely one of Michigan's attractions.

Two Hearted River

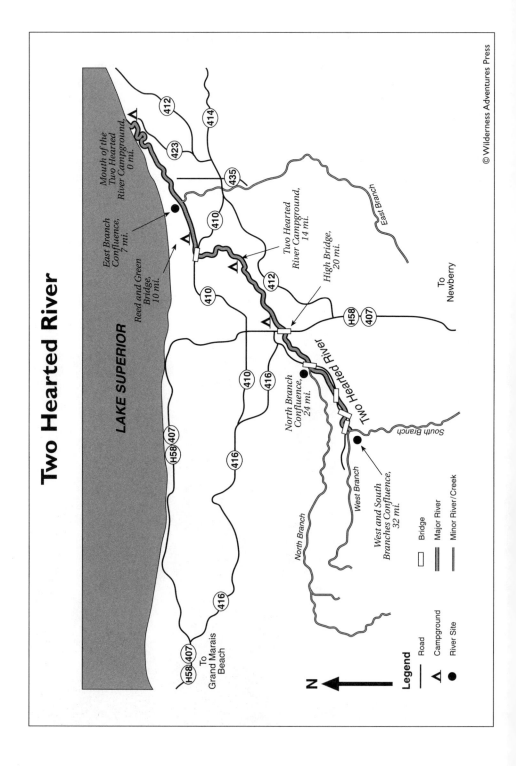

LAKE SUPERIOR

Mouth of the Two Hearted River Campground, 0 mi.

East Branch Confluence, 7 mi.

Reed and Green Bridge, 10 mi.

Two Hearted River Campground, 14 mi.

High Bridge, 20 mi.

North Branch Confluence, 24 mi.

Two Hearted River

West and South Branches Confluence, 32 mi.

West Branch

South Branch

North Branch

East Branch

To Newberry

To Grand Marais Beach

N

Legend

Road

Bridge

Major River

Minor River/Creek

Campground

River Site

© Wilderness Adventures Press

in the Two Hearted System. Nevertheless, I really like fishing this water. Whitewater rapids in the reach between the North Branch entry and High Bridge add spice to the fishing, and I like to fish and wade upstream from High Bridge for a couple of miles. This puts me close to County Road 418, either to be picked up or to walk back. County Road 418 crosses the North Branch and continues to parallel the river up to the confluence of the South and West Branches. The same road continues along the West Branch for a couple of miles. If fishing with a partner, one can start at High Bridge and wade to the North Branch juncture, and the other can park the vehicle and walk down the North Branch, fishing up the mainstream until the appointed time, and then cutting out to 418. This water is also a prime area for spring-run steelhead.

Fast water continues for a short distance below High Bridge, but then the stream begins to meander and has more sand than gravel on the bottom. Deep bend holes and undercuts with lots of wood offer plenty of hideouts for brook trout. Just a mile or so below High Bridge, Dawson Creek further increases the size of the Two Hearted. Fishing the area just below the mouth of this tributary and up into the creek can be productive for both brook trout and juvenile steelhead.

The state forest campground at Reed and Green Bridge serves as a central point for the lower Two Hearted. All day float-fishing trips can start or end here—proceed to the mouth if starting here or start at High Bridge to end here. If the fishing is good on the upper stretch, stop at the Two Hearted River Campground, about two-thirds of the way between High Bridge and Reed and Green. For a shorter float, launch at the Two Hearted River Campground and fish down to Reed and Green Bridge. The Coast Guard Line Road is a fairly rough two-track that follows the Two Hearted on the north side of the river but doesn't go all the way to the mouth.

The East Branch of the Two Hearted joins the river about 3 river miles downstream from Reed and Green Bridge. The East Branch has a good population of brook trout. It can be waded, which is good since logjams make it very difficult to float. County Road 410 crosses the East Branch, and a two-track road, called the East Branch of the Two Hearted River Road, parallels the river downstream on the east side. County Road 435 runs along the East Branch to the south. When it crosses the river, it is also called Camp Road.

There is a campground at the mouth of the Two Hearted River, which is an excellent place to try your hand at catching steelhead from the beach. Menominee (small whitefish) are also present in the spring and fall and respond well to small egg flies. This campground is accessible from the south on County Road 423.

Steelhead runs on the Two Hearted are among the best on Lake Superior tributaries. Good natural reproduction, coupled with an annual stocking of hatchery smolts at Reed and Green Bridge, keeps the silvery rainbows coming. The river is open all year below this bridge, and there are plenty of opportunities to catch steelhead above this point in the spring after trout season opens. Usually the run peaks in early May. A special attribute of the Two Hearted River is its strong fall run of steelhead. This run usually occurs in November, and fish keep hitting until river ice puts a stop to fishing. Modest runs of pink and coho salmon precede the steelhead run in September and October.

Stream Facts: Two Hearted River

Seasons
- Open all year below Reed and Green Bridge.
- Remainder open from last Saturday in April through September 30.

Special Regulations
- Size limit for all trout and salmon between October 1 and last Saturday in April is 15 inches.

Fish
- Resident brook trout and rainbow trout (juvenile steelhead and occasional adult rainbow trout).
- Anadromous steelhead, pink, coho, and chinook salmon.

River Miles
- Lake Superior—0
- East Branch Confluence—7
- Reed & Green Bridge—10
- Two Hearted River Campground—14
- High Bridge — 20
- North Branch confluence — 24
- South Branch and West Branch confluence — 32

River Characteristics
- Highly stained, meandering soft water river with four major branches.
- Bedrock rapids give way to sandy bottom in lower river; in between there are periodic gravel bars.

River Access
- Most of river flows through Lake Superior State Forest and access is gained by walking in from nearby unimproved (two-track) roads.
- Developed access sites at High Bridge, Reed & Green Bridge, and the river mouth.
- County Road 412 crosses the East and South Branches and Dawson Creek.

TWO HEARTED RIVER MAJOR HATCHES

Insect	Jan	Feb	Mar	Apr	May	Jun	July	Aug	Sep	Oct	Nov	Dec	Time	Fly Patterns
Hendrickson					██								M/A	Hendrickson #12–14; Quill Gordon; Red Quill; Adams
Blue-winged Olive				██	██	██	██	██					A	Blue-winged Olive #18–20; Sparkle Dun Baetis; Iron Dun; Olive CDC Mayfly Dun
Little Black Caddis				██	██	██	██	██	██				A	Little Black Caddis #16–18; Griffith's Gnat; CDC Emerging Caddis Brown; Black Ant
Grannom				██	██	██	██	██					M/A	Grannom #14–16; Medium Brown Sedge; Elk Caddis (brown-olive)
Net-building Caddis					██	██	██	██	██	██			M/A	Spotted Sedge #16–18; Eastern Elk Wing Caddis; Goddard Caddis
Sulphur Dun						██	██						A/E	Sulphur Dun #16; Pale Morning Dun; CDC Comparadun Yellow; Pale Evening Dun
March Brown					██	██	██						M/A	March Brown #12–14; Dark Cahill; Gray Fox; Ginger Quill
Gray Drake						██							E	Gray Drake #12–14; Gray Adams
Brown Drake						██							E	Brown Drake #10–12; Adams; CDC Brown Drake
Hexagenia							██						E	Hex #4–8; Great Olive-winged Drake; Spring's Wiggler; Wiggle-Hex Nymph
Trico								██	██	██			M	Tiny White Wing Black #24–28; Parachute Adams; CDC Trico; Spent Wing Trico
White Fly									██				E	White Fly #12–14; White Miller
Streamers	██	██	██	██	██	██	██	██	██	██	██	██	M/A/E	Woolly Buggers #6–12; Clouser's Minnow; Muddler Minnows; BC Craw; Zonkers
Terrestrials									██	██			M/A/E	Woolly Worm #8–12; BC Spider; Letort Cricket; Joe's Hopper; Dave's Hopper; Dropper Hopper

HATCH TIME CODE: M = morning; A = afternoon; E = evening.

TAHQUAMENON RIVER

Mention the Tahquamenon River, and most Michigan residents immediately think of its waterfalls. But there are many fishing opportunities in this good-sized tributary to Lake Superior. A wide range of species is present in the river, with brook trout predominating in the headwaters of the main stream and the East Branch. As the river warms up, brown trout and then smallmouth bass take over. Below the lower falls, walleyes and muskies add to the fine smallmouth fishery.

The Tahquamenon begins in Luce County, very close to the origins of the Fox and Two Hearted Rivers. It quickly grows in size, and by the time the Tahquamenon flows under County Road 421 (Eagle's Nest Bridge), there is enough room to cast. Wild brook trout are supplemented with hatchery fish, both at this bridge and at CR-442, which crosses the river about 9 river miles downstream. Although the river warms slowly over its course, brook trout can still be found, especially near the mouths of cold tributary creeks when the weather is warm.

Below Dollarville Dam, the main game fish species are smallmouth bass, northern pike, and walleye, with the chance at hooking a muskie. At this point, it is better to float than wade, and many fishermen use motors for more mobility. The river is highly stained, so large, flashy streamers are needed to get a fish's attention.

Near both the Upper and Lower Falls, you can put your boots back on because there are bedrock rapids associated with each cascade. Brown trout are planted at the Upper Falls, and some seem to carry over well, but smallmouth bass and walleye are also likely to grab a streamer. Below the falls, the Tahquamenon is slow and deep and does not lend itself to flyfishing. In fact, many troll this part of the river. Modest runs of salmon and steelhead ascend the lower Tahquamenon but again are only reachable with fly tackle at the base of the lower falls.

East Branch of the Tahquamenon

This branch provides the best flyfishing for wild brook trout in this river system. Even though the upper two-thirds of the East Branch provides fine brook trout habitat, it, too, becomes a warmwater stream before it joins the mainstream. There are possibilities, though, for some outsize trout in the lower river, especially during cooler periods of the season.

By definition the East Branch becomes flyfishable at the beginning of its designation as a blue ribbon trout stream at Strongs Corners, but a lot of roll casting and maybe even some dapping will be necessary. The stream grows slowly in size, and there is much more casting room by the time it flows under M-123. Access between these two bridges is difficult, but an ambitious angler can walk the abandoned railroad grade that runs between the two roads and reach the river across national forest land. The railroad grade crosses the river about 1 mile east of M-123, and you can fish about 3 miles of river up to this crossing and then hike back. Use woolly buggers and marabou muddlers to draw 10- to 15-inch brookies out of their hideouts.

Tahquemenon River

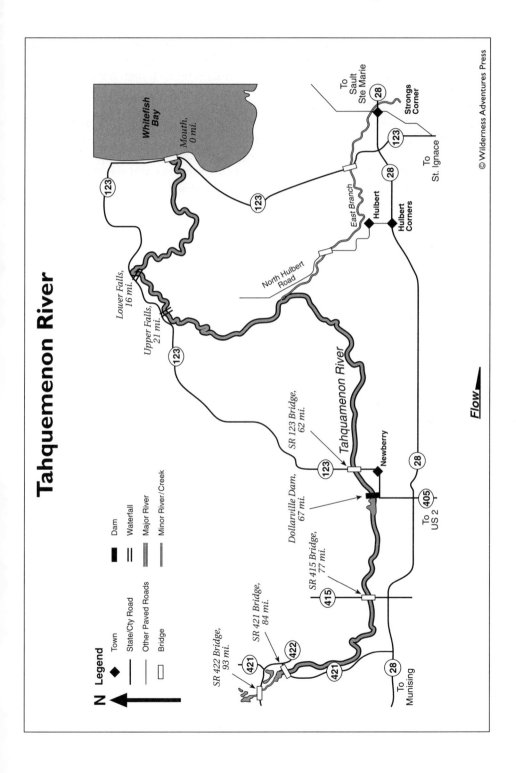

Legend

N

Town ◆

State/Cty Road —
Other Paved Roads —
Bridge ☐

Dam ▮
Waterfall ≡
Major River
Minor River/Creek

Whitefish Bay

Mouth, 0 mi.

123

123

123

Lower Falls, 16 mi.

Upper Falls, 21 mi.

123

East Branch

North Hulbert Road

Hulbert ◆

Hulbert Corners ◆

To Sault Ste Marie

28

Strongs Corner ◆

123

To St. Ignace

28

SR 123 Bridge, 62 mi.

Tahquemenon River

123

Newberry ◆

28

Dollarville Dam, 67 mi.

405

To US 2

SR 415 Bridge, 77 mi.

415

SR 421 Bridge, 84 mi.

SR 422 Bridge, 93 mi.

422

421

421

28

To Munising

Flow ◄

© Wilderness Adventures Press

There are no road crossings for about 10 miles below M-123, with the next bridge (North Hulbert Road) at the downstream edge of the blue ribbon water. There is some access in this long reach via two-track roads. Even though the upper half is on public forest land, you are likely to have plenty of river to yourself—just you and the brookies, that is. The lower East Branch's gentle current allows the use of a float tube or kickboat, which help make a quiet approach to the trout-holding bend holes.

Downstream from the bridge, the North Hulbert Road closely follows the river for several miles. Floating is again the best option for this water. There is the chance for some big brookies in this stretch, but smallmouth bass and northern pike are likely to be an increasing part of your catch as you move downstream.

Stream Facts: Tahquamenon River

Seasons
- Lower mainstream open all year.
- Bass must be released between January 1 and the Saturday before Memorial Day.
- Walleyes, northern pike, and muskellunge must be released between March 15 and the last Saturday in April.

Special Regulations
- Size limit for all trout and salmon between October 1 and last Saturday in April is 15 inches.
- Size limit for brook trout is 10 inches and brown trout 12 inches in the East Branch.

Fish
- Resident brook and brown trout, smallmouth and rock bass, walleyes, northern pike, muskellunge, and yellow perch.
- Anadromous steelhead, pink and chinook salmon.

River Miles
- Lake Superior (Whitefish Bay) — 0
- Lower Falls — 16
- Upper Falls — 21
- M-123 — 62
- Dollarville Dam — 67
- CR-415 — 77
- CR-442 — 84
- CR-421 — 93

River Characteristics
- It is highly stained with tannins and is a meandering river.
- Much of it is sand bottom, with the exception of the Tahquamenon Falls area.
- Becomes a large river, but tributary creeks and the headwaters are wadeable.

River Access
- Access is available at each landmark noted above with river miles.
- Additional access is available via back roads on public forest land.

Eastern Upper Peninsula Hub Cities

Sault Ste. Marie

Population – 14,689

ACCOMMODATIONS

Askwith Lockview Motel, 327 West Portage Avenue / 906-632-2491
Bambi Motel, 1801 Ashmun Street / 906-632-7881
Doral Motel, 518 East Portage Avenue / 906-632-6621
Lawson Motel, 2049 Ashmun Street / 906-632-3322
Ojibway Hotel, 240 West Portage Avenue / 906-632-4100
Plaza Motor Motel, I-75 Business Spur / 906-635-1881

CAMPGROUNDS

Brimley State Park, 9200 West 6 Mile Road (Brimley 49715) / 906-248-3422
Chippewa Campground, 412 East 3 Mile Road / 906-632-8581
City of Sault Ste. Marie Parks and Recreation, 435 East Portage Avenue /
906-635-5341

RESTAURANTS

Abner's Restaurant, 2865 I-75 Business Spur / 906-632-4221
The Antlers, 804 East Portage Avenue / 906-632-3571
Dream Catchers Restaurant, 2186 Shunk Road / 906-635-4773
Knife & Fork Restaurant, 3290 I 75 Business Spur / 906-635-1523
Riversedge Restaurant, 951 East Portage Avenue / 906-632-2050
The Ships Galley, 405 West Portage Avenue / 906-635-0350

FLY SHOPS AND SPORTING GOODS

Hank's Sport Shop, 3522 I-75 Business Spur / 906-632-8741
Superior Sports / 906-635-6220

AUTO SERVICE

Algonquin Service, 1610 West 4th Avenue / 906-632-3701
Merle's Garage & Towing, 301 East 3 Mile Road / 906-635-5725
Precision Automotive, 123 Maple Street / 906-635-1052
Roos Standard Service, 933 Ashmun Street / 906-632-2371
Rich Wood Service and Repair, 129-& West 1/2 Spruce / 906-632-7371

AIR SERVICE

Twin Cities Air, 228 West 14th Avenue / 906-635-0252

MEDICAL

Chippewa County War Memorial Hospital / 906-635-4460
Marquette General Hospital, 500 Osborn Boulevard / 906-632-0008

FOR MORE INFORMATION
Sault Area Chamber of Commerce
2581 I-75 Business Spur
Sault Sainte Marie, MI 49783
906-632-3301

St. Ignace
Population – 2,568

ACCOMMODATIONS
Aurora Borealis Motor Inn, 635 US 2 West / 906-643-7488
Birchwood Motel, 1809 Business Loop 75 / 906-643-7738
Cedars Motel, Evergreen Shores / 906-643-9578
Straits View Motel, 1177 US 2 West / 906-643-9355
Sunset Motel, 1034 US 2 West / 906-643-8377
Tradewinds Motel, 1190 North State Street / 906-643-9388

CAMPGROUNDS
Castle Rock Mackinac Trail Campark, 2811 Mackinac Trail / 906-643-9222
KOA Kampground / 906-643-9303
Lakeshore Park Campground, 416 Pte La Barbe Road / 906-643-9522
Straits State Park, 720 Church Street / 906-643-8620
Tiki Travel Park, 200 South Airport Road / 906-643-7808

RESTAURANTS
Bentley's Restaurant, 62 North State Street / 906-643-9031
Dockside Restaurant, 1101 North State Street / 906-643-7911
Driftwood Restaurant & Sports Bar, 590 North State Street / 906-643-9133
Galley Restaurant & Lounge, 241 North State Street / 906-643-7960
Northern Lights Restaurant, 645 US 2 West / 906-643-8250
Seafood Palace, 1160 US 2 West / 906-643-6966
Truck Stop Restaurant / 906-643-8076

FLY SHOPS AND SPORTING GOODS
Ace Hardware & Sporting Goods, 7 South State Street / 906-643-7721

AUTO SERVICE
Selden's Marathon Service, 709 North State Street / 906-643-8220
Fred Rowan's Automotive Repair / 906-643-8501
St. Ignace Automotive Supply Inc, 460 North State Street / 906-643-8038

AIR SERVICE
Mackinac County Airport, 180 North Airport Road / 906-643-7327

MEDICAL
Mackinac Straits Hospital, 220 Burdette Street / 906-643-8585

FOR MORE INFORMATION
St. Ignace Chamber of Commerce
560 North State Street
St. Ignace, MI 49781
906-643-8717

Newberry
Population – 1,873

ACCOMMODATIONS
Berry's Motel, South M-123 / 906-293-8911
Evening Star Motel, 965 Avenue / 906-293-8342
Falls Hotel, 301 Avenue / 906-293-5111
Gateway Motel, 980 South M-123 / 906-293-5651
Knollwood Inn, M-28 / 906-293-5007
Manor Motel, 123 Avenue / 906-293-5000

CAMPGROUNDS
Newberry KOA Kampground, M-28 / 906-293-5762
Northcountry Campground & Cabins, 94 M-123 / 906-293-8562
Tahquamenon Falls State Park, 41382 West M-123 (Paradise 49768) / 906-492-3415

RESTAURANTS
Moose Track Station, 1 North M-123 / 906-293-6667
Outpost Restaurant, 1151 Avenue / 906-293-6070
Poor Boy Restaurant, M-28 / 906-293-3151
Snook's Spot, 113 East John Street / 906-293-8591
Timber Charlie's Food & Spirits, 110 Avenue / 906-293-3363
Zellar's Village Inn, South M-123 / 906-293-5114

FLY SHOPS AND SPORTING GOODS
Duke's Sport Shop, 202 Avenue / 906-293-8421
Hilltop Sport & Bait, Avenue / 906-293-8856

AUTO SERVICE
Burbach Service, 202 East Helen Street / 906-293-8391
Newberry Motors, South M-123 / 906-293-5104

AIR SERVICE
Luce County Airport / 906-293-9956

MEDICAL
Helen Newberry Joy Hospital / 906-293-9233

FOR MORE INFORMATION
Newberry Area Chamber of Commerce
M-28 & M-123 Intersection
Newberry, MI 49868
906-293-5562

Manistique
Population – 3,456

ACCOMMODATIONS
Beachcomber Motel, East US 2 / 906-341-2567
Blue Spruce Motel, 1177 West Lakeshore Drive / 906-341-8543
Harbor Motel, 311 South Cedar Street / 906-341-5191
Mountain Ash Resort, RR 2 Box 2490 / 906-341-5658
Northshore Motor Inn, 1967 Lakeshore Drive / 906-341-2420
Star Motel, Lake Shore Drive / 906-341-5363

CAMPGROUNDS
Indian Lake Travel Resort, County Road 455 / 906-341-2807
Indian Lake State Park, Rt. 2, Box 2500 / 906-341-2355.
Woodstar Beach Campground (Little Harbor) / 906-341-6514

RESTAURANTS
Danny's Cafe, 220 Oak Street / 906-341-5772
Fireside Inn, RR 1 Box 1500 / 906-341-6332
Sunny Shores Restaurant, East Lake Shore Drive / 906-341-5582
Three Mile Supper Club, County Road 442 / 906-341-8048

FLY SHOPS AND SPORTING GOODS
Indian Lake Sports & Party Store (Indian Lake) / 906-341-5932

AUTO SERVICE
Bill's Automotive, 1001 West Lakeshore Drive / 906-341-6736
AAA, 323 South Maple Street / 906-341-2141
Pole Performance, 1863 Shunk Road / 906-341-8195
Bergy's Auto Repair, East US 2 / 906-341-2097
Ken's Auto Repair, M-94 / 906-341-5384

AIR SERVICE
Delta County Airport, 310 Delta County Airport (Escanaba 49829) / 906-786-
9037

MEDICAL
Manistique Medical Center, 115 North Lake Street / 906-341-2153

FOR MORE INFORMATION
Schoolcraft County Chamber of Commerce
US 2
Manistique, MI 49854
906-341-5010

Munising
Population – 2,783

ACCOMMODATIONS
Alger Falls Motel, M-28 East / 906-387-3536
Christmas Motel / 906-387-4652
Greenland Motel, 1410 High Street / 906-387-3396
Munising Motel, 332 East Onota Street / 906-387-3187
Terrace Motel, 420 Prospect Street / 906-387-2735

CAMPGROUNDS
Hiawatha Resort and Campground, Hwy 13 / 906-573-2933
Wandering Wheels Campground, M-28 East / 906-387-3315

RESTAURANTS
Country Connection, 208 East Superior Street / 906-387-4839
Dogpatch Restaurant, East Superior Street / 906-387-99480
The Navigator, 101 East Avenue / 906-387-4443
North Light Landing Restaurant & Co, M-28 East / 906-387-5400
Sydney's Restaurant, M-28 East / 906-387-4067

FLY SHOPS AND SPORTING GOODS
Curly's Hilltop Grocery and Party Store, H-58 / 906-387-3056

AUTO SERVICE
Hot Wrench Auto Repair, M-28 West / 906-387-5300
Lare Auto Repair, 1309 Commercial Street / 906-387-3091
Munising Auto Repair Inc, 9051 East M-28 / 906-387-5490

AIR SERVICE
Hanley Field, Hwy 13 / 906-387-3572

MEDICAL
Munising Memorial Hospital, 1500 Sandpoint Road / 906-387-4110

FOR MORE INFORMATION
Chamber of Commerce
PO Box 405
Munising, MI 49862
906-387-2138

Northwestern Lower Peninsula

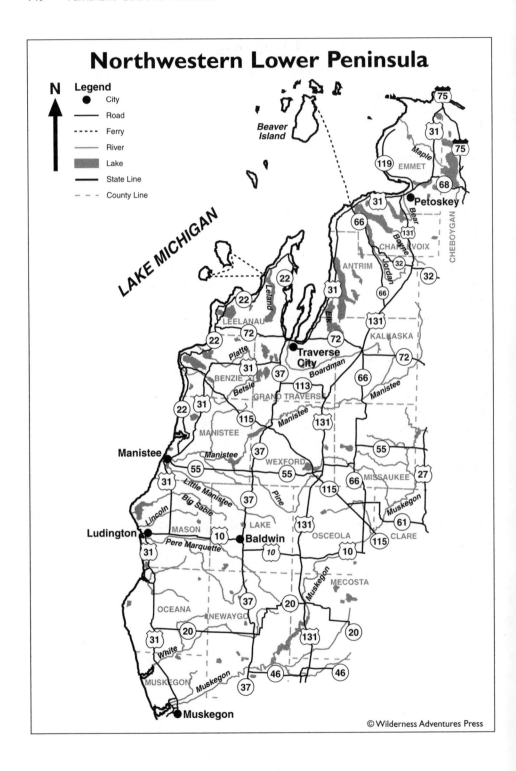

© Wilderness Adventures Press

Northwestern Lower Peninsula

The sandy soil and ample rainfall in this section of Michigan result in a large number of top quality trout streams. This is because a very high percentage of the precipitation soaks into the soil instead of running off, providing the rivers and creeks with a fairly constant flow of cold, spring water. Dr. Paul Seelbach, a fisheries research biologist for the Department of Natural Resources, states that the streams in this part of Michigan have some of the most stable river flows found anywhere in the world.

It is obvious that trout like this situation, as the state's highest concentration of blue ribbon trout streams are located here. While the Pere Marquette and Manistee Rivers are nationally famous, there are many others that offer equal or better fishing. It is really special to have "spring creeks" that are 50 to 100 feet wide and loaded with browns and brookies.

It's ironic that even with so much great trout water, this section of Michigan is much better known for its runs of steelhead and salmon. Of course, the Manistee and Pere Marquette are also among the best steelhead rivers, but the Betsie, Platte, Little Manistee, and Muskegon Rivers are just as famous for their runs of anadromous salmonids. It was in the Betsie River that I first experienced the power of a lake-run rainbow, and I can still go to the exact spot where my first steelhead came to net 34 years ago. This river continues to be one of the best-producing rivers that I fish, and even though it is a long drive from my lower Michigan home, I make a number of visits each year.

Warmwater angling opportunities also abound in this corner of Michigan. Walleyes and northern pike, which have fattened up in the drowned river mouth lakes of the Great Lakes tributaries, often move up into the rivers where they can be enticed with big streamers. This area also offers some of the best beach or surf fishing for steelhead, brown trout, and salmon.

MUSKEGON RIVER

The Muskegon River is one of the state's longest and largest. It begins as the outlet of Houghton Lake and meanders for about 230 miles to Lake Michigan at the city of the same name. The upper river is home to coolwater species, such as northern pike, rock bass, and a few walleyes, due to three factors: its warm start; a dam (Reedsburg) that is located just a short way from its beginning; and a relatively low gradient. The Muskegon River does have a number of tributaries that contain trout, however, it is essentially a warmwater river until it exits the dam at Croton.

The West Branch of the Muskegon joins the main river a few miles downstream from Reedsburg Dam. Even though this branch frequently warms into the low 70s, it contains a good population of brook trout. A cautious upstream approach is important on this stream, because its substrate is frequently composed of fine sand and silt. Wild brookies up to 14 inches are present and respond to the usual attractor flies. Plan

Muskegon River below Croton Dam.

Muskegon River
Croton to Lake Michigan

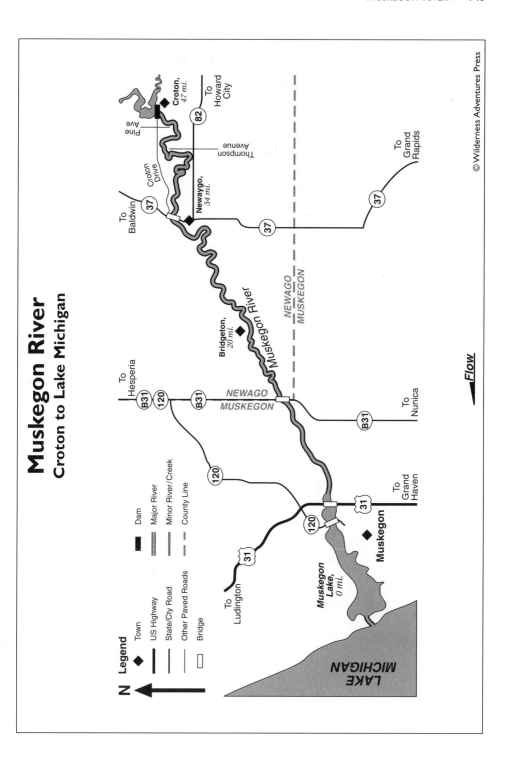

© Wilderness Adventures Press

N

Legend

◆	Town
	US Highway
	State/Cty Road
	Other Paved Roads
▭	Bridge
■	Dam
	Major River
	Minor River/Creek
	County Line

To Baldwin

Croton, *47 mi.*

To Howard City

Pine Ave

Thompson Avenue

Croton Drive

Newaygo, *34 mi.*

To Grand Rapids

Muskegon River

Bridgeton, *20 mi.*

NEWAGO
MUSKEGON

To Hesperia

NEWAGO
MUSKEGON

To Nunica

To Grand Haven

Muskegon

To Ludington

Muskegon Lake, *0 mi.*

LAKE MICHIGAN

Flow

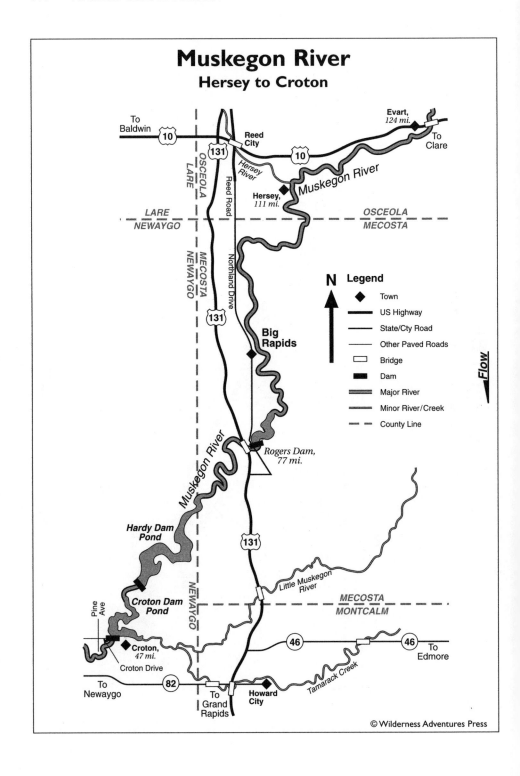

Muskegon River
Hersey to Croton

© Wilderness Adventures Press

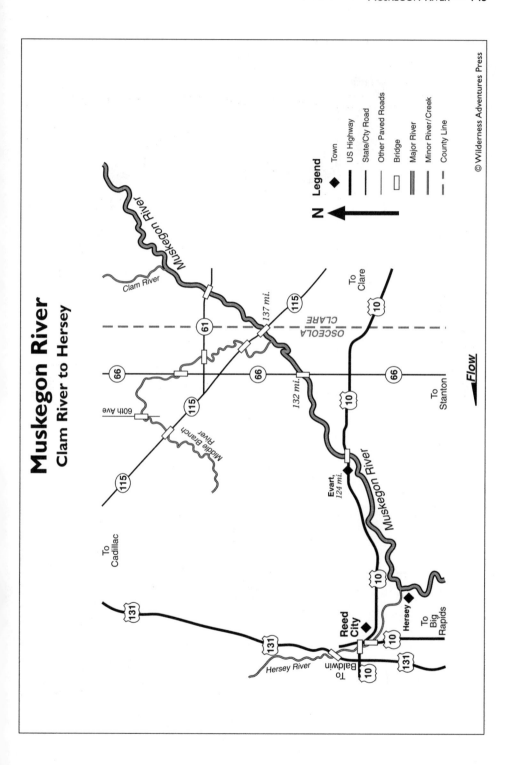

Muskegon River
Clam River to Hersey

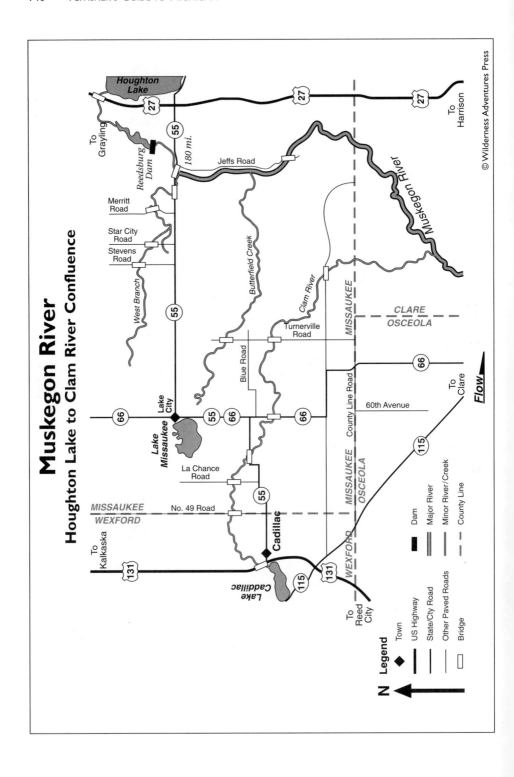

Muskegon River
Houghton Lake to Clam River Confluence

© Wilderness Adventures Press

to fish during cool weather and, because the river is full of minnows, try some stream-ers. Stevens, Star City, Young, and Merritt Road crossings offer access, as does M-55.

A bit farther downstream, Butterfield Creek joins the Muskegon and offers the small stream specialist a chance at a 2-pound brook trout. While there are plenty of open areas on this creek, the lunkers are likely to be found where there are lots of logs in the water and overhanging vegetation. This is definitely roll cast territory. While you can't expect to catch large numbers of brookies, streamers imitating creek chubs could draw out the largest brook trout of your season. Access is limited to road crossings.

The mainstream continues to grow in size from the numerous small creeks and swamp outlets that flow into it. Its size really increases when the Clam and Middle Branch Rivers join it. Although these are warmwater streams when they join the Muskegon, they do have blue ribbon sections in their upper reaches that will be described in more detail later. As the Muskegon becomes much wider and shallower, the primary predator fish switches from northern pike to smallmouth bass.

The river starts to flow faster, and the bottom changes to lots of rock and cobble that provide good habitat for insects and crayfish, as well as the smallies. Walleyes are also present, and the DNR adds a bonus fish in the reach between Evart and Hersey by planting some yearling browns. This means that when you drift a nymph or swing and twitch a streamer, you never know what's going to latch on. The river is beautiful here, and if it was just a bit colder, it would support a super trout population. North and South River Road (the same road that crosses the river in Evart) closely parallels the river, and Riverside Park offers access in Evart and is also a planting site for brown trout. Floating is a good option, and the Evart to Hersey reach is a fine all-day fishing trip. You can launch at M-66 for a slightly shorter trip to Evart.

The Hersey River joins the main river here and provides the opportunity to catch large brown trout with convenient access at road crossings. This is a small stream, but there is ample room to cast for browns over 20 inches. It fishes best when the water is up a bit and has some color. Crayfish-imitating streamers are my first choice for fooling one of its lunker brown trout.

Moving downstream toward Big Rapids, the river becomes deeper and walleyes are more numerous. There are still plenty of riffles in this stretch but a low head dam backs the water up a bit just above Big Rapids. Below Big Rapids three large dams—Rogers, Hardy, and Croton—greatly affect the river. Most of this reach is impounded, but there is some good smallmouth and walleye flyfishing to be found where it is still free flowing. In the spring walleyes move out of the impoundments and up into the river. This may happen before walleye season opens on the last Saturday of April, but they can still be fun to catch, even if you don't end up with some tasty filets. There is good access at the base of each dam.

Below Croton Dam, you will find what I like to call a pseudo tailwater trout fish-ery. The reason for the "pseudo" adjective is that there isn't a bottom draw here, and the water is frequently above 70 degrees in the summer. Run of the river operation of this hydroelectric dam greatly improved trout survival and growth below it, but it still gets too warm. The FERC relicensing agreement requires that water leaving the dam

*Butterfield Creek
is a tributary
of the Muskegon River.*

does not exceed 68 degrees, but so far, this requirement has not been enforced. There could be a world-class trout fishery here if there were a deeper draw or if a bubbler device to bring colder water up the inlet to the turbines were installed. The river is 200 feet wide and alternates between fast riffles and deep rocky runs. Springs that gurgle from the high banks lining the river between Croton and Newaygo help keep the water cool. Large numbers of brown and rainbow trout are planted each year, and young, future steelhead add to the mix.

Most of the fish here are small, but there is some carryover. The number of larger fish would be much greater if the water was colder. Trout can easily tolerate temperatures in the 70s for short periods, but warm water is stressful for them when they have to endure it around the clock for days at a time. Trout that are carrying over are likely finding cooler water near springs so they can to feed actively during warm spells.

Caddisflies are a primary food source on this beautiful section of river. Even though many of the trout are small, they can be quite selective at times. The cinnamon caddis seems to imitate the dominant species for most of the early to mid summer period. If you can figure out what the fish are feeding on as well as where in the water column, you can easily hook 20 or more trout in an afternoon. Crayfish are also common in this river, and fishing streamers in crayfish patterns is one of the best ways to catch the larger carryover trout.

There is excellent access to the Muskegon between Croton and Newaygo. There are developed sites at the dam and at the end of Pine and Thornapple Avenues. A county park (Henning) just upstream from Newaygo and a municipal park in town also provide access to the river. All of these sites have boat ramps. Anglers on foot can also get to the river at the High Rollaways Access Site off of M-82. While the stream's resident trout have recently become a big attraction in the lower Muskegon, steelhead and chinook salmon have been drawing anglers to this river for a long time. Large numbers of both species are planted annually, and run of the river dam operation has resulted in a huge contribution of wild fish.

The Muskegon River from Croton Dam downstream to Newaygo closely resembles Pacific Northwest steelhead rivers. The river is wide, the gradient is high, and there is gravel everywhere. Chinook salmon arrive in September, somewhat later than other northwestern Michigan rivers because the impoundments take a while to cool down. Steelhead, along with a few coho salmon and brown trout, join the kings in October. Because the river never freezes in this reach, you can chase steelhead all winter long if the weather permits. The main steelhead run arrives in March and April when big rainbows spawn. Walleyes up to 12 pounds join the steelhead, but most leave the river before their season opens. Still, there is great chance for a trophy and some photos.

Long, 4- to 8-feet deep runs result in most of the holding water being manageable without fast-sinking lines or lots of lead. There is time to get a fly down to the fish without resorting to chucking and ducking. This is a special feature of the Muskegon compared to many other Michigan rivers, where it's necessary to get a fly down very quickly because of sharp dropoffs and the presence of logs.

In contrast to the West, Midwest anglers commonly fish for spawning steelhead and salmon. Some anglers subtly intrude on spawning fish with small dark nymphs, while others try to anger or excite fish into striking a gaudy, fluorescent streamer. Egg flies also take the spawners. While I don't ignore spawning steelhead, I prefer to sweep or swing bright, fluorescent marabou streamers through the dark water above and below the spawning gravel. In the Muskegon, it's often possible to use a floating line with a fast-sinking leader and slightly weighted streamer to get down to the fish. There is lots of room to fight the fish, as well, and I have been led on many long, downstream chases in this river.

A few miles below Newaygo, gravel gives way to sand and holes become much deeper. Although steelhead and salmon can be intercepted here, flyfishing is more difficult. Floating is recommended because wading gets tough and the river is rarely crossable. During summer, smallmouth bass fishing is very good in the lower Muskegon.

Throughout its length and its seasons, a special feature of the Muskegon is that it is seldom out of shape. In a normal year, the river is unfishable only during the main spring snow runoff. Parsley's Sportshop in Newaygo and the Great Lakes Flyfishing Company in Rockford are good bets for the latest information.

Clam River

This is the first large tributary stream to join the Muskegon, starting out as a warmwater stream (the outlet of Lake Cadillac) and ending up the same way. In between, the Clam contains a lengthy stretch of high quality brook trout water. Between County Line Road (Wexford/Missaukee Counties) and Turnerville Road, the Clam is classified as a blue ribbon trout stream. Within this reach, between Blue and LaChance Roads, anglers are restricted to single hook lures and flies, and brook trout must be 10 inches long before they can be creeled. Beginning with the trout season in 2000, this regulation may be discontinued so that the flies-only reach on the Manistee River can be increased in length.

There are good numbers of brook trout in the 12- to 15-inch class in the Clam, and a trophy over 2 pounds is possible. There is a *Hexagenia* hatch, but brown drakes and Hendricksons are more dependable. Of course, classic attractor patterns, such as the Royal Coachman, also entice brookies into a take. The stream is relatively small but reasonably open. As is usually the case, roll and side arm casts that get a fly under the overhangs will increase your takes. In addition to the above-mentioned roads, M-66 and M-55 provide access to the prime trout water

Moving downstream toward the Muskegon, the water begins to warm and brook trout numbers decrease. While there are some brown trout in this transition water, once the West Branch of the Clam joins the mainstream, there are mostly pike and a few smallmouth.

Middle Branch River

The Middle Branch River is a fine, but often overlooked, trout stream that approximately parallels the Clam and joins the Muskegon about 4 miles downstream. It becomes flyfishable at 60th Avenue in Osceola County, which corresponds with the beginning of its designation as a blue ribbon trout stream. A dam in Marion prematurely terminates the top quality trout water. Even though this pond greatly warms the river, the water cools down enough to again hold trout about 3 miles downstream. The blue ribbon water is the place to hook lots of medium-sized browns along with a few brookies, while the lower water harbors some trophy brown trout.

The lower Middle Branch is loaded with both creek chubs and crayfish. Use durable flies because you will hook many chubs for each trout. A good crayfish pattern fished close to the logs is your best bet for enticing one of the 5-pound browns that lurk in this section of the river. Frequent road crossings provide good access to the entire stream.

Little Muskegon River

The Little Muskegon is the mainstream's third major tributary and is predominantly a smallmouth bass stream. There are some brook trout in its headwaters, and the DNR plants browns and rainbows in the middle section of the stream. Even though the stocked trout don't carry over very well, you never know when a lunker brown might surprise you.

Containing lots of rock and shallow riffles, the stream is easily waded. There are good hatches of riffle-produced mayflies and caddisflies, and crayfish are also abundant. The river joins the Muskegon in the Croton Dam Pond, with walleyes and northern pike becoming more common in the lower river.

Tamarack Creek flows into the Little Muskegon a few miles upstream from Croton and is regularly planted with both browns and rainbows. Downstream from Howard City, it is flyfishable and has produced brown trout in the 5- to 6-pound class. Crayfish again appear to be the key food item for larger trout. Just like the Little Muskegon, the lower Tamarack can produce a mixed bag. Pike are the most common nontrout predator, but once I was surprised by a tiger muskie that had migrated down from a headwater lake.

Clam River.

Stream Facts: Muskegon River

Seasons
- Open all year.
- Bass must be released between January 1 and the Saturday before Memorial Day.
- Walleye and northern pike must be released between March 15 and the last Saturday in April.

Special Regulations
- Size limit for all trout and salmon between October 1 and the last Saturday in April is 15 inches, and the possession limit is 3.
- No fishing below Rogers Dam downstream to below the southbound land of US 131 from March 16 to the last Saturday in April.

Fish
- Resident brown, brook, and rainbow trout; smallmouth and largemouth bass; walleye, northern pike, channel catfish, perch, and other panfish.
- Anadromous rainbow and brown trout, chinook and coho salmon, and walleye.

River Miles
- Muskegon Lake—0
- Bridgeton—20
- Newaygo—34
- Croton—47
- Rogers Dam—77
- Hersey—111
- Evart—124
- M-66—132
- M-115—137
- M-55—180

River Characteristics
- The upper river is slow, meandering, and sand-bottomed.
- The gradient gradually increases only to be intercepted by a number of dams.
- Below Croton Dam the river appears to have been transplanted from the Pacific Northwest, with long, gravel runs alternating with speedy riffles.
- The Muskegon again slows down as it nears Lake Michigan.

River Access
- Primary access is at road bridges, but there are a number of developed public access sites and boat launches.
- These are especially concentrated on the lower river and are noted on the river map.

MUSKEGON RIVER MAJOR HATCHES

Insect Species	Jan	Feb	Mar	Apr	May	Jun	July	Aug	Sep	Oct	Nov	Dec	Time	Fly Patterns
Black Stonefly			X	X									A	Early Black Stonefly #10–14
Hendrickson				X	X								M/A	Hendrickson #12–14; Rusty's Spinner; Red Quill; Adams; Quill Gordon
Blue-winged Olive					X	X	X	X					A	Blue-winged Olive #18–20; Sparkle Dun Baetis; Iron Dun; Olive CDC Mayfly Dun
Little Black Caddis				X	X	X	X	X					A	Little Black Caddis #16–18; Griffith's Gnat; CDC Emerging Caddis Brown; Black Ant
Grannom						X	X						M/A	Grannom #14–16; Medium Brown Sedge; Elk Caddis Brown-Olive
Net-building Caddis					X	X	X	X	X	X			M/A	Spotted Sedge #16–18; Eastern Elk Wing Caddis; Goddard Caddis
Cinnamon Caddis						X	X	X	X				M/A	Cinnamon Caddis #16–18; Woodchuck Caddis
Sulphur Dun					X	X							A/E	Sulphur Dun #16; Pale Morning Dun; CDC Comparadun Yellow; Pale Evening Dun
March Brown					X	X							M/A	March Brown #12–14; Dark Cahill; Gray Fox; Ginger Quill
Gray Drake						X							E	Gray Drake #12–14; Gray Adams
Brown Drake						X							E	Brown Drake #10–12; Adams; CDC Brown
Trico						X	X	X	X	X			M	Tiny White Wing Black #24–28; Parachute Adams; CDC Trico; Spent Wing Trico
White Fly								X	X				E	White Fly #12–14; White Miller
Streamers	X	X	X	X	X	X	X	X	X	X	X	X	M/A/E	Woolly Buggers #6–12; Clouser's Minnow; Muddler Minnows; BC Craw; Matukas
Terrestrials					X	X	X	X	X	X			M/A/E	Woolly Worm #8–12; BC Spider; Letort Cricket; Joe's Hopper #6–10; Dave's Hopper; Dropper Hopper

HATCH TIME CODE: M = morning; A = afternoon; E = evening.

WHITE RIVER

The White River begins as a cold brook trout creek north of White Cloud and quickly increases in size due to tributaries and springs. It is manageable with a fly rod for the last 7 or 8 miles above White Cloud, and this section has been designated a blue ribbon trout stream. Brook trout dominate in the headwaters, with brown trout increasing as you go downstream. These are all wild trout, and the browns grow to surprising size. Though the upper White tends to become stained with dark swamp water when it rains, it does not become turbid. This means that the prime time to be on the river with large attractor flies is during and following a hard shower. The stream also has a good brown drake hatch in June, and caddis species are numerous. Three Mile and Two Mile Roads, with M-20 in between, offer convenient access one-half mile apart. Three Mile Road does not cross the river any more, but it does put you right on the river. Walnut Avenue parallels the river farther upstream, and you can get to the river by walking a trail through the national forest. Van Buren and Six Mile Roads cross the river in the upper end of the blue ribbon water.

An impoundment in White Cloud warms the water, but the river continues to hold fairly good numbers of brown trout down to Hesperia. Martin and Mena Creeks cool the river and help make the trout fishing better closer to Hesperia. Road crossings again provide the access but they are a bit farther apart. A favorite reach of mine for big browns is upstream from Green Avenue, perhaps because the next bridge (2 Mile Road) is 3 miles upstream. M-20 and Luce and Baldwin Avenues are additional spots to get on the middle part of the White.

Another low head dam is present at Hesperia, but high gradient and springs keep the water cool enough for some trout survival below this dam. This is lunker brown territory, with crayfish and creek chubs present in large numbers. Actively sweeping and retrieving streamers that imitate these dominant, big trout food items is the key to getting hooked up to a large brown trout.

Continuing downstream, smallmouth bass and northern pike become more prevalent. The river remains quite fast and gravel-bottomed until Pines Point Campground, where it begins its transition to sand. Below the campground, White River becomes difficult to wade, and a floating craft of some kind is very helpful. Cushman Creek, a very good though small trout stream, and the North Branch of the White, which is described in more detail later, add their flows to the White River before it becomes a drowned river mouth lake at Whitehall.

The White receives an excellent run of chinook salmon in September. No salmon are planted in the river, so most of these fish are wild except for a few strays from other rivers. If there is cool weather in August, bright chinooks will arrive then. Because the river is normally very clear, hooking these behemoths can be a challenge. Egg flies and marabou speys are good choices for enticing a strike from these nonfeeding fish. Fluorescent chartreuse and green seem to be preferred colors most of the time. The fish tend to concentrate in the gravel runs below Hesperia but can be more cooperative if you can find/intercept them in the lower river.

*The blue-ribbon section
of the White River.*

The White is known for a very fine, spring steelhead run. As already mentioned, the river is likely to remain fishable during runoff periods, making it a very friendly place to visit when snow is melting and steelies are on the move. While the river gets a large annual plant of steelhead smolts, there are also a surprising number of wild fish contributing to the run. Some steelhead seem to find their way past the dam in Hesperia, perhaps with some help from anglers, because steelhead fingerlings can be caught when trout fishing above the dam.

The run usually gets under way in March and peaks in early April. Of course, spring weather can alter this schedule. While the biggest concentration of fish is usually found near the dam in Hesperia, this can also be an angling zoo. A better plan is to wander in at one of the bridges (M-20, Stone, and Garfield Roads) or access sites along 194th Avenue downstream and find a gravel run to call your own. The Pines

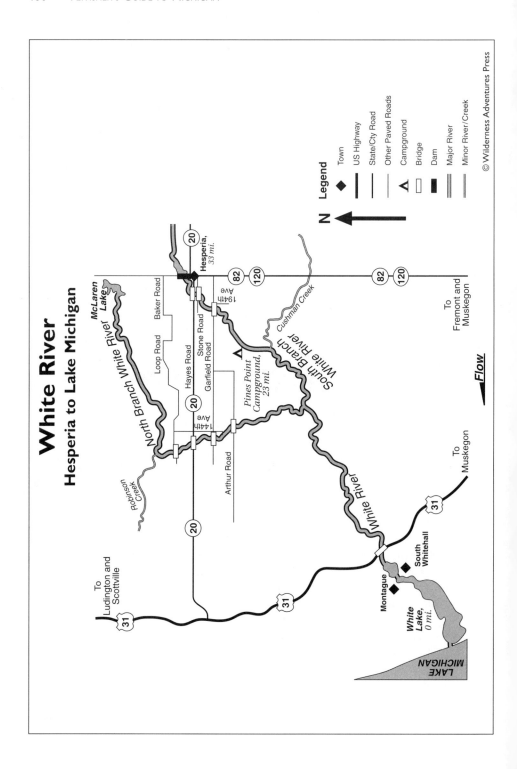

White River
Hesperia to Lake Michigan

Legend

Town ◆
US Highway
State/City Road
Other Paved Roads
Campground ▲
Bridge □
Dam ■
Major River
Minor River/Creek

N

Flow

© Wilderness Adventures Press

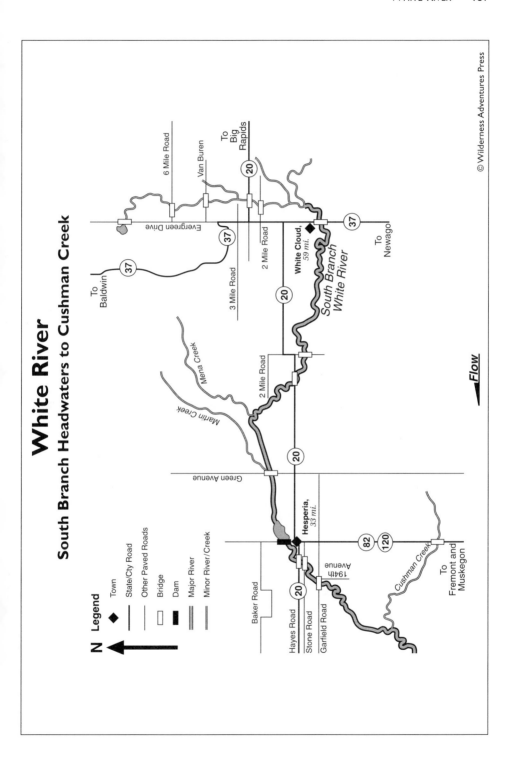

White River
South Branch Headwaters to Cushman Creek

Point area is a good place to intercept fresh steelhead before they get too interested in spawning.

Spring steelhead are pretty much turned off to feeding, although they remain opportunistic when an egg drifts too close. Taking advantage of the relatively clear water and drifting a large, dark nymph or twitching a bright streamer in their territory is a better way to get that electric grab.

A tremendous run of walleyes has joined the White's steelhead run in recent years, adding some spice to the early spring fishing. I saw a walleye that had to be pushing 15 pounds, but I was unable to convince it to take my offering. Because these fish are spawning and not very interested in eating, you need to goad them into hitting a bright streamer.

Depending on rainfall, steelhead also run the White in the fall. While this run is not very dependable, when it happens it can be fantastic. They are very aggressive and are easily fished to in the numerous deep gravel runs.

North Branch of the White

The North Branch becomes a good-sized stream before joining the mainstream, and it is very popular with spring steelheaders. Unlike the main White, the North Branch starts out as a warmwater stream due to lakes in its headwaters. When it gathers the water of Robinson Creek and makes a sharp turn to the south, it becomes large enough for flyfishing and cold enough to support a fine population of brown trout. Young steelhead are also present, and the occasional brook trout or two will snatch a fly.

There are many large holes created by logjams in the upper fly water, and lunker browns lurk in them. Large streamers are a good choice to lure them out of these lairs. Many of these trout are in the 20-inch class, so a reasonably strong tippet is required to extricate them from the wood. Loop, Hayes, Garfield, and Arthur Roads all cross the North Branch one mile apart from each other, so if you and a friend are into wading stretches of water, it is easy to jockey the car so neither angler has to walk back.

The gradient picks up below Arthur Road, and most of the stream's prime spawning riffles are found in the mile or two below this road. Arthur Road also marks the upstream limit for the steelhead extended season. While occasionally there will be a fishable number of steelhead in the fall, the prime time is April. This is one of the few steelhead streams that is closed in winter and has an April 1 opener, however, it is scheduled to be open all year after April 1, 2000. The stream can be very crowded on opening day, but a real quality outing can be had by visiting the river on a weekday in midmonth. Because it can be waded all the way to its mouth, the crowds can be avoided by trying to intercept steelhead in the lower river. Much of the lower North Branch flows through national forest land, and dirt roads from Arthur Road take you to the Bear Creek/North Branch juncture and the North Branch/Main White confluence. The former (144th Avenue) starts just west of the Arthur Road Bridge, while the path to the mouth starts just west of the Bear Creek Bridge on Arthur Road and parallels the small creek for about a mile before turning south.

Stream Facts: White River

Seasons
- Open all year below the dam in Hesperia and from the last Saturday in April until September 30 upstream from the dam and in the North Branch above Arthur Road.
- Below, the North Branch of the White is open from April 1 through December 31.
- Bass must be released between January 1 and the Saturday before Memorial Day.
- Walleyes and northern pike must be released between March 15 and the last Saturday in April.

Special Regulations
- Size limit for all trout and salmon between October 1 and the last Saturday in April is 15 inches.
- Possession limit is 3.

Fish
- Resident brown, rainbow and brook trout; northern pike, walleye, and smallmouth bass.
- Anadromous rainbow and brown trout, chinook and coho salmon, and walleye.

River Miles
- White Lake—0
- Pines Point—23
- Hesperia—33
- White Cloud—59

River Characteristics
- A classic gradation from blue ribbon trout water to marginal trout water, and then to smallmouth and northern pike as the river grows in size.
- It has an excellent gradient with deep gravel runs in the steelhead and salmon water below Hesperia.
- The river is slow to muddy and quick to clear.

River Access
- Primary access is from road bridges, but there are a number of public access sites, especially in the steelhead and salmon water.

PENTWATER RIVER

The Pentwater River is almost the shortest described in this volume. The mainstream is only about a mile long after it is formed at the confluence of the North and South Branches. It meanders through a marsh before widening into Pentwater Lake. The principal fishery in this short section is for steelhead. In addition to intercepting steelhead on their run upstream to spawn, there can also be an interesting feeding period when rainbows are staging in Pentwater Lake. Depending on winter weather, you might be able to drift flies that imitate both eggs and *Hexagenia* nymphs to fish that are still actively feeding. Streamers imitating shiners, smelt, and alewives also get the attention of big rainbows as they move in and out of Pentwater Lake. Access is from Long Bridge Road, which crosses the mainstream, or Monroe Road, which crosses the North Branch just upstream from the juncture.

The North Branch is loaded with both browns and future steelhead. Some argue that it is too small for a fly rod, but much of the diminutive stream is quite open. There will be times as you move upstream that even a roll cast is not practical, but be patient—the stream does open up again.

The same description fits the upper South Branch, except that there are no steelhead fingerlings because the Hart Hydro Dam blocks their migration. Brook trout are present along with browns, and 120th Avenue probably marks the upstream limit for flyrodding, just as it does on the North Branch. Huftile Creek is a small but good brook and brown stream that joins the South Branch a mile or so above Hart Lake, and fishing below the juncture can be good for larger trout.

Below Hart Dam, fishing centers on anadromous fish. Chinook salmon run the river in the fall, along with some steelhead when there is ample rain. The area just below Hart Dam is quite popular in the spring for steelhead, but there is more solitude to be found farther downstream. In spring when the South Branch can be difficult to wade, floating in a small craft is advised. Access to both branches is via road crossings.

PERE MARQUETTE RIVER

Next to the Au Sable, the Pere Marquette is probably Michigan's most famous trout stream. It was America's first river to receive brown trout and is special because it is still free flowing with no dams. However, this river and its fishery are not without controversy. Many anglers lament the presence of anadromous fish and their impact on the resident brown trout. Of course, there are just as many who love to do battle with giant chinook or a rampaging steelhead. Steelhead affect the brown trout population the most, because they have to reach 7 or 8 inches within the stream before they reach the smolt stage and head to Lake Michigan. Since the river can only hold so many trout, there are fewer brown trout now than there were before the lampreys were brought under control in the 1960s.

I think there is a good balance between the numbers of resident trout and anadromous species, allowing the river to provide a very diverse fishery throughout

*A stretch of steelhead
fishing on the
Pere Marquette.*

the year. The future steelhead keep summer trout fishermen busy while trying for
larger browns. And a trout angler can be pleasantly surprised by a chinook or summer steelhead in July or August. Conversely, there have been many times when resident browns have spiced up a slow day of winter steelheading for me.

The Pere Marquette begins near the town of Chase, where several creeks come
together, and is known as the Middle Branch until joined by the Little South Branch
south of Baldwin. The trout fishing gets better as you move downstream, and it
becomes easily fishable with the fly rod south of Nirvana. The blue ribbon water starts
a few miles farther downstream at Broadway Road and continues for 39 river miles.

The Middle Branch has all the major mayfly hatches, including the giant
Hexagenia, and also has the reputation of being a good hopper stream in mid to late
summer. Stoneflies and caddisflies are also common in this high quality stretch of
water. Angling pressure is usually lighter in the Middle Branch than it is in the mainstream below Baldwin, and there are certainly a lot fewer canoes. It can be a very

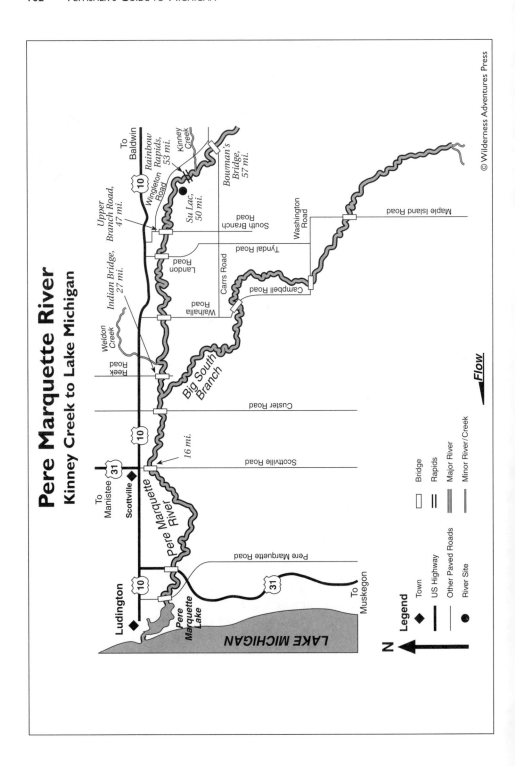

Pere Marquette River
Kinney Creek to Lake Michigan

Pere Marquette River
Headwaters to Kinney Creek

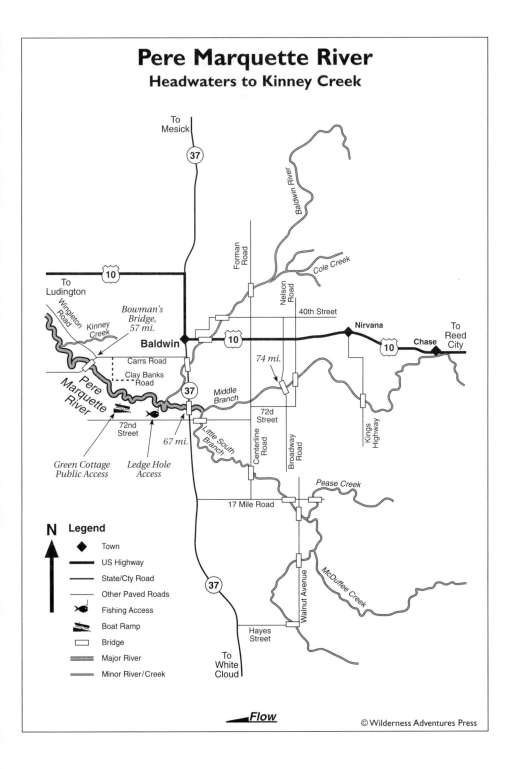

To
Mesick

37

Baldwin River

Forman
Road

Cole Creek

10

To
Ludington

Nelson
Road

40th Street

Nirvana

To
Reed
City

Wingleton
Road

Kinney
Creek

Bowman's
Bridge,
57 mi.

Baldwin

10

10

Chase

Carrs Road

74 mi.

Clay Banks
Road

Pere
Marquette
River

37

Middle
Branch

72d
Street

Kings
Highway

72nd
Street

67 mi.

Little South
Branch

Centerline
Road

Broadway
Road

Green Cottage
Public Access

Ledge Hole
Access

Pease Creek

17 Mile Road

N **Legend**

◆ Town

━━ US Highway

── State/Cty Road

── Other Paved Roads

✦ Fishing Access

🚤 Boat Ramp

▭ Bridge

▬ Major River

▬ Minor River/Creek

Walnut Avenue

McDuffee Creek

37

Hayes
Street

To
White
Cloud

Flow

© Wilderness Adventures Press

Pete Schantz fishes the Pere Marquette's fly-only water.

good place to fish on weekends. Good access occurs at road crossings. As you move downstream these include King's Highway (Nirvana Bridge), Rosa Road, Nelson Road, Broadway Road (Switzer Bridge), Forman Road, and James Road. Additional public access sites are located east (Roller Bridge) and west (Thompson's Spring) of Broadway Road.

Although it is not as cold as the Middle Branch, the Little South Branch is also a good trout stream. When McDuffee and Pease Creeks add their cold flows, the stream becomes large enough to navigate with a fly rod, and the Little South is classified as a blue ribbon trout stream below the next bridge downstream at Walnut Avenue. These streams are also the source of some brook trout that could add to your catch. Like the Middle Branch, it has diverse insect fauna, including enough silt-filled areas for good numbers of burrowing mayflies, such as *Hexagenia* and green drakes. This branch can also provide some refuge when the mainstream becomes too crowded. Centerline and 17 Mile Roads and 72nd Street crossings offer additional access, and where James Road crosses the Middle Branch, you can see the juncture with the Little South just downstream.

From Baldwin down to the end of the blue ribbon water at Reek Road in Mason County, the Pere Marquette has the water and the fish to satisfy just about anyone's taste. Many anglers decide where to fish based on their quarry and the river height. Below M-37 the river is almost the perfect combination of riffles and deep runs. Between the highway bridge and Gleason's Landing, fishing is restricted to artificial

Driftboating on the fly-only section of the Pere Marquette River.

flies only and will become catch and release in 2000. This is a very popular reach, especially for anadromous fish. There is prime spawning gravel for both chinook and steelhead, along with plenty of nearby dark water where they can hide and rest. Browns are plentiful, as well, and the river gains in size when the Baldwin River joins it in this stretch. Steve Fraley of Baldwin Bait & Tackle reports that some of the best dry-fly fishing occurs during the overlap of the early gray drake and *Hexagenia* hatches, which usually happens in mid-June. He also claims that streamer fishing for big browns is especially good when the steelhead run is winding down in May.

The upper part of the fly-only water is paralleled by 72nd Street on the south side of the river. Lumberjack, Ledge Hole, and the Green Cottage Public access sites are located on this road. Walking in at the Ledge Hole access puts you on the river just below the confluence of the Baldwin River and the Pere Marquette. This is a favorite of mine because it gives me the option of working up the Baldwin if canoe and drift boat traffic gets too heavy on the mainstream. Take Peacock Road north off of 72nd Street for a quarter mile to reach the parking lot of the Green Cottage access site. Access to the Claybanks and Gleason's Landing is from the north, following the signs from Carrs Road. If you cross the river (Bowman Bridge) coming from Baldwin, you missed the turns to these access points for the lower fly-only water.

At Gleason's Landing, the river makes a transition back to predominantly sand bottom, and this continues until Kinney Creek joins it. There are spotty sections of gravel here, but burrowing mayflies as well as mayflies and caddisflies that cling to woody debris are the predominant insects. There is a good *Hexagenia* hatch here, and browns over 20 inches are waiting to be fooled by your after dark presentation.

The gradient really picks up below Kinney Creek, and although there isn't any true whitewater, the flow is pretty darn quick in the Rainbow Rapids area. There is a good public access and boat launch at Rainbow Rapids, and the float from here down to Su Lac or the Upper Branch Bridge access sites is a fun and productive one. Choosing the takeout point usually is determined by how fast you want to cover the water, how much daylight you have, and the river level. This reach is a mix of rocks, gravel, sand, and lots of very slippery clay. All of this reach can be waded during normal summer and fall levels, but many still prefer to float it. If you do wade, a wading staff is a good idea even in low water because of the strong current and greasy clay.

Even though there are no additional major tributaries, the river continues to slowly grow as it winds its way down to the end of the blue ribbon water at Reek Road. Brown trout continue to be the dominant resident trout, with plenty of future steelhead inhabiting the faster water. You can continue to wade this water in the summer, but some of the crossings are difficult, so floating is a better idea. Between Walhalla and Reek Road, the river braids a lot, providing some interesting fishing and boating. An easier float is between Landon Road (Lower Branch Bridge) and Walhalla Bridge. Gravel becomes scarcer below Walhalla, so burrowing mayflies again make up the major hatches. Weldon Creek, which joins the mainstream above Reek Road, helps cool the water. It is also the source of some brown trout that move down into the Pere Marquette to grow bigger.

Below Reek Road, the river broadens and the bottom is mostly sand. There are some monster browns here, but you are also likely to encounter some hefty northern pike. The Big South Branch joins the Pere Marquette a couple of river miles below Reek Road and greatly increases the size of the river. Northerns increasingly become the dominant resident predator, but there is still a chance for a good-sized brown trout. Fishing large, colorful streamers here could net you either species. The river is also much better traversed by boat even during dry periods. There are parks and launch ramps at the Custer and Scottville Road crossings that provide access to the lower Pere Marquette.

Anadromous fish make up a very large part of the fishery on the Pere Marquette River. The principal species are chinook salmon and steelhead, but lake-run browns and coho can also show up in your catch. Essentially, you can find lake-run fish in the Pere Marquette every month of the year.

Summer steelhead were stocked in the past, but this was halted due to concerns that Skamania strain steelhead might interbreed and cause some problems with the Pere Marquette's wild steelhead. Because of straying and possibly some natural reproduction, summer steelhead are still encountered on a regular basis. They can enter the river as early as June but are most frequently hooked in July and August.

Confluence of the Middle Branch and Little South Branch
of the Pere Marquette River.

Needless to say, when a 10-pound summer-run steelhead clobbers a nymph that has been catching 12-inch browns, it gets real exciting in a hurry.

Because there have never been stockings of chinook salmon in the Pere Marquette, virtually all of its chinook are wild. They begin to enter the river in late July, and there are almost always fishable numbers by late August. The lower river is the place to intercept these salmon when they are still bright and very aggressive. Invading their territory by sweeping fluorescent marabou streamers is a good way to get hooked up to these hard-fighting fish. Expect to land only about one out of three that you hook. While these fish are usually more concentrated below the Big South Branch, they also linger in the water above this tributary, where it is easier to get a fly down to them.

While fresh chinook continue to enter the river through September, many anglers shift their attention to spawning chinook in September and October. It is pretty hard to beat the fly-only stretch for numbers of fish, but unfortunately, there are also lots of anglers. Coho salmon and lake-run brown trout also begin to move upriver in September, but because it rarely pays to target them, they tend to be bonus fish.

The Pere Marquette's wild steelhead begin to run in late September, with the fall run peaking in November. Paying attention to autumn rains is the key to finding them. During a dry fall, they stay in the lower river, but periodic heavy rains can cause them to move all the way up to the fly-only water. Covering lots of water with bright streamers is the best way to catch them. If you find a concentration of steelhead, egg flies and large, dark nymphs will also get you hooked up.

Winter steelheading can be fantastic in this river. Since there are no dams, fish spread out and don't get hammered like they do in rivers with dams. During very cold weather, when you won't want to be out anyway, a fair amount of ice builds up in the river. But the stretch between Kinney Creek and Upper Branch Bridge usually remains fishable and is a good stretch even when it is mild, because water is warmer here. At times in the dead of winter, resident browns become surprisingly active, providing spice to your action.

On one frigid day when the water was cooled below 32 degrees and there was lots of anchor ice, I was ready to surrender after sucking the ice out of the guides for a couple of hours. But then a steelhead hit and warmed me up. What followed made me forget all about the weather. Half a dozen brown trout between 12 and 17 inches grabbed my offering, along with another three steelhead. The water temperature never got above 32 degrees, but much of the anchor ice lifted off the bottom. My theory is that the slight warming of the water, combined with the dislodging of nymphs by the anchor ice, triggered the feeding activity of the browns.

Spring is spawning time for these fish, of course, and again, the biggest concentrations are found in the fly-only stretch. There is good gravel in the river above and below Branch, as well, and it is much less crowded in this downstream reach. Fluorescent streamers and egg flies are the most successful offerings. There will always be as many fish in the dark water near the redds as there are actually spawning, so fish these gravel runs hard. Though April is the peak month, fish can start spawning in late February and continue through May. Sometimes the spent fish linger in the river, and many times trout anglers are surprised by spawned out female steelhead in May and early June. Weather greatly affects timing of the run in the spring, and water conditions can vary a lot, so call ahead to make your trip more productive.

Big South Branch

The Big South Branch is the Pere Marquette's largest tributary. It is on the marginal side for trout because of warm summertime water temperatures. However, cold tributaries and spring holes allow year-round trout survival, and lunker browns are present. Some brook trout are also present in tributaries, such as Allen and Ruby Creeks, and they may move into the Big South during cool weather periods. Because it is not as good a trout river as the mainstream, it is not fished nearly as hard. The net result is that you can do quite well here if you are willing to put up with the creek chubs and cover lots of water.

The middle reach of the river between Dickinson Avenue and Walhalla Road is probably best for trout, but they are present throughout the stream. Hawley, Anthony, and Washington Road crossings offer additional access in this reach. You will not catch as many trout on the Big South as you do in the mainstem, but the average size will be larger. In the lower river, more pike than trout are found, especially in slow-moving side channels and bayous. The river alternates between gravel

Confluence of the Baldwin River (left) and the Pere Marquette.

runs and deep sandholes, with enough sand and silt to have a good population of *Hexagenia* and other burrowing mayflies. Imitating the stream's plentiful minnows with a streamer is also a good plan.

In early fall, chinook salmon run this stream in good numbers. There is also a steelhead run that is augmented by some planted smolts in Ruby Creek, a small but cold tributary. Fishing below this creek is a good plan when looking for silvery rainbows.

Baldwin River

The Baldwin River is a relatively small stream but provides excellent trout fishing. It starts as a brook trout creek in cedar swamps northeast of Baldwin and becomes large enough for flyfishing when it is joined by Cole Creek. Classified as a blue ribbon trout stream from here down to its mouth, much of the stream is fairly narrow, sand-bottomed, and deep. Because of this, wading is difficult, especially in the spring between Cole Creek and the 40th Street bridge. Below this reach the river becomes wider and shallower and has more gravel. It remains wader friendly all the way to its mouth, about 2 miles south of the village of the same name.

There is a very good population of medium sized brown trout in the Baldwin, along with the ever present future steelhead. The stream is not open during the extended season, so trout get a rest in the fall and winter. The Baldwin is known for a

Baldwin River.

late run of steelhead, which means there are still good numbers of anadromous rainbows in the river when trout season opens. This makes it a very popular destination for anglers seeking steelhead that haven't been fished over. Of course, any gullibility the steelhead might have had by not being fished for in the early spring is lost in about an hour on opening day. Hatches in the Baldwin coincide with those found in the Pere Marquette. It has a surprisingly good *Hexagenia* hatch upstream from Baldwin where it is not fished nearly as hard as the mainstream. Pete Schantz of Al and Pete's Sport Shop in Hastings routinely bypasses the main Pere Marquette and heads to the Baldwin when the big mayflies are hatching.

Stream Facts: Pere Marquette River

Seasons
- The main stream down stream from M-37 and the Big South Branch are open all year.
- The remainder of the river and its tributaries are open from the last Saturday in April through September 30.
- Bass must be released between January 1 and the Saturday before Memorial Day.
- Walleyes and northern pike must be released between March 15 and the last Saturday in April.

Special Regulations
- Size limit for trout and salmon between October 1 and the last Saturday in April is 15 inches, and the possession limit is 3 fish.
- All brown trout must be released during this period, as well.
- Between the M-37 Bridge and Gleason's Landing, it is artificial flies only, with a minimum size of 16 inches and a possession limit of 1 fish until April 1, 2000, when it becomes catch and release.

Fish
- Brown, rainbow, and brook trout; northern pike.
- Anadromous chinook and coho salmon, brown and rainbow trout, and walleye.

River Miles
- Pere Marquette Lake—0
- Scottville—16
- Indian Bridge—27
- Upper Branch Road Bridge—47
- Su Lac—50
- Rainbow Rapids—53
- Bowman's Bridge—57
- M-37 Bridge—67
- Broadway Road—74

River Characteristics
- Medium-sized coldwater river that is free of any dams.
- Excellent combination of resident trout and wild anadromous rainbows and chinook salmon.
- The Pere Marquette is a true four-season stream.
- The fly-only water contains some of the best spawning habitat in the entire river.

River Access
- Access available at each landmark noted above with river miles.
- Numerous public access sites along with road crossings provide additional access and are noted on the river map.

PERE MARQUETTE RIVER MAJOR HATCHES

Insect	Jan	Feb	Mar	Apr	May	Jun	July	Aug	Sep	Oct	Nov	Dec	Time	Fly Patterns
Black Stonefly		▓	▓	▓									A	Early Black Stonefly #10–14
Hendrickson					▓								M/A	Hendrickson #12–14; Rusty's Spinner; Red Quill; Adams; Quill Gordon
Blue-winged Olive				▓	▓	▓	▓	▓					A	Blue-winged Olive #18–20; Sparkle Dun Baetis; Iron Dun; Olive CDC Mayfly Dun
Little Black Caddis				▓	▓	▓	▓	▓					A	Little Black Caddis #16–18; Griffith's Gnat; CDC Emerging Caddis Brown; Black Ant
Net-building Caddis					▓	▓	▓	▓	▓	▓			M/A	Spotted Sedge #16–18; Eastern Elk Wing Caddis; Goddard Caddis
Sulphur Dun					▓	▓							A/E	Sulphur Dun #16; Pale Morning Dun; CDC Comparadun Yellow; Pale Evening Dun
March Brown					▓	▓							M/A	March Brown #12–14; Dark Cahill; Gray Fox; Ginger Quill
Gray Drake						▓							E	Gray Drake #12–14; Gray Adams
Brown Drake						▓							E	Brown Drake #10–12; Adams; CDC Brown
Green Drake						▓							E	Green Drake #10–12; Comparadun Green
Hexagenia						▓	▓						E	Hex #4–8; Great Olive-winged Drake; Spring's Wiggler; Hare's Ear
Trico							▓	▓	▓				M	Tiny White Wing Black #24–28; Parachute Adams; CDC Trico; Spent Wing Trico
White Fly								▓	▓				E	White Fly #12–14; White Miller
Streamers	▓	▓	▓	▓	▓	▓	▓	▓	▓	▓	▓	▓	M/A/E	Woolly Buggers #6–12; Clouser's Minnow; Muddler Minnows; BC Craw; Matukas
Terrestrials						▓	▓	▓	▓				M/A/E	Woolly Worm #8–12; BC Spider; Letort Cricket; Joe's Hopper #6–10; Dave's Hopper; Dropper Hopper

HATCH TIME CODE: M = morning; A = afternoon; E = evening.

SABLE RIVER

The Sable River, also known as the Big Sauble River, is often confused with the much more famous Au Sable. If there is such a thing as a sleeper trout stream in northwestern Michigan, this may be it. Even though there are lakes in its headwaters, many springs quickly cool it down and increase its size. It becomes a blue ribbon trout stream at USFS-5199 and keeps this designation down to Freesoil Road. The Little Sable River, which joins the main stream in this reach, contains a good population of brook trout. There are brookies in the mainstream but browns dominate here.

Below Freesoil Road the river widens, slows down and gradually becomes a bit warm for trout. Lunker browns remain a possibility, though, almost to the head of Hamlin Lake. This lake is formed by a dam close to Lake Michigan and provides excellent warmwater fishing. Pike from the lake move up into the lower part of the river where they can compete for streamers with the big browns.

An advantage this trout stream has over its neighbors is that the resident trout don't have to share the river with the offspring of anadromous fish. Of course, many anglers don't mind at all catching riffle rainbows between brown trout takes. Because this won't happen here, all the stream's bio-energy can go into growing resident trout.

Numerous bridges provide access. The lower river near Freesoil is crossed by six roads that are all a mile a part, perfect for a bridge-to-bridge streamer angler like me. Bridges are less numerous in the upper river, but there are two public access sites on Sauble Road south of Freesoil Road.

A beautiful 21-inch brown trout.

Sable River

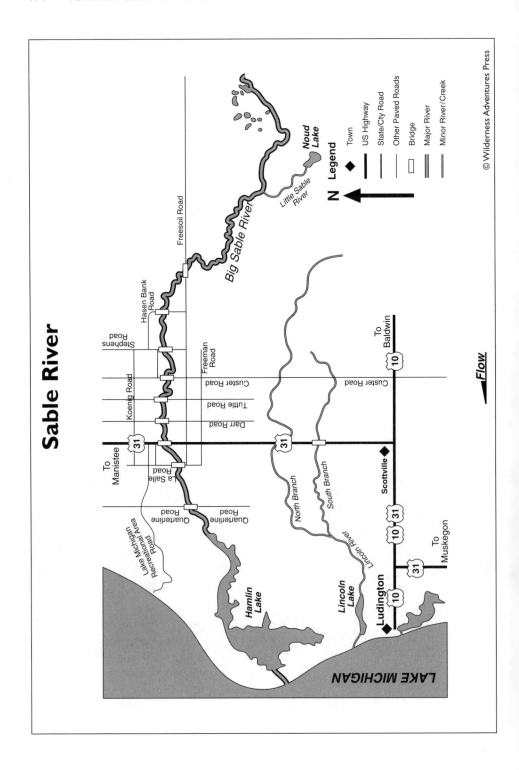

© Wilderness Adventures Press

The Sable has a good *Hexagenia* hatch in late June and usually is much less crowded than the nearby Pere Marquette. Other species of burrowing mayflies are also present, along with many caddis species. Crayfish are present in good numbers, especially in the lower reaches, which helps explain the lunker brown possibilities. Streamers imitating minnows or crayfish are good bets when there isn't a hatch. Even though there are not any anadromous fish in the Sable above Hamlin Lake, it is open to trout fishing year-round below Freesoil Road.

Chinook salmon and steelhead enter the short section of river between Lake Michigan and the Hamlin Lake dam. This is tough fishing because the river is mostly quite shallow and very clear. The chinook run is delayed in September until Hamlin Lake has cooled into the 60s. This stream can serve as a backup when heavy rains or spring runoff turn the nearby steelhead and salmon streams chocolate brown. It is always nice to have an "insurance policy" when you have traveled a long way to fish. The lower Sable is within the Ludington State Park, so you will need a current state parks permit or sticker.

The Lincoln River flows between the Sable and the Pere Marquette River into Lake Michigan. It has marginal flyfishing once the North and South Branches merge a few miles upstream from Lincoln Lake. While the brushy South Branch contains a good population of browns and brookies, the combined mainstream is on the warm side for trout. There is still a chance for a brown, and there are also some pike present. Steelhead and salmon also run this river, which is open year-round up to the forks. Pressure is usually light unless word gets out that there are a bunch of steelhead in the river.

LITTLE MANISTEE RIVER

The Little River, as the Little Manistee is commonly known, is a real jewel of a trout stream. It is the "mother river" for all of Michigan's and some neighboring states' hatchery steelhead. No steelhead are planted in the Little Manistee, and its wild fish do so well in this stream that the Michigan DNR is able to "borrow" a couple of thousand returning adults each year for their eggs and milt. This results in Michigan's hatchery steelhead always coming from wild parents and free of some of the inbreeding problems that can come from many generations of hatchery fish.

The Little Manistee starts a few miles south of the town of Luther, where several small creeks come together. It continues to increase in size with the influx of small creeks and springs as it flows northwest to Manistee Lake and then Lake Michigan. It becomes an official flyfishing stream at County Road 633, which is also where the blue ribbon trout water starts, but a small stream specialist can roll cast to the brookies upstream. As the stream meanders and grows in size, it alternates between sandy, slow stretches and fast gravel reaches. There is ample room for flycasting at M-37, and there is good access here at the Old Grade Campground. Brookies soon give way to browns as the resident trout. Small rainbows (future steelhead) abound throughout the river. Occasionally, you will encounter a rainbow of 12 to 16 inches that had steelhead parents but never smolted and became a river resident.

Little Manistee River

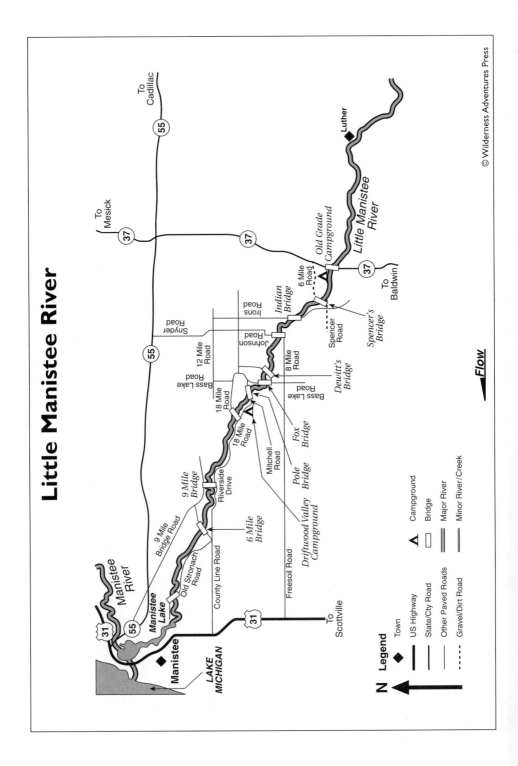

© Wilderness Adventures Press

*Linda Hayslette and Randy Worden admire a fine steelhead
from the Little Manistee River.*

The reach between Spencer's Bridge and Johnson's Bridge has been designated as fly-only, and in April 2000, it will become catch and release. For now, the minimum size for all trout is increased to 10 inches and the regular trout season is extended until October 31. Irons Road (Indian Bridge) bisects the fly-only stretch providing additional access. The Johnson Road Bridge is also the upstream limit for the extended steelhead and salmon season.

The blue ribbon water extends down to the Manistee County Line, but I strongly believe it should continue another 10 river miles to the site of the harvest weir. Lots of groundwater enters here, making the river cooler than it is upstream. Several years ago I caught and released a 28-inch resident brown in this stretch, and it still stands as my longest stream resident trout. Unfortunately, I caught the fish on my steelhead tackle after it had spawned in December. What a treat it would have been to hook this monster on a 4-weight the previous September.

Fran Gee proudly holds a November steelhead on the Little Manistee River.

The first bridge below Johnson's Bridge is called Dewitt's and is on Wills Road. Fox (Bass Lake Road) and Pole (Mitchell Road) Bridges provide nearby access just downstream. Gravel riffles abound between Fox and Dewitt's Bridges and attract spawning steelhead. Driftwood Valley Campground, just downstream from Pole Bridge, offers additional access and camping.

The Eighteen Mile Bridge to Nine Mile Bridge reach is mostly sand with some isolated patches of gravel. There are many deep bend holes and a modest *Hexagenia*, hatch along with brown drakes. Another U.S. Forest Service Campground, Bear Track, is located about a mile downstream from 18 Mile Road Bridge. At Nine Mile Bridge, the river begins a transition to all gravel and becomes very fast. Many a fairly experienced canoeist has capsized trying to negotiate this section's fast water that is punctuated by hairpin turns and log jams. It is a favorite place of mine to catch trout, since the trout have to make up their mind in a hurry as your fly drifts by.

As the water slows again at Six Mile Bridge, sand again becomes more prevalent than gravel and continues to prevail to the mouth. Logs and undercut banks provide cover for good-sized browns. The DNR salmon harvest weir is located about halfway between Six Mile Bridge and the river's mouth at Manistee Lake. This weir is used to block and harvest salmon in the fall. Eggs are taken from chinook salmon for the hatcheries, and the station also serves as a backup for coho salmon eggs. Steelhead and lake-run browns are counted and passed up stream. In spring, the steelhead egg take occurs. Green or unripe fish are passed upstream to spawn when they are ready, and even the steelhead that are stripped at the weir are released upstream for anglers to try to entice. You can gain access to the river at the weir but must not fish within 300 feet above or below the structure.

Even though the trout fishing is very good in this stream, I have to admit that it is the steelhead fishing that draws me to it each year. The presence of the weir allows me to fish for steelhead in the fall without the distraction of salmon or the anglers they attract. Actually, a fishable number of chinook salmon enter the Little Manistee in July and early August before the weir is closed, but they are done spawning for the most part by the time the steelhead arrive. These salmon do offer one of the best chances to hook a bright chinook in midsummer. Though they can be sightfished in the clear water, they are very difficult to catch under these conditions. Blind drifting bright streamers in the deeper holes when rain has stained the water is a much better bet.

The steelhead fall run in the Little Manistee varies greatly and is dependent, at least in part, on autumn rains and the level of Lake Michigan. Lots of rain and a high Lake Michigan facilitate the movement of steelhead over the shallow sand at the mouth of the river. Remember—these fish don't spawn until spring, so they don't have any urgent motivation to migrate in the fall if conditions are not right.

Over the last 30 years, the fall run has varied from a few hundred to over 7,000 fish. You can keep tabs on the number of steelhead and lake-run browns that have been passed by calling the Cadillac District Office of the DNR (616-775-9727, ext. 6072). Generally, about 500 or more fish will result in good fishing. Of course, if you can find the pulse of fish after a much smaller pass, you can have great action. The longer it has been since additional steelhead have been passed, the tougher the fishing will be.

Many anglers sightfish for steelhead in the fall, but I believe that if you can see them, the fish have spotted you. My preference is to fish blind in the runs and holes that have been good producers in the past. Both bright nymphs and streamers and large dark leech patterns will take these great fish.

Usually, the best fishing occurs in November. This is when the most steelhead are in the river and are still very active. Parts of the Little Manistee, especially around Six Mile Bridge, never freeze, so this can also be a spot for December fishing. The Little Manistee closed at the end of December and did not reopen until April 1. This will change in 2000, with the lower river open to angling all year. Hopefully, with the upstream limit at Johnson Road and the voluntary release of female steelhead by anglers, there will be sufficient numbers of steelhead that escape to spawn and keep the Little Manistee at its carrying capacity for young steelhead.

The Little Manistee is especially popular in the spring for steelhead—too popular for me! At midnight on April 1, there will be lanterns dancing along its banks with anglers jockeying for the best holes when daylight arrives. It is especially crowded below the weir. If you have sharpened your elbows and don't mind crowds, you have the potential to catch a number of steelhead on this river in early April. My preference is to visit this river on weekdays later in April after the egg take is finished and the weir is opened. I've found that steelhead that have not been handled at the weir or been harassed by hundreds of anglers are much easier to catch. Picking a cloudy, dark day will also increase your chances on this clear river. In years when spring weather is normal, steelhead linger in this stream well into May. Smaller numbers of fish coupled with fewer anglers translates into more steelies bending your rod.

MANISTEE RIVER

The Manistee is one of Michigan's largest and most famous rivers—only the Au Sable is better known. Interestingly, these two rivers start very close to each other on opposite sides of the Lower Peninsula divide. They parallel each other, a few miles apart, for about 20 river miles until they turn in opposite directions, with the Manistee flowing into Lake Michigan and the Au Sable flowing into Lake Huron.

Kelly Galloup, veteran guide, flyfisherman, and owner of the Troutsman in Traverse City, describes the upper Manistee as a "river created for flyfishing." He says, "Its stable flow and water temperature create superb insect activity and keep the trout feeding on the surface with good regularity." Kelly considers the fly-only reach on the Manistee as "a dream come true."

With the influx of groundwater and small creeks, the Manistee quickly grows to a stream large enough to negotiate with a fly rod. While it becomes "officially" fly-fishable at the beginning of its blue ribbon water near Deward, the river is open enough for flyfishing for a number of miles upstream. Brook trout are the dominant fish here and readily take flies on and below the surface in a wide range of patterns. This is a great area for the novice fly angler to gain confidence in his or her fishing ability. There is access at Deward and at Cameron Road and County Road 612 bridges. Below CR-612, there are three campgrounds providing good access all the way down to M-72. In addition, most of the upper Manistee flows through public land, so you can always hike in to the river.

The Manistee keeps its blue ribbon designation down to Sharon. It ends here not so much because of the quality of the trout fishing but because the river becomes large and difficult to wade. Brown trout slowly increase in numbers downstream, but brook trout continue to be present. Within this reach, there is a 7-mile section designated as flies only. Between Yellowtrees Landing and the C.C.C. Bridge, anglers must use artificial flies, and the minimum size for brown trout is raised to 12 inches. The season is extended through the month of October for this water, as well. Starting in 2000, the fly-only water will be extended up M-72, adding a full 6 miles. Access is somewhat limited to the fly-only water, with the only bridges on the ends of the reach and most of the river bank in private hands. Many landowners will give permission if asked, and you can float this reach as well.

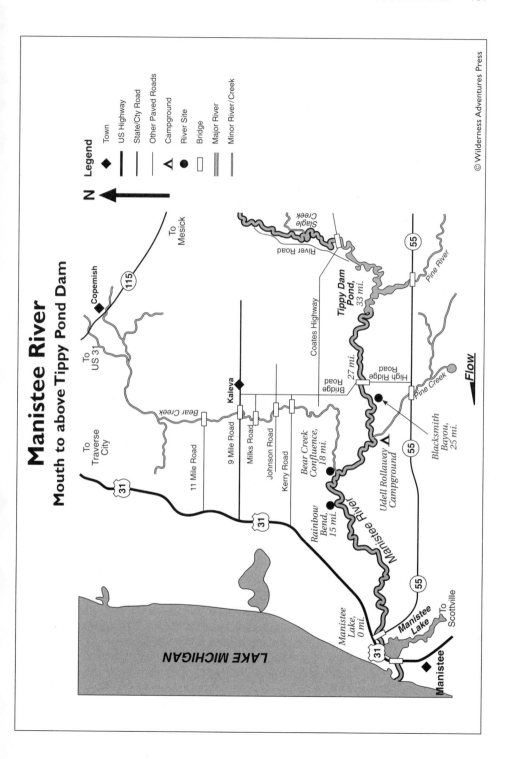

Manistee River
Mouth to above Tippy Pond Dam

Legend

N

Town
US Highway
State/Cty Road
Other Paved Roads
Campground
River Site
Bridge
Major River
Minor River/Creek

© Wilderness Adventures Press

To Traverse City

To US 31

To Mesick

Copemish

Kaleva

Bear Creek

11 Mile Road

9 Mile Road

Milks Road

Johnson Road

Kerry Road

Coates Highway

Bridge Road

High Ridge Road

River Road

Slagle Creek

Tippy Dam Pond, 33 mi.

Pine River

Pine Creek

Blacksmith Bayou, 25 mi.

27 mi.

Bear Creek Confluence, 18 mi.

Rainbow Bend, 15 mi.

Udell Rollaway Campground

Manistee River

Flow

LAKE MICHIGAN

Manistee Lake, 0 mi.

Manistee Lake

To Scottville

Manistee

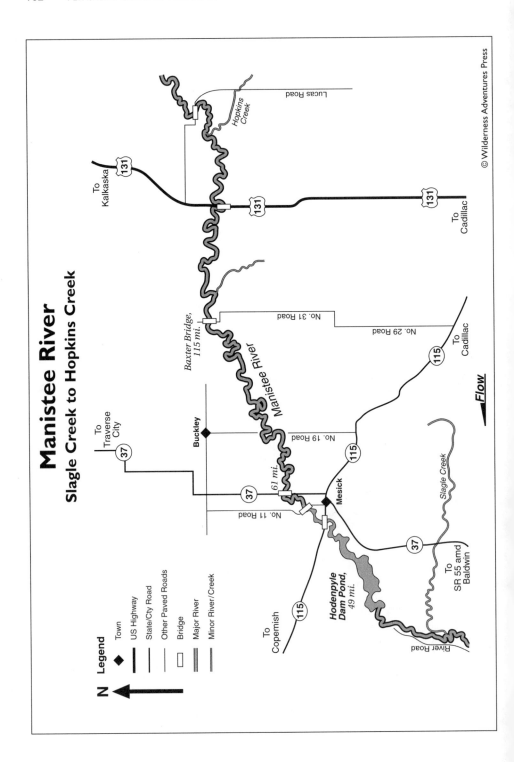

Manistee River
Slagle Creek to Hopkins Creek

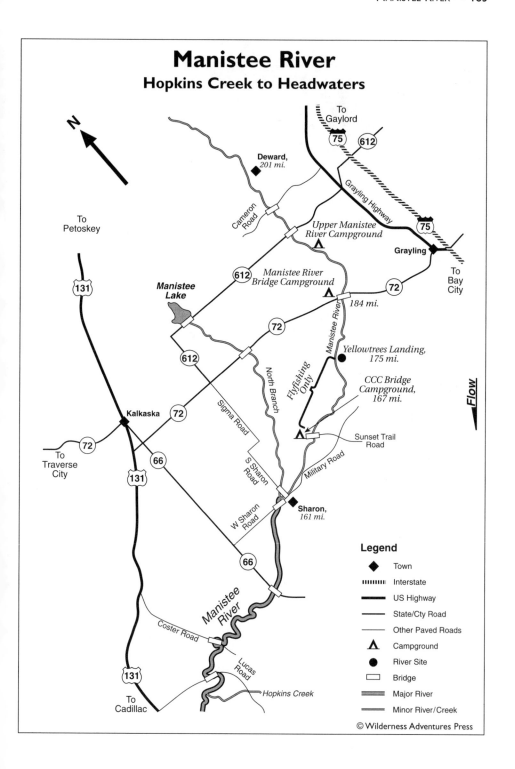

Manistee River
Hopkins Creek to Headwaters

N

To
Gaylord

75 612

To
Petoskey

Deward,
201 mi.

Cameron
Road

Grayling Highway

75

Upper Manistee
River Campground

Grayling

To
Bay
City

131

612

Manistee
Lake

Manistee River
Bridge Campground

72

184 mi.

72

Manistee River

Yellowtrees Landing,
175 mi.

612

North Branch

Flyfishing
Only

CCC Bridge
*Campground,
167 mi.*

Sigma Road

Kalkaska

72

Sunset Trail
Road

To
Traverse
City

72

66

S Sharon
Road

Military Road

Flow

131

W Sharon
Road

Sharon,
161 mi.

66

Manistee
River

Coster Road

Lucas
Road

131

To
Cadillac

Hopkins Creek

Legend

◆	Town
�IIIIIII	Interstate
▬▬	US Highway
—	State/Cty Road
—	Other Paved Roads
⋀	Campground
●	River Site
▭	Bridge
▬▬	Major River
▬▬	Minor River/Creek

© Wilderness Adventures Press

The fly-only water
on the Manistee River.

The North Branch of the Manistee joins the Manistee at Sharon. Although it is full of brook trout, it is relatively lightly fished because of a limited number of access sites. The first 4 miles upstream from the mainstream is classified as blue ribbon trout water. There is access at either end (Mecum and North Sharon Roads) of this water but none in between. This means that if you are willing to hike a little, you can have the river to yourself. There is room to roll cast upstream from Mecum Road, as well.

As is evident from the hatch chart, the upper Manistee's insect population is diverse. If there is no hatch, probing the water with streamers in muddler or small leech patterns is a good idea. Because trout love the wood in the Manistee, getting your imitation close to and in the logs is a key to success.

From Sharon down to the backwaters of the Hodenpyle Dam Pond, the river is best fished by floating. Large brown trout are present in this stretch, with smallmouth bass and walleyes joining the mix as you get closer to the backwaters. There are several high quality trout creeks that flow into the Manistee in this long reach. Most are too small to flyfish, but you can maneuver with the fly rod a bit in Silver, Buttermilk, and Hopkins Creeks where they enter the mainstream. Landing a canoe or boat and wading up one of these creeks adds variety to an outing and can provide some of the best fishing. Below these and other coldwater creeks, the Manistee is also likely to be productive, especially during warm weather. M-66, Coster Road, Lucas Road, US-131, CR-31 (Baxter Bridge), CR-19, M-37, and CR-11 crossings provide periodic access to this big water section of the Manistee. All of these accesses allow you to pick and choose how far you want to float. Some wading is also possible.

There are some very large browns in the short stretch between the Hodenpyle Dam and the backwaters of Tippy Dam, with some walleyes and smallmouth bass also present. Slagle Creek adds it cold flow in this reach, and focusing your efforts below it can increase your chances for brown trout hookups. Coates Highway crosses the Manistee in this reach near the backwaters of Tippy Dam and is the only road that does so.

The Manistee below Tippy Dam, nationally known for its anadromous fishery, is now usually called the Big Manistee. Since the state requires that the dam be operated at run of the river instead of peaking, a respectable trout fishery has been developed below it. Before the practice of peaking was stopped, the river essentially rotated between drought flow and a flood each day, which had devastating effects on the fish and the benthos.

There is still one hurdle to conquer before we can have a truly great tailwater fishery here, and that is temperature control. Like Croton Dam on the Muskegon, Tippy does not have a bottom draw, which means that the water temperature rises to the low 70s and stays there round the clock during summer hot spells. The FERC relicensing agreement specified that the water temperature below the dam be maintained at 68 degrees or lower in the summer. So far, that control has not been enforced, which is sad for the river and its anglers.

Run of the river has also helped the chinook, and to some extent, steelhead have increased their natural reproduction in the lower river. Couple this with very large plants of steelhead and chinook hatchery smolts, and it is easy to understand why this river has a world class fishery in the fall, winter, and spring.

In both summer and winter steelhead smolts (Little Manistee offspring) are planted in the Big Manistee. The Skamania strain summer-runs can enter the river as early as late June. A heavy rain and cool weather at any time in July or August are likely to trigger a run. When the weather is warm, angling for these fish can be difficult, because they do not strike well when the water temperature is above 68 degrees.

These fish tend to move quickly up the river and become concentrated below the dam. In summer the area below the coffer dam can be waded easily for about a mile downstream. The fish like to rest in deep riffles and runs under broken water, which means that bright, gaudy, marabou streamers work well, especially in orange and red hues. Crayfish patterns also seem to be attractive to these fish. When we had a cool

*Steelhead and salmon
water on the
Big Manistee River.*

summer a few years ago, the fishing was outstanding. With temperature control at
the dam, this could happen every summer. There is access on each side of the river
at the dam, with a boat launch on the north side. Additional access is found at
Suicide Bend, about a mile down from the dam on the north side of the river.

Chinook salmon begin to enter the river in August, with fishable numbers almost
always present by the end of the month. Unlike the Skamania steelhead, they linger
in the lower river and can be intercepted just up from Manistee Lake, on a section of
the river that needs to be floated. Streamers with lots of flash and fluorescent green
or chartreuse color work best. Pine River is a small stream that joins the Manistee
below High Bridge Road. It is usually at least 15 degrees colder than the mainstream,
and the long bend below it always holds salmon looking for cooler water. Access is
possible by walking to the mouth of Pine River at the Udell Rollaways Campground

This 17-inch brown trout was caught on the Manistee River.

on the south side of the river. To get to this coldwater influx, launch at High Bridge or Blacksmith Bayou and float down or motor up from Bear Creek.

As September progresses, chinook pile up more and more below Tippy Dam, where there is a lot of spawning gravel for the fish to build giant redds. Anglers can fish for sighted fish on the spawning beds or probe the dark water nearby. Using bright streamers that the salmon can readily see helps prevent accidental foul hooking. The salmon either attack the bright intruder or get out of its way. Even though snagging has been banned here for a number of years, you are still likely to encounter some unscrupulous "anglers" trying to force feed these fish. Moving downstream away from the dam is often helpful in getting fish to hit because they will not have been harassed as much.

Coho salmon and brown trout join the chinook later in September. While their numbers are not great, they add to the variety of fish present below the dam. Although both species spawn later than chinook, there may be some overlap.

Winter steelhead begin arriving in earnest in October, and their fall-run numbers peak in November. Because the Manistee is a very large river, its fall run is somewhat less dependent on good rainfall, although periodic downpours really help. In general, the lighter the rains the more you should concentrate on the lower river. Conversely, if the river comes up, head for the dam.

The river never freezes below the dam and usually remains fishable down to High Bridge except during severe arctic blasts when you won't want to be fishing anyway. Steelhead can become pretty dour during long periods of cold weather with no runoff. Thus, if you can time your trip after a thaw, your chances of success are better.

At Tippy, March and April are the peak months to fish for spawning steelhead. If the gravel areas are too crowded, you might want to move down to the Suicide Bend area. Here you can probe a deep bend from shore and hook steelhead right at your feet. The river will have some turbidity in the spring, and fish will be harder to spot. The good news is that this will make them less spooky and more likely to hit.

Bear Creek provides good steelhead fishing.

Bear Creek

Bear Creek, better described as a small river than a creek, is a major tributary to the Big Manistee. It joins the big river about halfway between Tippy Dam and Lake Michigan. There is very good natural reproduction of steelhead and coho and chinook salmon in Bear Creek, and the returning wild adults contribute to the Manistee fishery. I am sure some of these fish miss the turn and keep going to Tippy dam.

Brook trout are the principal fish as Bear Creek starts near the small town of Copemish. Creeks named First, Second, and Third add their water to the headwaters, and once Third Creek has joined the Bear, it is marginally flyfishable and classified as blue ribbon trout water. This designation continues down to Nine Mile Road. But even though the blue ribbon designation ends there, good trout fishing doesn't. Although the trout mix changes to mostly brown trout and future steelhead, there is good trout fishing down to about a mile below the Coates Highway Bridge.

*Another nice steelhead
brought to hand
on Bear Creek.*

While Bear Creek's trout numbers are not huge, there are a surprising number of big brown trout. There are *Hexagenia* and brown drake hatches, and I think the larger browns have gotten pretty good at dining on steelhead fingerlings. Bear Creek is perfect for the fly rodder who likes to keep moving. The stream can be easily waded, and there are a number of bridges that are one mile apart as the crow flies. Going bridge to bridge puts you into water that is not heavily pressured. Milks, Johnson, and Kerry Roads provide bridge accesses between Nine Mile Road and Coates Highway.

In September, Bear Creek receives a large run of wild chinook salmon. Mixed in with these fish will be a few stray summer steelhead. Although there are some areas that are dominated by sand, most of the stream has gravel riffles alternating with deep bend holes. You will usually have your choice of trying to tease spawning salmon into striking or hooking them in the holes.

Pine River

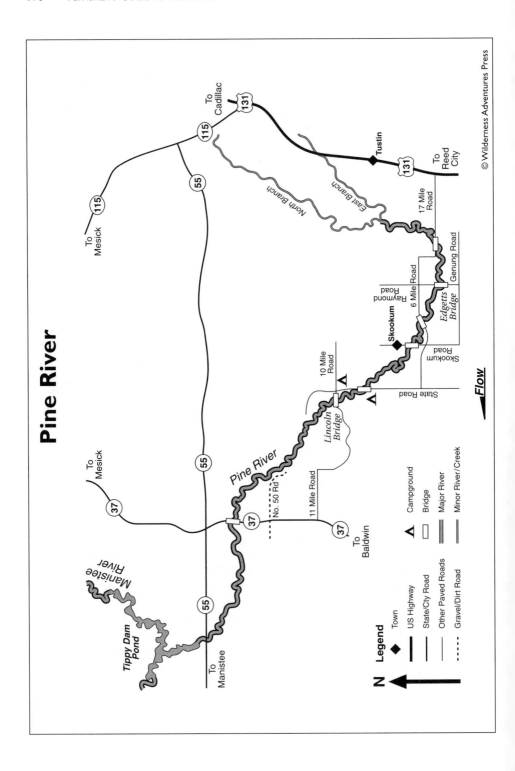

© Wilderness Adventures Press

Though the fall run of steelhead has been poor in recent years, the Bear can be counted on for good spring steelheading with a lot less competition compared to the Little Manistee and the Tippy Dam area of the Big Manistee. The good gravel starts below Coates Highway and is present in every section up to Eleven Mile Road. There is a big gradation in the clarity of Bear Creek upstream, and this is especially pronounced in the spring. It is quite possible to have only 6 inches of visibility because of clay-induced turbidity at Coates Highway yet be able to see chartreuse marabou streamer at a depth of 3 to 4 feet at Eleven Mile. Somewhere on the creek, you can usually find those ideal conditions, where the fish are not spooky but can see your offering.

Pine River

The Pine River is Manistee's largest tributary, joining the mainstream in the backwaters of Tippy Dam. This river is special in that it has Michigan's best population of wild, stream resident rainbow trout. These fish probably were originally young steelhead that became trapped above Tippy Dam when it was finished in 1918. Even today, they still have a steelhead look to them.

The Pine begins as two branches near the town of Tustin. When the North and East Branches join together, the stream becomes large enough to navigate with the fly rod. This also marks the beginning of the blue ribbon water. The Pine retains this classification all the way to Tippy Dam Pond. Only the mainstream of the Au Sable has more miles of blue ribbon water. Brook trout are fairly common in the upper Pine, with brown and rainbow trout numbers increasing downstream. The reach above and below Edgetts Bridge is one of the best for accomplishing the trout angler's "triple double" (catching at least one 10-inch or better trout of all three species on the same outing). The 17 Mile Road Bridge upstream and the 6 Mile Road Bridge downstream provide additional access in this area.

One of the fastest flowing streams of the Lower Peninsula, Pine River continues to grow in size as it moves downstream. The result is great habitat for both rainbows and canoes. I am sure the trout are used to the canoeists banging their way downstream, but if you want some solitude, you may want to time your outing on the lower river to minimize contact with the traffic — fish ahead of them in the morning and behind them in the afternoon.

Of course, sometimes the canoeists can add to the overall experience on the river. A friend was fishing the lower Pine a couple of years ago and was doing reasonably well, having landed and released a couple of rainbows and two nice browns. Rather abruptly, two canoes came around the bend. Each was paddled by a couple, with the ladies in the bow. It was a warm day and all the canoeists were getting a complete upper body tan. The guy in the second canoe asked my friend how the fishing was. Not satisfied with a mumbled, "OK," he pressed for how many trout had been caught. My buddy quickly answered, "Two pair!"

In the Pine's lower half there is a lot of clay that can make it tough to wade and also to color up quickly when it rains. It is also very cold. This means that even though there are good Hendrickson and other early spring hatches, the Pine can be tough to fish. However, these negatives turn into positives by midsummer. Trout actively feed on the surface even on the hot, bright afternoons when trout on neighboring low, clear rivers have run for cover. When there isn't a hatch, it is hard to beat actively fishing a muddler through the gravel and clay runs. Access continues to be provided by bridges, such as the Skookum Road, Walker (State Road), Lincoln (10 Mile Road), Dobson (No. 50 Road), and Peterson (M-37) Bridges. There is a public access site at Elm Flats downstream from Lincoln Bridge, and much of the river flows through public land, allowing anglers to hike in from the nearest road.

While it is possible to catch browns up to 20 inches in the Pine, most of the rainbows will be between 9 and 12 inches. While they are great fun to catch, it would be better if there were more large rainbows. Currently, the DNR is considering raising the minimum size and reducing the bag limit. If this happens, the fishing should improve. I would just love to be trying to land some 16- to 18-inch rainbows in the Pine's heavy current in a few years.

Stream Facts: Manistee River

Seasons
- Open all year downstream from US-131.
- Bass must be released between January 1 and the Saturday before Memorial Day.
- Walleyes and northern pike must be released between March 15 and the last Saturday in April.

Special Regulations
- Size limit for all trout and salmon between October 1 and the last Saturday in April is 16 inches, and the possession limit is 3 fish.
- During this extended season, all trout must be released between US 131 and Red Bridge.

Fish
- Resident brown, rainbow, and brook trout, smallmouth bass, northern pike, walleye, channel catfish, and panfish.
- Anadromous coho and chinook salmon; brown, rainbow, and lake trout; walleye.

River Miles
- Manistee Lake—0
- Rainbow Bend—15
- Bear Creek mouth—18
- Blacksmith Bayou—25
- High Bridge—27
- Tippy Dam—33
- Hodenpyle Dam—49
- M-37—61
- Baxter Bridge—115
- Sharon—161
- CCC Bridge—167
- Yellowtrees Landing—175
- M-72—184
- Deward—201

River Characteristics
- Major Lake Michigan tributary with many miles of prime wild brown and brook trout water in its upper half.
- Dams greatly influence lower river, but resident trout are present almost to its mouth.
- There is an excellent anadromous fishery to Tippy Dam and in a major tributary, Bear Creek.
- The Pine River is a major trout stream tributary that does not receive anadromous fish.
- The Little Manistee River, which joins the Big Manistee in Manistee Lake, has an excellent wild resident trout and steelhead fishery.

River Access
- Access is available at each landmark noted above with river miles.
- Many additional public access sites are found on the main stream and tributaries, along with numerous road crossings.

MANISTEE RIVER AND PINE RIVER MAJOR HATCHES

Insect	Jan	Feb	Mar	Apr	May	Jun	July	Aug	Sep	Oct	Nov	Dec	Time	Fly Patterns
Hendrickson				▮	▮								M/A	Hendrickson #12–14; Rusty's Spinner; Red Quill; Adams; Quill Gordon
Blue-winged Olive					▮			▮					A	Blue-winged Olive #18–20; Sparkle Dun Baetis; Iron Dun; Olive CDC Mayfly Dun
Little Black Caddis					▮			▮					A	Little Black Caddis #16–18; Griffith's Gnat; CDC Emerging Caddis Brown; Black Ant
Grannom							▮						M/A	Grannom #14–16; Medium Brown Sedge; Elk Caddis Brown–Olive
Net-building Caddis										▮	▮		M/A	Spotted Sedge #16–18; Eastern Elk Wing Caddis; Goddard Caddis
Sulphur Dun						▮							A/E	Sulphur Dun #16; Pale Morning Dun; CDC Comparadun Yellow; Pale Evening Dun
March Brown						▮							M/A	March Brown #12–14; Dark Cahill; Gray Fox; Ginger Quill
Gray Drake						▮							E	Gray Drake #12–14; Gray Adams
Brown Drake						▮							E	Brown Drake #10–12; Adams; CDC Brown
Hexagenia						▮	▮						E	Hex #4–8; Great Olive-winged Drake; Spring's Wiggler; Hare's Ear
Light Cahill							▮						A	Light Cahill #12; Ginger Quill
Trico							▮	▮	▮	▮			M	Tiny White Wing Black #24–28; Parachute Adams; CDC Trico; Spent Wing Trico
White Fly									▮				E	White Fly #12–14; White Miller
Streamers	▮	▮	▮	▮	▮	▮	▮	▮	▮	▮	▮	▮	M/A/E	Woolly Buggers #6–12; Clouser's Minnow; Muddler Minnows; BC Craw; Matukas
Terrestrials						▮	▮	▮	▮				M/A/E	Woolly Worm #8–12; BC Spider; Letort Cricket; Joe's Hopper #6–10; Dave's Hopper; Dropper Hopper

HATCH TIME CODE: M = morning; A = afternoon; E = evening.
Hatch times will be slightly later on the North Branch of the Manistee and the Pine.

An angler spends a pleasant afternoon on the Upper Betsie River.

BETSIE RIVER

The Betsie River is best known for its anadromous fishery, but there are also lots of opportunities for resident fish. It begins as the outlet of Green Lake near Interlochen, and soon after it leaves the lake, it flows through the Grass Lake Flooding. Thus, the Betsie starts out as a warmwater stream with largemouth and rock bass as the principal predators. For a number of years, there has been discussion about constructing a deep, coldwater draw out of Green Lake and then channeling the water quickly through the waterfowl flooding. If this could ever be accomplished, we would have a real topnotch trout stream—one loaded with wild trout possessing good growth potential.

Moving downstream, groundwater slowly cools the river, and brown trout start showing up. With the addition of the Little Betsie's cold water at Thompsonville, trout numbers greatly improve. This tributary, loaded with wild browns and steelhead fingerlings, is only sporadically open enough for flyfishing. If you wake up well rested and have a lot of patience, you might try to poke your way up this little gem of a trout creek. Many road bridges provide access to the Betsie above Thompsonville. King, Thompsonville, Carmean, Long, and Wallin Roads cross the river and divide it into two 1-mile sections and two shorter corner sections.

The Michigan DNR still considers the upper Betsie only a marginal trout stream and supplements its wild fish with some hatchery brown trout. In the reach between

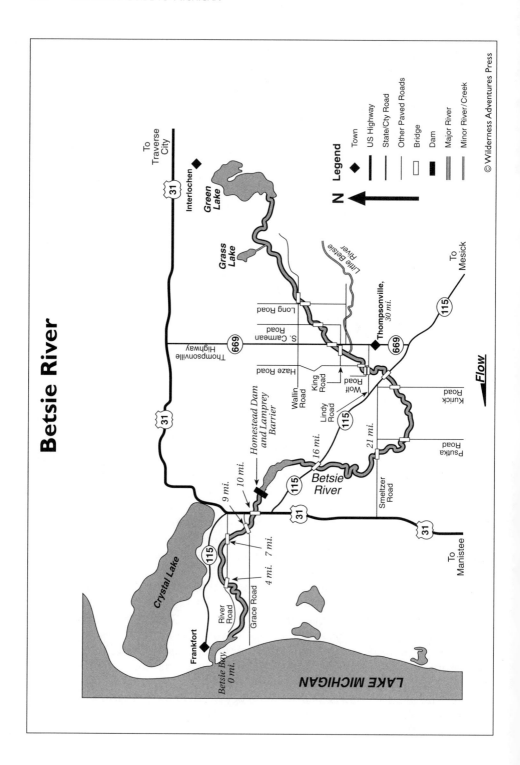

Betsie River

The upper Betsie River is a good place to try for spawning steelhead.

Thompsonville and the Homestead lamprey barrier, there is a good population of brown trout and future steelhead along with an occasional brook trout. There is a modest *Hexagenia* hatch and a good brown drake emergence, making 20-inch-plus browns on a dry fly a definite possibility.

Access is limited to bridges (Haze and Lindy Roads, M-115, Kurick, Psutka, and County Line Roads, and then M-115 again), but most of the water can be waded at summer levels, and you can fish as far from the bridges as you like. Gravel and clay runs alternate with log-infested deep sand holes, providing lots of cover for big trout. Floating from County Line to M-115 is a good way to fish water that doesn't see many anglers. If the trout are hitting at all, it will take all day. The lower end of the river above the lamprey barrier is the least desirable since it is still recovering from having been impounded by the old Homestead Dam. Lots of deep, soft sand and a lack of shade are found here.

Trout continue to be found below the lamprey barrier, but they tend to give way to smallmouth bass and northern pike as the water gets warmer and gravel becomes more and more scarce. Below Grace Road, the substrate is almost 100 percent sand, and the river warms well into the 70s in hot weather. Pike are present in good numbers, with some fish over 10 pounds to challenge your fish landing ability. There are some bayous and side channels where pike seem especially numerous, located between River Road and the Betsie's termination at its drowned rivermouth lake, Betsie Lake, at Lake Michigan.

When you pull up to one of the Lower Betsie's access sites in November and see license plates from Ontario and Minnesota, you start to get the idea that this must be a good steelhead river. And that would be the correct conclusion.

Actually, the Betsie's anadromous season gets started in August with the beginning of a fine run of wild chinook. This river has never been planted with salmon but has developed its own chinook and coho runs from earlier stray fish. Late August is the time to intercept kings in the lower river with bright or black marabou streamers. These fish move to the gravel in September. There will be lots of fish in the reach between US-31 and the Homestead Lamprey barrier, but there will also be lots of people. If the crowds get too heavy for your taste, try the upper river between the County Line Road Bridge and Thompsonville. Note that at the end of September the river is closed above Wolf Road, which is near Thompsonville.

Some summer steelhead stray from the Big Manistee River, adding variety to your August catch. Both the chinook and the summer-runs shock unsuspecting trout anglers each summer, usually stealing their fly.

The Betsie is known for a big run of "skippers" that begin to fill the river in late September. These are jacks (small mature males) and immature steelhead that head back up river after just one summer in Lake Michigan. They range from 15 to 19 inches long and are very aggressive. Many of them, especially the immature fish, are actively feeding, and egg patterns drifted in the holes and close to the logs will be readily snapped up by these small caliber silver bullets. Expect to have your hands full with a very strong, acrobatic battle. If the big adult steelhead fought as hard, pound for pound, we would never land any. Four- and 5-weight trout rods let you have maximum sport with these fish, but most are caught on heavier tackle because of the presence of chinook salmon.

Soon larger steelhead also enter the lower river. At this time, the Betsie also gets a pretty good run of "sea trout" (lake-run browns) and coho salmon at this time. So October is mixed bag time on the Betsie, and with the fall colors, it is a glorious time to be on the water.

As with other northwest rivers of the Lower Peninsula, the fall steelhead run peaks in November. You can continue to intercept them in the lower river or try the upper river where there are fewer fish but also fewer anglers. Cohos will be in the upper river and will add to your action, especially early in the month.

The Betsie is not usually a good choice for winter steelhead because it is prone to freezing. But when parts of it do open up during a thaw, the fishing can be quite good because the fish haven't seen an angler for a while. The lower river usually stays frozen until spring. Traditionally, there is some very hot fishing to be had when the ice goes out, but this is hard to hit unless you live nearby or have a contact who is willing to share this news.

Spring is prime time for Betsie River steelhead, and the stretch between US 31 and the lamprey barrier is the prime spot. Unfortunately, thousands of other anglers also know this. Still, lots of fish are hooked here because it is the first stretch of faster water with good spawning gravel that steelhead encounter. I jokingly think that the nearby Backcast Fly Shop in Benzonia is missing a good thing by not stocking special hones for sharpening elbows. But a sturdy wading staff might be a better idea for creating some casting room.

There are developed public access sites at each of the next four bridges downstream: US-31, Grace Road and the two River Road crossings. However, at the height of the spring run, even these sites will be quite busy with anglers. Still, there is more room than at Homestead and a good chance of intercepting fresh fish on their way to the gravel.

Just as you would during the fall chinook run, you will find fewer steelhead as you move upriver but also fewer anglers. For me this has always been the better formula for success. It should also be noted that the water near the upstream limit will always be clearer than at Homestead, so keep this in mind if spring rains have turned the lower Betsie to an opaque, yellow brown.

Stream Facts: Betsie River

Seasons
- Open all year downstream from Wolf Road.
- Bass must be released between January 1 and the Saturday before Memorial Day.
- Walleyes and northern pike must be released between March 15 and the last Saturday in April.

Special Regulations
- Size limit for all trout and salmon between October 1 and last Saturday in April is 15 inches, and the possession limit is 3 fish.
- No fishing is allowed within 100 feet upstream and downstream of the lamprey weir at the old Homestead Dam site.

Fish
- Resident brown, brook, and rainbow trout; smallmouth and rock bass; northern pike.
- Anadromous chinook and coho salmon; brown and rainbow trout; and walleye.

River Miles
- Betsie Bay—0
- River Road—4 and 7
- Grace Road—9
- US-31—10
- M-115—16
- County Line Road—21
- Thompsonville—30

River Characteristics
- The Betsie is a medium sized river that is especially known for its runs of anadromous fish.
- The middle part of the river has a good population of brown trout, while the lower river is primarily home to northern pike and some smallmouth bass.
- The river can be waded or floated throughout most of its length.

River Access
- Access is available at each landmark noted above with river miles.
- Road bridges provide additional access and there are several developed public access sites in the lower river that are noted on the map.

BETSIE RIVER MAJOR HATCHES

Insect	Jan	Feb	Mar	Apr	May	Jun	July	Aug	Sep	Oct	Nov	Dec	Time	Fly Patterns
Black Stonefly			█										A	Early Black Stonefly #10–14
Hendrickson				█									M/A	Hendrickson #12–14; Rusty's Spinner; Red Quill; Adams; Quill Gordon
Blue-winged Olive					█			█					A	Blue-winged Olive #18–20; Sparkle Dun Baetis; Iron Dun; Olive CDC Mayfly Dun
Little Black Caddis				█				█					A	Little Black Caddis #16–18; Griffith's Gnat; CDC Emerging Caddis Brown; Black Ant
Net-building Caddis									█	█			A	Spotted Sedge #16–18; Eastern Elk Wing Caddis; Goddard Caddis
Sulphur Dun						█							A/E	Sulphur Dun #16; Pale Morning Dun; CDC Comparadun Yellow; Pale Evening Dun
March Brown					█	█							M/A	March Brown #12–14; Dark Cahill; Gray Fox; Ginger Quill
Gray Drake						█							E	Gray Drake #12–14; Gray Adams
Brown Drake						█							E	Brown Drake #10–12; Adams; CDC Brown
Hexagenia						█	█						E	Hex #4–8; Great Olive-winged Drake; Spring's Wiggler; Hare's Ear
Trico							█	█					M	Tine White Wing Black #24–28; Parachute Adams; CDC Trico; Spent Wing Trico
White Fly									█				E	White Fly #12–14; White Miller
Streamers	█	█	█	█	█	█	█	█	█	█	█	█	M/A/E	Woolly Buggers #6–12; Clouser's Minnow; Muddler Minnows; BC Craw; Matukas
Terrestrials						█	█	█	█				M/A/E	Woolly Worm #8–12; BC Spider; Letort Cricket; Joe's Hopper #6–10; Dave's Hopper; Dropper Hopper

HATCH TIME CODE: M = morning; A = afternoon; E = evening.

Platte River

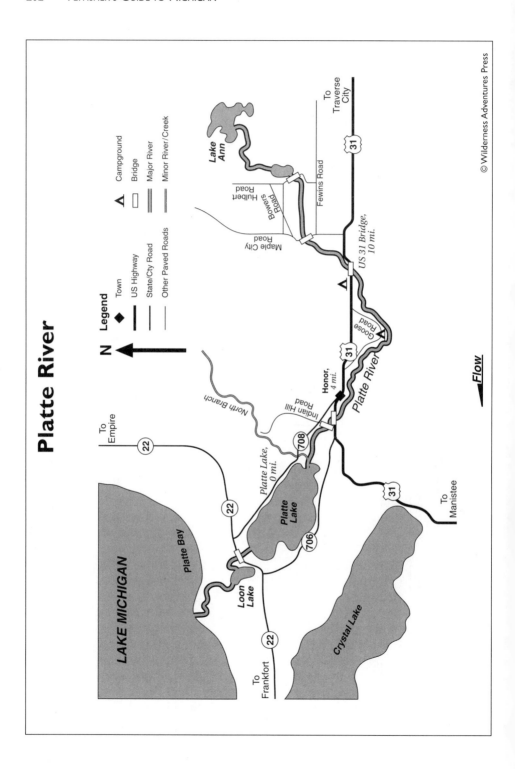

PLATTE RIVER

The Platte River is another stream that is better known for its visiting fish than its resident population. This is where coho salmon were introduced into Lake Michigan in 1966, and the salmon that return to it continue to be the source of eggs for future generations of silvers.

The Platte at first glance appears to be a rather small stream, but its very clear water disguises a strong flow. It begins as the outlet of Lake Ann, southwest of Traverse City. By the time it reaches Maple City Road, the Platte has both cooled down and become large enough to be classified a Blue Ribbon trout stream. This designation continues down to the town of Honor. There are some good-sized brown trout present, but it can be difficult getting a fly past the always-eager steelhead fingerlings.

The Platte is an ultra clear river, so a stealthy upstream approach is needed to fish its sophisticated browns. This is one stream where you don't need to hook trout on the surface to see them take. Fishing on and under broken water is almost a must in order to fool these fish when the sun is shining.

Between Indian Hill Road and Platte Lake, the river enters a swamp and slows down. Big silt beds provide good habitat for *Hexagenia limbata*. A float tube or kickboat is recommended here because the water gets deep and the bottom soft. Both resident and migrant browns come here to feed during the Hex hatch, making a very large trout a possibility.

Platte River.

While a few chinook run the Platte, coho salmon and steelhead are the primary anadromous visitors. There is a harvest weir on the lower Platte below Loon Lake where some of the coho are removed. Steelhead and fishable numbers of coho are passed upstream. Early in the run (September 1 through mid-October) the river is closed to fishing below the weir, but when it reopens, there is a chance for some excellent fishing. A light tippet is needed because of the very clear, slow-moving water.

I have always had better luck fishing the faster water near Honor. You can fish to spawning coho or try to lure a steelhead from under the logs from October through December. Starting in 2001, you can continue to fish the upper river during the first three months of the year. Expect a big crowd on the Platte on the first two weekends in April. I suggest visiting on a weekday later in April — in a normal spring, there will still be plenty of steelhead well into the month of May.

Keep this river in mind when the Betsie or Big Manistee are too muddy to fish. The upper river is usually fishable, and the reaches between Platte and Loon Lake and below Loon Lake virtually never go out. Road crossings provide most of the access, but there are campgrounds on the river below US 31 and on Goose Road. You can also gain access to the river at the fish hatchery, but fishing is not allowed within 300 feet of the salmon-blocking weir.

Stream Facts: Platte River

Seasons
- Open all year below Platte Lake.
- Open below the US 31 Bridge East of Honor from April 1 through December 31.

Special Regulations
- Size limit for all trout and salmon between October 1 and the last Saturday in April is 16 inches, and the possession limit is 3 fish.
- No fishing is allowed within 300 feet of either the upstream weir at the hatchery and the downstream weir below Loon Lake.
- In addition, no fishing is allowed between the lower weir and the river mouth between September 1 and October 14.

Fish
- Resident brown, brook, and rainbow trout in the upper river.
- Occasional pike and panfish below Platte Lake.
- Anadromous coho and chinook salmon; brown and rainbow trout.

River Miles
- Platte Lake—0
- Honor—4
- US-31—10

River Characteristics
- The Platte is a small, very clear river that has a surprisingly strong, stable flow.
- A large hatchery on the river raises Michigan's coho smolt along with some trout species.
- Large numbers of coho smolt are planted in this river to assure a continuing egg supply.
- Along with the coho, there is a strong run of wild steelhead and a good resident population of sophisticated brown trout.

River Access
- Access is available at each landmark noted above with river miles.
- Additional access can be found at road bridges and campgrounds on the river that are noted on the river map.

Boardman River

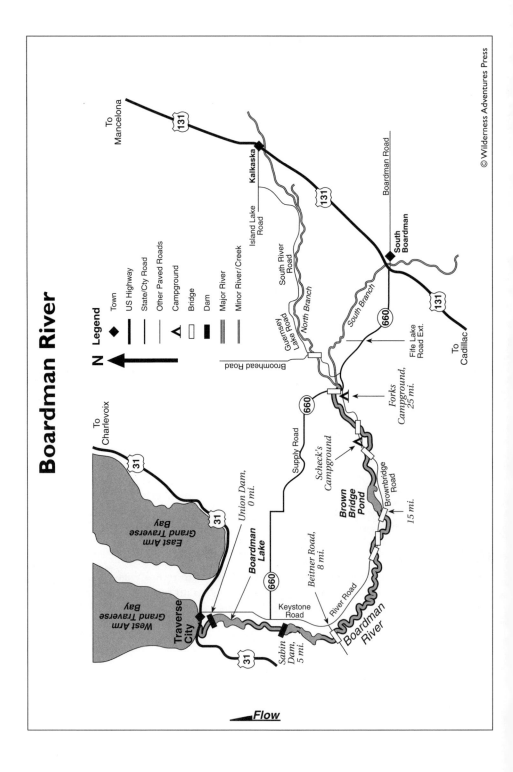

© Wilderness Adventures Press

BOARDMAN RIVER

The Boardman is an excellent wild brown trout stream that begins as two branches in western Kalkaska County. Brook trout are also plentiful, especially in the headwaters and tributary creeks. Although both the North and South Branches are relatively small, they can be flyfished for their last 8 or 10 miles. While the average trout size is probably somewhat smaller and the casting room can be tight, the branches provide a chance to fish with less competition from other anglers and no interference from canoeists.

Another testament to the influx of cold spring water and the high quality of this trout stream is that it retains its blue ribbon status through and below the Brown Bridge Pond impoundment. Below the forks, Boardman is easy to wade and read. The gradient is good, and lots of logs and streamside vegetation provide cover for the trout. All the mayflies, caddisflies, and stoneflies that would be expected in a high quality cold-water stream are present. The season begins with a good Hendrickson hatch, and brown drakes, sulphurs, and *Hexagenia* follow. Kelly Galloup of the nearby Troutsman Shop says that the Boardman is slow to warm in the spring, and thus the hatches are set back a bit. But he thinks this slow start is one of the main reasons why the Boardman sustains such good numbers of wild trout and has a good late-season fishery. Kelly claims the Hex hatch can last almost two months, which is rare for Michigan streams—or any other for that matter. Below Brown Bridge Pond, crayfish numbers increase and are probably one of the reasons that a 22-inch brown is possible.

The Boardman River at the forks.

Dead-drifting on the Boardman River.

Supply Road crosses the river just below the convergence of the two branches and, along with the Forks Campground, provides access to this part of the river. Broomhead Road crosses both the North and South Branches. Guernsey Lake and then South River Road parallel the North Branch upstream from Broomhead Road. There are a number of pulloffs, and much of the land is state forest. Although more of the South Branch flows through private property, access to the middle part of the stretch is possible by driving straight north from Supply Road on the Fife Lake Road extension, a sandy two-track, until it ends at the river. You can get on the upper part of the Blue Ribbon water at Boardman Road and at a public access about a mile downstream. Boardman Road also crosses the North Branch.

On the mainstream, Brown Bridge Road crosses Boardman three times, and there is also access where it nears the river about a mile below the forks. Scheck's Campground on this road also gets you on the river. Downstream Brown Bridge becomes River Road and crosses the river twice again in big trout country. Two-and-a-half miles below the last crossing there is a public access off River Road for anglers and canoeists.

Despite two more impoundments, brown trout are still present below the Sabin Dam. Their numbers are not great, but growth is good and there is a chance to catch some really nice trout, especially during the *Hexagenia* hatch. There is one more dam, Union, which forms Boardman Lake. Union Dam has a fish passage that allows steelhead and salmon to move upstream as far as Sabin.

The Boardman flows right through the heart of Traverse City before it empties into Grand Traverse Bay. The in-town fishery is primarily for anadromous species, with winter steelhead the primary quarry. At one time, summer steelhead were planted in the river, and there continues to be a modest run of these fish. A friend of mine who works in downtown Traverse City regularly hooked summer-runs during his lunch hour in the past. He continues to vertically drift his attractor patterns under a strike indicator for them, but his success rate is down because of the reduced run. I don't know of anyone who has hooked more steelhead with a sport coat and tie on than this guy.

The salmon run is relatively sporadic because the Boardman is not planted. Lake-run browns also move up river in fall. Sometimes in the spring, lake trout move into the rivermouth, probably on the trail of the smelt run. For the most part, these other salmonids end up being bonus fish for anglers targeting steelhead. There is little gravel for spawning, so the best plan is to drift exciter patterns through the holes and runs. Fish concentrate below the dams, but when the run is on, they become too crowded for me.

Streams Facts: Boardman River

Seasons
- Open all year below the Sabin Dam.

Special Regulations
- The size limit for trout and salmon between October 1 and the last Saturday in April is 15 inches, and the possession limit is 3 fish.
- No fishing between the Union Street Dam and the US-31 bridge between September 1 and October 31.

Fish
- Brown and brook trout.
- Anadromous chinook and coho salmon, rainbow and brown trout.

River Miles
- Grand Traverse Bay—0
- Sabin Dam—5
- Beitner Road—8
- Brown Bridge Pond—15
- Forks—25

River Characteristics
- Wide variety of wild brown and brook trout fishing opportunities are found in the upper Boardman, with small stream fishing in its two branches, and changing habitat and gradient in the mainstream.
- Trout fishing continues despite several impoundments, with large browns possible.
- The river provides urban fishing opportunities for anadromous fish in Traverse City.

River Access
- Access is available at each landmark noted above with river miles.
- Access is available at road bridges and campgrounds shown on map.

BOARDMAN AND JORDAN RIVERS MAJOR HATCHES

Insect	Jan	Feb	Mar	Apr	May	Jun	July	Aug	Sep	Oct	Nov	Dec	Time	Fly Patterns
Black Stonefly			X	X									A	Early Black Stonefly #10–14
Hendrickson					X								M/A	Hendrickson #12–14; Rusty's Spinner; Red Quill; Adams; Quill Gordon
Blue-winged Olive							X	X					A	Blue-winged Olive #18–20: Sparkle Dun Baetis; Iron Dun; Olive CDC Mayfly Dun
Little Black Caddis							X	X					A	Little Black Caddis #16–18; Griffith's Gnat; CDC Emerging Caddis Brown; Black Ant
Net-building Caddis									X	X			M/A	Spotted Sedge #16–18; Eastern Elk Wing Caddis; Goddard Caddis
Grannom							X						A	Grannom #14–16; Medium Brown Sedge
Sulphur Dun						X							A/E	Sulphur Dun #16; Pale Morning Dun; CDC Comparadun Yellow; Pale Evening Dun
March Brown					X	X							M/A	March Brown #12–14; Dark Cahill; Gray Fox; Ginger Quill
Gray Drake						X							E	Gray Drake #12–14; Gray Adams
Brown Drake						X							E	Brown Drake #10–12; Adams; CDC Adams
Hexagenia						X	X						E	Hex #4–8; Great Olive-winged Drake; Spring's Wiggler; Hare's Ear
Trico								X	X	X			M	Tiny White Wing Black #24–28; Parachute Adams; CDC Trico; Spent Wing Trico
White Fly									X				E	White Fly #12–14; White Miller
Streamers	X	X	X	X	X	X	X	X	X	X	X	X	M/A/E	Woolly Buggers #6–12; Clouser's Minnow; Muddler Minnows; BC Craw; Matukas
Terrestrials						X	X	X	X				M/A/E	Woolly Worm #8–12; BC Spider; Letort Cricket; Joe's Hopper #6–10; Dave's Hopper; Dropper Hopper

HATCH TIME CODE: M = morning; A = afternoon; E = evening.
Jordan River hatches occur slightly later than the Boardman's. Maple and Boyne are similar to Jordan, and the Platte is similar to the Boardman.

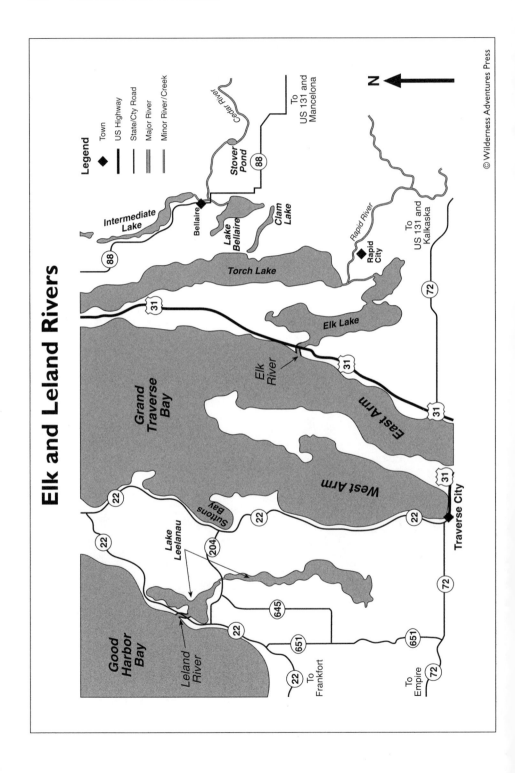

Elk and Leland Rivers

Legend

◆ Town
— US Highway
— State/Cty Road
— Major River
— Minor River/Creek

© Wilderness Adventures Press

N

Cedar River

Stover Pond

88

To US 131 and Mancelona

Intermediate Lake

Bellaire

88

Lake Bellaire

Clam Lake

Torch Lake

Rapid River

Rapid City

To US 131 and Kalkaska

72

31

Elk Lake

Elk River

31

East Arm

31

Grand Traverse Bay

West Arm

Suttons Bay

22

204

Lake Leelanau

22

22

31

Traverse City

22

72

Good Harbor Bay

Leland River

22

645

651

651

72

To Frankfort

To Empire

22

Elk and Leland Rivers

On either side of Boardman and Grand Traverse Bay are two rivers that are the outlets of large lakes, Leelanau and Elk. Both of these rivers travel only a short distance until they enter Lake Michigan, and lake level control dams block fish migration. They are mentioned here because they are always clear enough to fish and have runs of anadromous fish. The Elk River is known for a late spring run of steelhead but is frequently crowded just below the dam. The Leland River's claim to fame is its big fall run of lake trout. Unfortunately, because of snagging problems, you cannot fish for them, but it is quite a spectacle to see hundreds of 6- to 25-pound gray trout milling about in a crystal clear river. Both rivers attract fish to their adjacent beaches, and you can fish for trout and salmon there in the spring and fall.

Two small streams that are inlets to the Torch/Elk Lake system provide some opportunities for trout fishing with a fly rod. Rapid River near the town of Rapid City contains both browns and rainbows. It also receives a run of rainbows from the large inland lakes it feeds and is open until December 31 in the fall and reopens on April 1.

The Cedar River near Bellaire is a small, pristine brook trout stream. It has been in the center of some battles over this area's development into year-round resorts. The stream is classified as blue ribbon trout water between Bellaire and Stover Pond, and road crossings provide access.

Jordan River

The Jordan River is one of Michigan's most pristine trout streams and was the first to be protected under the state's Natural Rivers Act and to be designated a National Scenic River. It is fed by many creeks and large springs and attains an amazing size in a relatively short distance. I am sure that the ample groundwater flows were a strong influence when the upper Jordan River was selected as a site for a national fish hatchery.

As is typical for streams in this section of Michigan, brook trout are common in the headwaters of the Jordan, slowly giving way to brown trout downstream. Steelhead reproduce in this river, adding small rainbows to the trout mix. The Jordan is designated as a Blue Ribbon trout stream from the confluence of its largest tributary, the Green River, almost to its mouth. I am sure that the reason the blue ribbon water doesn't start until the Green River is because of its size relative to being flyfishable. While the river is relatively small, it flows through mature forest, so anglers with reasonable fly casting skills will do fine well upstream from the designated water.

The Jordan River Pathway, a hiking trail, meanders along the upper river, as does Pinney Bridge Road. If the river gets a little tight, just hike a little farther until things open up or you find an inviting beaver pond. Trout, though not large, do live in a very clear river, so stealth is important. There are lots of logs for cover, necessitating many very short drifts while also actively moving the fly to draw trout out.

Upper Jordan River.

Below the Green River confluence, the Jordan is 40 to 50 feet wide with enough current and deep holes to require careful wading. Wood and undercut banks hide good-sized brook trout and larger browns. A wide variety of stoneflies, caddisflies, and mayflies inhabit the Jordan, as would be expected from a high quality stream. Rather than match the naturals, it often pays to offer something a bit bigger to get their attention. Muddlers and *Hexagenia* nymph imitators are good searching patterns.

Trout exist in good numbers all the way to Lake Charlevoix, but the river slows and becomes difficult to wade because of the depth and the soft substrate below Rogers Road. In between Rogers Road and the Jordan River Trail area, access to the river is possible at Graves Crossing Campground, Old State Road (Chestonia Bridge), and Webster Bridge. There is a good Hex hatch in the lower river, and it not only brings large resident browns to the surface but trout from Lake Charlevoix that have moved upstream to take advantage of the feast. If you think your heart can take it,

Jordan River

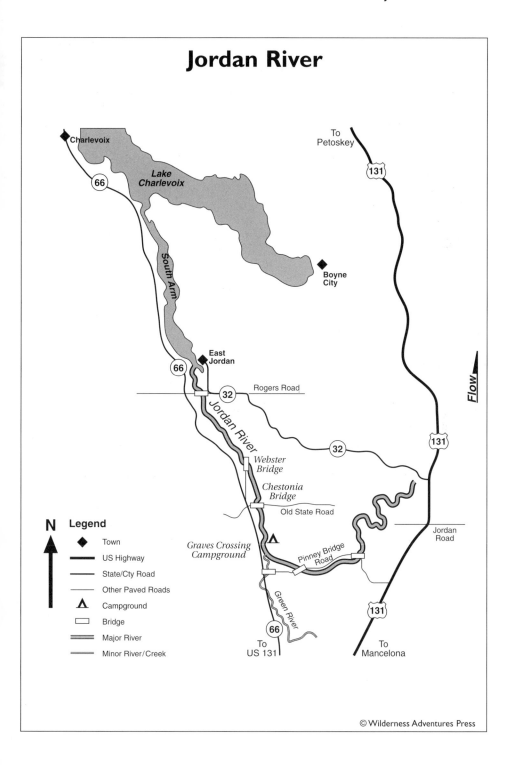

Charlevoix

Lake
Charlevoix

South Arm

66

66

East
Jordan

Boyne
City

To
Petoskey

131

Flow

Rogers Road

32

32

131

Jordan River

Webster
Bridge

Chestonia
Bridge

Old State Road

Jordan
Road

Graves Crossing
Campground

Pinney Bridge
Road

131

Green River

66

To
US 131

To
Mancelona

N

Legend

◆ Town

▬ US Highway

── State/Cty Road

── Other Paved Roads

▲ Campground

▭ Bridge

▬ Major River

── Minor River/Creek

© Wilderness Adventures Press

this is your chance to catch a 10-pound brown on the surface. It is important to scout the area you are going to fish during daylight so that you can maneuver safely after dark. The lower river's gentle flow is ideal for prams and kickboats.

Because of snagging problems in the past, a blocking weir is installed at the mouth of the river each September and October in order to keep the bulk of the chinook salmon run out of the Jordan. Some kings move up before the weir is put in, and coho salmon, brown trout, and steelhead move up after its removal. Most of the lower river (up to Graves Crossing) is open all year for steelhead and salmon fishing. Steelhead numbers peak in mid-November and stack up in the deep bend holes of the lower river. Despite the northern latitude of this river, ice rarely prevents winter fishing here. Because it is an extra hour's drive for downstate anglers, it is normally less crowded in the spring. The Jordan's clear water is a plus when trying to excite a steelhead into striking a bright, marabou spey. In many rivers, the streamers would swing by unnoticed in a 5-foot-deep run—but not the Jordan.

BOYNE RIVER

The Boyne is a relatively small stream that flows into a different arm of Lake Charlevoix north of the Jordan River mouth. Lake Charlevoix is directly connected to Lake Michigan with no barriers. For half of its length, it is split into two branches, and when the branches come together the Boyne is soon impounded.

The lower 4 or 5 miles of each branch are large enough to fish with a fly rod and contain good populations of small- to medium-sized brown trout. An occasional brook trout is also encountered in these very clear, stable streams. Each branch is relatively shallow with firm sand and gravel bottoms, making them easy to wade. Logs and streamside vegetation provide cover for the wary browns. Roads at conveniently spaced distances cross each branch of the Boyne. Cherry Hills, Metros, and Greigar Roads pass over the lower South Branch, while access to the North Branch can be made at US 131 and Thumb Lake, Denise, and Springbrook Roads.

A small dam blocks the upstream migration of steelhead on the Boyne. Even with the combination of the two branches, the Boyne still provides an intimate steelhead experience. You can usually see fish, even when they are in a 5-foot-deep hole. While there is a fall run of steelhead along with a few salmon, the main anadromous fishery occurs in the spring. The nature of the stream changes drastically at the Dam Road Bridge.

The half-mile of river between the bridge and the dam is relatively wide and shallow, with excellent spawning gravel. Cover is lacking, which makes it difficult for steelhead to find a place to hide when they are not spawning. Below the bridge, the river is narrower, with lots of wood in the water. Gravel is present for about a half–mile, then the river substrate becomes mostly sand for the rest of its length. To avoid spooking fish in either direction, casting from your knees can be the order of the day.

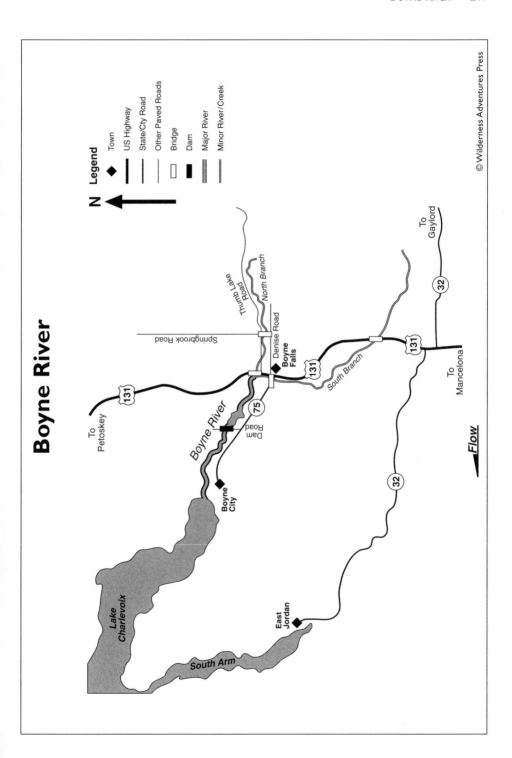

Boyne River

Bear River

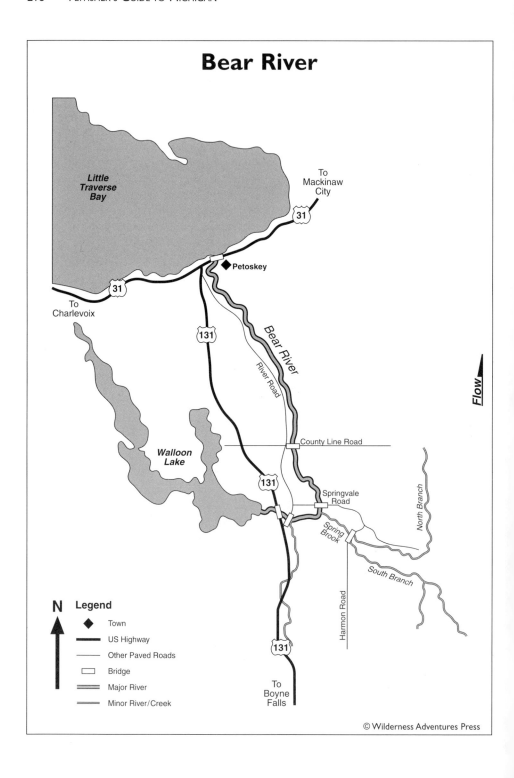

Little Traverse Bay

To Mackinaw City

31

Petoskey

31

To Charlevoix

131

River Road

Bear River

Flow

Walloon Lake

County Line Road

131

Springvale Road

131

Spring Brook

North Branch

South Branch

Harmon Road

131

To Boyne Falls

Legend

N

- ◆ Town
- US Highway
- Other Paved Roads
- ☐ Bridge
- Major River
- Minor River/Creek

© Wilderness Adventures Press

The Boyne's steelhead are some of the latest to spawn in the Lower Peninsula. Normally, the run doesn't peak until early May. Several years ago, trout were not cooperating very well for me upstream on Memorial Day Weekend, so I decided to check things out at Dam Road. After landing two steelhead and not seeing another angler, I knew that I had made a good decision.

Bear River

The Bear River is a relatively small stream that joins Lake Michigan in the town of Petoskey. In spite of the fact that it has a number of low head dams and is fed by the warm surface waters of Walloon Lake, it manages to support brook trout with the help of some fingerling stockings. The main reason for this is that Spring Brook counterbalances the warming effect. This stream is loaded with wild brook trout and helps supply the downstream reaches with brookies. Once the two branches of Spring Brook come together, it is marginally large enough to fish with a fly rod, especially when there is an open meadow or new beaver pond. Harmon Road provides access at the confluence.

The mainstream below Spring Brook is a bit marginal for trout but is rich in food, so trout can grow fast. In addition to imitating the aquatic insects, you will also want to be armed with streamers that match the abundant crayfish and minnows present in the lower river. Road crossings provide good access to the Bear, with County Line Road and County Road 630 putting you on the upper trout water below Spring Brook.

There is an anadromous fishery on the Bear, but it is very limited because of a dam just upstream from the mouth. Steelhead and chinook run this stream, but things get real hectic in the limited amount of available water when the run is going strong. A better plan might be to ply the bay (Little Traverse) in a small boat or kickboat and swim streamers near the mouth of the river. Though this river is not normally a destination spot for me, I sometimes stop to see what's going on when on my way to or from another river.

MAPLE RIVER

The Maple River near Michigan's "icebox," Pellston, is quite a different river, both in geography and in water quality, from the southern Maple River. The river is relatively small but gathers a fair amount of groundwater before emptying into Burt Lake. If we were using watersheds to delineate sections, this river would be in the Northeast section of the Lower Peninsula because its water ends up in Lake Huron via the Cheboygan River. This is surprising since it is located only about 10 miles from Little Traverse Bay on Lake Michigan.

The West Branch of the Maple is loaded with a fine mix of wild brown and brook trout. Even though it is quite small, it can be navigated with a fly rod in its lower sections near Pellston, where Camp Road, Robinson Road, and US 31 provide access. Fishing upstream from Robinson Road, I encountered good numbers of medium-sized browns and caught an 18-inch lunker. The strong flow of cold water from this branch manages to counteract the relatively warm water of the smaller East Branch

Maple River

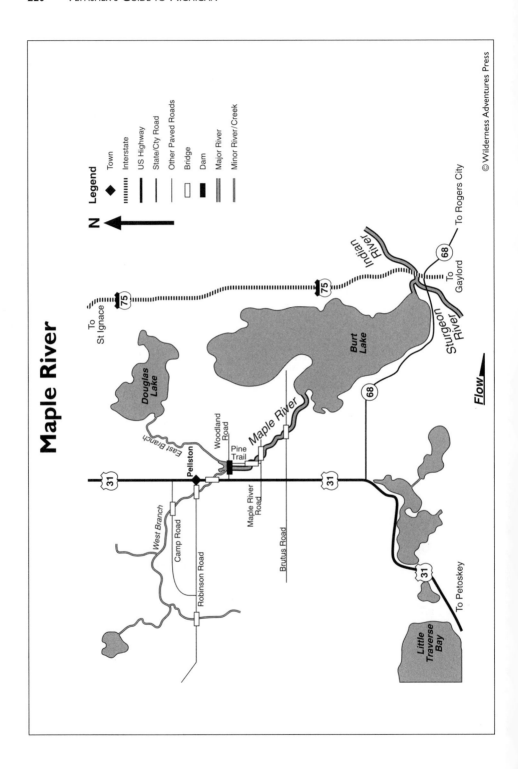

and the effects of a small impoundment. The result is a fine blue ribbon fishery for brown trout and some brookies below the dam. Some rainbow trout, offspring of lake-run rainbows, also rise to a fly here. Though there is no extended season on the Maple, rainbows from Burt Lake can still be found in the river when opening day rolls around. There are also occasions in the summer when both brown and rainbow trout move up from Burt Lake, either to cool off or feed. This movement is sometimes hampered by the fact that the river braids and is very shallow when it flows into Burt Lake. Access to the lower river can be found at Woodland Road, just below the dam, and downstream at Maple River and Brutus Road Crossings. Additional access is found north of Maple River Road on Pine Trail.

Northwestern Lower Peninsula Hub Cities
Muskegon
Population – 40,283

ACCOMMODATIONS
Alpine Motel, 4262 Airline Road / 231-733-1323
El Royal Motel, 4610 Airline Road / 231-733-2511
Orchard Inn, 3450 Hoyt Street / 231-733-2601
Pines Motel, 1507 Whitehall Road / 231-744-3640
Seaway Motel, 631 West Norton Avenue / 231-733-1220
Oakridge Motel, 9145 Mason Drive (Newaygo 49337) / 231-652-1288
Riverside Resort, 5757 Division Street (Newaygo 49337) / 231-652-1292

CAMPGROUNDS
Camp Lor-ray, 5218 Rousell Street / 231-766-3152
Henning County Park, 500 Croton Drive (Newaygo 49337) / 231-652-1202
Mystery Creek Campground, 9419 Wisner (Newaygo 49337) / 231-652-6915
Day in the Park, 6585 Lake Harbor Road / 231-798-2251
Fisherman's Landing Inc. (Giddings) / 231-726-6100

RESTAURANTS
Aron's, 1437 Whitehall Road / 231-744-1666
Brownstone Restaurant, 99 Sinclair Drive / 231-798-2273
Carmen's Cafe, 315 West Clay Avenue, Muskegon, MI 49440, 726-6317
Chesapeake Crab House, 939-3 Reed Avenue / 231-728-2204
Diversions, 2353 Holton Road / 231-744-3722
Hearthstone, 3350 Glade Street / 231-733-1056

FLY SHOPS AND SPORTING GOODS
Flies for Michigan, 409 East Circle Drive / 231-744-1524
Springs Sporting Goods, 280 Ottawa Street / 231-722-7107
Parsley's Sport Shop, 70 State Street (Newaygo 49337) / 231-652-6986
Lakeland Outfitters Inc., 116 West Colby Street (Whitehall 49461) / 231-894-4670

AUTO REPAIR
Laird Automotive, 3445 Russell Road / 231-766-2111
Affordable Auto Repair, 2107 Henry Street / 231-726-7283
Bill's Automotive & Transmission, 2501 Peck Street / 231-733-8592
Le Barons Service Center, 575 West Hume Avenue / 231-733-1565
Zack's Automotive, 2294 South Getty Street / 231-728-2886

AIR SERVICE
Muskegon County Airport, 105 Sinclair Drive / 231-798-4596

MEDICAL
Hackley Hospital, 1700 Clinton Street / 231-726-3511

FOR MORE INFORMATION
Chamber of Commerce
250 Morris Avenue, Ste. 230
Muskegon, MI 49440
231-722-3751

Baldwin

Population – 821

ACCOMMODATIONS
Johnson's Pere Marquette Lodge, M-37 / 231-745-3972
Osceola Inn, 110 East Upton Avenue (Reed City 49677) / 231-832-5537
Reed City Motel, 781 South Chestnut Street (Reed City 49677) / 231-832-5373

RESTAURANTS
All Seasons Restaurant, Corner of South M 37 & 68 / 231-745-7731
B T Food & Spirits, 3247 South M-37 / 231-745-3571
Main Stream Cafe, 396 Michigan Avenue / 231-745-3377
Mother's Cupboard, 2677 South M-37 / 231-745-3720
Sporties Bar & Grill Inc, 867 North Michigan Avenue / 231-745-3932
Dolly's Family Dining, 1075 Washington Street / 231-745-7361
Village Coffee Shop Restaurant, 825 North Michigan Avenue / 231-745-7710

FLY SHOPS AND SPORTING GOODS
Baldwin Bait & Tackle Inc, 3223 South M-37 / 231-745-3529
Streamside Woman, 765 East Fifth Street / 231-745-9680
Ed's Sport Shop, 712 North Michigan Avenue / 231-745-4974
Johnson's, An Orvis Shop, M-37 / 231-745-3972
Pere Marquette River Lodge, RR 1, Box 1290 / 231-745-3972

AUTO REPAIR
A A Collision, 3 miles south on M-37 and south M-3 / 231-745-7771
Gene's Service, 3380 North M-37 / 231-745-4692
North End Auto, 2240 West US 10 / 231-745-2339

AIR SERVICE
Mason County Airport, E Avenue (Ludington 49431) / 231-843-2049

MEDICAL
Family Health Care Medical, 4967 North Michigan Avenue / 231-745-4624

FOR MORE INFORMATION
Chamber of Commerce
911 Michigan Avenue
Baldwin, MI 49304
231-745-4331

Ludington
Population – 8,507

ACCOMMODATIONS
Four Seasons Lodging & Breakfast, 717 E Avenue / 231-843-3449
Blue Spruce Motel, 109 North Ferry Street / 231-843-9537
Lakewood Motel, 1934 North Lakeshore Drive / 231-843-3884
Tumble Inn Motel, 5005 West US 10 @US 31 / 231-843-2140
Vista Villa Motel, 916 E Avenue / 231-843-9320

CAMPGROUNDS
Cartier Campgrounds, 1254 North Lakeshore Drive / 231-845-1522
Kibby Creek Travel Park, 4900 West Deren Road / 231-843-3995
North Woods Campground, 4565 West US Highway 10 / 231-845-7106
Poncho's Pond RV Park, 5335 West Wallace Lane / 231-845-7711
Tamarac Village, 2875 North Lakeshore Drive / 231-843-4990

RESTAURANTS
Beamers at the Lanes, 2253 West US Highway 10 / 231-757-0008
Chuck Wagon, 971 North Lakeshore Drive / 231-843-2852
Del's Restaurant, 404 South Washington Avenue / 231-843-8894
The Main Sail, 4079 West US Highway 10 / 231-845-7311
Maria's Cuisine, 120 W Avenue / 231-845-1466
Sportsman's Restaurant & Bar, 111 W Avenue / 231-843-2138

FLY SHOPS AND SPORTING GOODS
North Bayou Resort, 4849 North Lakeshore Drive / 231-845-5820
Pere Marquette Sport Center, 214 W Avenue / 231-843-8676
Provisions Sport Shop, 112 W Avenue / 231-843-4150

AUTO REPAIR
Ludington Car Care Center, 215 North Jebavy Drive / 231-845-7363
Parkview 76 Service, 302 W Avenue / 231-843-3329
Northland Performance Service & Repair, 302 South James Street / 231-845-7124

AIR SERVICE
Mason County Airport, E Avenue / 231-843-2049

MEDICAL
Memorial Medical Center of West Michigan, 1 North Atkinson Drive /
    231-845-2355

FOR MORE INFORMATION
Ludington Area Chamber of Commerce
5827 West US Highway 10
Ludington, MI 49431
231-845-0324

Manistee
Population – 6,734

ACCOMMODATIONS
Hillside Motel, 1599 Manistee Hwy / 231-723-2584
Lake Shore Motel, 101 Lakeshore Drive South / 231-723-2667
Moonlite Motel & Marina, 111 US 31 / 231-723-3587
Riverside Motel & Marina, 520 Water Street / 231-723-3554
Garlet's Restaurant & Motel, 8037 M-37 (Wellston 49689) / 862-3500

CAMPGROUNDS
Coho Bend Campground, 5025 River Road / 231-723-7321
Insta Launch Campground & Marina, 20 Park Street / 231-723-3901
Orchard Beach State Park, 2064 Lakeshore Road / 231-723-7422
Coolwater Camp Grounds, 9424 West 48½ Road (Wellston 49689) / 862-3481
Twin Oaks Campground, 233 Moss Road (Wellston 49689) / 848-4710

RESTAURANTS
Dockside, 445 River Street / 231-723-3046
Four-forty West, 440 River Street / 231-723-7902
Gregory's Restaurant at the Carriage Inn, 200 Arthur Street / 231-723-4661
Old Town Restaurant, 155 8th Street / 231-723-4581
Dam Site Inn, 5073 Highbridge Road (Brethren 49619) / 477-5005
The Kozy Kitchen, 16938 Caberfae Hwy (Wellston 49689) / 848-4632

FLY SHOPS AND SPORTING GOODS
Schmidt Outfitters, 918 Seaman Road (Wellston 49689) / 231-848-4191
Fisherman's Center, 263 Arthur Street / 231-723-7718
Northwind Sports, 400 Parkdale Avenue / 231-723-2255

AUTO REPAIR
Erdmann's Car Care, 1628 Cedar Road / 231-723-5860
North Bridge Auto, 147 Cleveland Street / 231-723-4841
Parkdale Tire & Auto Center, 418 Parkdale Avenue / 231-723-8329
Wellston Auto Salvage & Repair, 1339 South Baker Road (Wellston 49689) / 848-4371

AIR SERVICE
Manistee Blacker Airport, 2323 Airport Road / 231-723-4351

MEDICAL
West Shore Hospital, 1465 East Parkdale Avenue / 231-723-3501

FOR MORE INFORMATION
Manistee Area Chamber of Commerce
11 Cypress Street
Manistee, MI 49660
231- 723-2575

Cadillac
Population – 10,104

ACCOMMODATIONS
American Inn, 312 East Cass Street / 231-779-9000
Birchwood Resort and Campgrounds, 6553 East M-115 / 231-775-9101
Blue Gingham Inn & Motel, 8560 M-115 Street / 231-775-7949
Driftwood Lodge, 5475 West M-55 / 231-775-2932
Olson's Motel & Cottages, 1423 North Mitchell Street / 231-775-7281
Pine Knoll Motel, 8072 South Mackinaw Trail / 231-775-9471

CAMPGROUNDS
Birchwood Resort and Campgrounds, 6553 E M-115 / 231-775-9101
Camp Cadillac, 10621 East Thirty Four Road / 231-775-9724
Lake Billings Camp Grounds, 221 East Elmore Street (Manton 49663) /
    231-824-6454

RESTAURANTS
Merry Inn Restaurant, 204 South Michigan Avenue (Manton 49663) / 824-3600
Bread Basket Cafe, 126 M-55 Hwy / 231-779-1058
Charlene's Restaurant, 1034 North Mitchell Street / 231-775-1861
Frosty Cup Family Restaurant, 2257 Sunnyside Drive / 231-775-7451
Hillcrest Family Restaurant, 1250 South Mitchell Street / 231-775-4191
Marina Restaurant & Lounge, 2404 Sunnyside Drive / 231-775-9322
Timbers Restaurant, 5535 East M-115 / 231-775-6751

FLY SHOPS AND SPORTING GOODS
JD's Sport Shop, 301 North Mitchell Street / 231-775-8787
Ron's Sporting Goods, 1531 North Mitchell Street / 231-779-0750
Pilgrim Village Fishing Shop, 301 S. Lake Mitchell Drive / 231-775-2401

AUTO REPAIR
Mitchell's Auto Service, 522 North Mitchell Street / 231-775-6115
Westside Auto Service, 6732 West Division Street / 231-775-3323
Roy's Auto Repair, 1130 West 13th Street / 231-779-3839
Willis Automotive, 8860 34 Road / 231-779-4045

AIR SERVICE
Wexford Airport, 8040 East Thirty Fourth Road / 231-779-9525

MEDICAL
Mercy Hospital, 400 Hobart Street / 231-876-7200

FOR MORE INFORMATION
Cadillac Area Chamber of Commerce
222 North Lake Street
Cadillac, MI 49601
231-775-9776

Traverse City
Population – 15,155

ACCOMMODATIONS
Briar Hill Motel, US 31 North at East 8th Street 461 Munson Avenue /
   231-947-5525
Buena Vista Motel & Cottages, 1639 North US 31 / 231-938-1440
Driftwood Motel, 1861 North US 31 / 231-938-1600
Grand Traverse Motel Williams, 1010 East Front Street / 231-947-9410
Moonlight Bay Resort, 4095 Harolds Road / 231-946-5967
Pinestead Reef Motel, 1265 North US 31 / 231-947-4010
Sleepy Hollow Motel, 939 South US 31 / 231-943-4740

CAMPGROUNDS
Jellystone Park Camp Resort, 4050 Hammond Road East / 231-947-2770
Lakeside Resort and Party Store, 9851 Sperrins Landing Drive / 231-946-6994
Michigan Air Streamers Park, 4860 South US 31 / 231-943-4410
Kalkaska Campgrounds, 580 M-72 SE (Kalkaska 49646) / 231-258-9863
Rapid River Campground, 7182 US 131 NE (Kalkaska 49646) / 231-258-2042

RESTAURANTS
Country Skillet Cafe, 10945 72 NE (Kalkaska 49646) / 231-258-8899
Dill's Olde Towne Saloon, 423 South Union Street / 231-947-7534
The Diner, 1103 South Garfield Avenue / 231-946-0789
Larry's Place, 1265 North US 31 / 231-929-1044
Long Lake Inn, 7208 Secor Road / 231-946-3991
Reflections Restaurant & Lounge, 2061 North US 31 / 231-938-2321
Scott's Harbor Grill, 12917 South West Bay Shore Drive / 231-922-2114

FLY SHOPS AND SPORTING GOODS
Austin & Nelson, 104 S. Union St., Ste 211 / 616-933-4649
Can Am Angler, 536 Washington / 616-946-7477
Gander Mountain, 3500 Marketplace Circle / 321-929-5590
Riverborne Angler, 535 West Front Street / 231-941-3474
Tackle Town, 13680 South West Bay Shore Drive / 231-941-5420
The Troutsman, 4386 North US 31 North / 231-938-3474
Jack's Sport Shop, 212 South Cedar Street (Kalkaska 49646) / 231-258-8892
Backcast Fly Shop, 1675 Benzie Hwy (Benzonia 49616) / 231-882-5222
Streamside Orvis Shop, 4400 Grand Traverse Village (Williamsburg 49690) /
   231-938-5338
Aries Tackle, 7567 Michigan Avenue (Thompsonville 49683) / 231-378-4520
Fieldsport Ltd., 3313 West South Airport Road / 231-938-3474
M.C. Sports, 848 US 31 South / 231-943-8280

AUTO REPAIR

Lodi Garage, 4915 M-66 SE (Kalkaska 49646) / 231-369-2805
B & L Automotive, 1045 Oak Terrace Drive / 231-941-0405
Car Repairs Inc, 701 West Front Street / 231-947-9011
Cramer's Auto Repair, 820 Robinwood Court / 231-946-2990
Dresnek Auto Repair, 3180 Keystone Road North / 231-929-1117
Parkway Auto Service, 2960 Cass Road / 231-946-2228

AIR SERVICE

Cherry Capital Airport / 231-947-2250

MEDICAL

Munson Medical Center, 1105 6th Street / 231-935-5000

FOR MORE INFORMATION

Chamber of Commerce
202 East Grandview Parkway
Traverse City, MI 49684
231-947-5075

Petoskey
Population – 6,056

ACCOMMODATIONS
Apple Tree Inn, 915 Spring Street / 231-348-2900
Baywinds Inn, 909 Spring Street / 231-347-4193
Coach House Motels, 1011 North US 31 / 231-347-8281
Green Roof Motor Inn, 1420 South US 131 / 231-348-3900
Petoskey Motel, US 31 / 231-347-8177
Boyne City Motel, 110 North East Street (Boyne City 49712) / 231-582-6701

CAMPGROUNDS
KOA Kampground of Petoskey, 1800 North US 31 / 231-347-0005
Petoskey State Park, 2475 M-119 / 231-347-2311

RESTAURANTS
Andante, 321 Bay Street / 231-348-3321
The Bistro, 423 Michigan Street / 231-347-5583
Northwood Restaurant, 4769 Oden Road / 231-347-3894
Park Garden Cafe, 432 East Lake Street / 231-347-0101
Schelde's Restaurants, 1315 North US 31 / 231-347-7747
Country Star Restaurant, 1113 East Division Street (Boyne City 49712) /
    231-582-2751

FLY SHOPS AND SPORTING GOODS
The Troutsman, 217 Howard Street / 231-348-3474
Whippoorwill Fly Shop, 1844 M-119 / 231-348-7061
Jordan River Fly Shop, 105 Main Street (East Jordan 49727) / 231-536-9925

AUTO REPAIR
Bill's Auto Clinic, 2175 Howard Road / 231-347-8545
Brown's Auto Clinic, 4106 Hiawatha Trail / 231-347-4466
Epsilon Auto Service, 7680 Mitchell Road / 231-347-3111
Roger's Auto Service & Repair, 1445 Standish Avenue / 231-347-5312

AIR SERVICE
Harbor Springs Airport, 8656 M-119 / 231-347-2812

MEDICAL
Northern Michigan Hospital Emerge, 416 Connable Avenue / 231-348-4520

FOR MORE INFORMATION
Petoskey Regional Chamber of Commerce
401 East Mitchell Street
Petoskey, MI 49770
231-347-4150

Northeastern Lower Peninsula

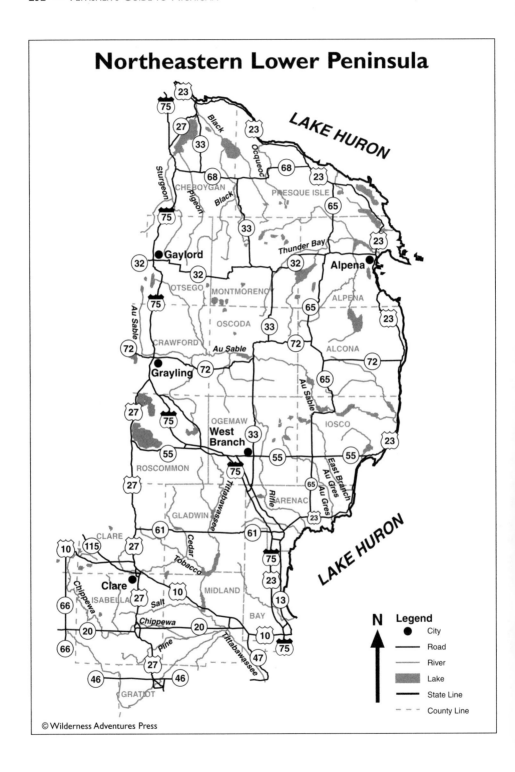

N

Legend
● City
— Road
— River
▮ Lake
— State Line
--- County Line

© Wilderness Adventures Press

Northeastern Lower Peninsula

The northeastern part of the Lower Peninsula is home to Michigan's most famous trout stream, the Au Sable. And while the sunrise side of the northern Lower Peninsula is not quite as blessed with trout water as the western side, there are still lots of other opportunities for some great fishing.

The Sturgeon, Pigeon, and Black Rivers eventually join before flowing into northern Lake Huron, providing us with over 100 miles of blue ribbon trout water. As we shall see, they offer a large diversity of fishing opportunities. There are also a number of rivers that provide good trout fishing without the blue ribbon label.

Steelhead and salmon play a big role in the northeast, and the tributaries to Saginaw Bay host big runs of walleyes. Steelhead usually run later on the northern Lake Huron tributaries, so the nomadic steelheader can make a clockwise migration to maximize opportunities for these silver fish. Starting with southern Lake Michigan runs, moving north, and then swinging east will keep your arm pleasantly tired from March through May.

The Saginaw River is the dividing line between the north and south sections of the eastern Lower Peninsula, so I will describe its northern tributaries in this section and cover its southern watershed in the southeastern section. While the Saginaw is very large and doesn't offer much, if any, opportunity for the fly angler, it certainly gathers some fine water from the north.

TITTABAWASSEE RIVER

The Tittabawassee River is the Saginaw's largest tributary and, in turn, the bulk of its flyfishing opportunities are found in its feeder streams. The river starts as three branches that are not only marginal trout creeks but marginal in size for flyfishing. When they join together, they are impounded by the Secord Dam. A series of dams keeps most of the river from being free-flowing all the way down to Sanford. Except for a low head dam at Dow Chemical in Midland, the river is now free from dams down to its confluence with the Saginaw River in the city of the same name. Anadromous fish and resident fish are able to get around the Dow Dam.

The lower Tittabawassee is best fished from a boat, but there are some limited areas that can be carefully waded during low water. The Chippewa River adds a lot of water to the mainstream, so wading possibilities are mostly upstream from Midland.

Walleyes, both resident fish and migratory marble eyes from Saginaw Bay, are the main attraction of the lower Tittabawassee, but there are also good numbers of smallmouth bass. Because of the big walleye run in the spring and to protect spawning walleyes, the Tittabawassee is closed to fishing from March 16 to the last Saturday in April between the Sanford Dam and the mouth of the Salt River and

Smallmouth bass are great fun on a fly rod.

Tittabawassee River
Wixom Lake to Second Lake and Branches

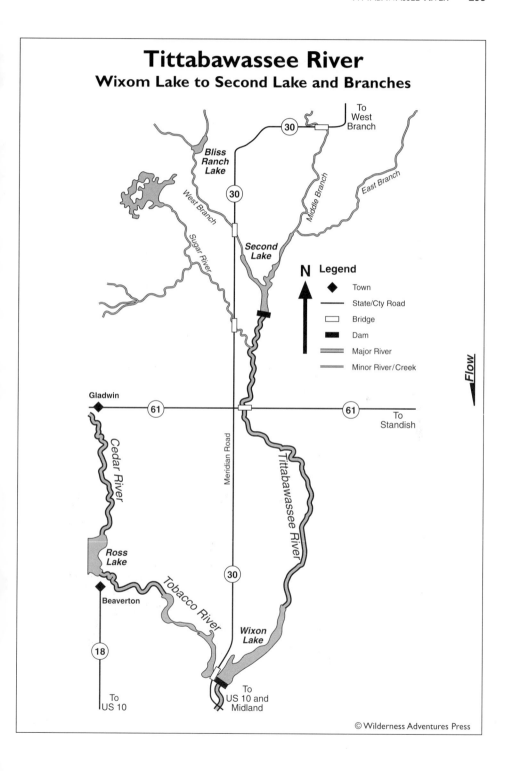

To
West
Branch

30

Bliss
Ranch
Lake

West Branch

30

Middle Branch

East Branch

Sugar River

Second
Lake

N   Legend

◆   Town
───   State/Cty Road
▭   Bridge
■   Dam
═══   Major River
───   Minor River/Creek

Flow

Gladwin

61

61

To
Standish

Cedar River

Meridian Road

Tittabawassee River

Ross
Lake

30

Beaverton

Tobacco River

18

Wixon
Lake

To
US 10

To
US 10 and
Midland

© Wilderness Adventures Press

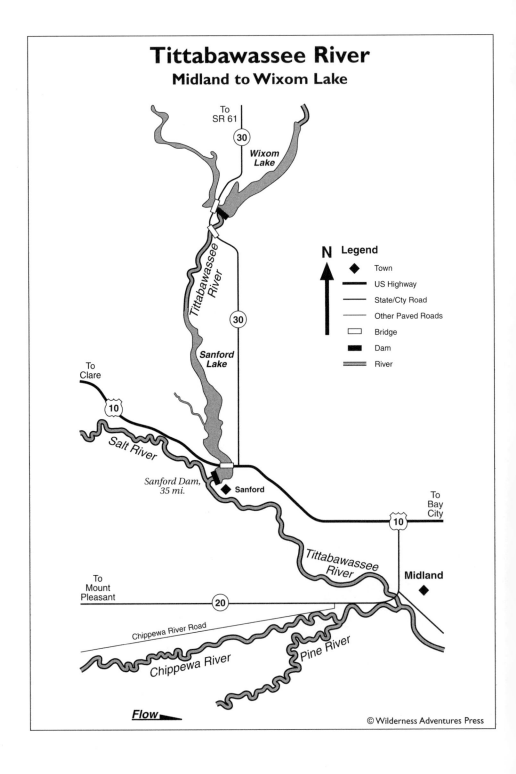

Tittabawassee River
Midland to Wixom Lake

To
SR 61

30

Wixom
Lake

N Legend

◆   Town
──   US Highway
──   State/Cty Road
──   Other Paved Roads
▭   Bridge
■   Dam
━   River

Tittabawassee River

30

Sanford
Lake

To
Clare

10

Salt River

Sanford Dam,
35 mi.

◆ Sanford

To
Bay
City

10

Tittabawassee River

Midland ◆

To
Mount
Pleasant

20

Chippewa River Road

Chippewa River

Pine River

Flow ▶

© Wilderness Adventures Press

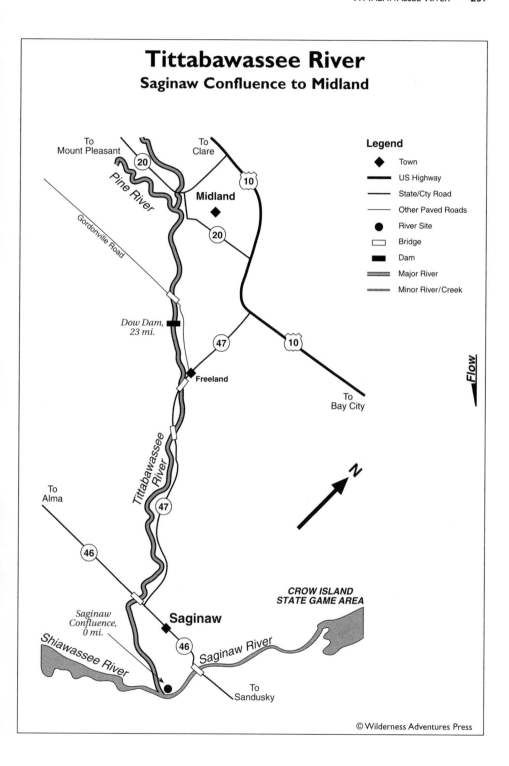

Tittabawassee River
Saginaw Confluence to Midland

To
Mount Pleasant

To
Clare

20

10

Legend

◆ Town

▬ US Highway

── State/Cty Road

── Other Paved Roads

● River Site

▭ Bridge

■ Dam

≈≈ Major River

══ Minor River/Creek

Pine River

Midland
◆

Gordonville Road

20

Dow Dam,
23 mi.

■

47

10

Freeland
◆

To
Bay City

Flow

Tittabawassee
River

To
Alma

47

N

46

CROW ISLAND
STATE GAME AREA

47

Saginaw
Confluence,
0 mi.

Saginaw
◆

46

Saginaw River

Shiawassee River

●

To
Sandusky

© Wilderness Adventures Press

between the Dow Dam and the Gordonville Road Bridge. This was implemented because of the tremendous fishing pressure on them even though keeping them is not allowed at this time.

You can still attempt to intercept walleye with streamers below these concentration points, although the DNR seems to be discouraging even catch and release. A better time to target anadromous walleyes in the Tittabawassee is in the fall. The water will be lower and clearer than it is in the spring, and walleyes are on a feeding run, so they will be much easier to entice into taking your offering. During fall, walleyes fatten up on gizzard shad and shiners in anticipation of the long winter and early spring spawning.

Fishing a large river like this for walleyes is pretty much an uncharted course for fly anglers. Swinging and then slowly retrieving streamers that imitate shad is a viable technique. You might also try some vertical drifting with a weighted fly under a floating line with a strike indicator. One thing is for sure: if you can figure out a presentation that works, bring your camera because there is an excellent chance of catching a 10- to 14-pound trophy walleye.

The Tittabawassee also hosts a modest run of steelhead and chinook salmon. Most of these fish are headed for the Chippewa River. Good places to intercept them are below the Dow Dam and at the juncture of the two rivers. Access is very good between Sanford Lake and the Saginaw River. In Sanford the Village Park and the

An average brown trout.

Sanford Lake County Park get you on the river. In Midland there is a boat launch at Emerson Park on the east side of the river, and the Golf Side Boat Launch is located on the west side north of M-20. Chippawassee Park offers access at the juncture with the Chippewa River. Caldwell Boat Launch on Gordonville Road south of Midland allows you to put your boat in below the Dow Dam. A boat launch at the Center Road crossing south of Saginaw gets you on the lower river.

Chippewa River

This large tributary to the Tittabawassee begins as the outlet of Cranberry Lake west of Clare. There are some browns and brookies in the headwaters, but the stream is quite small. There is enough room to maneuver with a fly rod upstream from M-66 and past the confluences with Rattail and Butts Creeks. M-66 crosses the river twice, and access to the upper river is available at Hoover Road.

The West or South Branch (depending on which map you are looking at) joins the river at Barryton, where the two are impounded by a dam. This branch's warm water in combination with the impoundment make the Chippewa home to small-mouth and rock bass instead of trout downstream from Barryton. Although the reach below Barryton does offer some fast action for smallies, they tend to be little fish. Colley Creek, a small brook trout stream, joins the Chippewa here. During spring when the water is still cool, you could be surprised by a good-sized brook trout grabbing your nymph or streamer instead of a bass. Brookies move into the mainstream to take advantage of the food supply and then retreat to cold water in the summer. Numerous county road bridges provide good access below Barryton.

The dam that forms Lake Isabella is the last barrier that blocks fish movement. With the addition of the Coldwater River, the Chippewa gains some size and so do the smallmouth, both in numbers and average length. The bottom is firm here, with numerous large rocks scattered in the sand and gravel, and abundant crayfish and a good minnow population keep smallmouth well fed. Again, there is a road crossing almost every mile, providing lots of opportunities to get on the river.

The North Branch of the Chippewa adds to the flow just upstream from Mt. Pleasant. This branch drains mostly agricultural land, and much of it is dredged. In the spring and when it rains, the North Branch adds a lot of sediment and turbidity. If the water becomes too dirty to fish downstream, the water is likely to be clearer farther upstream.

As the Chippewa passes through Mt. Pleasant and continues its journey east, it grows slowly but continues to have a firm bottom and good gradient. Some walleyes add to the catch in the lower river, and when you find some slow deep holes, there will be northern pike present. There are many bridges about the same distance apart on the river, making it possible to spot cars and wade or float whatever length of water you choose.

Steelhead are planted at Winn Road about 6 miles upstream from Mt. Pleasant. There is good spawning gravel here in the spring, so this is a good place to look for the silvery migrants. Some fish also stack up below the Lake Isabella Dam. Steelhead

Chippewa River
Mount Pleasant to Cranberry Lake (North Branch)

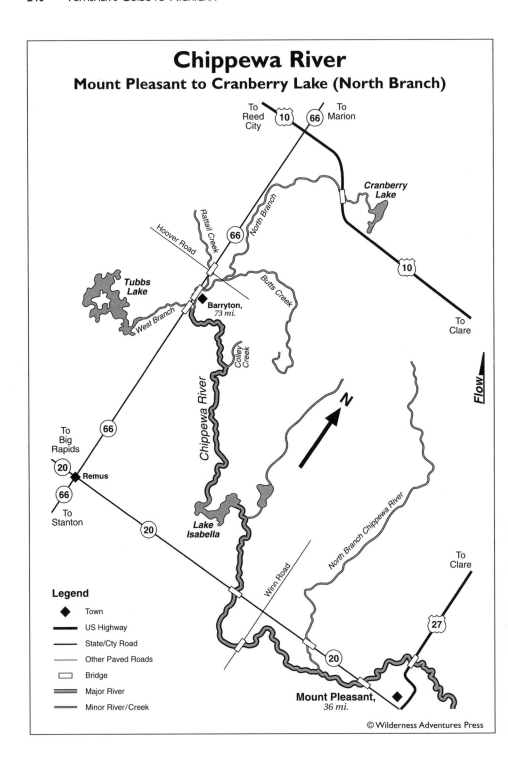

Legend

◆ Town

▬ US Highway

— State/Cty Road

— Other Paved Roads

▭ Bridge

▬ Major River

▬ Minor River/Creek

© Wilderness Adventures Press

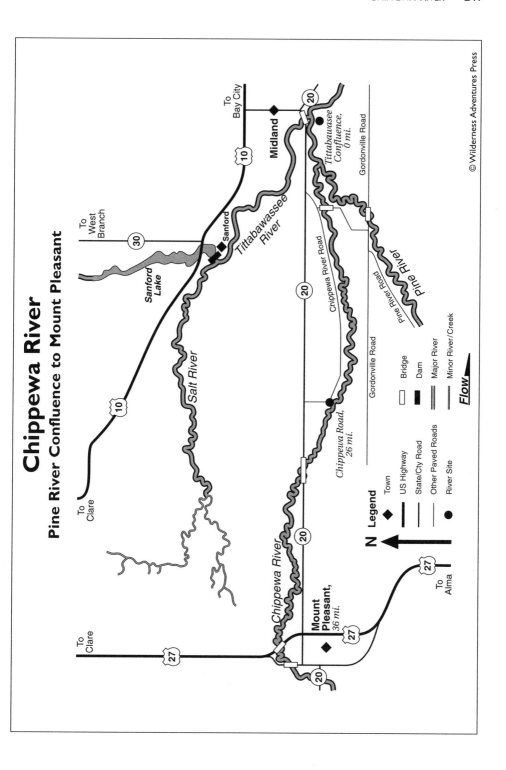

Chippewa River
Pine River Confluence to Mount Pleasant

© Wilderness Adventures Press

Legend

Town — ◆

US Highway

State/Cty Road

Other Paved Roads

River Site — ●

Bridge — ▭

Dam — ■

Major River

Minor River/Creek

Flow ➤

N

also enter the Chippewa in the fall, but there is a lot of river to search for relatively few fish. Covering lots of water is the key to finding steelies, and smallmouth will hit the same streamers used to interest steelhead.

Pine River

This is the southernmost of Michigan's Pine Rivers, and it merges with the Chippewa just before the "Chip" flows into the Tittabawassee. The Pine pretty much parallels the Chippewa and is often less than 10 miles south of it.

Pine River' headwaters, found southeast of Mecosta, hold wild browns and brookies. By the time it becomes flyfishing water with the addition of its South Branch and Pony Creek, it is somewhat marginal for trout. Browns and brook trout are still present, and some browns of surprising size have been caught in the upper Pine. I witnessed a huge brown in the 10-pound class caught from under a bridge at night. But, alas, it had succumbed to garden hackle.

When the Pine dips into Montcalm County, the gradient increases and so do the trout. Wolf (aka Cedar) Creek adds its cool waters, and the Pine widens into a very pleasant river to cast a fly. There is an excellent brown drake hatch at the end of May, and the bottom crawls with crayfish. Much of the first mile of Wolf Creek up from the

Thick cover crowds the banks of Pine River.

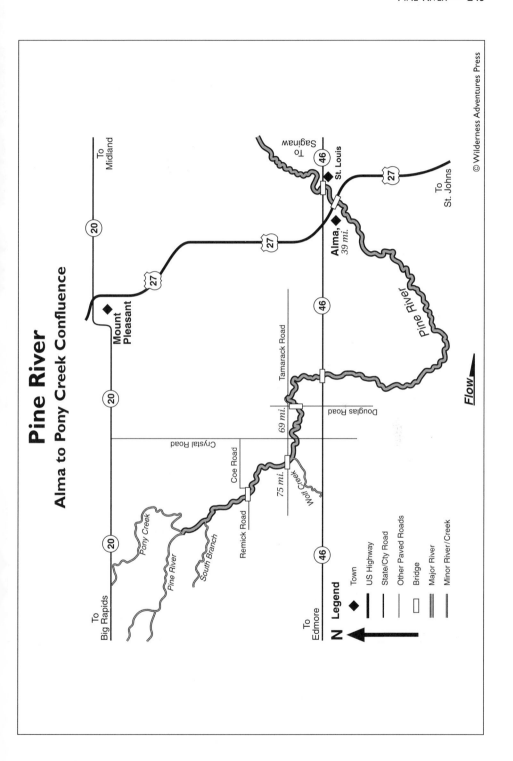

Pine River
Alma to Pony Creek Confluence

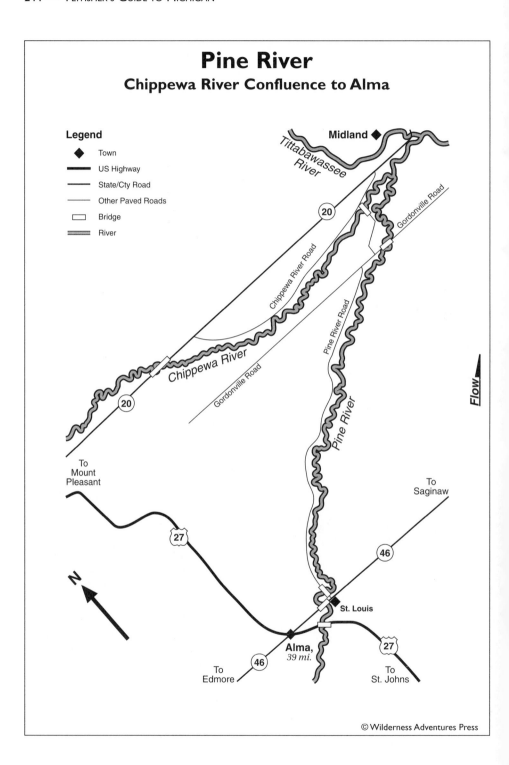

Pine River
Chippewa River Confluence to Alma

Legend
- ◆ Town
- US Highway
- State/Cty Road
- Other Paved Roads
- ☐ Bridge
- ▨ River

Midland ◆

Tittabawassee River

20

Gordonville Road

Chippewa River Road

Pine River Road

Chippewa River

Gordonville Road

20

Pine River

Flow

To
Mount
Pleasant

To
Saginaw

27

46

N

St. Louis

27

Alma,
39 mi.

46

To
Edmore

To
St. Johns

© Wilderness Adventures Press

Pine juncture is also open enough to fish with flies, and there are wild browns and brookies present. Fishing downstream from Tamarack Road on the Pine and then upstream on Wolf Creek from the confluence lets you try out both streams. Try above and below Crystal, Schmeid, and Remick Roads for more trout action.

Trout fishing continues down to M-46 with the help of some planted browns. Though there is still a chance to catch a lunker brown below the highway, the fish population is definitely shifting in favor of smallmouth bass and northern pike. There is a good population of rock bass, as well, to keep you busy. Good warmwater fishing continues until the backwaters of an impoundment in Alma. From below the dam in Alma, the remainder of the river has a black cloud hanging over its head in terms of eating fish. A chemical company in the next town downstream, St. Louis, severely contaminated the river sediment in the impoundment there with DDT and PBB. The fish continue to have concentrations of these compounds and carry very high levels.

This is not bad news for the catch-and-release angler. There is still very good smallmouth fishing to be had all the way to the Chippewa, and it is relatively lightly fished because of the fish consumption advisory. There is good access at numerous road crossings, and the Pine River Road parallels the river.

You might also want to investigate the area below the St. Louis dam in the spring. Some of the Chippewa's steelhead seem to make a wrong turn and end up in the Pine. There is also a modest salmon run in the fall.

Tobacco River

The Tobacco River is another large tributary of the Tittabawassee that joins the mainstream in the Wixom Lake impoundment. There are three branches to the Tobacco, and they all provide some fine flyfishing opportunities. Once they come together in the impoundment at Beaverton called Ross Lake, there is very little of the mainstream that is not impounded.

Beginning east of Farwell, the South Branch is the largest and most popular of the tributaries. Below the Mill Pond in Farwell, the stream is marginal for trout water and flyfishing. Because there are brook trout in the headwaters, fishing would likely improve if the Mill Pond dam were removed. A few miles downstream, Newton Creek adds its cold water and nearly doubles the flow. The lower few miles of Newton Creek are open enough for the fly rod, and it has a good population of wild brown trout, along with a few brookies.

The South Branch is noted for having good-sized brown trout but not in any great numbers. Even with the addition of Newton Creek, it remains a bit marginal for trout, due in part to a very healthy population of creek chubs that compete with trout. However, crayfish are present in good numbers, so the trout that do survive the competition have a chance to grow really large. The Grant Road to M-115 is a favorite stretch of mine, and the fishing is also good upstream from M-115. This is not wilderness fishing—you will catch more creek chubs than trout, but a lunker brown is always a possibility. A dam in Clare that creates Lake

Tobacco and Cedar Rivers

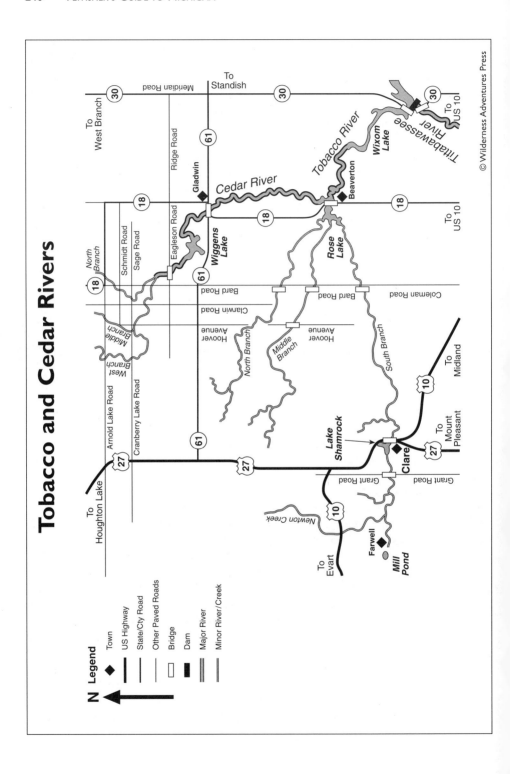

© Wilderness Adventures Press

Cedar River is a tributary of the Tobacco River.

Shamrock pretty much terminates the trout water. There have been some attempts to stock trout below this lake, but the survival rate has been poor. The lower river is pretty with lots of bend holes, but you will have to be content with catching mostly bass and pike.

If you are looking for a sleeper stream with large brown trout, try the Middle Branch. Though it is the smallest and least fished of the Tobacco's three branches, it holds some quality trout. When I first fished this stream, my first hour was spent unhooking a few chubs and shiners with no sign of a trout. However, in the next hour I landed a brace of 19-inch browns and lost a larger fish. The moral of this story applies throughout Michigan: If the water doesn't look good at the bridge and you don't start catching them right off the bat, give the stream a chance and keep going for a few more bends. A little perseverance could get you into some prime fishing that others have passed up.

While it's flow is quite small, you can start flyfishing the Middle Branch at Rodgers Road. There are brushy sections here as well as downstream. There are a few brook trout in the headwaters, but it is wild browns that make up most of the catch. The best water is between Calhoun and Athey Avenue, with three bridges for access.

There will be more and more chubs and shiners as you go downstream, and the reach between Bard and Calhoun has been badly degraded by cattle, however you can still encounter trout all the way to the headwaters of the impoundment.

The best population of wild trout in the Tobacco system resides in the North Branch, where the small fish will be browns and brookies, not creek chubs. Like the Middle Branch, the North Branch can be flyfished in places starting at about Mannsiding Road, but a lot of roll casting will be required. Because this stream never becomes "large," roll casting is the main presentation technique throughout its length. There is a chance for some good-sized brook trout in the headwaters and, following the typical pattern, browns become more and more prevalent as you move toward Beaverton. Bridges provide access, and fishing from one to the next will get you into lightly fished water.

Cedar River

This tributary to the Tobacco River at Beaverton is also a river of three branches. The West and Middle Branches are pretty small for flyfishing but not impossible because of their meadow and mature forest sections. The blue ribbon section of the Cedar River starts where these two branches come together and continues down to Bard Road. This section, as well as the branches above, is loaded with wild brown trout. Most are relatively small, ranging from 8 to 12 inches, but there are some larger fish present in the deeper holes. If you have only a couple of hours, fishing from Hoover Avenue up to the confluence of the two branches is a good section to try. You can walk or fish up the Middle Branch to Sage Road for an easy walk back to your vehicle. If you have more time and a partner to move the car, there are three adjacent stretches of about equal length for a half-day jaunt between Eagleson, Bard, Clarwin (no bridge, access to the river is from the south), and Hoover Roads. Aquatic insects are abundant on the Cedar, especially species that inhabit gravel riffles.

The North Branch is larger than either the Middle or West Branch and has fewer trout. As usual, there are some brook trout in its headwaters that give way to browns downstream. While you will frequently encounter heavy streamside vegetation, you can flyfish the North Branch up to M-18. Schmidt, Sage, and Bard (twice) Roads provide good access to the North Branch. When the North Branch joins the West branch below Bard Road, the combined flow offers lots of room for a fly rod. Chances for larger trout increase here, as well, although there won't be the constant action that is available in the blue ribbon water.

An indirect testament to the quality of the trout fishing in the Cedar was related to me by Tom Huggler. He said that when he was working on his *Fish Michigan Rivers* book, he was threatened by one of the local anglers when he decided to include this river.

The Wiggins Lake impoundment terminates the trout water. From this dam down to Beaverton, there are some opportunities for warmwater species, including smallmouth bass, rock bass, and pike. In general, the fish are small, and I can't help

*North Branch
of the Cedar River.*

thinking that this stretch, like the lower part of the South Branch of the Tobacco, would be much better as a trout river—damn dams.

Close to the Cedar and a tributary to the upper Tittabawassee, the Sugar River also offers an opportunity to cast a fly to brown trout. It is much less popular than the Cedar, so if your favorite bridge on the Cedar already has two vehicles parked there, you might consider venturing a few miles to the east and try the Sugar above or below Meridian Road.

Stream Facts: Tittabawassee River

Seasons
- Open all year except for short reaches below Sanford and Dow Dams that are closed from March 16 to the last Saturday in April.
- Bass must be released between January 1 and the Saturday before Memorial Day.
- Walleyes, muskellunge, and northern pike must be released between March 15 and the last Saturday in April.
- In designated trout stream tributaries, trout must be released between October 1 and the last Saturday in April, and most cannot be fished during this time.

Special Regulations
- Size limit for all trout and salmon between October 1 and last Saturday in April is 15 inches, and the possession limit is 3.

Fish
- Resident northern pike, muskellunge, walleye, smallmouth and largemouth bass, channel catfish, panfish, carp, suckers.
- Anadromous rainbow and brown trout, chinook and coho salmon.
- Resident brown and brook trout in tributaries.

River Miles
Tittabawassee River
- Saginaw River—0
- Dow Dam—23
- Sanford Dam—35

Chippewa River
- Tittabawassee River—0
- Chippewa Road—26

Pine River
- Chippewa River—0
- Alma—39
- Douglas Road—69
- Tamarack Road—75

- Mount Pleasant—36
- Barryton—73

River Characteristics
- It is a large, slow, relatively deep river in the lower half.
- Much of the upper river is impounded.
- Headwater branches and tributaries can be waded and provide the best flyfishing opportunities.

River Access
- Numerous bridges on mainstream and tributaries provide access.
- Boat launches and public access sites are noted on maps.
- Access is available at each landmark noted above with river miles.

TITTABAWASSEE RIVER AND COLDWATER TRIBUTARY MAJOR HATCHES

Insect	Jan	Feb	Mar	Apr	May	Jun	July	Aug	Sep	Oct	Nov	Dec	Time	Fly Patterns
Hendrickson				■									M/A	Hendrickson #12–14; Rusty's Spinner; Red Quill; Adams; Quill Gordon
Blue-winged Olive					■	■	■	■					A	Blue-winged Olive #18–20; Sparkle Dun Baetis; Iron Dun; Olive CDC Mayfly Dun
Little Black Caddis				■	■	■	■	■					A	Little Black Caddis #16–18; Griffith's Gnat; CDC Emerging Caddis Brown; Black Ant
Grannom					■	■	■						M/A	Grannom #14–16; Medium Brown Sedge; Elk Caddis Brown-olive
Net-building Caddis					■	■	■	■	■	■			M/A	Spotted Sedge #16–18; Eastern Elk Wing Caddis; Goddard Caddis
Sulphur Dun						■							A/E	Sulphur Dun #16; Pale Morning Dun; CDC Comparadun Yellow; Pale Evening Dun
March Brown						■							M/A	March Brown #12–14; Dark Cahill; Gray Fox; Ginger Quill
Gray Drake						■							E	Gray Drake #12–14; Gram Adams
Brown Drake						■							E	Brown Drake #10–12; Adams; CDC Brown
Trico						■	■	■	■	■			M	Tiny White Wing Black #24–28; Parachute Adams; CDC Trico; Spent Wing Trico
White Fly									■				E	White Fly #12–14; White Miller
Streamers	■	■	■	■	■	■	■	■	■	■	■	■	M/A/E	Woolly Buggers #6–12; Clouser's Minnow; Muddler Minnows; BC Craw; Matukas
Terrestrials						■	■	■	■				M/A/E	Woolly Worm #8–12; BC Spider; Letort Cricket; Joe's Hopper #6–10; Dave's Hopper; Dropper Hopper

HATCH TIME CODE: M = morning; A = afternoon; E = evening.
Note: See hatch chart for Grand River for hatches on Tittabawassee mainstream and the lower reaches of the Chippewa and Pine Rivers.

Rifle River

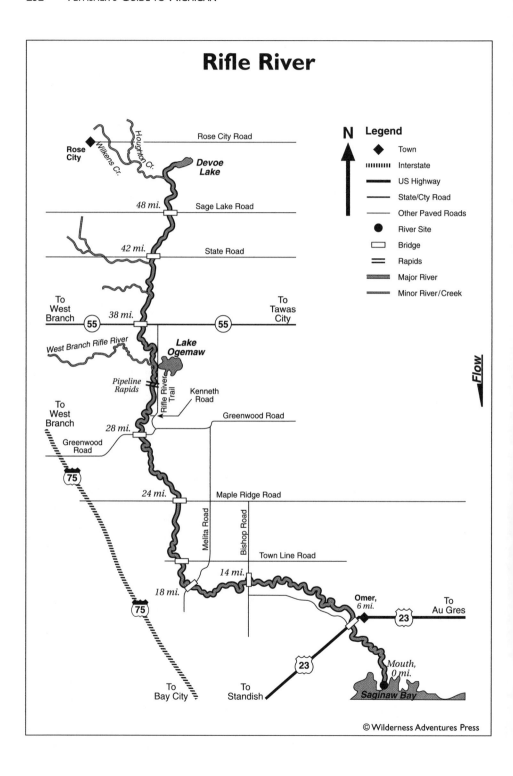

Legend

Town

Interstate

US Highway

State/Cty Road

Other Paved Roads

River Site

Bridge

Rapids

Major River

Minor River/Creek

N

Rose City Road

Rose City

Houghton Cr.

Wilkens Cr.

Devoe Lake

48 mi.

Sage Lake Road

42 mi.

State Road

To West Branch

55

38 mi.

To Tawas City

55

West Branch Rifle River

Lake Ogemaw

Pipeline Rapids

Rifle River Trail

Kenneth Road

Greenwood Road

To West Branch

28 mi.

Greenwood Road

75

24 mi.

Maple Ridge Road

Melita Road

Bishop Road

Town Line Road

18 mi.

14 mi.

75

Omer, 6 mi.

23

To Au Gres

23

To Bay City

To Standish

Mouth, 0 mi.

Saginaw Bay

Flow

© Wilderness Adventures Press

RIFLE RIVER

Now that my feeling about dams on trout streams is stated officially in the section on the Cedar River, I am pleased to report that the Rifle River flows for over 60 miles with no dams. It is located to the north and east of the Tittabawassee River and flows directly into the north side of Saginaw Bay. A feature of this river is the presence of a number of bedrock rapids, a relatively rare occurrence in Lower Peninsula rivers. One of my favorite phrases is, "The Rifle is loaded." When I get this report, it's time to get to the river and attempt to catch some of the silver bullets that have moved in from Lake Huron.

The Rifle River starts in a state game area of the same name as the outlet of Devoe Lake and is quickly joined by Houghton Creek. Below this juncture, the Rifle can be flyfished all the way to its mouth.

Houghton Creek contains some rather large browns relative to its size and is open enough at least for roll casts between the Rifle and where Wilkins Creek flows into it. There are meadow sections, where dropping your favorite hopper pattern next to the

An angler trying his luck on the Rifle River.

grassy undercuts can get you hooked up to a husky brown. Schmitt and Flynn Roads offer access at bridges, and Houghton Creek Road crosses the stream twice.

Devoe Lake has a deepwater draw that helps keep the upper Rifle cool. The river never attains blue ribbon status, but you can catch resident browns all the way down to Greenwood Road. This is fairly high gradient water with lots of gravel and occasional bedrock rapids. There is access at the bridges, along with a number of developed public access sites that are shown on the map.

On a recent August day, I started fishing at the Klacking Creek access site and was working my way up the Rifle to the mouth of the creek. A huge brown in the 8- to 10-pound class came out of a logjam and nailed my streamer. Unfortunately, it came unhooked almost immediately. I was astounded by what I thought had to be the mother of all resident brown trout in the Rifle. Later, I learned from Mike Batchelder, owner of the Spool and Fly Shop on the river at State Road, that some browns run up the river from Lake Huron in the summer, and the fish I had encountered was probably one of those.

Klacking Creek has a good population of wild brown trout, and while it is relatively small and narrow, it can be flyfished up from the Rifle. You will likely find a beaver dam or two, as well as some deep undercut bank holes that hide 10- to 16-inch browns.

The West Branch of the Rifle also has a good brown trout population. It, too, is not very wide, but you can easily navigate it with a fly rod for the first 10 miles or so up from the mainstream. In general, the best fishing is found near the main Rifle. The West Branch joins the main Rifle just downstream from the Ogemaw Lake public access site. For about a mile, the branch parallels the mainstream, which makes it possible to fish up one and down the other. There are public access sites at the Pipeline Rapids and at the end of Kenneth Road downstream from Lake Ogemaw. All three can be reached from the Rifle River Trail.

Even before you get to Greenwood Road, northern pike start showing up in the Rifle. But, by the same token, you can continue to catch browns farther downstream. When the locals catch a pike in the Rifle's trout water, they have a rule that the pike must walk back to the stream after it is released. While warmwater species continue to increase downstream, their numbers are not great, so few anglers fish the lower river in the summer.

One of the characteristics of the Rifle is that there is a fair amount of "empty" water in each reach. It is important to move along and not get bogged down in wide, shallow, slow-moving sections that have no cover. This is especially true when fishing for anadromous fish.

And speaking of migrants, the Rifle gets a very good run of steelhead and brown trout, along with a modest run of wild chinook. In the fall, the brown trout run is the highlight that makes the river special. In the majority of Great Lake tributaries, brown trout are just an occasional bonus fish, but in the Rifle you can count on catching them. These fish spawn in October and early November and seem most eager to grab a bright streamer after they are done spawning. Many stay in the river all winter, even though the Rifle is very prone to freezing. In general, browns utilize

A Rifle River brown trout.

some of the first available gravel, so the gravel stretches in the lower river between Maple Ridge Road and US-23 are good locations to find them. Because bridges are quite far apart on the lower river, it is necessary to commit to an all-day fishing trip when wading. Consequently, many anglers opt to float the river, which is probably a better plan considering the extensive reaches of flat water. Maple Ridge down to Melita Road and Bishop Road to Omer are full-day floats. Melita Road to Bishop Road can be floated and fished in about 6 hours unless the fish are in heavy and aggressively attacking streamers and egg flies.

Although some steelhead run in the fall, the main surge comes in spring, normally peaking in late April and early May. One obstacle to catching these fish is that the Rifle gets a huge run of white suckers right in the middle of the steelhead migration that can be so thick that you almost can't fish. They spook ahead of you, in turn

*A pleasant float
on the Rifle River.*

spooking steelhead before you can make a presentation. Timing a trip before or after the sucker run is a good idea. Luckily, the main part of the sucker spawning only lasts a week or so. Of course, if you end up arriving at the same time the suckers do, they will readily hit egg flies, and you can practice on them.

The upper river is the place to concentrate your fishing for spring steelhead. Smolts are planted in the upper river, and the best spawning gravel is between Sage Lake Road and M-55. In addition, the lower river runs quite turbid in the spring due to all the clay in the system. Peters and State Roads offer access in this reach, along with the Klacking Creek access site. In addition, there is a campground downstream from Sage Lake Road off of Twin Lake Road. Egg patterns, Hex nymphs, and bright streamers are prime choices for the Rifle's spawning steelies and those resting in the dark water.

Stream Facts: Rifle River

Seasons
- Open all year below the junction of the Rifle River and the Devoe Lake outlet.
- Walleyes and northern pike must be released between March 16 and the last Saturday in April.
- Bass must released between January 1 and the Saturday before Memorial Day.
- Brook and brown trout must be released between October 1 and the last Saturday in April upstream from the Melita Road (old M-70) Bridge.

Special Regulations
- Size limit for all trout and salmon between October 1 and the last Saturday in April is 15 inches. and the possession limit is 3 fish.

Fish
- Resident brown, rainbow, and brook trout, smallmouth bass, northern pike, walleye, suckers, and carp.
- Anadromous rainbow and brown trout, chinook salmon, white suckers.

River Miles
- Lake Huron—0
- Omer (U.S.-23)—6
- Bishop Road—14
- Melita Road—18
- Maple Ridge Road—24
- Greenwood Road—28
- M-55—38
- State Road—42
- Sage Lake Road—48

River Characteristics
- A medium-sized river with long shallow, flat sections intermingled with rapids/riffles and deep bend holes.
- It is easily waded throughout,except during high water events.
- It is prone to freezing in winter and quickly turns muddy with heavy rain.
- There are no dams or other barriers to hinder fish movement.
- It is heavily canoed in the summer.

River Access
- Excellent access at numerous developed public access sites and road crossings.
- Access available at each landmark noted above with river miles.

Au Gres River

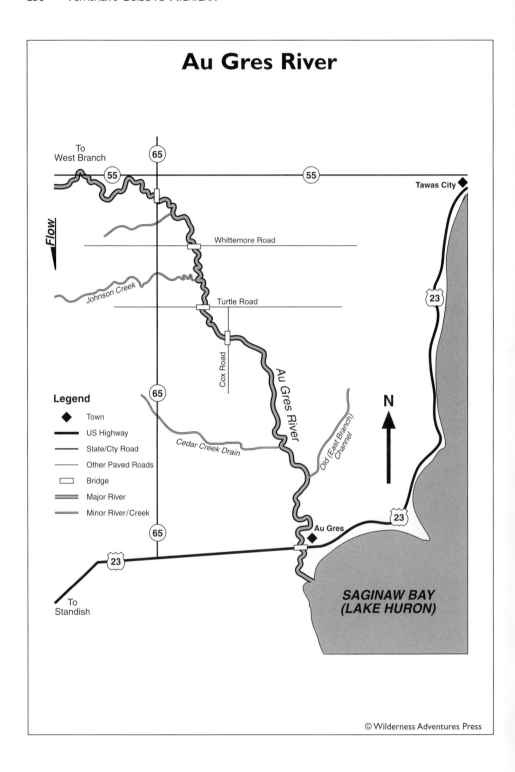

© Wilderness Adventures Press

AU GRES RIVER

The Au Gres River flows in the right latitude of Michigan to be a trout stream, but there are lakes in its headwaters, and the clay soils it runs through doesn't offer up much spring water. So it is primarily a warmwater river with smallmouth bass being the main resident game fish. In the lower river there are some walleyes and perch that move in from Saginaw Bay, and there is a chance for a surprise brown trout in the upper river during summer.

While on the narrow side in places, the Au Gres is roomy enough for fly casting below M-55. The bottom is mostly firm sand interlaced with gravel and clay runs. In addition to resident smallmouth bass, there have been reports of Saginaw Bay smallmouth bass moving up into the river in June. This would coincide with their spawning time. Perch and walleyes provide a spring and fall fishery in the lower river. Since minnows appear to be an important part of the diet of all three species, streamers imitating shiners, chubs, and sculpins are good choices. Bridges provide access, and M-65, Whittemore, Turtle, and Cox Roads are good places to try.

Even though steelhead, brown trout, and chinook salmon all run the Au Gres, they are relatively lightly fished, with the exception of salmon at the river's mouth. This is because most anglers gravitate toward the Rifle and the East Branch of the Au Gres. The formula that fewer fish and a lot fewer anglers makes better fishing often works here.

Dennis Dann fishes the East Branch of the Au Gres River.

East Branch of the Au Gres River

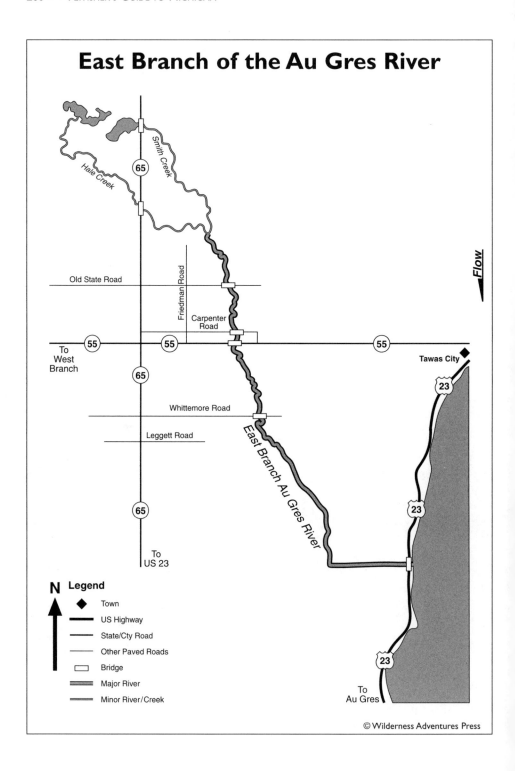

© Wilderness Adventures Press

In September, the chinook run is closely followed by a modest run of Lake Huron browns. As in most cases, finding some good gravel and fishing the runs and holes near it continue to be the keys for success. Chinook seem to hit best before they are ready to spawn, while browns are more aggressive later in the fall. Steelhead are mostly a spring proposition. The Au Gres tends to muddy easily from snowmelt or rain, so it is best to wait for several days after the last runoff event before fishing it. Even when the water is low, it always seems to have a little turbidity, and this can be helpful when sneaking up on spawning steelhead or salmon. Excite these fish into striking with bright or black leech and spey patterns.

East Branch of the Au Gres

It usually surprises the visiting angler to learn that the East Branch of the Au Gres does not flow into the Au Gres. Well, it used to, but in order to reduce flooding in the town of Au Gres, the East Branch was cut off and channeled straight out to Lake Huron. The channelized section is called Whitney Drain and is famous for the smelt runs that occur there.

The East Branch parallels the mainstream for most of its length but starts with the gathering of several cold creeks rather than lake outlets. Thus the headwaters are home to brown and brook trout, along with the offspring of steelhead and salmon. When Hale and Smith Creeks come together to form the East Branch, it is large enough to flyfish. This is also the beginning of the blue ribbon section that continues for 12 miles down to Whittemore Road. In terms of flow, the stream never gets very large, but there is lots of room in most of this reach, because it is relatively shallow with lots of gravel. Old State Road is the first crossing below the confluence of Hale and Smith Creeks and is about equidistant between the juncture and M-55. It can be fished a long way in either direction, and it is likely that you will have the stream to yourself in midsummer. Carpenter Road crosses the river a half-mile upstream from M-55 and provides additional access to the prime trout water.

Cover is at a premium, so when a hatch is not happening, it is best to drift a nymph near any log or overhanging vegetation that might hide a trout. Because terrestrials seem to be quite important in this stream, casting a hopper, ant, or beetle pattern close to the bank will likely be successful. Broken water also hides small to medium size trout, and when browns and brookies are found in this type of water, the are usually feeding. Though access is limited to the road crossings, there is a nice parking area at M-55. Because the stream is easily waded, you can fish as far as you want.

Steelhead are the East Branch's main draw, but the river also lures some lake-run browns in the fall. In a wet autumn, there will also be a fall steelhead run, but most of the rainbows arrive between early April and mid-May. For a mile on either side of Whittemore Road, there is relatively little gravel but there is good holding water for fish not quite ready to spawn. The farther upstream you go, the more gravel you will find, with the 2 miles below M-55 containing some outstanding spawning water. The stream is closed above M-55 until April 1, 2000. There is lots of good gravel here, as well, and steelhead anglers will be able to fish up to the confluence of Smith and Hale Creeks all year in the future.

*East Branch
of the Au Gres.*

Stealth is important when fishing steelies in the East Branch. Even when they are resting in the runs and not spawning, they are spooky. The reason is both the skinny water and the number of anglers. Many times, making an approach on your knees can pay off here, along with smaller, less gaudy flies. It is also best to present the nymph or streamer so that fish notice it without spooking.

Just upstream from Legget Road, there is a lamprey barrier that allows steelhead to move upstream, but most of the suckers are stopped by it. This is good news when fishing for steelies because the large numbers of suckers can alert the steelhead when you spook them. It should be noted that you are not allowed to fish in the area just below the lamprey barrier until trout season opens. Whittemore Road is the next bridge above the Lamprey Barrier, and fishing above and below it is a good plan early in the run or any time you want to try to intercept steelhead on their way to the gravel.

The East Branch's proximity to the main Au Gres and the Rifle offers the steelheader many options. For example, as just described above, when the suckers chase you off the Rifle, you can move to the East Branch. This river also clears faster than the Rifle or Au Gres. Conversely, if it is a beautiful April Saturday, you probably want to avoid the very crowded East Branch of the Au Gres. The Rifle will give you lots more room, and if it is a bright day, you might opt for the dingier and even less fished waters of the Au Gres. This trio of streams covers all the bases, especially in late April and early May.

Another close river is the Tawas River. It is a very short, slow-moving stream that is the outlet of Tawas Lake. Much of it flows through the towns of Tawas City and East Tawas and is an option when other rivers are too dirty, not to mention that there is a fairly good beach fishery at its mouth.

Au Sable River

Michigan's most famous trout stream is actually a large river system with many branches and a mainstream that changes greatly in character as it winds its way from the middle of the state to Lake Huron. Almost 180 miles of the mainstream Au Sable and its tributaries are classified as blue ribbon trout water. In this system you can fish for small to medium-sized browns, rainbows, and brookies, trophy browns, the largest steelhead run from Lake Huron, and everything in between.

The famous Au Sable River.

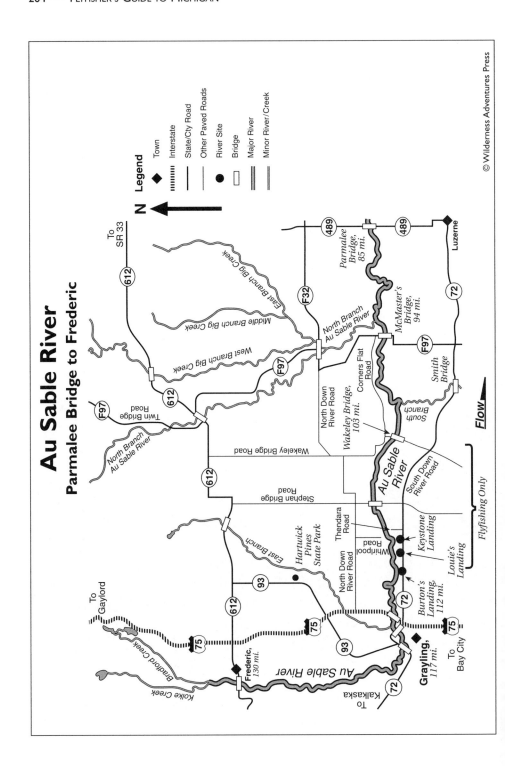

Au Sable River
Parmalee Bridge to Frederic

Legend

- ◆ Town
- Interstate
- State/Cty Road
- Other Paved Roads
- ● River Site
- ☐ Bridge
- Major River
- Minor River/Creek

N

To SR 33

To Gaylord

To Kalkaska

To Bay City

Frederic, 130 mi.

Grayling, 117 mi.

Luzerne

Parmalee Bridge, 85 mi.

McMaster's Bridge, 94 mi.

Smith Bridge

Wakeley Bridge, 103 mi.

Burton's Landing, 112 mi.

Keystone Landing

Louie's Landing

Hartwick Pines State Park

Flyfishing Only

Flow

Au Sable River

North Branch Au Sable River

East Branch Big Creek

Middle Branch Big Creek

West Branch Big Creek

North Branch Au Sable River

South Branch

East Branch

Bradford Creek

Kolke Creek

Twin Bridge Road

Corners Flat Road

North Down River Road

Wakeley Bridge Road

Stephan Bridge Road

Thendara Road

Whirlpool Road

North Down River Road

South Down River Road

© Wilderness Adventures Press

Au Sable River
McKinley to McMaster's Bridge

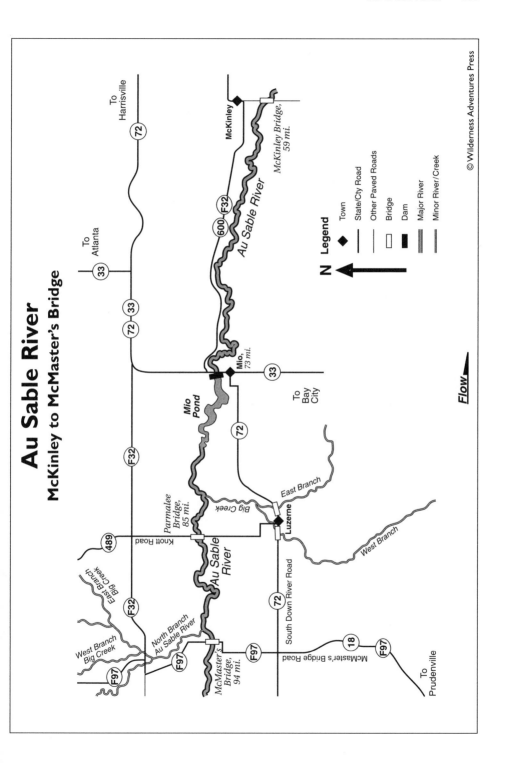

Legend

◆ Town

| State/City Road

| Other Paved Roads

□ Bridge

■ Dam

Major River

Minor River/Creek

N

© Wilderness Adventures Press

To Harrisville

72

To Atlanta

33

33

72

F32

McKinley

600 F32

Au Sable River

McKinley Bridge, 59 mi.

Mio Pond

Mio, 73 mi.

33

72

To Bay City

East Branch

Luzerne

West Branch

Parmalee Bridge, 85 mi.

Big Creek

Knott Road

489

F32

Au Sable River

West Branch Big Creek

East Branch Big Creek

North Branch Au Sable River

F97

F97

McMaster's Bridge, 94 mi.

South Down River Road

72

F97

McMaster's Bridge Road

18

F97

To Prudenville

Flow

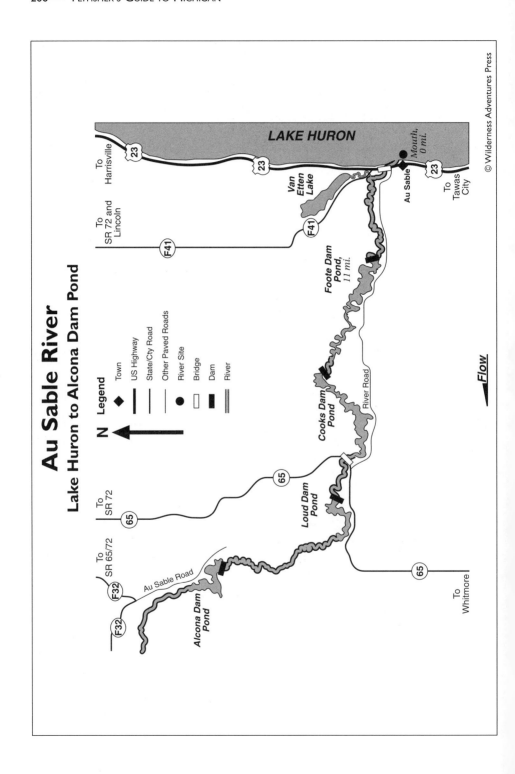

Flyfishing's next generation gets some mentoring on the Au Sable River.

The Au Sable begins when Kolke and Bradford Creeks come together just north of Frederick. In a few short miles, groundwater further cools the water, and the river becomes large enough to be flyfished at County Road 612 just west of Frederick. This is also the beginning of a 79-mile stretch of blue ribbon trout water. While brook trout dominate in this headwater stretch, browns are also present. Somewhat limited access and the presence of many other nearby choices result in relatively light fishing pressure on this section of the Au Sable.

The river makes a sharp turn to the east just above the storied fishing town of Grayling. Here the East Branch adds its cold water to the river and is also the location of probably the heaviest aluminum hatch in the state. Luckily, trout are used to the canoes, so you can still have a great day on the water.

The "Holy Waters" of the Au Sable begin a few miles downstream from Grayling at Burton's Landing. From here to Wakeley Bridge, fishing is limited to flies only, and all trout must be released. It is, however, open to fishing year-round. Louie's and Keystone Landings provide additional access just downstream from Burton's Landing, and all three are reached from South Down River Road. Thendara Road also provides access to the Holy Water from the south. From North Down River, the river can be reached from the end of Whirlpool Road and downstream about a mile at Trout Unlimited's Guide's Rest. Stephan's Bridge Road crosses the Au Sable in the center of the fly-only water and provides good access to this special reach. Gates Au Sable Lodge is located at Stephan's bridge and features a full service Orvis shop in case you need some flies or tackle. Recently, I was treated to their fine hospitality as an instructor for a youth fishing and conservation school sponsored by Trout Unlimited. The kids fished the river in front of the lodge and had a great time.

Downstream from Stephan's Bridge, access to the remaining fly-only water is more limited, but this can mean more room to fish for the ambitious angler. Pine River Road off of the North Down River Road provides access about a mile downstream from Stephan's Bridge. This is fine trout water, and floating from Stephan's to Wakeley Bridge is a great way to see it all and fish where you like.

Even though trout numbers in the upper Au Sable are good, growth has been below average in recent years. This is a reversal for what used to be one of the reaches where many large browns could be caught. Ironically, the Clean Water Act is probably the main reason that trout don't grow as fast in the "Holy Waters" as they used to. The poorly treated sanitary sewage from Grayling added lots of nutrients to the river, and trout responded to the enriched food chain. Of course, with a higher population this same situation might result in dissolved oxygen sags and fish kills. Currently, there are discussions on how to fertilize the Au Sable naturally in order to increase trout production and growth, possibly through the controlled addition of leaves.

At any rate, there is still excellent fishing to be found in the fly-only reach. The Hendrickson hatch starts the season off, and a diverse aquatic insect population keeps hatches happening all summer. Because of the good gradient and scarce silt beds, the only hatches that are relatively sparse here are the burrowing mayflies, such as the Hex and drakes. Not to worry, though, as nearby waters have good hatches of these mayflies that bring big fish to the surface. As you might expect, trout are quite sophisticated in this reach, so it is important to match the hatch well, both in size and color.

A few miles below Wakeley Bridge, the Au Sable changes character, becoming wide, slow, and sand-bottomed. Known as the "stillwaters," this reach is where the South Branch of the Au Sable adds its strong flow. The deep bend holes hide large brown trout, and there is a good Hex hatch in this part of the river. Access is provided at the White Pine Campground on the north side of the mainstream near the South Branch mouth and at Conner's Flat, on the road of the same name, about 2 miles upstream from McMasters Bridge Road on the north side of the river. You can also reach the river at the Rainbow Bend Campground, about a mile upstream from McMasters Bridge Road.

Above McMasters Bridge, there is once again gravel and good current at Rainbow Bend access site. The even faster North Branch joins the mainstream about a mile

*Plying the Au Sable
River from a boat.*

below McMasters, creating what amounts to a 150- to 200-foot-wide spring creek. An awesome trout river! Big water means big trout, and browns in the 20- to 25-inch range are caught here during the Hex hatch each year. Big Creek helps keep the river cool with a shot of cold water below Parmalee Bridge. Even though the blue ribbon designation officially ends at Luzerne Township Park, there are big brown trout down into the upper backwaters of Mio Pond. The prolific *Hexagenia* hatch continues down into this water. There is a campground and access at both Parmalee Bridge and the Luzerne Township Park.

While the river can still be waded here in the summertime, it can be tough to cross. Because of this and the relatively few access sites, many opt to float it in crafts ranging from float tubes to Au Sable River boats, which are specially designed flat-bottomed boats that are poled down the river. The pole gives the stern man great boat control, while the angler in front casts to rising trout or likely holding spots.

Despite the large impoundment created by the Mio Dam, the Au Sable continues to support trout below it. Trout numbers are not as high here, but they do grow fast. For this reason, there are special regulations for the reach between Mio and McKinley Bridge. Only flies and artificial lures are allowed, and the possession limit is 2 trout per day with a 15-inch minimum size for browns and 12 inches for rainbows and brookies. Floating all the way from Mio to McKinley Bridge doesn't leave much fishing time unless you start early and take all day. Pulling out at Comins Flat, about halfway through the stretch, gives you a lot more time to fish. My penchant for moving right along swimming streamers caused me to do the whole bridge-to-bridge reach the last time I fished it. County Road 600 (McKinley Road) parallels the river on the north side, and there is mostly national forest land between the road and the river, with forest service roads and two-tracks leading to the water, making the walk shorter.

With each dam, trout numbers continue to decrease, but there are some really large browns below Alcona Dam, due to the cooling water that flows from the South Branch River into this reach. There is hardly any free-flowing river from the backwaters of the Loud Dam to Foote Dam. Below Foote Dam, there is a tremendous fishery for anadromous fish, which will be covered after checking out the flyfishing opportunities on the Au Sable's major tributaries.

East Branch of the Au Sable

The East Branch of the Au Sable could probably be described as the forgotten branch. While there is no special "quality water" or fame for this small stream, the water is cold and trout are there. The East Branch starts out warm due to lakes in its headwaters north of Grayling but soon cools down to brook trout water. By the time the stream exits Hartwick Pines State Park, it is large enough to fish with a fly rod and is classified as a blue ribbon trout stream for the rest of its length.

Brown trout become increasingly numerous downstream, but brookies continue to be part of the catch all the way to the mainstream. Most hatches that appear on the mainstream, including the Hex hatch, also occur on the East Branch. Remember that the water is colder, so the peaks might occur a few days later on the East Branch.

There is one hatch that is almost nonexistent on the Au Sable's uppermost large tributary—the aluminum. Thus, if the canoe traffic drives you off the "Holy Water" but you still want to do some midday fishing, keep the East Branch in mind. There are some nice trout to fool here despite the fact that it is "catch and keep" water with no limitations on gear. North Down River Road in Grayling at the old fish hatchery provides access to the East Branch. If you can get somebody to drop you off, you can enter a lightly fished area of the river from I-75. Babbitt Road crosses the river about a mile upstream from the expressway, and Lewiston Grade Road provides access at the beginning of the blue ribbon water.

South Branch of the Au Sable

The South Branch is best known for its big browns and the Hex hatch. Ironically, it gets off to a real poor start as a trout stream. As the outlet of Lake St. Helen, it remains too warm for trout almost all the way to Roscommon. Robinson and Beaver

A fish well worth recording—a 26-inch, 6.5-pound stream-resident brown trout.

Creeks help cool down the river at Roscommon, and it really becomes a first rate trout river at Chase Bridge. This coincides with the beginning of the fly-only water that continues all the way to the mouth of the river. For the first 4 miles below Chase Bridge until the signs at the Lower High Banks, it is catch and release. Starting with the opener in 2000, the entire fly-only reach will be catch and release.

A special feature of the South Branch between Chase and Smith Bridges is the land along both banks that was donated by George Mason. Appropriately called the Mason Tract, development and logging are not permitted along the river here, so it will remain wild and natural. Access is excellent from the west side of the river throughout the Tract, however, most of the primitive but easily driven roads will leave you with a short walk to the river.

Because hatches on the South Branch are prolific and varied, something is usually happening throughout the season. The real draws to the South Branch are the brown drake and *Hexagenia* hatches in the lower half of the river. From early June into July, these large, burrowing mayflies bring big browns to the surface. The Hex hatch usually happens after dark, but you can catch browns 20 inches and larger rising to brown drakes in the evening and the first hour of daylight the next morning. Like the commercial, sometimes they "can't stop eating 'em." I have caught browns looking as though they had a big abdominal tumor that regurgitated flies in my hand when I unhooked them. Because it is a usually a bit warmer than the "Holy Water" and the North Branch, hatches can start a few days earlier on the South Branch.

South Branch of the Au Sable River

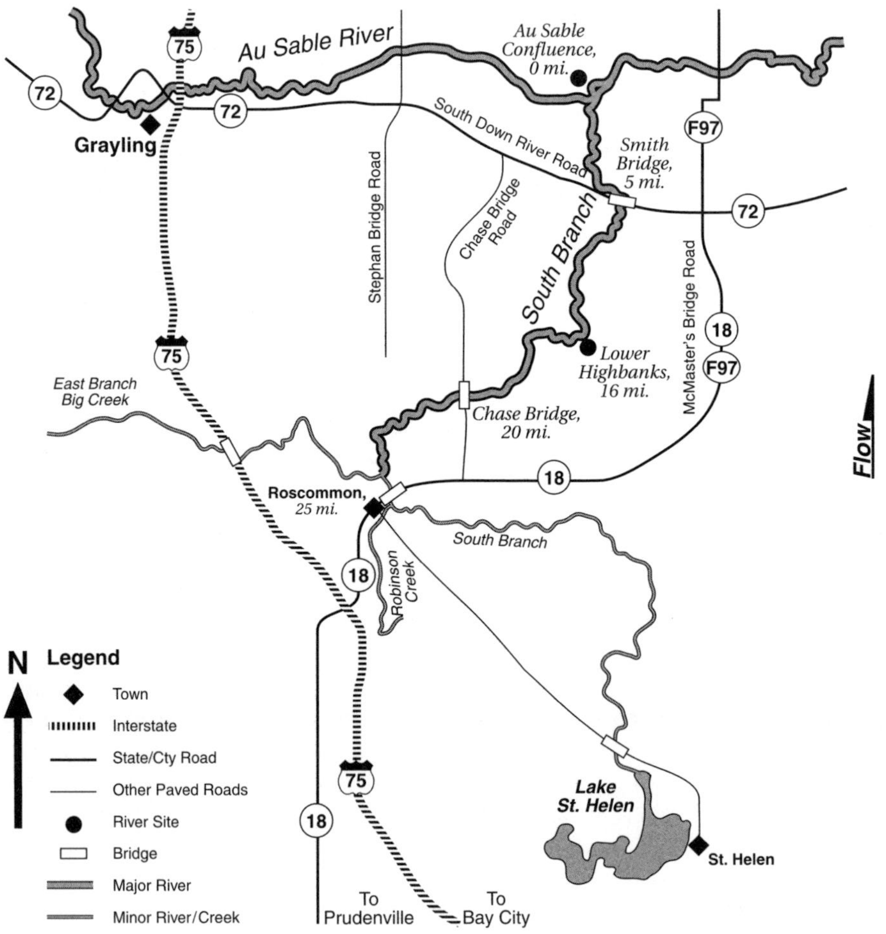

Au Sable River

75

72

72

Grayling

Au Sable Confluence, 0 mi.

South Down River Road

F97

Smith Bridge, 5 mi.

72

Stephan Bridge Road

Chase Bridge Road

South Branch

18

Lower Highbanks, 16 mi.

F97

McMaster's Bridge Road

75

East Branch Big Creek

Chase Bridge, 20 mi.

18

Roscommon, 25 mi.

18

South Branch

Robinson Creek

N

Legend

◆ Town

|||||||| Interstate

—— State/Cty Road

—— Other Paved Roads

● River Site

▢ Bridge

▬ Major River

▬ Minor River/Creek

75

18

To Prudenville

To Bay City

Lake St. Helen

St. Helen

Flow

© Wilderness Adventures Press

South Branch of the Au Sable.

Upstream from Smith Bridge, wading is relatively easy, but the river can be a bit tougher to navigate as you get closer to the mainstream. This, coupled with more private land along the banks, makes floating a good option. While brown trout are the dominant species throughout most of the South Branch, there are also lots of brookies, especially in the upper river. As you get nearer the mainstream, some rainbows are likely, as well.

There are sections in the lower reaches of both Robinson and Beaver Creeks that can be flyfished. Good-sized brook trout, along with some browns, are present in these small streams. During hot spells, trout can be found moving out of the South Branch and into these tributaries to cool off, which means that there can be a real concentration of big trout in the lower ends of both creeks. In addition to fishing up the creeks from the river, you can get on Beaver Creek at Stephan Bridge Road and Robinson Creek at numerous road crossings in Roscommon.

North Branch of the Au Sable River

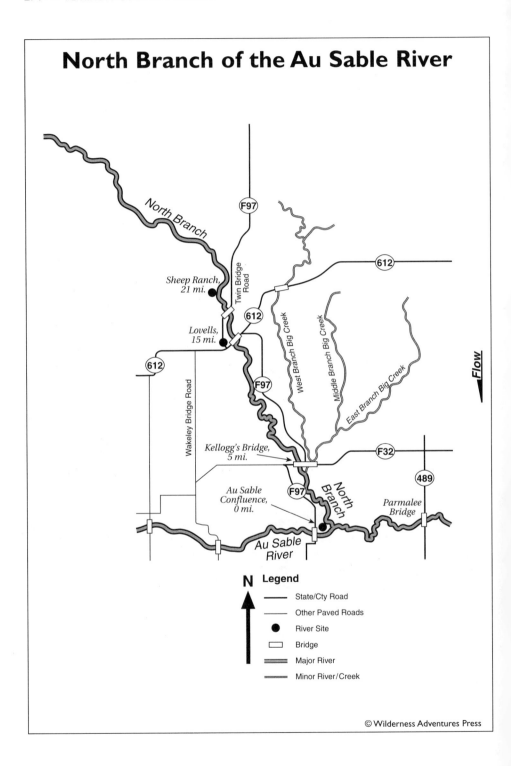

North Branch

F97

612

Sheep Ranch, 21 mi.

Twin Bridge Road

612

Lovells, 15 mi.

West Branch Big Creek

Middle Branch Big Creek

East Branch Big Creek

Flow

612

Wakeley Bridge Road

F97

Kellogg's Bridge, 5 mi.

F32

489

Au Sable Confluence, 0 mi.

F97

North Branch

Parmalee Bridge

Au Sable River

N

Legend

— State/Cty Road

— Other Paved Roads

● River Site

▭ Bridge

▨ Major River

— Minor River/Creek

© Wilderness Adventures Press

North Branch of the Au Sable

Like the other branches and mainstream, the North Branch starts out warm near Otsego Lake. Springs slowly cool it down, and it becomes a first rate trout stream when it enters Crawford County. The Sheep Ranch public access site, just above the county line, also marks the beginning of the artificial flies only stretch that continues to the mouth of the North Branch. At 21 miles, this is the longest reach of fly-only water in the state.

Brook trout are the dominant species in the upper river and continue to be numerous all the way to the mouth. Brown trout are also present throughout the stream, with increasing numbers as you go downstream. This river is very wader friendly and does not receive as much angling pressure as the South Branch and the mainstream Au Sable. Because much of the upper river is shallow with lots of gravel and rocks, it is not canoed heavily either. In general, trout are not as big in the North Branch, but there are still lunker brown possibilities in the mid and lower reaches. Twin Bridge Road and County Road 612 crossings provide additional access to the upper North Branch.

Excellent fly hatches occur throughout the season on the North Branch, with Hendricksons, sulphurs, and brown drakes leading the parade. There is a modest Hex hatch, but it is mostly limited to the lower river near the mouth. Caddis hatches are also very good, and anglers do well fishing them as emergers throughout the season.

A major tributary to the North Branch is Big Creek, a stream that flows in below Kellogg Bridge and is colder than the North Branch. Big Creek splits into two branches, the East and West, a short distance upstream from North Down River Road and only about a mile from the North Branch. Luckily, both branches of Big Creek are still pretty open and large enough to flyfish. In fact, they are both classified as blue ribbon trout water for about 6 miles up from their juncture. The East Branch splits again, but the best fishing is found before this happens. Brook trout are present in good numbers in both branches, while browns tend to take over in the combined reach. While most of the trout are small to medium-sized in Big Creek, their numbers are good and they respond well to the abundant hatches in this stream. And you won't have as much competition because of the relatively tight casting quarters.

Big Creek

For unknown reasons, this sizable tributary to the Au Sable downstream from the juncture of the North Branch is also called Big Creek. It flows northward into the mainstream about 2 miles below Parmalee Bridge and really helps keep the Au Sable cool.

The water quality in Big Creek is very good, clear, and cold and consequently difficult to fish because of its transparency. To continue the similarity and confusion, this Big Creek also has an East and a West Branch. Because of mature forest and good flow, both branches can be flyfished, but the West Branch is a bit larger and has more miles of blue ribbon water. Brook trout abound in the upper reaches of Big Creek, especially the West Branch. They continue to be present in the combined stream, but browns and some rainbows also respond to presentations.

The fly hatches are good in Big Creek, but stealthy approaches coupled with long leaders and light tippets are the order of the day. Keep this stream in mind when the water gets on the warm side in the mainstream or when rains cloud the water in the bigger water. Brown Cabin and Randall Roads provide access to the mainstream, while M-72 crosses both the East and West Branches.

Another small tributary to the Au Sable is the South Branch River. Again, it seems like those who named the streams intended to keep us confused. This feeder joins the Au Sable well downstream from the famous tributary with a similar name. Even though there are lakes and ponds on the upper river, it supports a good brown trout population. Undercut banks and logs provide cover, and there are good hatches of mayflies and caddisflies.

Lower Au Sable

The Au Sable receives the largest stocking of steelhead smolts in the state below the last of its dams. Chinook salmon are also planted in this river, so the fly angler chasing anadromous fish can look to the Au Sable from September through May. The downside is that most of this water is difficult to wade. While the area below Foote Dam is fairly wadeable and there are some gravel bars downstream, an angler can be hard pressed to find a place to cross the river even in low water. In short, floating is the way to cover all the water. There is public access at Rea Road, half of a river mile below the dam, and at the Whirlpool Public Access Site on the south side of the Au Sable on River Road.

Chinook don't enter the river until September because it takes awhile to cool down all the impounded water upstream. A temporary weir diverts a portion of the chinook run into Van Etten Creek near the mouth where they are harvested, but plenty get upstream for a good fishery. Even though they don't allow fishing from the dam or in the river within 175 feet of it, there always seems to be a crowd there. Intercepting chinook downstream is a better way to fish, and chinook are more likely to strike bright streamers in the lower river.

There is a fairly good run of steelhead in the Au Sable in the fall, peaking in November and early December. Because the river doesn't freeze near the dam, fishing can continue all winter. The steelhead spring run occurs later than it does in some of the nearby streams because it takes awhile for ice to leave the impoundments and for the water to warm up. This fact, along with a large run, makes the Au Sable one of the best for May steelhead.

Due to natural reproduction and some straying, the Pine River, which flows into Van Etten Lake and then connects to the Au Sable as Van Etten Creek, also has a steelhead run. Even though this river is relatively short and small, there is room for flyfishing. The upstream limit for year-round fishing is Road F-41. A number of county road bridge crossings provide access.

In summer the South Branch of the Pine provides the best trout fishing. Browns and brookies are present, along with juvenile steelhead. There are also some goodsized browns in the short main branch, but the Pine becomes fairly marginal for trout because of the addition of warm water from the East Branch and other warm tributaries. A plus for the lower Pine is that a Hex hatch occurs there. The stream also has good Hendrickson and brown drake hatches.

Stream Facts: Au Sable River

Seasons
- Open all year below Foote Dam.
- Also open all year between Burton's Landing and Wakeley Bridge, but all trout must be released.
- Most of the remainder of the Au Sable and its tributaries are designated trout streams and are open from the last Saturday in April through September 30.

Special Regulations
- Size limit for all trout and salmon below Foote Dam between October 1 and last Saturday in April is 15 inches, and the possession limit is 3.
- The fly-only reaches on the North and South Branches of the Au Sable allow fishing all year starting April 29, 2000. Part of the South Branch water is catch and release.
- The size limit is increased to 10 inches for brown and rainbow trout, and the possession limit is reduced to 5 trout.
- Between Mio Dam and McKinley Bridge, the minimum size limit is 15 inches for brown trout and 12 inches for rainbow and brook trout.

Fish
- Resident brook, brown, and rainbow trout.
- Resident smallmouth and largemouth bass, northern pike, walleye, and channel catfish in the lower river and impoundments.
- Anadromous rainbow and brown trout, and chinook salmon below Foote Dam.
- Occasional lake trout and coho salmon.

River Miles
- Lake Huron — 0
- Foote Dam — 11
- McKinley Bridge — 59
- Mio — 73
- Parmalee Bridge — 85

- McMaster's Bridge — 94
- Wakeley Bridge — 103
- Burton's Landing — 112
- Grayling — 117
- Frederick — 130

South Branch
- Mainstream — 0
- M-72 Bridge — 5
- Lower Highbanks — 16

- Chase Bridge — 20
- Roscommon — 25

North Branch
- Mainstream — 0
- Kellogs Bridge — 5

- Mainstream — 0
- Lovells — 21

River Characteristics
- A classic trout stream — sand and gravel-bottomed with a wide variety of habitat.
- It is a moderate to fairly high gradient stream that greatly increases in size through the influx of tributaries and springs.
- The lower river is almost completely impounded.
- There is a big water anadromous fishery below Foote Dam.

River Access
- Access available at all the landmarks on the mainstream and tributaries noted above with river miles.
- Many developed public access sites in addition to the road crossings, and these are noted on maps.

AU SABLE RIVER MAJOR HATCHES

Insect	Jan	Feb	Mar	Apr	May	Jun	July	Aug	Sep	Oct	Nov	Dec	Time	Fly Patterns
Hendrickson				▓	▓								M/A	Hendrickson #12–14; Rusty's Spinner; Red Quill; Adams; Quill Gordon
Blue-winged Olive					▓	▓	▓	▓					A	Blue-winged Olive #18–20; Sparkle Dun Baetis; Iron Dun; Olive CDC Mayfly Dun
Little Black Caddis				▓	▓	▓	▓	▓					A	Little Black Caddis #16–18; Griffith's Gnat; CDC Emerging Caddis Brown; Black Ant
Grannom					▓	▓	▓						M/A	Grannom #14–16; Medium Brown Sedge; Elk Caddis Brown-olive
Net-building Caddis				▓	▓	▓	▓	▓	▓	▓			M/A	Spotted Sedge #16–18; Eastern Elk Wing Caddis; Goddard Caddis
Sulphur Dun						▓	▓						A/E	Sulphur Dun #16; Pale Morning Dun; CDC Comparadun Yellow; Pale Evening Dun
March Brown						▓							M/A	March Brown #12–14; Dark Cahill; Gray Fox; Ginger Quill
Gray Drake						▓							E	Gray Drake #12–14; Gray Adams
Brown Drake						▓							E	Brown Drake #10–12; Adams; CDC Brown
Hexagenia						▓	▓						E	Hex #4–8; Great Olive-winged Drake; Spring's Wiggler; Hare's Ear
Trico							▓	▓	▓	▓			M	Tiny White Wing Black #24–28; Parachute Adams; CDC Trico; Spent Wing Trico
White Fly								▓	▓				E	White Fly #12–14; White Miller
Streamers	▓	▓	▓	▓	▓	▓	▓	▓	▓	▓	▓	▓	M/A/E	Woolly Buggers #6–12; Clouser's Minnow; Muddler Minnows; BC Craw; Matukas
Terrestrials					▓	▓	▓	▓	▓				M/A/E	Woolly Worm #8–12; BC Spider; Letort Cricket; Joe's Hopper #6–10; Dave's Hopper; Dropper Hopper

HATCH TIME CODE: M = morning; A = afternoon; E = evening.

Thunder Bay River

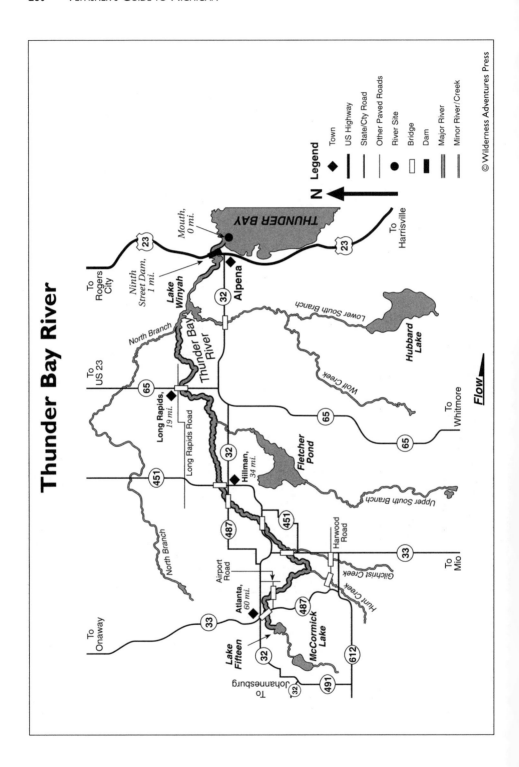

Legend

N

Town
US Highway
State/Cty Road
Other Paved Roads
River Site
Bridge
Dam
Major River
Minor River/Creek

© Wilderness Adventures Press

THUNDER BAY

Mouth, 0 mi.
Ninth Street Dam, 1 mi.
Lake Winyah
To Rogers City
To 23
Alpena
32
To 23
To Harrisville

Lower South Branch
North Branch
Thunder Bay River
Hubbard Lake
To US 23
65
Long Rapids, 19 mi.
Wolf Creek

Flow

Long Rapids Road
65
451
32
Hillman, 34 mi.
Fletcher Pond
65
To Whitmore
65

North Branch
Upper South Branch
487
451
Harwood Road
33
To Mio

Airport Road
Gilchrist Creek
Atlanta, 60 mi.
33
487
Hunt Creek
McCormick Lake
To Onaway
Lake Fifteen
32
612
To Johannesburg
32
491

THUNDER BAY RIVER

The Thunder Bay is a river of many branches. Unfortunately, dam builders have also impounded it frequently. The upper main stream flows through both McCormick Lake and Lake Fifteen in its headwaters and is then impounded at Atlanta. Despite all of this stillwater, there are some trout present below Atlanta, where it can be flyfished.

Between Atlanta and Hillman, Thunder Bay River gathers the icy waters of Hunt and Gilchrist Creeks, which help cool the mainstream and offset the fact that it becomes much wider and more exposed to the sun. Fair to good trout fishing, mainly for browns along with brook trout and a few rainbows, continues until the river is impounded by a power dam in the small town of Hillman. If the weather is hot, concentrating near the mouths of Hunt and Gilchrist Creeks can pay dividends. The river is relatively lightly fished despite good access at a number of bridges. County Road 487 in Atlanta, Airport Road, Red Bridge, and Eichorn Bridge divide the upper river into three approximately equal sections of about a mile in length.

Hunt Creek deserves strong mention here as an excellent small wild brook and brown trout stream, with an emphasis on brookies in its upper reaches. There is a fisheries research station on the headwaters of this creek, and once it leaves the station, it is classified as a blue ribbon trout stream. Though casting room is tight, the mature forest bordering much of the creek helps provide enough room to properly

Thunder Bay River at the 9th Street Dam.

present a fly. Schmallers Road provides access to the lower end of Hunt Creek, where you can also wade down to the Thunder Bay River from the bridge. Harwood and CR-612 cross the creek farther upstream.

Gilchrist Creek, which parallels Hunt Creek and also offers excellent small stream trout action, offers a good chance to accomplish the triple double — catching 10-inch or better brown, brook, and rainbow trout on the same outing. Despite its relatively small size, its lower reaches are also classified as blue ribbon water, where there is a chance for some browns pushing 20 inches. Access is available at several bridges (CR-451 and Harwood and CR-612 also cross the Gilchrist) and a county park along M-33.

Getting back to the Thunder Bay, the river gets on the warm side for trout below Hillman. While there is still a chance to hook a large brown below this town, you are more apt to be exercising smallmouth and rock bass along with a few pike. In the spring, some walleyes also move up to Hillman from the Seven Mile Dam impoundment. The addition of the Upper South Branch's warm waters ends the chance for any trout, but the increased flow enhances the smallmouth and walleye possibilities.

Thunder Bay River even looks like a smallmouth stream at this point, with lots of big rocks and logs providing cover. Despite becoming a really good-sized river, it is quite wadeable. There is good access at the Long Rapids County Park where M-65 crosses the river, and this site is probably the middle of the best smallmouth water. Floating is also a promising option, especially where bridges are quite far apart. There is a good crayfish population as well as minnows and burrowing mayflies, so take crayfish and minnow imitating streamers, along with some brown drake and *Hexagenia* nymphs and dries.

The North and Lower South Branches of the Thunder Bay join the mainstream in the Seven Mile Pond. Each of these branches is a warmwater stream. The better fishing occurs in the Lower South Branch, but smallmouth bass and northern pike can be caught in each, along with some walleyes. Wolf Creek, a major tributary to the Lower South Branch, is marginal trout water due to its temperature, being somewhat similar to the West Branch of the Muskegon. So the fact that it has some big brook trout, although not in any great numbers, is surprising since browns are usually considered better suited for marginal trout water. The best bet for brook trout in lower Wolf Creek is early in the season. Once summer arrives, it is principally a smallmouth stream on sections where it is large enough to flyfish.

The now quite large Thunder Bay River is pretty much continuously impounded from Seven Mile Pond down to the Ninth Street Dam in Alpena. Below this dam, the river is soon slowed by Lake Huron. At normal lake levels, the perceptible current runs out only a few hundred feet below the Ninth Street Bridge.

Even though there is relatively little water to drift or swim a fly, fishing can get quite exciting here for steelhead, chinook salmon, and lake-run brown trout. A modest run of pink salmon also occurs here, along with walleyes and suckers. In September, all four species of anadromous salmonids can be caught, but chances for steelhead are pretty slim, and browns will just be getting started. October is probably

Chinook salmon.

a better month for a grand slam. Because Lake Huron is so close, fish may move back and forth when they are not quite ready to make a spawning run.

November is the prime month for fall steelhead, and brown trout numbers also peak at this time. In winter the river stays open near the dam, but fishing can be kind of spotty. I would not travel to Alpena in winter just to fish the Thunder Bay River, but if I were going to be in the area, I would have my gear. This is definitely a fishery that caters to local anglers who can go down and try the river during a thaw and find out in a relatively short time whether it is going to be boon or bust.

In the spring, there is a good steelhead and walleye fishery. Water conditions are usually pretty stable, but during major snowmelt and rain runoff periods, even the impoundments will be muddy, and they will have to release more water. Steelhead normally continue to run the Thunder Bay River well into May. There is good access to the river at the dam on its southwest side.

Black seems to be Michigan's favorite river name, and there is a small stream south of Alpena that bears this name and is an option when larger anadromous rivers are unfishable. A good run of wild steelhead enters this river in the spring, but it quickly splits into two branches that are only marginally fishable with fly tackle. High Lake Huron levels make the lower river become unsuitable for wading, and most of the river flows through private land, making access a problem. Anglers solve this problem by launching a small boat or canoe at the public boat launch at the mouth and then paddling upstream into the river.

Stream Facts: Thunder Bay River

Seasons
- Open all year except for the parts of the upper river and tributaries that are designated trout streams. There the open season is from the last Saturday in April through September 30.
- Bass must be released between January 1 and the Saturday before Memorial Day.
- Walleye and northern pike must be released between March 15 and the last Saturday in April.

Special Regulations
- Size limit for all trout and salmon between October 1 and the last Saturday in April is 15 inches, and the possession limit is 3 fish.

Fish
- Brook, brown, and rainbow trout, smallmouth and largemouth bass, panfish, northern pike, walleye, and channel catfish.
- Anadromous rainbow and brown trout, chinook and pink salmon, occasional lake trout and coho salmon.

River Miles
- Lake Huron—0
- Ninth Street Dam—1
- Long Rapids—19
- Hilllman—34
- Atlanta—60

River Characteristics
- Considering latitude, it has a relatively short reach of trout water due to impoundments and warm tributaries.
- It has a moderate gradient with diverse habitat.
- When not impounded, most of upper river and tributaries can be waded and floated.

River Access
- Not as well developed as some northern Michigan rivers.
- Most access is at bridges.
- Access is available at the landmarks noted above with river miles.

THUNDER BAY RIVER AND OCQUEOC RIVER MAJOR HATCHES

Insect	Jan	Feb	Mar	Apr	May	Jun	July	Aug	Sep	Oct	Nov	Dec	Time	Fly Patterns
Black Stonefly			■	■									A	Early Black Stonefly #10–14
Hendrickson					■								M/A	Hendrickson #12–14; Quill Gordon; Red Quill; Adams
Blue-winged Olive					■	■	■	■					A	Blue-winged Olive #18–20; Sparkle Dun Baetis; Iron Dun; Olive CDC Mayfly Dun
Little Black Caddis					■	■	■	■					A	Little Black Caddis #16–18; Griffith's Gnat; CDC Emerging Caddis Brown; Black Ant
Grannom					■	■	■						M/A	Grannom #14–16; Medium Brown Sedge; Elk Caddis Brown-olive
Net-building Caddis						■	■	■	■	■			M/A	Spotted Sedge #16–18; Eastern Elk Wing Caddis; Goddard Caddis
Sulphur Dun						■	■						A/E	Sulphur Dun #16; Pale Morning Dun; CDC Comparadun Yellow; Pale Evening Dun
March Brown						■							M/A	March Brown #12–14; Dark Cahill; Gray Fox; Ginger Quill
Gray Drake						■	■						E	Gray Drake #12–14; Gray Adams
Brown Drake						■							E	Brown Drake #10–12; Adams; CDC Brown Drake
Hexagenia						■	■						E	Hex #4–8; Great Olive-winged Drake; Spring's Wiggler; Hare's Ear
Trico							■	■	■				M	Tiny White Wing Black #24–28; Parachute Adams; CDC Trico; Spent Wing Trico
White Fly									■				E	White Fly #12–14; White Miller
Streamers	■	■	■	■	■	■	■	■	■	■	■	■	M/A/E	Woolly Buggers #6–12; Clouser's Minnow; Muddler Minnows; BC Craw; Matukas
Terrestrials					■	■	■	■	■				M/A/E	Woolly Worm #8–12; BC Spider; Letort Cricket; Joe's Hopper #6–10; Dave's Hopper; Dropper Hopper

HATCH TIME CODE: M = morning; A = afternoon; E = evening.

Ocqueoc River

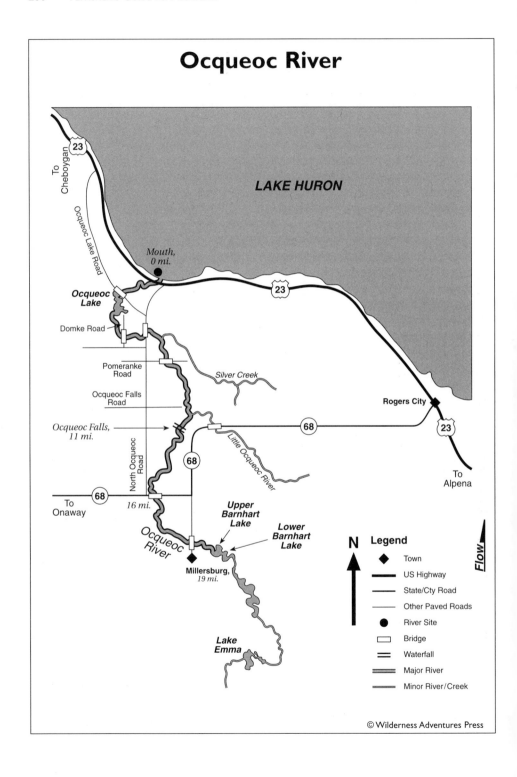

LAKE HURON

To Cheboygan

Ocqueoc Lake Road

Mouth, 0 mi.

Ocqueoc Lake

Domke Road

Pomeranke Road

Silver Creek

Ocqueoc Falls Road

Ocqueoc Falls, 11 mi.

North Ocqueoc Road

Little Ocqueoc River

Rogers City

To Alpena

To Onaway

16 mi.

Upper Barnhart Lake

Lower Barnhart Lake

Ocqueoc River

Millersburg, 19 mi.

Lake Emma

N

Legend
- ◆ Town
- ━━ US Highway
- ── State/Cty Road
- ── Other Paved Roads
- ● River Site
- ▭ Bridge
- ═ Waterfall
- ▬ Major River
- ── Minor River/Creek

Flow

© Wilderness Adventures Press

OCQUEOC RIVER

The Ocqueoc River in the northeast corner of the Lower Peninsula doesn't cause any identity problems with any other river in the state, or for that matter, the country. Starting out as a warmwater stream, this small river ends up the same way. But in between, it provides marginal habitat for trout and cascades over a falls.

Above the falls there are some opportunities to try for warmwater fish, such as smallmouth bass, northern pike, and panfish, but these fish tend to be small. Below the falls, both the Little Ocqueoc River and springs cool the river down. While it is classified as marginal trout water, there is a carryover of browns and brook trout. There is some natural reproduction of trout, steelhead, and salmon in the Little Ocqueoc. With Silver Creek's additional cold water farther downstream, browns are present in logjams all the way down to Ocqueoc Lake. Below this natural lake, the river again supports some bass and pike.

A number of bridges provides good access to the Ocqueoc. There are hiking trails and a campground at the falls. US 23 and Ocqueoc Lake Road crossings allow access to the river below Ocqueoc Lake, while Domke, Ocqueoc, and Pomeranke Roads cross the river between the lake and the falls.

Most anglers travel to the Ocqueoc to fish its runs of anadromous fish. Steelhead smolts are stocked, and there is natural reproduction of chinook, coho, and pink salmon. Lake Huron browns also migrate up the river. In the fall, you can often can see your quarry in the Ocqueoc, making for some interesting sightfishing. This stream is a very easy to wade, and locating the holding water is also a breeze. Chinook and pink salmon enter the river in early September, and cohos and browns follow later in the month. Steelhead runs in the fall are not dependable, but when good rains do come, there can be a fine run of silver rainbows. Spring is a better time to catch these fish, and because the river is small and has headwater lakes, it clears relatively quickly after a runoff event in the spring.

Though you can float in a canoe all the way from the falls to the mouth, you could be dragging it when there is low water. And on top of that, Ocqueoc Lake can be a long paddle when there is a headwind. All in all, the river is so small that I think wading is a better way to fish it.

Stream Facts: Ocqueoc River

Seasons
- Open all year downstream from Barnhart Lake.
- Bass must be released between January 1 and the Saturday before Memorial Day.
- Walleyes and northern pike must be released between March 15 and the last Saturday in April.

Special Regulations
- Size limit for all trout and salmon between October 1 and the last Saturday in April is 15 inches, and the possession limit is 3.

Fish
- Resident smallmouth and largemouth bass, northern pike, walleye; brown, brook, and rainbow trout.
- Anadromous brown and rainbow trout; chinook, coho, and pink salmon.

River Miles
- Lake Huron—0
- Ocqueoc Falls—11
- M-68—16
- Millersburg—19

River Characteristics
- This is a small river with a relatively low gradient except for Ocqueoc Falls, which is about a 10-foot drop.
- There are several natural lakes in the river system.
- Riverine sections are easily waded, but the stream is on the small side for floating.

River Access
- Access is mostly limited to bridges, but they are fairly numerous and evenly spaced.
- Access is available at each landmark noted above with river miles.

BLACK RIVER

For Michigan's brook trout anglers, this is *the* Black River. There may be a half dozen other Black Rivers in Michigan, but when you are talking about *Salvelinus fontinalis*, this is the river that anglers think of. The upper part of this Black has long had the reputation of being Michigan's premier wild brook trout stream.

The Black rises in the northeast corner of Otsego County and becomes "officially" large enough to flyfish at McKinnon's Bend, where there is a public access site off of Black River Trail. Above here, you can coax brookies out with a fly rod, but this location marks the beginning of the river's blue ribbon water. At this point, the Black is less than 2 miles from the Pigeon River, and these two streams, along with the Sturgeon, join before flowing into Lake Huron.

A very long time ago just a short distance from McKinnon's Bend, I caught my first significantly sized brook trout. This event sticks in my mind because I thought it was a bass as I was fighting it. The trout had a real green cast to it, and at 13 inches, it was about 4 inches longer than any brookie I had caught up to that time. I just couldn't believe it was a trout until I had the speckled beauty in my net. Tin Shanty Bridge on the road of the same name and the Town Corner Public Access Site also provide access to the upper Black River.

As it swings into the northwest corner of Montmorency County, the river's size continues to grow slowly. The East Branch of the Black flows in here and almost

Breached beaver dam on the Black River.

Black River

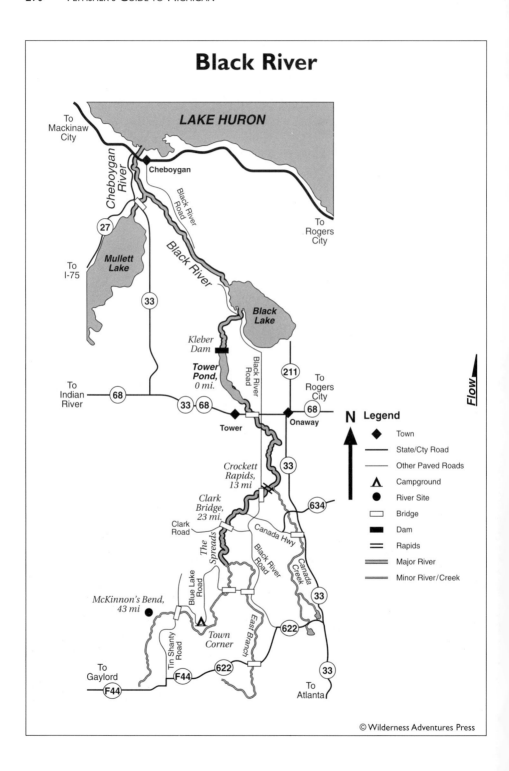

© Wilderness Adventures Press

The tight banks of the Black River.

doubles the size of the mainstream. This is a very high quality tributary that is generally cooler than the mainstream. The East Branch is also classified as a blue ribbon trout stream and is readily fished with a fly rod below County Road 622 (Shingle Mill Bridge). When the weather is real warm, the East Branch might be a better choice for fishing in the afternoon and evening. Blue Lake Road crosses both the East Branch and the main Black for access.

Downstream from the East Branch, the Black braids in a reach called The Spreads. From here it starts to warm significantly, and brook trout begin to be joined by some smallmouth bass and northern pike. Large brook trout continue to be present, and the Crockett Rapids area is a good one for brook trout in the mid teens. Clark Road crosses the river below the spreads, and Black River Road provides access just below Crockett Rapids. Attractor flies, such as the Royal Coachman and Adams, work on the Black River just as they do for any other brookie population. There are some creek chubs in the system, and streamers that imitate them are a good way to hook larger brook trout.

Canada Creek joins the Black a couple of miles downstream from Crockett Rapids and provides a welcome shot of cold water. This stream is also blue ribbon trout water and has a very good population of brook trout. It is fishable with a fly rod for about 12 miles up from the mainstream. Some of the large brook trout in the lower Black River move into Canada Creek during hot weather. Use a thermometer to check the temperature. As the main Black edges up near 70 degrees, you may want to try Canada Creek or the East Branch for more cooperative brook trout. Access is somewhat limited to Canada Creek, and much of it flows through private Canada Creek Club property. County Road 634 and Canada Highway provide some access, and ambitious anglers who wade a long way from the access point are likely to find exceptional fishing for wild brook trout.

While the DNR manages the Black as a brook trout stream, you may encounter some browns in the lower reaches. About 20 years ago, the DNR electrofished about 20 miles of the Black, removing all of the browns they caught and transplanting them into a nearby lake. Today, brookies continue to dominate, but the DNR suggests harvesting of legal-sized brown trout caught here. In order to encourage harvesting of northern pike, there is no size limit on these fish in the trout water of the Black.

Moving down to the town of Tower, the Black River is impounded, letting pike and smallmouth become the dominant species. Below the next dam, Kleber, where the river moves more rapidly, there is some good bass fishing. This is the reach where Michigan's largest lake sturgeon population spawns, and consequently, there is no angling allowed here in April and May. If you time it right, you can take a break from trout fishing and watch huge sturgeon go through their spawning ritual.

The river next flows into Black Lake, and below it, the river offers fishing for smallmouth, walleye, northern pike, and a few muskies. This is big, deep water, but its clarity allows the use of fly tackle and streamers. Finally, the Black joins the Cheboygan River, which is the combination of the Pigeon and Sturgeon Rivers.

Stream Facts: Black River

Seasons
- The upper river is open to fishing between the last Saturday in April until September 30.

Special Regulations
- Below Kleber Dam to Black Lake, the river is closed to fishing in April and May to protect spawning sturgeon.
- There is no size limit on northern pike.

Fish
- Brook and brown trout, northern pike, smallmouth bass, walleye, lake sturgeon.

River Miles
- Tower Pond—0
- Crockett Rapids—13
- Clark Bridge Road—23
- McKinnon's Bend—43

River Characteristics
- The upper river is not affected by impoundments and has a moderate gradient.
- Lots of bends and streamside vegetation provide good trout habitat.
- Easily waded in the upper reaches and floatable below the junction with the East Branch.
- The lower river is influenced by low head dams and the very large Black Lake.

River Access
- Access is available at road crossings, and there is a fair amount of public land with forest service roads and trails.
- Access is available at each landmark noted above with river miles.

Pigeon and Sturgeon Rivers

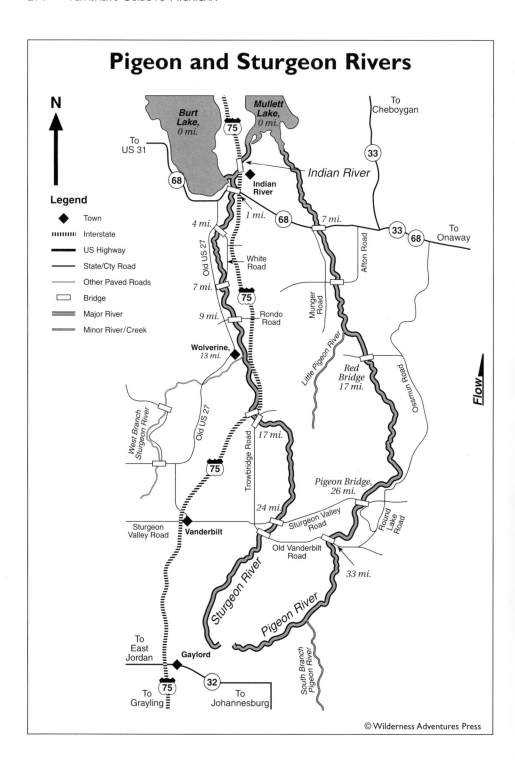

N

Legend

◆   Town

▦   Interstate

━   US Highway

─   State/Cty Road

─   Other Paved Roads

▭   Bridge

▓   Major River

▒   Minor River/Creek

Burt Lake, 0 mi.

Mullett Lake, 0 mi.

75

To Cheboygan

33

To US 31

68

Indian River

Indian River

1 mi.

68

7 mi.

33 68

To Onaway

4 mi.

Old US 27

White Road

Afton Road

7 mi.

75

Munger Road

9 mi.

Rondo Road

Little Pigeon River

Wolverine, 13 mi.

Red Bridge 17 mi.

Ossmun Road

Flow

West Branch Sturgeon River

Old US 27

Trowbridge Road

17 mi.

75

Pigeon Bridge, 26 mi.

24 mi.

Sturgeon Valley Road

Round Lake Road

Sturgeon Valley Road

Vanderbilt

Old Vanderbilt Road

33 mi.

Sturgeon River

Pigeon River

To East Jordan

Gaylord

South Branch Pigeon River

To Grayling

75

32

To Johannesburg

© Wilderness Adventures Press

PIGEON RIVER

The Pigeon is the namesake river for one of Michigan's best-known tracts of state land, the Pigeon River State Forest. This is elk country, and more people come to see elk than fish the river. This is good news for the avid trout chaser.

The Pigeon is the center river of the three north-flowing blue ribbon trout streams at the "Tip of the Mitt." There is a fairly even balance of all three species of trout in the crystal clear waters of the Pigeon. Interestingly, while the Sturgeon to the west is primarily inhabited with brown trout, along with rainbows that are the off-spring of lake-run fish, the Black holds mostly brook trout. It is as if you took the average numbers of all the trout in its two neighbors and placed them into the Pigeon.

The Pigeon's headwaters are just east of Gaylord, and it becomes classified as a blue ribbon trout stream just above Old Vanderbilt Road. You can flyfish the river upstream from here because of numerous meadow areas and mature forest, but there are also some real brushy cedar tangles intermingled with the more open areas. The only dam on the river occurs just a few miles downstream from Old Vanderbilt Road. While this small impoundment doesn't seem to overly warm the stream, the dam blocks fish movement.

The prime trout water starts at Pigeon Bridge and continues all the way to M-68. While there is access at a number of bridges, most of this reach flows through state forest land. There are also four state forest campgrounds spread out along the Pigeon's blue ribbon trout water. The stream has good gradient, with gravel and rocks being more common than sand. Abundant insect life is present in the cobble, and all the normal northern Michigan hatches occur. Spring comes later in this part of Michigan, so the hatches are usually a week or two behind those in the Manistee/Au Sable latitude. While brown drakes and *Hexagenia* are present, their numbers are not very high because of the lack of silt beds.

The Pigeon's size does not change much because of a lack of large tributaries. Rather, it grows slowly as springs flow in from the sides. The Little Pigeon joins the river below Red Bridge and does noticeably enlarge the flow. This tributary is a good but small trout stream and flows mostly through private land.

You can catch trout all the way to Mullett Lake, but the river braids some near the lake and starts to warm a bit. There are more silt beds here, providing more habitat for burrowing mayflies. There is an extended fall season until December 31 and an early spring opener on April 1 below M-68 that allows fishing for a modest run of browns and rainbows from Mullet Lake. This also gives the hardy stream angler more days to fish for the stream's resident trout.

Stream Facts: Pigeon River

Seasons
- Open from the last Saturday in April until September 30.
- Below M-68 the river will be open all year starting April 1, 2000.

Special Regulations
- Size limit for trout from October 1 through December 31 and April 1 through last Saturday in April is 16 inches, and the possession limit is 3 trout.

Fish
- Resident brook, brown, and rainbow trout, plus lake-run rainbows and browns.

River Miles
- Mullet Lake—0
- M-68—7
- Red Bridge—17
- Shingle Mill Bridge—26
- Old Vanderbilt Road—33

River Characteristics
- This is a small to medium-sized river with a moderate to brisk current and very clear water.
- It can be waded throughout, and the lower half can be canoed.
- Most of the adjacent land is undeveloped.

River Access
- Access is available at each landmark noted above with river miles.
- Many additional public access sites and public campgrounds are found on the river.

STURGEON RIVER

The Lower Peninsula's Sturgeon River stands out as one of Michigan's finest trout streams. From its headwaters to its mouth, it is a real gem. Basically a large spring creek, the Sturgeon is home to resident wild brown, rainbow, and brook trout. Burt Lake, a large, cold inland lake, provides runs of browns and rainbows that can attain weights up to 10 pounds.

The Sturgeon Bridge on Sturgeon Valley Road east of Vanderbilt is the beginning of the blue ribbon water and, by definition, where the stream becomes fishable with a fly rod. You can poke around above this bridge, making roll casts and dapping in the maze of logs that provide trout cover. Even below Sturgeon Bridge, you will earn your trout and get lots of exercise climbing over the wood. All three species are available in the upper reaches. The Green Timbers access site is located about 3 river miles downstream from Sturgeon Valley Road and is reached by a gravel road about a mile-and-a-half east of the bridge.

Once you near Trowbridge Road, the river becomes much faster with more room to cast. From here on down to the mouth, brown trout, along with the ever-present small rainbows, dominate. Occasionally, offspring of Burt Lake rainbows stay in the river, and a 12- to 16-inch, high-flying, red-striped beauty could surprise you. Trowbridge Road crosses the river again and then parallels it for most of the Sturgeon's lower water. One of my favorite outings is to wade from the lower to the upper bridge, which provides lots of fishing with an easy, short walk back to the car. For a shorter wade, fish from Secord Road up to the lower Trowbridge Road crossing.

The river is flows very quickly from here all the way to Burt Lake. Though it makes for some tough upstream wading, this is the best way to keep the wily browns in this stretch from knowing you are there. Swinging and twitching muddler, crayfish, woolly bugger, and other streamer patterns by the logs, root wads, and overhanging brush is a great way to catch the bigger brown trout. Because browns have to make a snap decision or the fly will be gone in the fast water, hard strikes are the rule. For this reason ,visible patterns that look good to eat are more important than an exact imitation.

While the current can make drag-free floats difficult, the fact that trout have little time to make up their mind results in some real fun fishing on top. There are good hatches of Hendrickson's, Cahills, and Tricos, along with many stoneflies and caddisflies. Enough logs trap silt and sand behind them that brown and gray drakes and *Hexagenia* mayflies are also present.

Just upstream from Wolverine, the West Branch joins the mainstream and increases the Sturgeon's size considerably. The river can be waded all the way to Burt Lake at summertime levels, but at this point the river is large enough to add floating to your options. Of course, canoeists have also discovered that the brisk current of the Sturgeon is fun to navigate with their sleek vessels, and most begin their trips in Wolverine. From here, a wading staff is an important accessory when you are on foot, and I even use one upstream when the river level is up.

Wolverine is also the upstream limit for the extended season on the Sturgeon's anadromous visitors from Burt Lake. Besides their spawning runs in the Sturgeon, browns and rainbows make what is called a "temperature run" in July and August. When the food-rich shoal areas of Burt Lake become uncomfortably warm, trout move into the cold flow of the Sturgeon, both to cool off and continue feeding. Believe me, 4- to 10-pound browns and rainbows rising to the Hex hatch is plenty exciting. I've found the best fishing for these lake-fattened trout is just up from the M-68 crossing in Indian River. At night here, you must use caution because the currents are strong and there are plenty of deep holes. Fishing streamers during the day for temperature-run trout from here all the way up to the first White Road crossing is a marathon wade. But you certainly put the odds in your favor for several encounters with monster trout.

Browns usually spawn in October, and many stay in the river until spring. A modest number of Burt Lake rainbows also run in the fall. These inland lake steelhead spawn in April and May. Opening day anglers often find these steelhead are still in the upper parts of the river. Since these trout are not actively feeding during their spawning run, streamers and large nymphs in bright exciter patterns often work best. Of course, they remain opportunistic, so egg flies work in the runs adjacent to spawning riffles.

West Branch of the Sturgeon

The West Branch could be described as a narrow version of the lower main Sturgeon River. Most of the time, you will be casting in the direction of the flow, and roll casts are needed on a frequent basis. The upstream limit for conventional flyfishing is probably at the Shingle Mill Bridge (Wilderness Road). You can still present a fly in meadow sections above this point, and the upper West Branch has more brook trout than the mainstream.

Several creeks and springs add their water to the West Branch, resulting in more room to cast from the old US-27 Bridge down to Wolverine. In general, trout are smaller here compared to the main Sturgeon, but what they lack in size they make up for in eagerness. The West Branch runs a bit colder than the Sturgeon, and this sometimes results in trout being attracted into its lower reaches during very hot weather. The West Branch can also be a good place to avoid canoes during the middle part of the day. Fishing the mainstream early and late and the West Branch during the middle of the day is a good plan, unless the Sturgeon's current makes you opt for a siesta instead.

When the Sturgeon leaves Burt Lake, it is called the Indian River until it flows into Mullet Lake. This is a short, slow stretch of water that doesn't really offer much for the fly angler. When it leaves Mullet Lake, it is called the Cheboygan River and continues to be called this all the way to Lake Huron. When the Black River joins it, this is really big, deep water that doesn't lend itself to flyfishing. It should be mentioned, though, that a dam blocks steelhead movement in the town of Cheboygan, and there is some opportunity to drift large, weighted flies here when other rivers are too muddy.

Stream Facts: Sturgeon River

Seasons
- Open all year below Afton Road Bridge in Wolverine and from the last Saturday in April until September 30 upstream from Afton Road.
- The Cheboygan River, the combination of the Sturgeon, Black and Pigeon Rivers, is also open all year below the Cheboygan Dam.

Special Regulations
- Size limit for trout between October 1 and the last Saturday in April is 15 inches, and the possession limit is 3 trout.

Fish
- Brook, brown, and rainbow trout.

River Miles
- Burt Lake—0
- M-68—1
- White Road—4
- White Road –7
- Rondo Road—9
- Wolverine—13
- Trowbridge Road—17
- Sturgeon Valley Road—24

River Characteristics
- The lower river is a high gradient, gravel-bottomed chute, while the upper river is slower moving and characterized by lots of logs in the water.
- A special run of lake-dwelling browns and rainbows occurs in mid to late summer.
- Careful wading is needed on one of Michigan's best and quickest trout streams.

River Access
- Access is available at each landmark noted above with river miles.
- Additional access is at road crossings, and there is a campground (Haakwood), downstream from Wolverine.

STURGEON, PIGEON, AND BLACK RIVERS MAJOR HATCHES

Insect	Jan	Feb	Mar	Apr	May	Jun	July	Aug	Sep	Oct	Nov	Dec	Time	Fly Patterns
Hendrickson					▮								M/A	Hendrickson #12–14; Quill Gordon; Red Quill; Adams
Blue-winged Olive								▮					A	Blue-winged Olive #18–20; Sparkle Dun Baetis; Iron Dun; Olive CDC Mayfly Dun
Little Black Caddis				▮					▮				A	Little Black Caddis #16–18; Griffith's Gnat; CDC Emerging Caddis Brown; Black Ant
Grannom								▮					M/A	Grannom #14–16; Medium Brown Sedge; Elk Caddis Brown-olive
Net-building Caddis					▮					▮			M/A	Spotted Sedge #16–18; Eastern Elk Wing Caddis; Goddard Caddis
Sulphur Dun						▮							A/E	Sulphur Dun #16; Pale Morning Dun; CDC Comparadun Yellow; Pale Evening Dun
March Brown						▮							M/A	March Brown #12–14; Dark Cahill; Gray Fox; Ginger Quill
Gray Drake						▮							E	Gray Drake #12–14; Gray Adams
Brown Drake						▮							E	Brown Drake #10–12; Adams; CDC Brown Drake
Hexagenia							▮						E	Hex #4–8; Great Olive-winged Drake; Spring's Wiggler; Hare's Ear
Trico								▮					M	Tiny White Wing Black #24–28; Parachute Adams; CDC Trico; Spent Wing Trico
White Fly									▮				E	White Fly #12–14; White Miller
Streamers												▮	M/A/E	Woolly Buggers #6–12; Clouser's Minnow; Muddler Minnows; BC Craw; Matukas
Terrestrials					▮				▮				M/A/E	Woolly Worm #8–12; BC Spider; Letort Cricket; Joe's Hopper #6–10; Dave's Hopper; Dropper Hopper

HATCH TIME CODE: M = morning; A = afternoon; E = evening.

Northeastern Lower Peninsula Hub Cities

Gaylord

Population – 3,256

ACCOMMODATIONS

Wildwood Chalet Motel Resort, 15665 Valley Drive (Wolverine 49799) / 616-525-8321

Alpine Motel, 2731 Old 27 South / 517-732-5733

Cedars Motel, 701 North Center Avenue / 517-732-4525

Hamlet Motel, 2418 Old 27 South / 517-732-4913

Hub Motel, 4349 Irma Avenue / 517-732-5668

Northernaire Motel & Cottages, 5119 Old 27 South / 517-732-4782

CAMPGROUNDS

Gaylord Alpine RV Park & Campground, 1315 West M-32 / 517-731-1772

Lakes of the North Campground / 517-616-585-6828

Michaywe Campground & Travel Trailer / 517-939-8723

Circle S Campground, 15247 Trowbridge Road (Wolverine 49799) / 616-525-8300

Raywood Campground, 2733 Lance Lake Road (Wolverine 49799) / 616-525-8373

Burt Lake State Park, 6635 State Park Drive (Indian River 49749) / 616-238-9392

Onaway State Park, 3622 M-211 (Onaway 49765) / 517-733-8279

RESTAURANTS

Albie's Pasties Subs Chicken & Salad, 1403 West Main Street / 517-732-8000

Arlene's Diner, 324 West Main Street / 517-732-5654

The Chatterbox, 610 South Otsego Avenue / 517-732-4880

Knickers, 833 West Main Street / 517-732-2431

Sweet Basil Restaurant & Lounge, 137 West Street / 517-732-8644

Willabee's Restaurant, 1961 South Old 27 / 517-732-1788

Country Lane Restaurant, 4853 Afton Road (Wolverine 49799) / 616-525-8311

FLY SHOPS AND SPORTING GOODS

Alphorn Sport Shop, 137 West Main Street / 517-732-5616

Wolverine True Value & Quiet Sports, 13386 Straits Hwy (Wolverine 49799) / 616-525-8370

AUTO SERVICE

R & R Auto Service & Repairs, 12420 Straits Hwy (Wolverine 49799) / 616-525-8388

Dr. John's Auto Clinic, 819 South Illinois Avenue / 517-732-7720

Fred's Garage, 1035-& W 1/2 Main / 517-732-8736

Rick's Auto Repair, 3967 Old 27 South / 517-732-4999

Ron's Auto & Wrecker Service, 611 W 4th Street / 517-732-3142

MEDICAL
Otsego Memorial Hospital / 517-732-1731

FOR MORE INFORMATION
Gaylord Otsego County Chamber of Commerce
125 South Otsego Avenue
Gaylord, MI 49735
517-732-4000

Grayling
Population – 1,994

ACCOMMODATIONS
AuSable Motel, 1348 I-75 Business Loop / 517-348-2825
Cedar Motel, 606 North James Street / 517-348-5884
Hospitality House, 1232 Business Loop / 517-348-8900
Warbler's Way Inn, I-75 North Business Loop / 517-348-4541
Woodland Motel, 267 South I-75 Business Loop / 517-348-9094
Fawn Motel, 8160 North Harrison Road (Roscommon 48653) / 517-821-6658
Spruce Motor Lodge, 900 Lake Street (Roscommon 48653) / 517-275-5781

CAMPGROUNDS
Great Circle Campground, 5370 West Marl Lake Road (Roscommon 48653) / 517-821-9486
Higgins Lake East Campgrounds, 2380 West Burdell Road (Roscommon 48653) / 517-821-6891
Heart of the North Jellystone, 370 West 4 Mile Road / 517-348-2157
River Park Campgrounds, 2607 Peters Road / 517-348-9092
Whispering Pines Rustic Cabins & RV, CR-612 / 517-348-8113
Hartwick Pines State Park, R #3, M-93 / 517-348-6373

RESTAURANTS
Bears Country Inn, 1081 South I 75 Business Loop / 517-348-5516
Breakers Steak House, 2123 Industrial Drive / 517-348-5181
Grayling Restaurant, 211 East Michigan Avenue / 517-348-2141
Lone Pine Restaurant, 1164 South I-75 Business Loop / 517-348-7312
Baum's AuSable Cafe, 802 Lake Street (Roscommon 48653) / 517-275-8540
Cut River Restaurant Dining & Cocktails, 1136 East Higgins Lake Drive (Roscommon 48653) / 517-821-9521

FLY SHOPS AND SPORTING GOODS
Cartwright & Danewell Provisioners, M-72 West / 888-857-6500
Fly Factory, The Hatch Line, 200 Ingham Street / 517-348-7108
Gate's AuSable Lodge & Pro Shop, 471 South Stephan Bridge Road / 517-348-8462
Hartman's Fly Shop, 6794 East County Road 612 / 517-348-9679
Bill's Au Sable Rod & Fly Shop, Route 3 (Lovells 49738) / 517-348-7111
Ray's Canoeing & The Fly Factory / 200 Ingham St / 517-348-5844
Skip's Sport Shop, 5875 West M-72 Hwy / 517-348-7111
Sports Barn, 9475 North Cut Road (Roscommon 48653) / 517-821-9511

AUTO SERVICE

Fenton's Auto Service, 602 North James Street / 517-348-5242
Grayling Auto Repair, I-75 Business Loop / 517-348-8123
Moshier's Auto Repair, 104 Ogemaw Street / 517-348-2471
Great Lakes Service Equipment, 11855 Ellison Drive (Roscommon 48653) / 517-275-6005
Roscommon Automotive Parts & Service, 111 North 5th Street (Roscommon 48653) / 517-275-5097

AIR SERVICE

Grayling Airport / 517-348-5845

MEDICAL

Northern Michigan Health Services, 308 East Michigan Avenue / 517-348-4110

FOR MORE INFORMATION

Grayling Regional Chamber of Commerce
City Park
Grayling, MI 49738
517-348-2921

Alpena
Population – 11,354

ACCOMMODATIONS
Alpena Motel, 3011 US 23 South / 517-356-2178
Bay Motel, 2107 US 23 South / 517-356-6137
Dew Drop Inn Motel, 2469 French Road / 517-356-4414
Forty Winks Motel, 1021 South State Avenue / 517-354-3915
Presque Isle Motel, 385 North Bradley Hwy (Rogers City 49779) / 517-734-3392
Rogers City Motel, 220 North Bradley Hwy (Rogers City 49779) / 517-734-3707

CAMPGROUNDS
Campers Cove Campground, 5005 Long Rapids Road / 517-356-3708
Clear Lake State Park, Box 51 (Atlanta 49709) / 517-785-4388
Harrisville State Park, 248 State Park Road (Harrisville 48740) / 517-724-5126
Hoeft State Park, US-23, North (Rogers City 49779) / 517-734-2543

RESTAURANTS
Delynn's Family Restaurant, 1284 M-32 / 517-354-6190
Grove Restaurant, 1001 US 23 North / 517-354-4191
Lud's Restaurant, 1201 West Chisholm Street / 517-356-2314
The Portage, 5529 Grand Lake Road / 517-595-6051
Black Bear Cafe, 136 East Erie Street (Rogers City 49779) / 734-2007
Karsten's Restaurant & Ice Cream Parlor, 1072 West Third Street
    (Rogers City 49779) / 517-734-2050

FLY SHOPS AND SPORTING GOODS
Adrian's Sport Shop, 335 North Bradley Hwy (Rogers City 49779) / 517-734-2303
Buck's Bait & Tackle, 8501 US 23 North / 517-595-2121

AUTO SERVICE
Dick's Auto Service, 2298 Diamond Point Road / 517-356-2368
G M's Auto Repair, 610 West Campbell Street / 517-354-6832
J & S Auto Repair, 610 River Street / 517-354-8918
Car Care Clinic, 1074 West Third Street (Rogers City 49779) / 517-734-7314
Lutz Auto Repair, 4108 US 23 North (Rogers City 49779) / 517-734-2140

AIR SERVICE
Rogers City Airport, 658 South Bradley Hwy (Rogers City 49779) / 517-734-7037
Alpena County Regional Airport / 517-354-2907

MEDICAL
Alpena General Hospital, 1501 West Chisholm Street / 517-356-7390

FOR MORE INFORMATION
Alpena Area Chamber of Commerce
235 West Chisholm Street
Alpena, MI 49707
517-354-4181

West Branch
Population – 1,914

ACCOMMODATIONS
Dale Motel, 1086 North Huron Road (Tawas City 48763) / 517-362-6153
Harbor View Motel, 1008 North Huron Road (Tawas City 48763) / 517-362-3971
Riverside Resort Motel & Charter Service, 730 West Lake Street (Tawas City 48763) / 517-362-5052
La Hacienda Motel, 969 West Houghton Avenue / 517-345-2345
Red Rose Motel, 836 South M-33 / 517-345-2136
Tri Terrace Motel, 2259 South M-76 / 517-345-3121

CAMPGROUNDS
Lake George Campground, 3070 Elm Drive / 517-345-2700
Troll Landing, 2660 Rifle River Trail / 517-345-7260
Shady Oaks Campgrounds, 115 Proctor Road (Tawas City 48763) / 517-362-3947
Tawas Point State Park, 686 Tawas Beach Road (East Tawas 48730) / 517-362-3113

RESTAURANTS
Bay View Restaurant, 637 West Lake Street (Tawas City 48763) / 517-362-5851
Lakeside Too, 448 West Lake Street (Tawas City 48763) / 517-362-4887
Sonny's on the Bay, 175 Lake Street (Tawas City 48763) / 517-362-6378
Charbonneau's Family Restaurant, 503 East Houghton Avenue / 517-345-9317
Logmark's Family Restaurant, 2980 Cook Road / 517-345-3503
North Country Junction, 2463 Vern Court / 517-345-4340

FLY SHOPS & SPORTING GOODS
Batchelder Spool & Fly, 1434 East State Road / 517-345-8678
Nordic Sports, 218 West Bay Street (East Tawas 48730) / 517-362-2001
J & P Sporting Goods, 3275 West M-76 / 517-345-3744
Zettel's Sport Center, 3091 West Houghton Avenue / 517-345-3159
All Season Sporting Goods, 1131 North Huron Road (Tawas City 48763) / 517-362-4512

AUTO SERVICE
Bill's Wrecker & Snow Plowing, 1033 West Lake Street (Tawas City 48763) / 517-362-5642
Bud's Garage, 4805 West M-76) / 517-345-2314
Gene's Garage, 3274 West M-76 / 517-345-2831
Harold's Auto Rental, 2665 South Flowage Lake Road / 517-345-1633
Sanford Service Center, 2789 South M-76 / 517-345-8761

AIR SERVICE
West Branch Community Airport, 1519 West Airport Road / 517-345-1453

MEDICAL

Mid-Michigan Regional Medical, 455 South Quarter Street / 517-426-9286
Tawas St. Joseph Hospital, 200 Hemlock (Tawas City 48763) / 517-362-7862

FOR MORE INFORMATION

West Branch Area Chamber of Commerce
422 West Houghton Avenue
West Branch, MI 48661
517-345-2821

Tawas Area Chamber of Commerce
402 West Lake Street
Tawas City, MI 48763
517-362-8643

Clare
Population – 3,021

ACCOMMODATIONS
Gladwin Motor Inn, 1003 West Cedar Avenue / 517-426-9661
Northwoods Motel, 5810 North M 30 / 517-426-4021
Stag Haven, 1749 Bowmanville Road / 517-345-7774
Doherty Motor Hotel, 604 North McEwan Street / 517-386-3441
Lone Pine Motel & Restaurant, 1508 North McEwan Street / 517-386-7787
Northgate Motel, 3785 East Colonville Road / 517-386-9004

CAMPGROUNDS
River Valley RV Park, 2165 South Bly Lake Avenue (Gladwin 48624) /
    517-386-7844
Herrick Lake Family Park, 6320 East Herrick Road / 517-386-2010
Jan's Secord Lake Campground, 2616 Lakeshore Drive / 517-426-4020
Sugar Hills Campgrounds, 2540 Cemetery Road / 517-426-3800

RESTAURANTS
Country Home Restaurant, 680 North M-18 / 517-426-1784
Northwoods Restaurant and Lounge, 5810 North M-30 / 517-426-9420
Pepper Mill Restaurant, 217 West Cedar Avenue / 517-426-8922
Brassie, 7795 South Clare Avenue / 517-386-9747
Town & Country Lounge, 1395 North McEwan Street / 517-386-7567
Whitehouse Restaurant, 613 North McEwan Street / 517-386-9551

FLY SHOPS AND SPORTING GOODS
Little Forks Outfitters, 143 East Main Street (Midland 48640) / 517-832-4100
Jay's Sporting Goods, 8800 South Clare Avenue / 517-386-3475
Larry's Bait & Sport Shop, 5449 Round Lake Road / 517-426-7205

AUTO SERVICE
Kidd's Service, 301 East Cedar Avenue, Gladwin, MI 48624, 426-1991
Larry's Auto Repair, 1330 West Sun Oil Road / 517-426-5985
Benchley Brothers Body Shop, 821 East 5th Street / 517-386-4452
Dick's Complete Collision, 11453 North Mission Road / 517-386-9460
Kidd's Car Clinic, 103 Schoolcrest Avenue / 517-386-7374

AIR SERVICE
Gladwin Zettel Airport, 735 South State Street / 517-426-4201

FOR MORE INFORMATION
Clare Area Chamber of Commerce   Gladwin County Chamber of Commerce
609 North McEwan Street   608 West Cedar Avenue
Clare, MI 48617   Gladwin, MI 48624
517-386-2442   517-426-5451

Southwestern Lower Peninsula

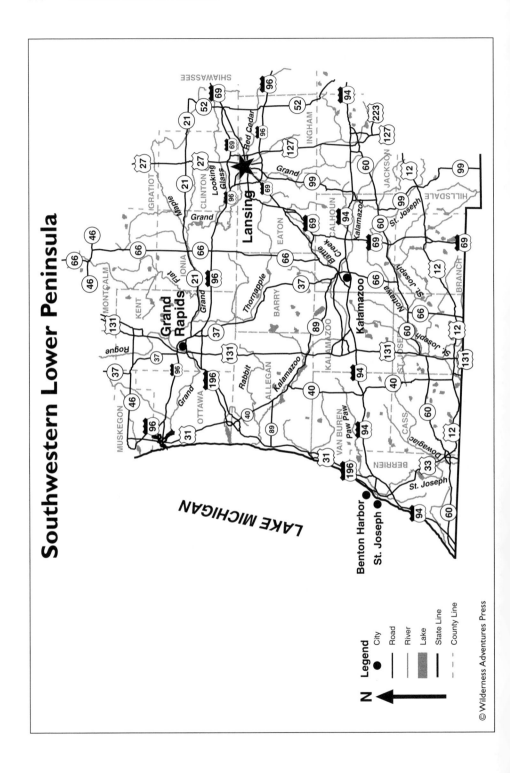

Legend

● City
— Road
— River
▓ Lake
— State Line
--- County Line

N ←

© Wilderness Adventures Press

Southwestern Lower Peninsula

Three large rivers gather most of the water in the southwestern part of the Lower Peninsula and carry it to Lake Michigan. Just as the water quality of the St. Joseph, Kalamazoo, and Grand Rivers has improved greatly over the past 30 years, so has the fishing. One could easily say that the good old days are right now for these beautiful streams.

Because of their size and gentle gradient, these are warmwater streams, but sandy soil found in much of this region results in many springfed tributaries that harbor good numbers of trout. Flyfishing for smallmouth bass is outstanding throughout these river systems, and walleyes, northern pike, channel and flathead catfish, and carp spice up the action. During the fall, winter, and spring, lake-run steelhead and brown trout are found in these rivers. In the fall you can add lake trout and chinook and coho salmon to your catch.

Each river has large metropolitan areas on it banks: Lansing and Grand Rapids on the Grand, Battle Creek and Kalamazoo on the Kalamazoo, and Benton Harbor/St. Joseph on the St. Joseph. Despite the presence of these population centers, fishing is rarely crowded, and greenbelts along the rivers buffer the sights and sounds of urban bustle.

My home river is the Grand, and my boyhood playground was the Red Cedar River, a sizable tributary that joins the Grand in Lansing. Back then, pollution damaged the river and periodic fish kills occurred when there were heavy thunderstorms. When sewer catch-basin overflow entered the river, the biochemical oxygen demand robbed the river of all of its dissolved oxygen. Today, it gives me great pleasure to return to this river and catch smallmouth after smallmouth on crayfish streamers or tease coho salmon and steelhead into striking a gaudy offering.

GRAND RIVER

The Grand River is Michigan's longest, flowing approximately 250 miles across seven counties before emptying into southern Lake Michigan at Grand Haven. The best flyfishing occurs in its middle reaches between a small city and a large one with names influenced by the river: Eaton Rapids and Grand Rapids.

The Grand is a very sluggish stream for its first 30 or so miles in Jackson County. Its soft bottom makes wading difficult, and the fishing is only fair. But the river begins changing to a classic smallmouth bass stream as it nears Eaton Rapids. It widens, the bottom firms up, and boulders poke their round tops above the surface. Except for impoundments and occasional slow-moving stretches, the river maintains this character all the way to Grand Rapids. Most of the dams on the Grand are of the low head variety, but the hydroelectric dams (Smithville, Moores Park, and Webber) do create long backwaters. Both fish and human populations are high at the dams for two reasons: the fish are blocked and concentrate in the waters below, and the fishermen are provided good access at each site. In addition, there are many

Author with a 16-inch smallmouth bass from the Grand River.

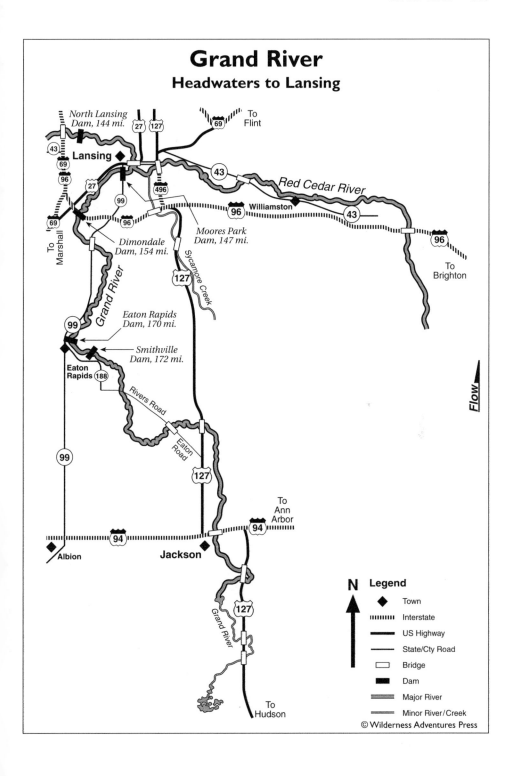

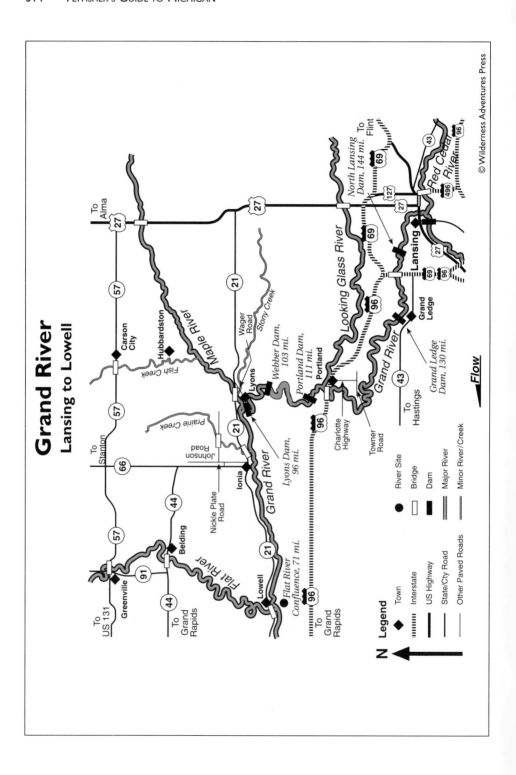

Grand River
Lansing to Lowell

© Wilderness Adventures Press

Legend

Town	River Site
Interstate	Bridge
US Highway	Dam
State/Cty Road	Major River
Other Paved Roads	Minor River/Creek

N

Flow

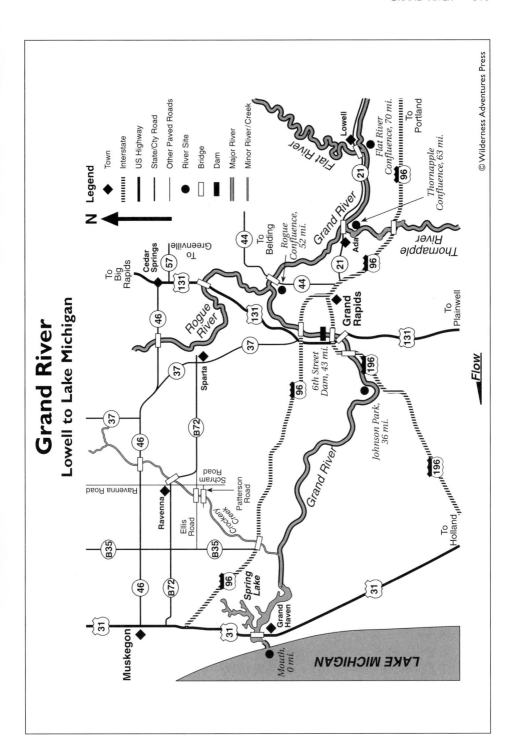

© Wilderness Adventures Press

Tony Paglei caught this carp on a fly in the Grand River.

road bridges providing access. Developed public access sites with launch ramps are noted on the maps. The Portland State Game Area just upstream from the town of Portland provides another public access. For ambitious flyfishers, launching a canoe or kickboat at Charlotte Highway or Turner Road and floating through the entire state game area is a great trip. The riverside park in Portland provides a place to take out. Smallmouth bass will wear your arm out, so you might need help with your watercraft at the end of the float.

Smallies are the prime target between Eaton Rapids and Portland, but walleyes and channel catfish are also present in good numbers. If you have not caught channel catfish on a fly rod, you are in for a pleasant surprise. They will put just as deep a bend in your rod as a smallmouth, and they don't give up easily. All three are often caught in the same pool or deep riffle, because they all like the same rocky substrate. Smallmouth come to the surface for poppers as well as mayfly and grasshopper patterns, but streamers imitating crayfish and minnows are best for catfish and walleyes.

Working into the shaded banks of the Grand River.

The upper Grand tends to remain clear during the summer and settles fairly rapidly after a rain, providing the opportunity for another special warmwater fishery: sightfishing for carp. These fish definitely use their eyes to feed, and nymphs that imitate damselflies and mayflies, as well as crayfish streamers, will catch these fish. A stealthy approach and accurate casts are necessary for these surprisingly wary fish. Ten-pounders can be expected, and 20-pounders are definitely possible, so gear up your tackle accordingly.

Tony Paglei of BC Outfitters introduced me to this great sport. The carp eagerly attacked red squirrel nymphs, and I soon found out that hooking one of these large, scaled fish did not guarantee landing it. It was almost as much fun hearing Tony shout out, "carp on," as it was hooking into one myself.

Plankton blooms in the impoundment behind Webber Dam and the turbid flow from the Maple River combine to decrease the clarity of the Grand's middle and lower reaches. This decreases the dry fly opportunities, but there is still a lot of sport to be found beneath the surface. While smallmouth continue to reign, walleyes and channel catfish become more numerous. There is also the chance of hooking a flathead.

A successful angler on the Grand River.

The areas below Webber and Lyons Dams are very easy to wade during summer flows, but once the Maple joins the Grand, floating becomes a better way to fish the river. Some of the Grand's most productive water can be fished by wading between the mouth of Maple and the Lyons Dam.

The exception to this is the rapids in the city of Grand Rapids below the Sixth Street Dam. For more than a mile, the now 400-foot-wide river becomes essentially a giant riffle. There are some holes, such as the quarry hole where bedrock was blasted for construction material, but during summer flows, the river is easily waded. A number of city bridges, along with their abutments, add structure and cover. In addition, there are four coffer dams ranging from 1 to 3 feet in height that provide resting and feeding locations for fish. In the summer, smallmouth are still the dominant species, but catfish and walleye are very numerous. There are public access sites on both sides of the river at the dam as well as river walks along both sides.

As the Grand gets closer to Lake Michigan, it slows down, changing the species mix a bit. Largemouth bass and northern pike become more prevalent. There are bayous and side channels that are more like lakes than a river, and their inhabitants include the largemouth bass, pike, and panfish mix you would expect to find in a warmwater lake.

Prime months for the Grand's resident fish are May through September, although they remain active into October until the water temperature falls below 50 degrees. The Grand's second season—the first in the minds of many anglers— begins as soon as the water temperature cools into the 60s in late August or early September. Chinook salmon are the first of five anadromous species to run this river, arriving in Grand Rapids after water temperatures below 70 degrees have occurred for about five days. A cold, late summer rain hastens this charge upriver.

Some brown trout and a few stray summer steelhead usually tag along with the kings. Within a couple of weeks, coho salmon join the kings, and the number of lake-run browns continues to increase. A few winter steelhead are found in the river by the first of October, with the peak of the fall run occurring in November. Lake trout are the last fish to begin their migration, with the run concentrated within a week or two before and after November 1. With the exception of steelhead, all of these fish are fall spawners, but many brown trout stay in the river after spawning and are frequently a bonus catch when fishing for steelhead in winter. Although the steelhead's main run occurs in spring, high water usually makes flyfishing tough in the main river, so it is best to focus on the tributaries at this time.

Anadromous fish are not actively feeding, but many anglers experience success by using nymphs and baitfish imitating streamers that appeal to the fish's memory of eating. Egg flies also take many fish, especially those that are fresh in the river. My favorite tactic is to invade their territory with a gaudy streamer or, if the water is very clear, a black marabou leech. The goal is to make the fly appear alive, triggering an aggressive response.

The biggest concentration of migrating fish occurs below Sixth Street because the fast water and the dam both slow the fish down. Ladders at all of the dams below the Moore Park Dam in Lansing provide many opportunities to catch salmon and steelhead farther upstream. Each dam temporarily concentrates the migrants and are good places to focus your efforts. Only the lake trout seem reluctant to ascend the river past Grand Rapids. Coho salmon proceed quickly to their planting site in Lansing, with females usually still shiny bright, while chinook tend to find all the spawning gravel they need by the time they reach Portland. Steelhead also run the whole length of the river, but the tributaries that attract many fish along the way make the number that reaches Lansing much smaller than the river's total run. Brown trout are caught incidentally to the others, and while they do ascend the Sixth Street Dam with regularity, not many are hooked upstream.

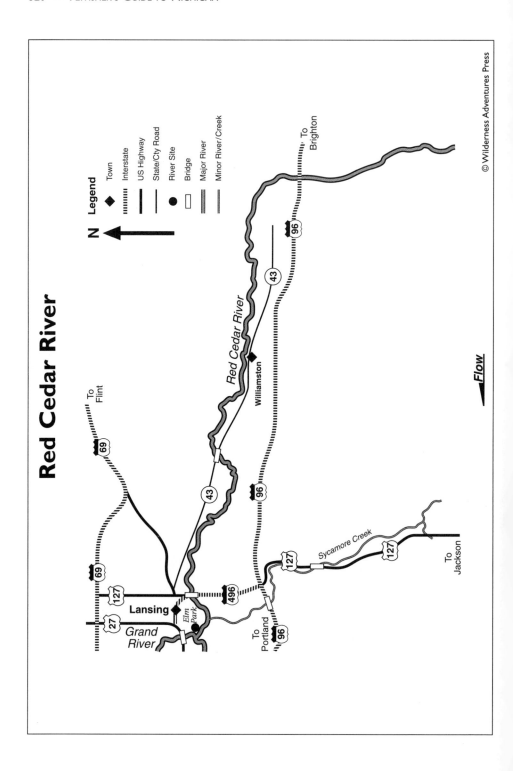

Red Cedar River

Legend

- Town
- Interstate
- US Highway
- State/Cty Road
- River Site
- Bridge
- Major River
- Minor River/Creek

N

Red Cedar River

Williamston

To Flint

To Brighton

To Jackson

To Portland

Sycamore Creek

Lansing

Elm Park

Grand River

Flow

© Wilderness Adventures Press

Red Cedar River

The Red Cedar River is the first major tributary to add its flow to the Grand. The prime water for both resident and anadromous fish is between the town of Williamston and its confluence with the Grand in Lansing. There is a dam in Williamston that has been modified to provide a short run of whitewater for paddle sports enthusiasts, and the entire stretch of river is floatable by canoe or small boat. The Red Cedar can be waded except for a mile or two above a low head dam on Michigan State University's campus and the last 3 miles above the confluence with the Grand, where the North Lansing Dam impounds the tributary. It should be noted that MSU has a rather strange local ordinance prohibiting fishing from the bank, but this should not affect fishing since wading or floating provide better casting room.

The principal resident game fish in the Red Cedar are smallmouth bass and northern pike. They are both found throughout the river, with pike more dominant in the slow, deep water and smallmouth preferring rocks and logs in moderate current. The insect fauna is similar to the Grand except for the presence of a somewhat higher population of the *Hexagenia* mayfly. I don't know how well the smallmouth might come to surface during the Hex hatch, but they are not bashful about taking poppers during the day. Shiner imitating streamers are just the ticket for the northerns.

Coho salmon run the Red Cedar in October, and steelhead visit the river in spring. Neither fish is planted in the river, but quite often smolts that are planted in the Grand at Lansing move into the Red Cedar and become imprinted there before leaving for Lake Michigan. The reason for this is that the discharge from the Lansing power plant makes the Grand uncomfortably warm for these fish. It's also possible that adults, especially cohos, find the Grand too warm when they return and make a left turn at Lansing. Sightfishing is most often employed when fishing for spawning anadromous species, but they can also be intercepted in holes by using brightly colored streamers and nymphs. At Elm Park, a municipal facility, the Red Cedar merges with the Grand, and cohos tend to concentrate here. This is fairly deep water, but weighted, brightly colored streamers should get you into fish at what local anglers call "The Point." Check with Wayne Werner in the fly shop of Grand River Bait and Tackle for the latest information on the run and what flies are working.

Sycamore Creek, a fairly good-sized stream that joins the Red Cedar in Lansing,, also attracts some of the lake-run migrants. This creek clears faster after a rain than the Grand or Red Cedar, and there are several areas of gravel in the first few miles upstream from its confluence with the Red Cedar. Scott Woods and Biggie Munn Parks in Lansing offer good access. Northerns are the dominant resident predator, and there is enough room to do some flyfishing in the lower third of the stream.

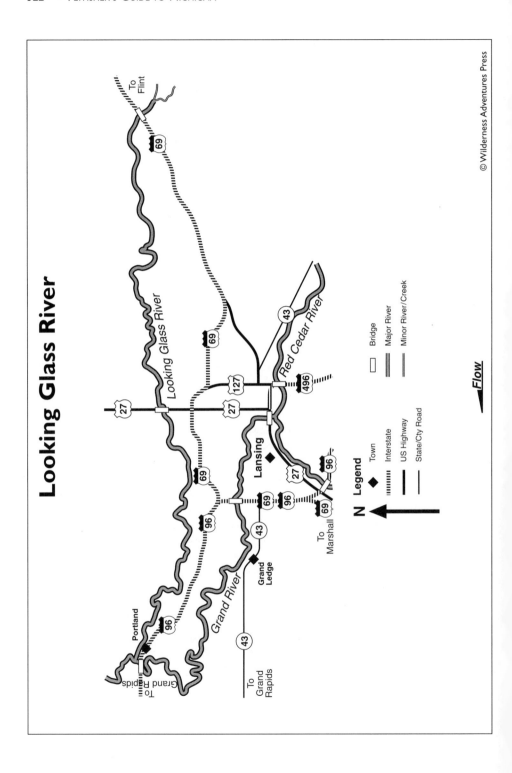

Looking Glass River

Looking Glass River

Similar to the Grand, the Looking Glass River begins as a slow, soft-bottomed stream. Gradually, the current begins to quicken and the stream widens as it proceeds downstream. By the time the river reaches the US 27 crossing, it has a firm gravel and cobble bottom with numerous large boulders. The Looking Glass retains this character all the way to its confluence with the Grand in Portland. Smallmouth are the main quarry, with rock bass and northern pike to add variety. Pike are more common in the slower water upstream, and there is room to fish for them in the 4 or 5 miles of river upstream from US 27.

In general, cover and deep holes are lacking in the lower Looking Glass. This makes it necessary to cover a considerable distance of the river in order to fish a number of the good holes. Bridges are conveniently located every mile or two, and fishing from bridge to bridge, whether floating or wading, is a good tactic. As you would expect, fish are quite concentrated, and multiple encounters are likely in a good pool. Sightfishing for carp in these pools is also a way to add to the sport.

Insect species and hatch times in the Looking Glass are similar to the Grand. It is also important to remember that bass, as they grow larger, really key in on crayfish and minnows. Even though northerns are almost exclusively fish eaters, it is not uncommon to hook them on streamers imitating crayfish.

Anadromous fish have access to the Looking Glass, but none are planted in it. Coho and steelhead do stray into it, but normally it's better to cast an offering in the

A lake-run brown caught with a streamer.

Maple River

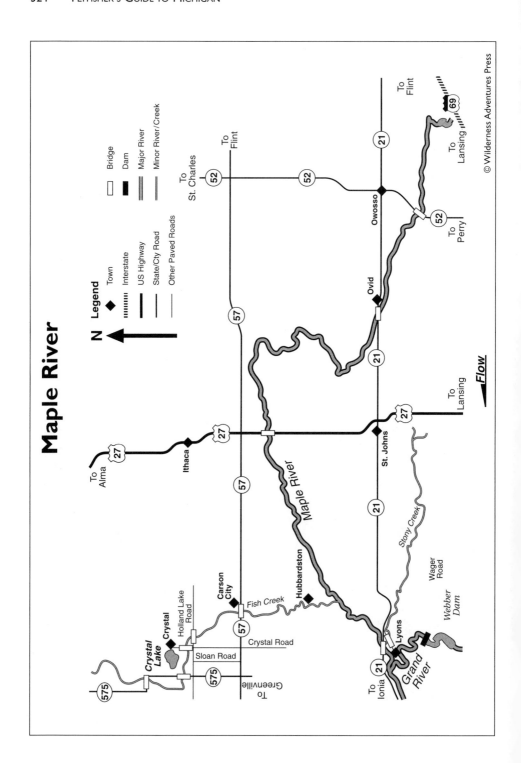

© Wilderness Adventures Press

Grand. The exception might be when the Grand is still too high after a rain when the Looking Glass has dropped and cleared. There is usually no temperature difference between the rivers. Fishing the Looking Glass just upstream from its confluence with the Grand or in the main river just below the merger is a good bet when the run is on. Access is available from the previously mentioned municipal park in Portland.

Maple River

Even during low flows, the Maple River suffers from high turbidity due to the soil types in its drainage basin. This is unfortunate, because although there is good population of channel catfish along with some pike, smallmouth bass, and walleyes, flyfishing is difficult due to poor visibility. Some success can be achieved by slowly pulsing large marabou streamers in the reach between Maple Rapids and the Grand. Short casts quartering downstream and very slow movement of the fly are keys to success.

A better plan for the Maple River would probably be to fish its two largest tributaries, Stony Creek and Fish Creek. Both of these creeks join the Maple just a short distance above where the Maple enters the Grand. Fishing the Maple at the mouths of these feeder streams can also be productive.

Stony Creek is a good smallmouth stream producing bass of remarkable size. The nature of this small stream makes it relatively easy to fish with a fly rod. The rock-strewn pools are large, and much of the creek flows through open farmland. The first few miles above the Maple are best, with the M-21 and Wagar Road Bridges providing access.

Fish Creek offers even more fly angling opportunities. The lower creek between Carson City and the mouth has a good population of smallmouth bass with a sprinkling of northern pike and walleye. Above Carson City, the stream is regularly stocked with brown trout. While the overhanging vegetation can limit casting in some areas, most of the creek between Vickeryville Road and Carson City is flyfishable. This reach is scheduled to be open all year, starting at the beginning of April 2000. Bridges at Sloan, Crystal, and Holland Lake Roads provide access to some of the better trout water. The creek's headwaters produce both wild brown and brook trout. Occasionally, a good-sized brookie can be encountered that has moved down from the upper creek, an always welcome surprise.

A prolific brown drake hatch occurs in late May on Fish Creek, and brown trout feed heavily during this time. There are fish up to 26 inches in the stream, and this hatch gives you an excellent chance to hook a 20-inch brown on the surface during daylight hours. Crayfish are also very numerous in this stream and are a staple in the diet of larger browns.

Steelhead are stocked in Fish Creek and can ascend the stream as far as Hubbardston, where there is a small hydroelectric dam. Although this is mostly a spring fishery, during wet autumns, some fish do enter the river in November. A modest number of both coho and chinook salmon run this stream in the fall. In this stretch, there are several prime gravel riffles where fish spawn, and concentrating on either the spawning fish or the nearby runs will put a bend in your rod. A park in Hubbardston provides parking and access. The farther downstream you wade and walk, the more room there is to fish, both in terms of people and overhanging brush.

Flat River

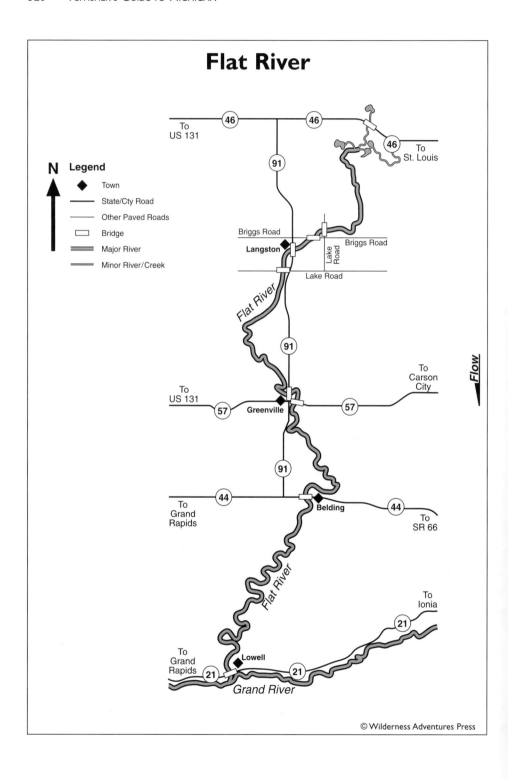

© Wilderness Adventures Press

Even though Prairie Creek does not flow into the Maple, it joins the Grand just downstream from the mouth of the Maple and deserves mention here. Its flow is about the same as Fish Creek, and it has a resident brown trout population. Its other similarities to Fish are that it also has a brown drake hatch and a healthy crayfish population. Steelhead successfully reproduce in Prairie Creek, and small rainbows can also keep you busy when browns are not taking. In addition, a small percentage of steelhead parr do not smolt, becoming resident rainbows. I've caught them up to 17 inches or so, and they definitely spice up the summer action.

As it is on Fish Creek, the steelhead fishery is mostly a spring event. April is usually the peak time, but a mild winter can bring good steelheading in March. Prairie is also known for a late spurt of steelies that extend the fishing into May. The stream is now open for fishing to Nickel Plate Road year-round, and the entire stream is scheduled to have no closed season and a 10-inch limit for browns and rainbows starting in April 2000. There is a low head dam at the first bridge (Main Street) that slows fish down in low water. The DNR is trying to have the dam removed, but there is local political pressure to keep it in place. In the past, some "anglers," who had less than honorable intentions, frequently blocked a small "steep pass" fish ladder device on the dam. Even when the fish ladder is open, steelhead tend to stack up below this dam. Many fish are caught on flies below the dam, but this is definitely combat fishing when the run is in full swing. Anglers can only hope the future will bring better fish passage at this location, because there is some real quality fishing to be had upstream. Of course, there are some advantages to having fewer fish, and that is fewer anglers. Bridges provide the only access, and wading from one to the next can help you find fish that have had little or no fishing pressure.

Flat River

A very good smallmouth stream, the Flat River joins the Grand at the town of Lowell. Its most special trait is that it is the slowest to muddy and the quickest to clear after a heavy rain, and moderate rains don't seem to affect its fishablilty. This makes the Flat River your insurance policy when other rivers are too muddy.

While the entire stream is classified as a warmwater river, there is a chance to catch brook trout in the spring. There are a number of small brook trout creeks north of Greenville that feed the Flat, and brookies up to 16 inches move down into the Flat to feed. Usually, the water temperature stays cool enough for them until late May. While all traditional brook trout patterns catch these fish, remember that brookies have moved down to take advantage of the abundant food in the Flat, so use flies that are a bit larger than would normally be used. Good access spots to try for these seasonal brookies include the M-91, Lake Road, and Briggs Road bridges upstream from Langston.

The prime smallmouth water is between Greenville and the mouth. Except where the river is impounded, the boulder-strewn stream has perfect habitat for bronzebacks. Fishing the Grand just below the mouth of the Flat is also a good plan. Crayfish and shiner streamer patterns in sizes 6 and 8 work well, and the clear water makes it easier to bring bass to the surface for poppers.

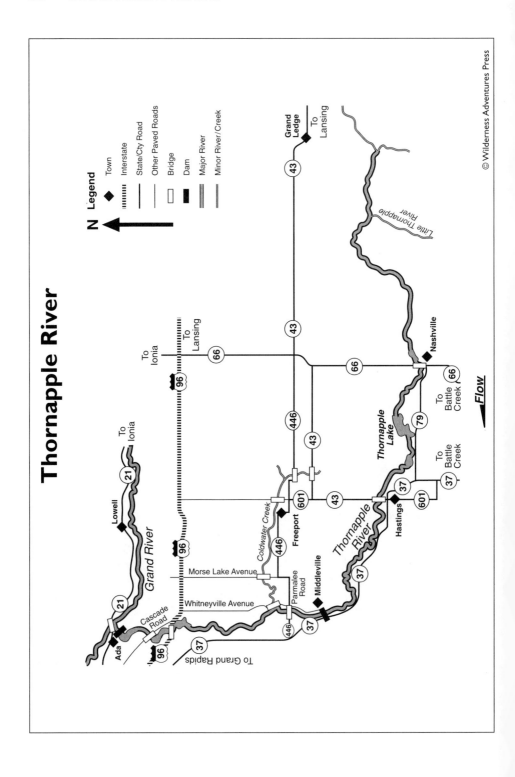

The Flat River is planted with steelhead, and a few salmon also stray into it. A dam in Lowell limits the fishing for anadromous species to the lower mile of river. Much of this section flows over prime spawning gravel. The clear water and the fact that the river is very popular with anglers tends to make the steelies more spooky here — to increase the chances for hookups, use stealth and pick dark days for fishing. Smaller but still bright streamers and nymphs can aggravate spawning rainbows into striking. April is the prime month, but steelhead can arrive in good numbers in March.

Thornapple River

This tributary, joining the Grand from the south at the small town of Ada, is well known as a fine smallmouth bass stream. Even though much of the lower river is impounded and several low head dams are located upstream, the free flowing reaches between Nashville and the junction with Coldwater Creek are loaded with smallmouth bass. Northern pike, rock bass, and a few walleyes are also present. Muskellunge and largemouth bass inhabit Thornapple Lake, a natural widening of the river, and sometimes move up and down into the river. There are a number of small trout streams that add that flow into Thornapple, and later in the season when the weather is cool, an occasional brown trout can surprise a smallmouth angler.

Insect species on the Thornapple are similar to the Grand and other tributaries. Streamers that imitate crayfish and creek chubs, once again, can produce hookups with the river's larger smallmouths. Most of the river can be waded and floated during normal summer flows, with good access at frequent county road crossings. The reach between the Middleville Dam and Parmalee Lake Road is a good one to float.

The largest tributary and the only trout stream in the drainage that is large enough to be comfortably angled with a fly rod is Coldwater Creek. Much of this river has been dredged, but it still offers good fishing for both browns and rainbows. A large number of "Half Logs" have been placed in the creek, and plans are in the works to add more stream improvement structures to augment its relatively sparse cover. This took some doing since the stream is classified as a county drain — usually the drain commissioner's goal is to keep the drain clean rather than allowing angler groups to add logs and other impediments to the flow.

Starting out as a lake outlet and a warmwater stream, Coldwater Creek cools off enough for trout about 4 miles upstream from the town of Freeport and continues to hold trout almost to its confluence with the Thornapple. Below Freeport, the stream will be open all year starting in April 2000; and on the upper creek, size limits will be raised to 12 inches because of good growth rates. Natural reproduction is very limited, so small browns and rainbows are stocked each year. There are many county road bridges and a county park at Morse Lake Avenue for access, as well as Trout Unlimited property that is open to the public upstream from Baker Avenue. Riffle-loving insects predominate in this stream, with good hatches of caddisflies and baetis mayflies. Crayfish are also abundant.

Even though anadromous fish are not regularly planted in the Thornapple, some do stray into the short reach at Ada below a hydroelectric dam. This part of the river

Rogue River

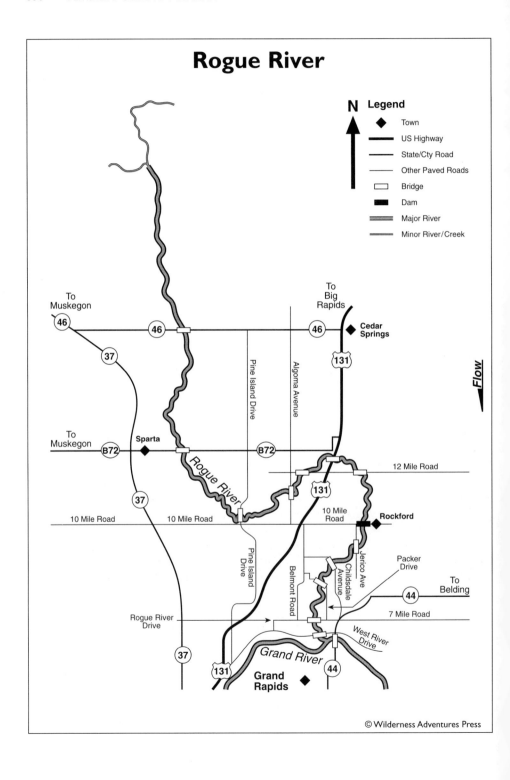

Legend

N

◆ Town
— US Highway
— State/Cty Road
— Other Paved Roads
▭ Bridge
▬ Dam
▬ Major River
▬ Minor River/Creek

To Muskegon

46

37

To Big Rapids

46 46 ◆ Cedar Springs

131

Flow

Pine Island Drive

Algoma Avenue

To Muskegon

B72 ◆ Sparta B72

Rogue River

12 Mile Road

37

131

10 Mile Road

10 Mile Road 10 Mile Road

10 Mile Road ◆ Rockford

Pine Island Drive

Jerico Ave

Packer Drive

To Belding

44

Belmont Road

Childsdale Avenue

Rogue River Drive

7 Mile Road

West River Drive

37

131 Grand River 44

Grand Rapids ◆

© Wilderness Adventures Press

is difficult to wade, but there are areas near the dam where it's possible to wade out far enough for a backcast. Usually, I only fish here on my way back from Sixth Street or another tributary.

Rogue River

The Rogue is the Grand's only large coldwater tributary. Though relatively marginal for trout, both browns and rainbows survive year-round in the lower river. Following the trend of many smaller Grand River trout stream tributaries, the Rogue begins as a warm stream draining muck farms and small lakes. There are limited opportunities to fish for northern pike and the occasional brown trout in the stretch from M-46 down to Pine Tree Avenue. But the stream's real draw is the trout fishing from Algoma Avenue down to the confluence with the Grand. Through here, the river changes from a relatively narrow, soft-bottomed stream to one that is broad with a firm gravel and sand substrate.

About 2½ miles of the Rogue between the two 12 Mile Road bridges have been restricted to flies and artificial lures with a 16-inch size limit. This restriction, however, is scheduled to end in 2000. Nevertheless, fishing will probably continue to be good in this reach, where many anglers practice catch and release. Here, the river is easy to wade, offering the fly angler a great chance to fool some sizable browns and rainbows. The nutrient rich Rogue has a large population of mayflies with an especially prolific brown drake hatch in late May. Other hatches include Hendrickson,

Waist deep in the Rogue River.

blue-winged olives, sulphurs, white mayflies, and a modest *Hexagenia* emergence. Crayfish are also a very important part of the diet of larger browns.

There is a small impoundment formed by a dam in Rockford. Trout seem to move back and forth between this impoundment and the shallow gravel reach above it. Despite the impoundment's slight warming effect, trout survive year-round below the dam. Part of the reason for this is that additional spring water and small, cold creeks join the river on its journey to the Grand.

By far, the Rogue receives the largest tributary plant of steelhead in the Grand River system. It is famous for its spring steelhead run, and when there is ample rain in the fall, even better fishing can be expected in November. The dam in Rockford blocks migration and creates the biggest concentration of steelhead. There are excellent spawning riffles right in town, so when fish are unable to swim farther upstream, they drop back to dig their redds. The fishing is usually crowded, but if there are lots of fish, you can still be very successful.

Luckily, if you don't enjoy the elbow-to-elbow scene, you can move a few bridges downstream and still catch fish. Quietly wading upstream from one bridge to the next allows you sneak up on holding fish that haven't been cast over continuously. For me, this is more of a quality experience: less fish but fewer anglers, so the success ratio is about the same. There are five bridges (Jericho, Childsdale, Packer, Rogue River, and West River Roads) below Rockford that allow you to pick the distance you want to wade. As with most southern Michigan streams, the run can ordinarily be expected to peak in early April and extend into early May.

Salmon are not planted in the Rogue, but fishable numbers of both coho and chinook enter the stream in late September and October to spawn. Because the river is normally quite low and clear at this time of year, stealth and long casts are helpful in aggravating the spawning fish to grab your fly. Many anglers opt for small "intruder flies," such as the Spring's Wiggler and early black stoneflies.

Crockery Creek

Crockery Creek is the Grand's first sizable tributary upstream from Lake Michigan. From the junction of its two branches in Ravenna, it is large enough to flyfish all the way to its juncture with the big river. Unfortunately, the creek soon becomes too warm for trout downstream from Ravenna. For those who like to roll cast and don't mind some brush, the stream can still be fished upstream past the forks, with the North Branch having the most room and better trout fishing. There are still some trout below Ravenna, but they give way to modest numbers of smallmouth bass and northern pike.

Steelhead are planted at Ravenna and are the main draw of Crockery Creek. The spring run is both early and good. This is a flashy stream that rises and muddies up in a hurry when it rains or the snow melts. But it is also quick to clear, and getting to the stream as it comes down and becomes fishable is a key to success. Steelhead arrive following the first major runoff in the spring, which usually occurs in March. Access is available at the bridges, with Ravenna, Schram, Ellis, and Patterson Roads good places to try when steelhead are running. Use gaudy marabou streamers and concentrate on the runs near good gravel.

ROGUE RIVER MAJOR HATCHES*

Insect	Jan	Feb	Mar	Apr	May	Jun	July	Aug	Sep	Oct	Nov	Dec	Time	Fly Patterns
Black Stonefly		X	X										A	Early Black Stonefly #10–14
Blue-winged Olive				X	X	X	X	X					A	Blue-winged Olive #18–20; Adams #18–20; Pheasant Tail Nymph #18–20; Iron Dun #18–20
Hendrickson				X	X								M/A	Hendrickson #14; Red Quill #14
Brown Drake					X	X							E	Brown Drake #10–12; Brown Drake Paradun #10–12
Sulphurs					X	X							M/A/E	Pale Morning Dun #14–16; Light Cahill #14–16; Roberts Yellow Drake #14–16
Hexagenia						X	X						E	Giant Mayfly #6–8; Hex Nymph #6–8
White Mayfly								X	X				E	White Miller #14; White Fly #14
Crayfish				X	X	X	X	X	X				M/A/E	BC Craw #4–10

HATCH TIME CODE: M = morning; A = afternoon; E = evening.
*This chart can also be applied to the other coldwater streams in the Grand River's watershed, such as Prairie, Fish, and Coldwater, as well as other trout streams in southwest Michigan.

Stream Facts: Grand River

Seasons
- Open all year.
- Bass must be released between January 1 and the Saturday before Memorial Day.
- Walleyes, muskellunge, and northern pike must be released between March 15 and the last Saturday in April.

Special Regulations
- Size limit for all trout and salmon between October 1 and the last Saturday in April is 15 inches.

Fish
- Resident smallmouth and largemouth bass, northern pike, muskellunge, walleye, channel catfish, panfish, carp.
- Anadromous rainbow trout, brown trout, lake trout, chinook salmon, coho salmon —fall through spring.
- Brown, rainbow, and brook trout in tributaries.

River Miles
- Lake Michigan—0
- Johnson Park—36
- Sixth Street Dam—43
- Rogue mouth—52
- Thornapple mouth—63
- Flat mouth—71
- Lyons Dam—96
- Webber Dam—103
- Portland Dam—111
- Grand Ledge Dam—130
- North Lansing Dam—144
- Moores Park Dam—147
- Dimondale Dam—154
- Eaton Rapids Dam—170
- Smithville Dam—172

River Characteristics
- This is a large, broad, relatively shallow river in most of the reach described.
- Exceptions are the impoundments and the upper and lower 30 miles of river.
- It has a gentle current for the most part, with numerous large boulders.

River Access
- Access is available at each landmark noted above with river miles.
- Additional boat launches are noted on maps.
- Access is also available at numerous road bridges on both the mainstream and tributaries.

GRAND RIVER MAJOR HATCHES*

Insect	Jan	Feb	Mar	Apr	May	Jun	July	Aug	Sep	Oct	Nov	Dec	Time	Fly Patterns
Caddis						█	█	█					M/E	Goddard Caddis #12–16; Elk Hair Caddis (olive) #12–18; Caddis Pupa (olive or green) #14–18
Mayflies				█	█	█	█	█					M/A/E	Light Cahill #12–16; Pale Morning Dun #14; Blue-winged Olive #14–18; Mahogany Dun #12–12; Gold Ribbed Hare's Ear Nymph #12–16; Pheasant Tail Nymph #12–16
White Mayfly								█	█				E	White Fly #14; White Miller #14
Terrestrials						█	█	█	█				M/E	Dave's Hopper #6–10; Joe's Hopper #6–10; Letort Cricket #8–12; BC Spider #8–12; Black Ant #12–16; Woolly Worm #8–12
Streamers				█	█	█	█	█	█	█			M/A/E	Woolly Buggers (white, black, & chartreuse) #6–12; Muddler Minnow #6–10; Clouser Minnow (black or blue/white) #6–10; Whitlock's Eelworm (black, chartreuse, & brown) #6–10; Matuka (olive or black) #6–10
Carp Flies						█	█	█	█				M/A/E	BC Hex #6–10; Red Squirrel Nymph #10–14; BC Damsel #8–10; BC Craw #6–8; Teeny Leech (black, brown, & dark olive) #6–8

HATCH TIME CODE: M = morning; A = afternoon; E = evening;.
*This chart can also be applied to the Grand's warmwater tributaries and the St. Joseph and Kalamazoo Rivers and their warmwater tributaries.

KALAMAZOO RIVER

Interestingly, the Kalamazoo River's headwaters are very near the origin of the Grand River. The streams then approximately parallel each other on their journey to Lake Michigan. Ironically, the Kalamazoo is both a fine warmwater fishing river and a Superfund site. More on this when we get to the stretch of river carrying this label.

The river begins as two branches, both with considerable flyfishing opportunities, that join in Albion to form the main Kalamazoo. The North Branch looks like a classic spring creek: the water is very clear, with watercress beds and other aquatic weeds growing luxuriantly. One might expect huge, sophisticated brown trout to be lurking in the undercut banks, but there is one problem. Headwater lakes and an impoundment at Concord render the stream too warm for trout, however, there is a good population of smallmouth bass and northern pike in the river and plenty of room for the flyrodder downstream from Concord. The stream flow is very stable and stays clear unless there

*North Branch
of the Kalamazoo.*

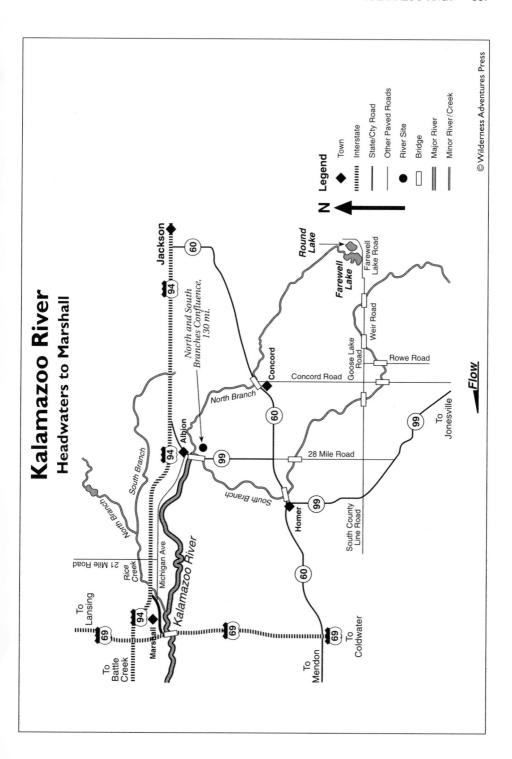

Kalamazoo River
Headwaters to Marshall

North and South Branches Confluence, 130 mi.

Jackson

Round Lake

Farewell Lake

Farewell Lake Road

Weir Road

Rowe Road

Goose Lake Road

Concord Road

Concord

North Branch

28 Mile Road

South Branch

South Branch

Albion

To Jonesville

Homer

South County Line Road

To Mendon

To Coldwater

To Lansing

To Battle Creek

Marshall

21 Mile Road

Rice Creek

Michigan Ave

Kalamazoo River

North Branch

South Branch

Flow

N

Legend

◆	Town
	Interstate
	State/Cty Road
	Other Paved Roads
●	River Site
▢	Bridge
	Major River
	Minor River/Creek

© Wilderness Adventures Press

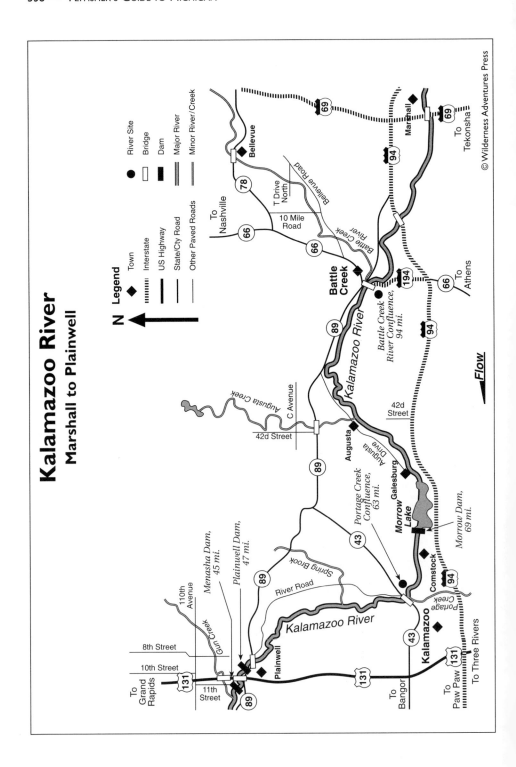

Kalamazoo River
Marshall to Plainwell

Legend

N

Town — ◆
Interstate
US Highway
State/Cty Road
Other Paved Roads

River Site — ●
Bridge — ▭
Dam — ▮
Major River
Minor River/Creek

© Wilderness Adventures Press

Battle Creek River Confluence, 94 mi.

Portage Creek Confluence, 63 mi.

Morrow Dam, 69 mi.

Menasha Dam, 45 mi.

Plainwell Dam, 47 mi.

Flow

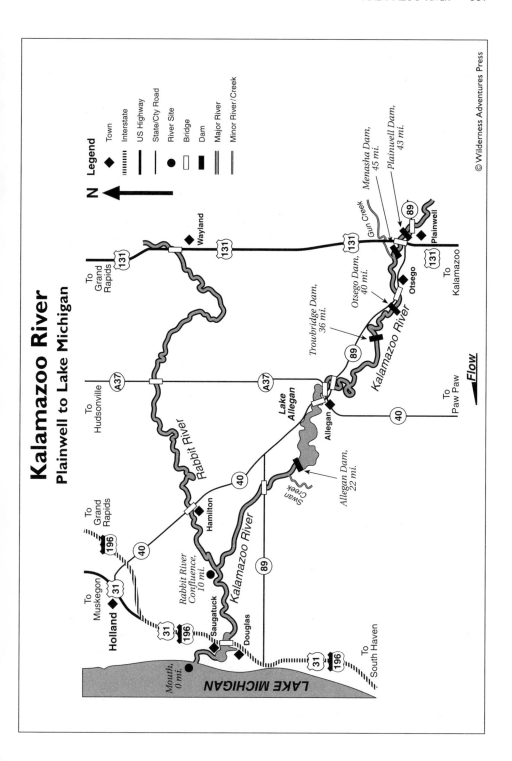

Kalamazoo River
Plainwell to Lake Michigan

Northern pike caught with an egg-sucking leech.

is extremely heavy rainfall. The river is rich with insect species as well as a good cray-fish population. The North Branch is easy to wade and is also floatable below Concord.

The South Branch is very similar in nature, with this bonus: a large influx of groundwater where the stream dips into Hillsdale County creates a short stretch of water loaded with wild brown trout. Unfortunately, the narrow brushy nature of the stream here makes flyfishing very difficult. There is, however, a meadow section at the lower end of the trout water, downstream from Rowe Road, where a fly rod can be brandished. Several lake outlets join the river in this reach, so by the time it reaches Concord Road, trout are real scarce and northern pike and smallmouth bass take over as the stream's predator fish. However, for about half a mile of stream, anglers have the chance to fool browns up to 22 inches long with a fly.

Except for a small impoundment at Homer, the South Branch flows freely to Albion. There are lots of bridge crossings that provide convenient access to this smallmouth- and pike-infested river. Its clear water is easy to read, allowing you to see a bass or pike come out and take your streamer or nymph.

Below Albion, the Kalamazoo broadens, averaging close to 100 feet in width, with the bottom continuing to be firm with lots of gravel and cobble. This part of the river provides fine habitat for smallmouth and rock bass. The water becomes a bit more enriched and is not quite as clear as the branches. There is still enough visibility to sightfish for the carp that are quite numerous here. The Kalamazoo is first impounded at Marshall, and dams appear periodically thereafter, although many of them have been drawn down and have little or no backwater.

Marshall is also where one of the Kalamazoo's larger trout streams joins the river. Rice Creek is regularly stocked with brown trout and is large and open enough to flyfish for the first 5 miles or so above the Kalamazoo. The best fishing is found

South Branch of the Kalamazoo.

between Michigan Avenue and 21 Mile Road. Although part of the stream has been dredged and straightened, enough trees have fallen into the water to provide trout cover. In addition, large rocks are plentiful, and the stream has undercut some of the large trees on the bank. Crayfish, a favorite brown trout food, are abundant. One of my first really large browns (25 inches) was caught in this stream, and after 30 years, I can still vividly remember being able to feel the lumpy crayfish that filled the trout's belly.

With additional water contributed from the Battle Creek River at the city of the same name, the Kalamazoo continues to grow in size. Remarkably, except for the impounded reaches, this now good-sized river can still be waded in the summer all the way to Allegan. This is due to the river's wide, firm rocky bottom.

Augusta Creek is the next sizable tributary to join the Kalamazoo. The water quality of this tributary meets all the requirements of a prime trout stream except for its temperature. Nevertheless, the Michigan DNR still manages it as a trout stream, and there is carryover of stocked brown trout. However, if it were just a few degrees colder in the summer it would be much better. Even so, it provides some small

Working in close on the South Branch of the Kalamazoo.

stream trout fishing opportunities for fly anglers, especially in the Kellogg Forest area below M-89. Some areas are pretty tight and require roll casting, but in the mature forest and extensive meadows downstream, it really opens up. The Forest, which belongs to Michigan State University, is open to the public, and access is available from a number of bridges and points within it. The next bridge above M-89 at C Avenue is probably the upstream limit for comfortable fly casting. Wading from M-89 to C Avenue has been a favorite tactic of mine, and although most of the trout encountered were under 12 inches, there were occasional hookups with 16- to 19- inch carryover fish. Below the forest, EF Avenue provides access, and Forty-second Street parallels the stream on the west side.

Walleyes are stocked in Morrow Lake, a large impoundment upstream from the river's namesake city, as well as in the river below, and they now add to the catch. Channel catfish are also becoming more abundant in the river downstream.

The reach that grows the biggest smallmouth starts in Comstock below the dam that creates Morrow Pond. Unfortunately, it is also the beginning of the Superfund site, which is both bad and good news for flyfishers. The bad news is that residual PCBs in the sediment translates to high enough residues in fish that the Michigan Department of Community Health advises anglers not to eat fish caught in the lower river. The fish consumption advisory goes on to emphasize that larger fish are usually more heavily contaminated and are therefore more toxic to eat. The good news is that the river is continuing to clean up and that state and federal agencies are working to hasten this process. The other obvious good news is that lots of big fish are being released to grow bigger. Fred Lee, a river guide and manager of the flyfishing shop in the Fishing Memories Outdoor Store, related that he and his clients regularly encounter smallmouth in the 20-inch class in the river above and below Kalamazoo. He also mentioned the time that a client hooked a "steelhead-sized" smallmouth that they managed to get to the boat three times, but on the third trip, the 6- to 7-pound fish jumped and tossed the streamer.

Portage Creek joins the Kalamazoo in the city of the same name, and the lower part of the creek is also part of the Superfund site. The upper creek is stocked with brown trout and gives the urban angler a chance to bend a fly rod. Most of the creek is fairly open, and hiking paths along parts of it provide access. It will be open all year beginning in April 2000, with a 10-inch size limit. One word of caution, in some areas, especially around Milham Road, wading can be difficult due to the soft bottom.

Downstream from Kalamazoo the river is wide and rocky—prime smallmouth habitat, with lots of bass in the reach. Though the river is still negotiable on foot in summer, a canoe or small boat makes it easier. Several dams in the Plainwell/Otsego area have been drawn down so that some of the PCB-contaminated sediment can be removed or treated to accelerate the breakdown of the PCBs. These dams can hold large concentrations of fish, but if you are floating, they also must be portaged.

Just below Kalamazoo, a small trout stream empties its cold, clear water into the big river. Most would not consider Spring Brook large enough to fish with fly tackle, but the Kalamazoo Valley Chapter of Trout Unlimited has brushed out a section of the creek downstream from DE Avenue. An abandoned railroad trail provides access. This stream is teeming with small- to medium-sized wild brown trout that respond well to a stealthy upstream approach. Brown sedge caddis larva imitations work well when there is no hatch. Above and below Riverview Road, the stream runs through backyards with lots of casting room, but permission, which may not be easy to get, is necessary.

Another trout stream joins the Kalamazoo a bit farther downstream. Gun Creek starts as the warmwater outlet of Gun Lake, but by the time it reaches 110th Avenue, it supports large trout and is large enough to flyfish. This sandy stream is strictly put, grow, and take/release, but the browns carry over and can reach the 20-inch mark. There is a relatively long reach below 110th Avenue without bridges for access, but from the next bridge at 7th Street, three more follow at 9th, 10th, and 11th Streets that are all about the same distance apart and an easy wade. Of course, being the active wader and streamer swimmer that I am, the long stretch below 110th is pretty enticing. Woolly buggers, matukas, and crayfish streamers are good bets to lure a large trout from cover.

The hydroelectric Allegan Dam, downstream from the town of the same name, forms a large impoundment, Allegan Lake. Below the dam, walleye, as well as channel and flathead catfish, become much more numerous. The river is deeper and starts to slow down as it gets closer to Lake Michigan. While it is more difficult to flyfish this section, there are lots of fish.

Battle Creek River

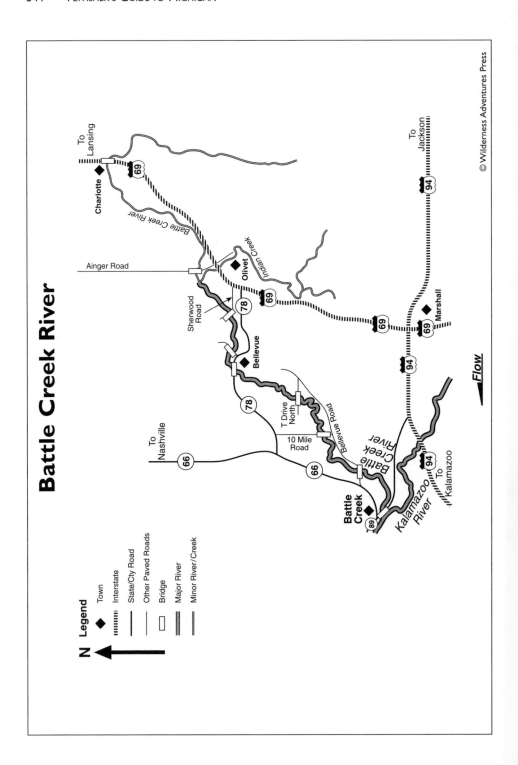

Swan Creek enters the Kalamazoo a couple of miles below Allegan Dam and is another stream stocked with brown trout. Even though the water temperature is fine for trout, the lack of spawning habitat requires regular supplements of hatchery fish. Burrowing mayflies are common in the stream, and there is a good brown drake hatch in late May. Most of the stream travels through the Allegan State Game Area, providing hike-in access in addition to the bridges. Mature forest along the banks of this modestly sized stream helps provide casting room.

Like the Grand River, the Kalamazoo becomes more like a lake near Lake Michigan, with largemouth bass and northern pike becoming more numerous. The depth and turbidity of the water necessitate a boat and make flyfishing difficult. The Rabbit River further increases the river's flow near the mouth.

Steelhead and chinook salmon are planted in the Kalamazoo, and there is also a modest run of lake trout in the fall. Brown trout are stocked at the mouth, and a portion of these fish also run upstream. Allegan Dam blocks upstream movement, greatly limiting the amount of river available to fish them.

If there is a period of cool weather that drops the water temperature to 70 degrees or below, summer steelhead, planted in the St. Joseph River and Indiana Creeks, stray into this river. This usually happens once or twice in July and August, and some of these fish tag along with chinook in September. After they have run and if the weather warms back up, check out Swan Creek. Its cool water will be a magnet for the summer runs when the Kalamazoo's water temperature gets too warm.

Large, gaudy marabou streamers are the ticket in late summer and early fall, because the water will be murky. While chartreuse seems to be the best color for chinook salmon, Skamania steelhead really turn on to fluorescent orange flies.

The Kalamazoo stays ice free below the dam for a fair distance, so hardy flyfishers can fish for steelhead and lake-run browns throughout the winter. The spring steelie run is usually accompanied by high muddy water, making flyfishing very difficult. A better bet at this time is its tributary, Rabbit River, described below.

Battle Creek River

Battle Creek River is a real sleeper, because it is relatively lightly fished by anglers of all persuasions. Although northern pike are present in good numbers throughout the river, they tend to be the dominant predator in the upper river. As the river broadens downstream from Bellevue, smallmouth and rock bass become more numerous. The best flyfishing starts north of Olivet and continues to the mouth. While most of the river can be waded, the impoundments in Bellevue and Battle Creek have some areas that are quite deep with a soft bottom. Even though this is a small river, a small johnboat, canoe, kickboat, or float tube can be very helpful. There are some good 4- to 6-hour floats, including: Ainger Road to Sherwood Road above Bellevue, and T Drive North to 10 Mile Road below this town. For a longer float, try launching at the M-78 bridge just west of Bellevue and taking out at T Drive North.

Northerns in the 6- to 15-pound class are numerous in this stream, so even if you are targeting smallmouth, it is a good idea to add a bit of wire to your tippet. Stainless steel wire with a dull brown finish in .014 or .016 diameters can be formed into 6-inch

Rabbit River

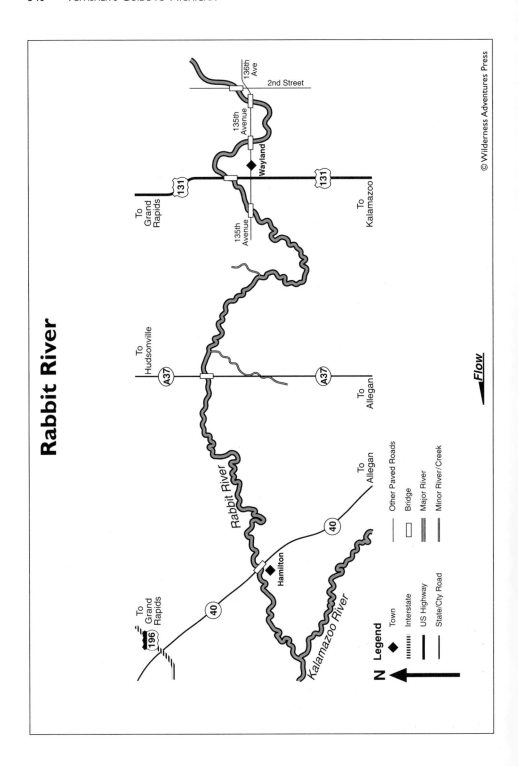

© Wilderness Adventures Press

leaders that don't detract from casting or the streamer's action. If you put a tiny black snap on the end of the leader, you will be able to quickly change flies as well.

Indian Creek, which joins the Battle Creek River north of Olivet, is a bit tight for flyfishing but loaded with pike. If the main river is not producing, try roll-casting up this feeder stream. Fish upstream, twitching the streamer through holes with a downstream retrieve.

Rabbit River

Of principal interest to the fly angler is the Rabbit River's steelhead run. This relatively small river, which is planted with steelhead each year, joins the Kalamazoo nears its mouth. It probably siphons off a portion of the Kalamazoo's planted fish, as well, and there is a small amount of natural reproduction in its headwaters. A low head dam slows anadromous rainbows a bit at Hamilton, making this a good place to try to intercept steelhead in the fall and early spring. There is a long reach of prime spawning riffles above and below Second Avenue west of Wayland, which is a good area to concentrate your efforts in March and April.

Upstream from Wayland, a good population of brown trout can be found, but the stream is very small and brushy. However, there are a few marsh/meadow areas that can be fished in the spring before the grass flattens all the way across the narrow creek. Of course, if you are really into jungle angling, you can poke your rod through the brush and dap your fly. Browns to 7 pounds are possible, but I must warn you that even ultra light spinning enthusiasts have left the creek muttering unintelligibly.

There are resident pike and smallmouth bass in the lower river, but in fall chinook salmon enter the Rabbit, as well. Big salmon head for the same spawning gravel as steelhead, but low water can make them very difficult to approach. When you do tease one into taking a nymph or streamer, it will be a very satisfying but long chase before the salmon tires out.

Stream Facts: Kalamazoo River

Seasons
- Open all year.
- Bass must be released between January 1 and the Saturday before Memorial Day.
- Walleyes and northern pike must be released between March 15 and the last Saturday in April.

Special Regulations
- Size limit for all trout and salmon between October 1 and the last Saturday in April is 15 inches.

Fish
- Resident: Largemouth and smallmouth bass, northern pike, walleye, channel catfish, panfish, and carp. Brown and brook trout in some tributaries.
- Anadromous: Summer- and winter-run steelhead, brown trout, lake trout, chinook salmon, and coho salmon (late summer through spring).

River Miles
- Lake Michigan — 0
- Rabbit River mouth — 10
- Allegan Dam — 22
- Trowbridge Dam — 36
- Otsego Dam — 40
- Menasha Dam — 45
- Plainwell Dam — 47
- Portage Creek mouth — 63
- Comstock (Morrow) Dam — 69
- Battle Creek River mouth — 94
- North and South Branch confluence, Albion — 130

River Characteristics
- Slow and deep below Allegan Dam, the river is broad and relatively shallow river for most of its length.
- The upper river has a very stable flow.
- Clear water in the South and North Branches allows some sightfishing opportunities.

River Access
- Access is available at many county and state road bridges.
- Launch ramps are at New Richmond and Allegan Dam.
- Small boats and canoes can be launched at bridges.

ST. JOSEPH RIVER

Outside the state of Michigan, the St. Joseph is probably Michigan's best known warmwater river. Ironically, this is due to its tremendous anadromous trout and salmon fishery. There are more guides and charter boats on this river than any other southern stream, and most of them focus on the lower river.

The St. Joseph's headwaters are surprisingly close to those of the Grand and Kalamazoo Rivers. The river dips into Indiana for about a 50-mile loop and then flows north into Lake Michigan. As it is on the Grand, fishing in the upper reaches is not very exciting. However, the Coldwater River's contribution greatly increases the size of the river, and below Union Lake, it becomes a fine smallmouth bass stream with walleyes, pike, and channel catfish adding to the possible catch. You can gain access to the river at Riley Road just below the dam and at Athens, Arney, and Stowell Roads farther downstream.

The St. Joseph has many impoundments, but where the river is freeflowing, warmwater flyfishing opportunities are very good. An excellent example of this is the stretch above Mendon. Three 2-mile reaches of the river are delineated by Nottawa Road (in Mendon), M-66, Jacksonburg, and Farrand Roads. These are convenient half-day floats or somewhat longer wades. The Nottawa River joins the St. Joe in this reach, offering flyfishing opportunities that we will focus on later.

As the St. Joseph continues toward Indiana, it gathers the water of several more small rivers: the Portage, Rocky, Prairie, Fawn, and Pigeon Rivers, which all flow into the St. Joe before the big river crosses the state line. Each stream is large enough to flyfish, and all offer an alternative to the mainstream when it is too high or turbid. Mostly offering a mixed bag of warmwater species, a couple of rivers also hold a few browns, as well. The Fawn is especially good for smallmouth bass, and there is still the chance for a brown trout in the Rocky, although it is no longer stocked. The Prairie River used to be planted with browns above Prairie River Lake, but the DNR lost a battle with the Drain Commissioner on the upper river. Once this reach was dredged, stocking was stopped. On my last excursion to this river,

This summer steelhead from the St. Joseph River was caught with an egg-sucking leech.

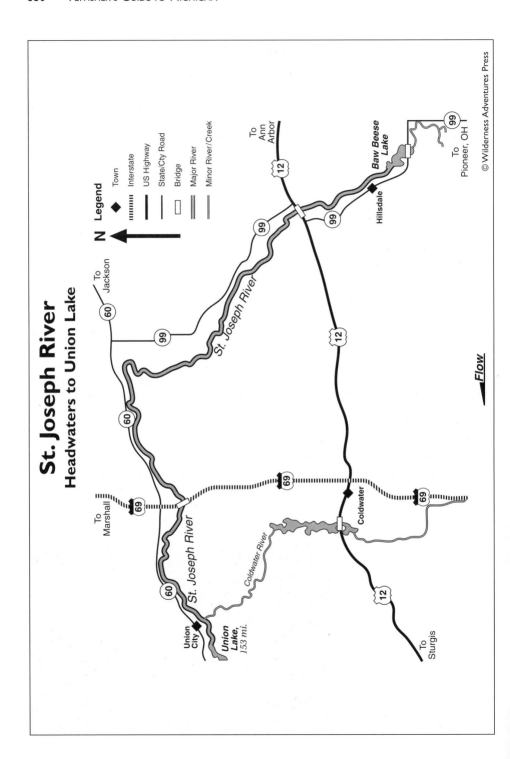

St. Joseph River
Headwaters to Union Lake

Legend

◆ Town
▪▪▪▪▪ Interstate
━━ US Highway
─── State/Cty Road
☐ Bridge
━━ Major River
─── Minor River/Creek

N

© Wilderness Adventures Press

Flow

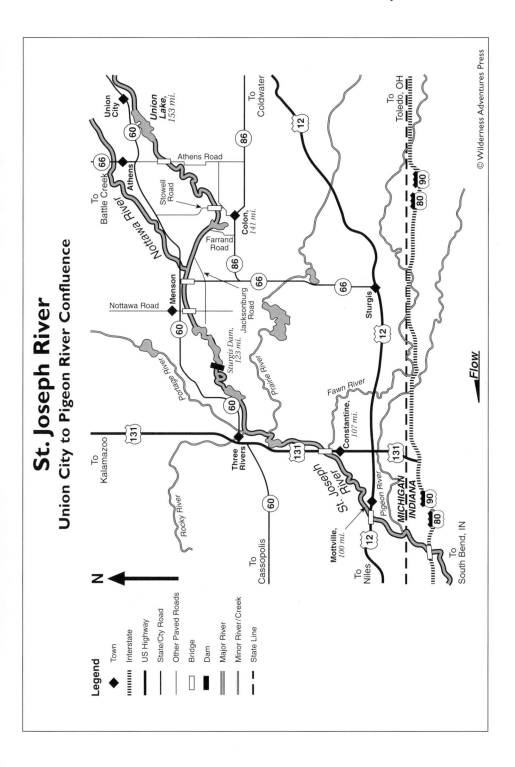

St. Joseph River
Union City to Pigeon River Confluence

© Wilderness Adventures Press

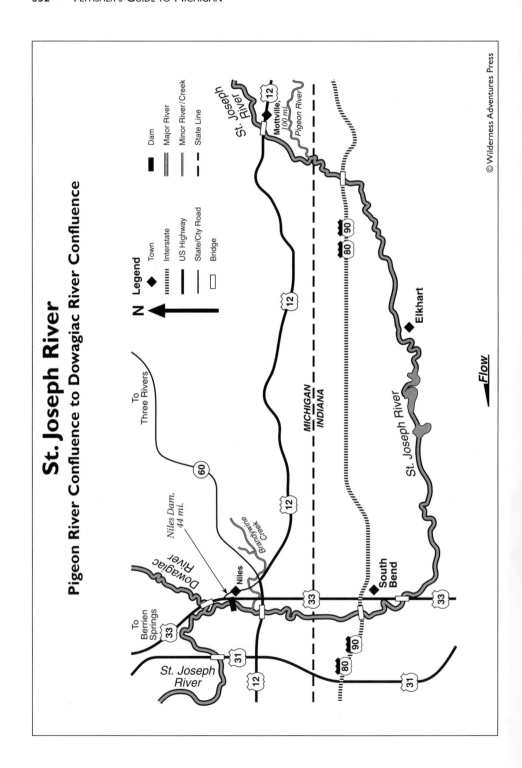

St. Joseph River
Pigeon River Confluence to Dowagiac River Confluence

© Wilderness Adventures Press

St. Joseph River
Dowagiac River Confluence to Lake Michigan

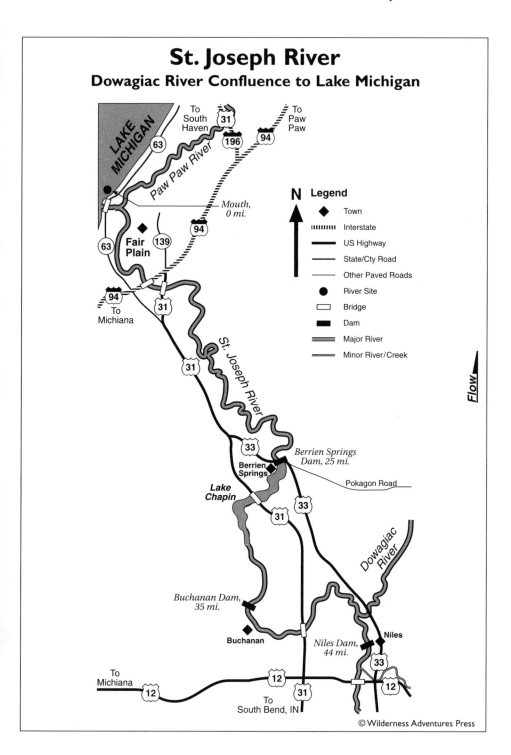

Legend

◆ Town

|||||||| Interstate

━━ US Highway

── State/Cty Road

── Other Paved Roads

● River Site

▢ Bridge

■ Dam

━ Major River

━ Minor River/Creek

N

Mouth, 0 mi.

Berrien Springs Dam, 25 mi.

Pokagon Road

Buchanan Dam, 35 mi.

Niles Dam, 44 mi.

Lake Chapin

Fair Plain

Berrien Springs

Buchanan

Niles

To South Haven

To Paw Paw

To Michiana

To Michiana

To South Bend, IN

Flow

© Wilderness Adventures Press

I still managed a brace of 15-inch browns along with a 17-inch smallmouth—not a bad mixed catch. The St. Joseph River now is much better floated than waded, with bridges providing the access.

When the St. Joseph comes back to Michigan, it has become a very large river, making wading even more limited except when it is very low. A number of dams continue to impound portions of the river, but they also tend to concentrate game fish below them. Brandywine Creek, which flows into the St. Joe upstream from Niles, is large enough to fish with a fly rod in its lower reaches and contains a good population of brown trout. The Michigan DNR recently purchased land between the first (Bond Street) and second (Third Street) bridges for additional access.

The Dowagiac River joins the St. Joseph downstream from Niles. A relatively large trout stream for southwest Michigan, it will be discussed in more detail later. Dams at Buchanan and Berrien Springs keep most of the river impounded, but below Berrien Springs, the river is freeflowing to Lake Michigan. This reach of river provides prime habitat for smallmouth bass, walleyes, and channel catfish. Flathead catfish and a few northern pike also add to the resident mix of game fish. Since crayfish and minnows make up the majority of the fish's diet here, nymphs and wet flies take a back seat to streamers imitating crayfish, shiners, sculpins, and creek chubs.

The big appeal of the lower St. Joseph River is the large influx of anadromous salmonids each year. Winter steelhead, brown trout, and chinook salmon are stocked by Michigan, while Indiana adds a summer-run Skamania strain steelhead, along with more salmon and winter steelhead, to the mix.

Although the idea of planting summer steelhead in a warmwater river has been questioned by many, the St. Joseph is Indiana's only large tributary to Lake Michigan. Since Indiana has had much success with this fish in its creeks, they decided to put them in the St. Joe after ladders were completed that made it possible for the fish to return to Indiana. The St. Joseph's summer water temperature is usually in the high 70s and routinely gets into the 80s. When water temperature drops to near 70 degrees after a cool spell, Skamania steelhead make their run. This creates big concentrations of fish below the dams, but I don't think they bite well because they are stressed while trying to get upstream. Many seek the cooler water of tributaries, such as the Dowagiac River, and either move up them or hold around the mouths.

There is a much better chance of enticing a summer-run fish to grab a gaudy streamer when it is holding in water 65 degrees or colder. This means fishing in the lower Dowagiac River or at the mouths of such feeders as Farmers, Lemon, Love, Pipestone, Hickory, and Big Meadow Creeks is a better bet than the main river below a dam. It is often possible to get out of the boat and wade where these creeks flow into the main stream. Polarized glasses can help in spotting these fish, and a careful stalk and good presentation of a fluorescent orange or pink nymph or a streamer can result in an exciting visual take.

These fish fight a very exciting but short-lived battle in the relatively warm stream. It is not unusual for Skamania strain steelhead to leap 5 feet out of the water —I almost always get wet from the splashdowns before I get them corralled. Use a strong tippet of 10- or 12-pound test so that you can horse the fish in near the end of the battle and release it before it becomes too fatigued.

In September, the water temperature usually drops into the 60s and stays there. New runs of summer steelhead, along with chinook salmon, invade the river and offer some exciting possibilities for the flyrodder. The water, usually relatively low at this time, continues to clear as fall progresses. Coho salmon, brown trout, winter steelhead, and lake trout join the party below Berrien Springs by mid to late October. Exciter and egg patterns entice strikes from all species, and the best area for flyfishing is along the west side of the island below the dam. There is good access with lots of parking on this side of the river at the dam. All of these fish, with the exception of lake trout, can also be caught below the upstream dams in Buchanan and Niles, but wading areas are limited.

Nottawa River

Even though the Nottawa River has been dredged for most of its length, it remains an important tributary to the St. Joe because its middle reach supports trout year-round. The trout fishing is best near and upstream from the town of Athens, south of Battle Creek. Channelized many years ago, the stream now has mature trees growing out of its dredge banks. A number of these have blown into the stream, creating cover and causing the flow to be concentrated periodically. There is usually plenty of casting room, but a tight roll cast is needed to get into some of the nooks and crannies where big browns lurk.

Because the stream is mostly sand-bottomed with very little suitable spawning gravel, it is dependent on DNR stocking of brown trout. During hot spells the Nottawa warms into the 70s, which make it best to fish in the morning or wait for cooler weather. Various caddis species and burrowing mayflies are present, but, as is

A beautiful brown trout comes to hand.

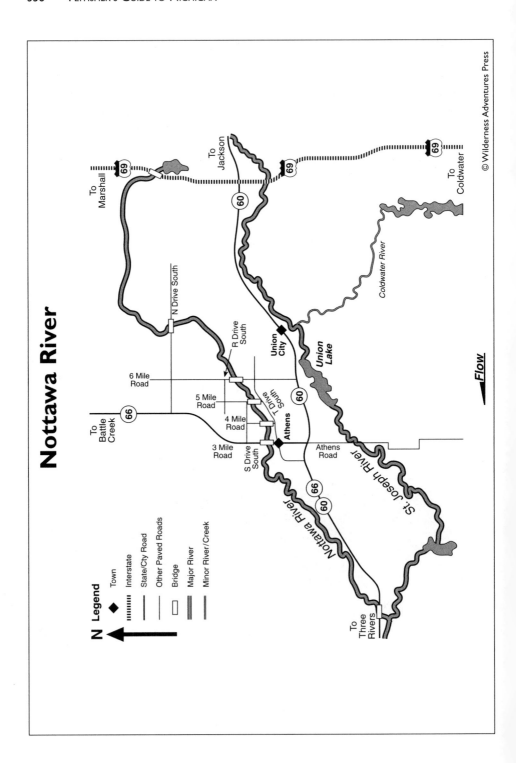

often the case with southern Michigan trout streams, crayfish are the staple in the diet of larger trout. As should be obvious by their names, 3 Mile, 4 Mile, 5 Mile, and 6 Mile Roads cross the Nottawa at 1-mile intervals. If you and a partner want to wade a stretch and cover water with streamers or nymphs, you can drop your partner off at the lower bridge and park the car at the next bridge. The downstream fisherman fishes to the car and picks up the upstream angler who has fished up to the next bridge. This eliminates walking back to the car or fishing back downstream, which is not very productive because of the river's sand and silt. Plan on about four to five hours to fish these dredged and straightened sections.

When Pine Creek joins the Nottawa below Athens, it becomes too warm for trout. There are smallmouth and pike here, and its stable flow often keeps it fishable when the mainstream is out of shape.

Dowagiac River

If it were in its natural state, the Dowagiac River would probably be a blue ribbon trout stream. The problem is that virtually the entire stream was dredged and straightened in the 1920s to lower the water table for farming the organic soils that bordered it. That's the bad news. The good news is that a partnership has been formed to rehabilitate the river, and it has a very appropriate acronym: MEANDRS— Meeting Ecological and Agricultural Needs within the Dowagiac River System. One of its main goals is to recreate the riffles, pools, and sinuosity of the stream within the dredge banks. By the time you read this, some of these projects might already have been completed.

Even as a "drain," the Dowagiac offers trout fishermen some fine sport for stocked brown trout, up to 6 or 8 pounds. It is a good-sized stream that is floatable and has a strong current. Trees have fallen in, and undercut banks and overhanging streamside vegetation provide cover. Crayfish and terrestrial patterns serve best in this stream, although there are sporadic caddis and mayfly hatches.

The headwaters are on the warm side for trout, but the stream cools off as it grows in size. The best reach for trout is the section near Sumnerville, where Peavine, Pokagon, and McKenzie Creeks add their flows. All three of these small streams, which contain good numbers of wild brown trout, are not stocked. Although they are a bit tight for flycasting, give them a try if things aren't happening in the main river. Access in this reach is provided by bridges at Peavine, Sink, Pokagon, and Sumnerville Roads.

One tributary that doesn't help cool the mainstream but does have room for fly-fishing is Dowagiac Creek. For the first 4 or 5 miles upstream from LaGrange Lake, there are carryover browns up to 20 inches and a fairly open stream, considering its size. Both the lake and an impoundment turn the creek into a warmwater stream before it reaches the Dowagiac River. The prime trout stretch is between Kelsey Lake Road and Goodenough Road, with Dutch Settlement Street, Griffis Road, McKenzie Street, Decatur Road, and Marcellus Highway bridges providing access in between.

In general, the hatches are more consistent here than on the Dowagiac River. Sulphurs in early May and brown drakes in late May are a couple of the best mayfly

Dowagiac River

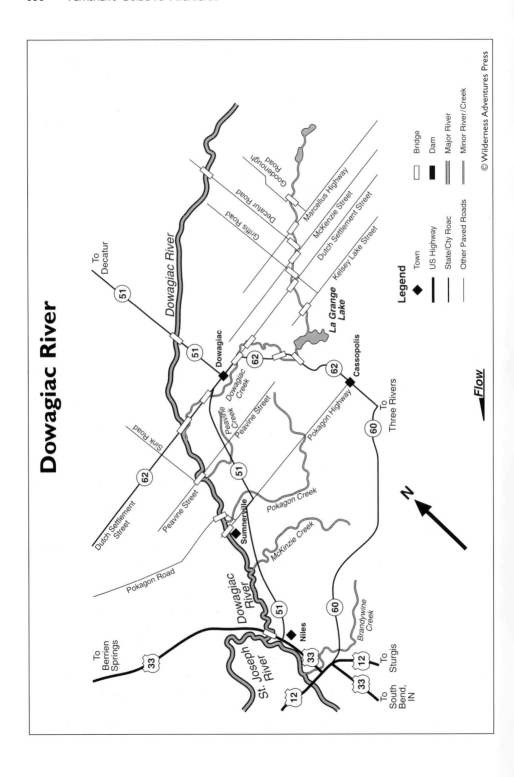

hatches. Caddisflies seem to be hatching all the time, and you can't go wrong with streamers imitating creek chubs and crayfish for larger trout. Northern Indiana and Illinois fly anglers seem to have adopted this stream, and cars bearing their license plates can often be seen at the bridges.

There is a dam a few miles upstream from the mouth of the Dowagiac River that blocks the migration of fish but does not warm the river too much. When conditions are right, this is the very best place in the St. Joseph system to fish for summer steelhead. If the St. Joe stays cool enough for good numbers of Skamania to get through both the Berrien Springs and Buchanan Dam fish ladders, they will often stray into the Dowagiac. Other anadromous species also stray into the Dowagiac, providing a mixed bag during fall and winter. Resident brown trout are also present. Below the dam, the river is open to fishing all year, but watch for the "potato hatch" (floaters on innertubes) in the summer. Because of its relatively fast current, this is a very popular stream for tubers.

Paw Paw River

The St. Joseph's largest tributary is the Paw Paw River, but it doesn't join the big river until just before it enters Lake Michigan. While the Paw Paw is a warmwater river, it is generally cooler than the St. Joe and occasionally attracts some summer steelhead. This river also runs clearer than the mainstream and is a good backup if it rains.

The Paw Paw starts out as three branches that all hold trout. In fact, if it were not for the dam that forms Maple Lake in the town of Paw Paw, the upper river would probably be a fine trout stream of considerable size. Of the three branches, the South (aka West) Branch is probably the only one large enough to flyfish, and it will require a lot of roll casting. The bottom is mostly sand, and much of it has been dredged, but there is a good carryover of stocked brown trout. Try fishing it at the 60th and 64th Avenue Bridges. The Wolf Lake Fish Hatchery and a Fisheries Interpretive Center are located near the headwaters of the North Branch, and they are definitely worth a visit if you are in the area.

Smallmouth and northern pike are the predominant resident species of the mainstream, but walleyes and rock bass are also present. In the lower river, channel catfish also add to the mix. The stream is floatable and most of it can be waded, but there may be deep sections that require a detour to the bank. Numerous bridges provide access. The river bends a lot, so when floating or wading, plan a little extra time for getting from point A to point B.

Steelhead are planted in the Paw Paw, and while a low head dam in Watervliet tends to slow them down, it doesn't stop their upstream migration. There is good gravel below this dam, making it a good spot to try for steelhead in the spring and some stray salmon in the fall. In fact, gravel riffles are not too numerous in the river, so whenever you find one, concentrate your fishing in nearby holes and runs. In spring, it's likely that there will be steelhead lurking in these places.

Two small rivers near the St. Joseph flow directly into Lake Michigan, and each has a branch offering some fly angling opportunities. The Galien River hits the beach

Paw Paw River

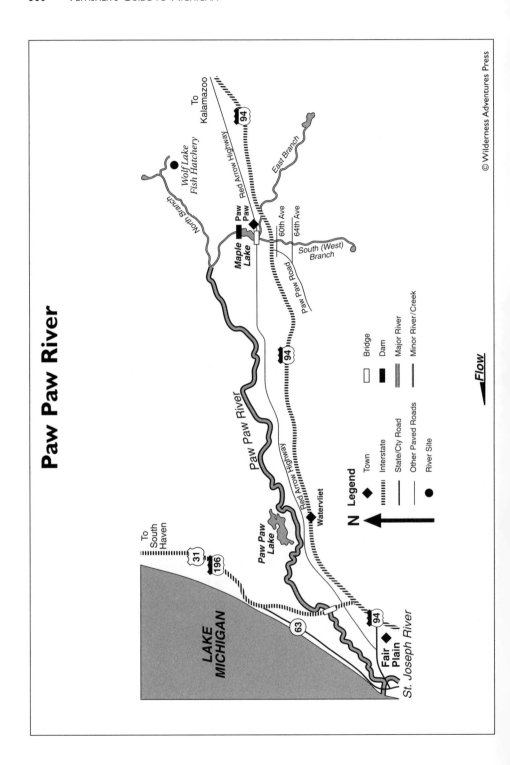

just north of the state border in the town of New Buffalo. The South Branch of this river is planted with brown trout, and summer steelhead routinely stray into it because of its cooler water. The 3 miles of stream south of US 12 are where you should concentrate your efforts. Though the stream isn't large, much of it flows through mature hardwoods where there is room to cast.

One of Michigan's many Black Rivers flows into Lake Michigan at South Haven, about 20 miles north of the St. Joseph mouth. The mainstream is very short, as its three branches don't come together until just a couple of miles from Lake Michigan. The primary resident predator in all three branches is the northern pike. Because the Middle Branch is the coolest, it sometimes attracts a good run of straying summer steelhead. When I have fished it, pike usually outnumbered the summer-runs and were almost as big as the steelhead, 5 to 9 pounds, and were exciting in the stream's very clear water. You will have to decide whether your streamers merit protection with a light wire leader. Old scissormouth definitely made quick work of some of my offerings. There are many county road bridges for access.

Stream Facts: St. Joseph River

Seasons
- Open all year.
- Black bass must be released between January 1 and the Saturday before Memorial Day.
- Walleyes and northern pike must be released between March 15 and the last Saturday in April.

Special Regulations
- Size limit for all trout and salmon between October 1 and the last Saturday in April is 15 inches.
- Possession limit is an aggregate of three.

Fish
- Resident: smallmouth and largemouth bass, walleye, northern pike, channel catfish, panfish, carp.
- Anadromous: summer and winter steelhead, lake trout, brown trout, coho and chinook salmon—late summer through spring with spurts of summer steelhead during cold spells in summer.
- Brown and brook trout in selected tributaries.

River Miles
- Lake Michigan—0
- Berrien Springs Dam—25
- Buchanan Dam—35
- Niles Dam—44
- Mottville—100
- Constantine—107
- Sturgis Dam—123
- Colon—141
- Union Lake—153

River Characteristics
- This is a large warmwater river, with difficult wading in the lower river.
- Many dams are sprinkled through out.

River Access
- Primary access is at road bridges and most of the dams.
- Developed boat launches are present at several locations below Berrien Springs and are noted on the map.

Southwestern Lower Peninsula Hub Cities

Grand Rapids
Population – 189,126

ACCOMMODATIONS
Cascade Inn, 2865 Broadmoor SE / 616-949-0850
Colonial Motel, 330 Northland Drive (Rockford) / 616-866-1585 / Near the Rogue River
Amway Grand Plaza Hotel, 187 Monroe Avenue SW / 616-776-6450 / On the Grand River
Plainfield Motel, 3709 Plainfield NE / 616-361-6603

CAMPGROUNDS
Grand Rogue Campgrounds & Canoes, 3747 Hordyk NE / 616-361-1053
Hungry Horse Campground, 2016 142nd (Dorr) / 616-681-9836
Indian Valley Campground & Canoe, 8200 108th SE (Caledonia) / 616-891-8579
Woodchip RV Park, 7501 Burlingame SW (Byron Center) / 616-8789050
Holland State Park, 2215 Ottawa Beach Road (Holland) / 616-399-9390

FLY SHOPS AND SPORTING GOODS
Great Lakes Fly Fishing Co., 2775 10 Mile Road (Rockford) / 616-866-6060
Thornapple Orvis Shop, 1200 East Paris (Ada) / 616-676-0177
Al & Pete's Sport Shop, 111 South Jefferson (Hastings) / 616-945-4417
American Tackle Outfitters, 360 Douglas Avenue (Holland) / 616-392-6688
Al & Bob's Sports, 3100 South Division Avenue / 616-245-9156
Gander Mountain, 2890 Acquest Avenue SE / 616-975-1000
Michigan Sporting Goods, 3160 28th St / 616-949-8510

RESTAURANTS
The Gathering Place, 6886 Cascade Road SE / 616-949-3188
Ada Bridge Inn, 7586 East Fulton (Ada) / 616-676-2114 / Near Thornapple River
Backwater Café, 109 Riverside Drive (Lowell) / 616-897-6370 / Flat River
Dockside Pizza, 8451 Belding Road NE (Rockford) / 616-874-7292 / Rogue River

AIR SERVICE
Kent County International, 5500 44th SE / 616-336-4500

MEDICAL
Blodgett Memorial Medical Center, 1840 Wealthy SE / 616-774-7444
Butterworth Hospital, 100 North Michigan NE / 616-391-1720
Saint Mary's Health Services, 200 Jefferson SE / 616-456-1453

FOR MORE INFORMATION

Grand Rapids Chamber of Commerce
111 Pearl NW
Grand Rapids, MI 49503
616-771-0300

Lansing
Population – 127,321

ACCOMMODATIONS
Burkewood Inn, 3216 West Main / 517-487-9119 / 78 Units
West View Motel, 15713 South US 27 (Dewitt) / 517-484-4439 / Near Looking
Glass River
Williamston Inn, 1133 E. Grand River (Williamston) / 517-655-3773 / Red Cedar
River
Willow Lakes Motel & Grocery, 7113 Saginaw Hwy (East Lansing) / 517-339-9021

CAMPGROUNDS
Lansing Cottonwood Campground, 5339 Aurelius / 517-393-3200 / On
Sycamore Creek
Hickory Lake Campgrounds, 11433 South Beardslee Road (Perry) / 517-625-3113
Wheel Inn Campground, 240 Fogg, Leslie / 517-589-8097
Sleepy Hollow State Park, 7835 Price Road (Laingsburg) / 517-651-6217

FLY SHOPS AND SPORTING GOODS
BC Nymph Co., 302 S Waverly / 517-321-3800
M. Chance Fly Fishing Specialties (Orvis), 5100 Marsh (Okemos) / 517-349-6696
Gander Mountain, 430 Market Placw Blvd. / 517-622-5700
Grand River Bait & Tackle, 536 East Grand River / 517-82-4461
BC Nymph Co., 302 South Waverly / 517-321-3800
Four Seasons Bait & Tackle, 1210 North Cedar Street / 517-487-0050

RESTAURANTS
Beggar's Banquet, 218 Abbott Road (East Lansing) / 517-351-4540
Clara's Restaurant, 637 East Michigan Avenue / 517-372-7120
Apple Jade Restaurant, 505 Frandor / 517-332-8010
Sammy's, 301 East Jolly / 517-394-3447

AIR SERVICE
Capital City Airport, 4100 Capital City Boulevard / 517-321-6121

MEDICAL
Ingham Regional Medical Center, 401 West Greenlawn / 517-334-2121
Sparrow Hospital, 1215 East Michigan / 517-483-2700

FOR MORE INFORMATION
Lansing Regional Chamber of Commerce
300 East Michigan
Lansing, MI 48933
517-487-6340

Benton Harbor/St. Joseph
Population – 22,032

ACCOMMODATIONS
Benton Harbor Comfort Inn, 1598 Mall Drive (Benton Harbor) / 616-925-1880
Village Inn, 9008 US 31 (Berrien Springs) / 616-471-1354
Best Western Golden Link, 2723 Niles Avenue (St. Joseph) / 616-983-6321
Quality Inn, 2860 M-139 (Benton Harbor) / 616-925-3234
Super 8 Motel, 1950 East Napier (Benton Harbor) / 616-926-1371

CAMPGROUNDS
Benton Harbor KOA, 3527 Colon Road (Riverside) / 616-849-3333
Paw Paw River Campground and Canoe Livery, 5355 M-140 (Watervliet) /
    616-463-5454
Oronoko Lakes Campground (Berrien Springs) / 616-471-7389
Warren Dunes State Park, 12032 Red Arrow Hwy (Sawyer) / 616-426-4013

FLY SHOPS AND SPORTING GOODS
Lunker's, 26296 East US 12 (Edwardsburg) / 616-663-3745
Dick's Place, 7100 West Territorial Road (Camden) / 517-368-5283
Tackle Haven, 741 Riverview Drove (Benton Harbor) / 616-925-0341

RESTAURANTS
McLaughlin's, 2699 M-139 (Benton Harbor) / 616-925-3333
Chickhaven Restaurant, 2675 Niles Road (St. Joseph) / 616-429-0151
Clementine's Too, 1235 Broad Street (St. Joseph) / 616-983-0990
Zitta's at the Depot, 410 Vine Street (St. Joseph) / 616-983-7541
Roma Pizzeria-Restaurant, 121 West Ferry Street (Berrien Springs) / 616-471-7755

AIR SERVICE
Southwest Michigan Regional Airport, 1123 Territorial (Benton Harbor) /
    616-927-3194

MEDICAL
Sister Lakes Medical Center, 67892 West M-152 (Benton Harbor) / 616-944-3500

FOR MORE INFORMATION
Lakeshore Chamber of Commerce
P.O. Box 93
Stevensville, MI 49127
616-429-1170

Kalamazoo
Population – 80,277

ACCOMMODATIONS
Stuart Avenue Inn, 229 Stuart Avenue / 616-342-0230
Kalamazoo Hampton Inn, 1550 East Kilgore Road / 616-344-7774
Radisson Plaza Hotel, 100 West Michigan / 616-343-3333
Kalamazoo Motel 6, 3704 Van Rick Road / 616-344-9255

CAMPGROUNDS
Curtis Trailer Center (Plainwell) / 616-685-6837
Van Buren State Park, 23960 Ruggles Road (South Haven) / 616-637-2788.

FLY SHOPS AND SPORTING GOODS
Angling Outfitters, 3207 Stadium Dr / 616-372-0922
Fishing Memories, 8842 Portage Road (Portage) / 616-329-1803
Doc's Custom Fly Tackle, 1804 Thrushwood (Portage) / 616-327-8917
D & R Sports Center, 8178 West Main / 616-49009, 372-2277

RESTAURANTS
Lafontanella Restaurant, 678 Maple Hill Drive / 616-344-6918
Demeyer's Country Kitchen, 6375 Stadium Drive / 616-375-7113
Russ Restaurant, 7225 South Westnedge (Portage) / 616-323-1750
Olive Tree Restaurant, 2307 East Main / 616-345-4321
Gum-Ho Restaurant, 5222 Portage Road / 616-343-1990

FOR MORE INFORMATION
Kalamazoo County Chamber of Commerce
P.O. Box 51169
Kalamazoo, MI 49005
616-381-4000

Battle Creek
Population – 53,540

ACCOMMODATIONS
McCamly Plaza Hotel, 50 Capital Avenue SW / 616-963-7050
Michigan Motel, 20475 Capital Avenue NE / 616-963-1565
Red Carpet Inn, 11081 East Michigan / 616-964-3000
Economy Inn, 90 North Division / 616-966-4000

CAMPGROUNDS
Cereal City Campground / 616-968-8248

FLY SHOPS AND SPORTING GOODS
Dickerson Sporting Goods, 95 Sigel Avenue / 616-963-7429
Creekside Bait & Tackle, 22551 Bedford Road North / 616-721-8990

RESTAURANTS
Jack's, 1346 West Michigan / 616-964-1995
Shrank's Cafeteria, 85 West Michigan / 616-964-7755
TE-KHI Truck Auto Plaza, 15874 Eleven Mile Road / 616-965-7721
Homespun Restaurant, 210 East Columbia Avenue / 616-962-5323
Mr. Cribbins, 5050 Beckley Road / 616-979-1100

AIR SERVICE
W K Kellogg Airport / 616-966-3470

FOR MORE INFORMATION
Battle Creek Area Chamber of Commerce
34 West Jackson Street
Battle Creek, MI 49017
616-962-4076

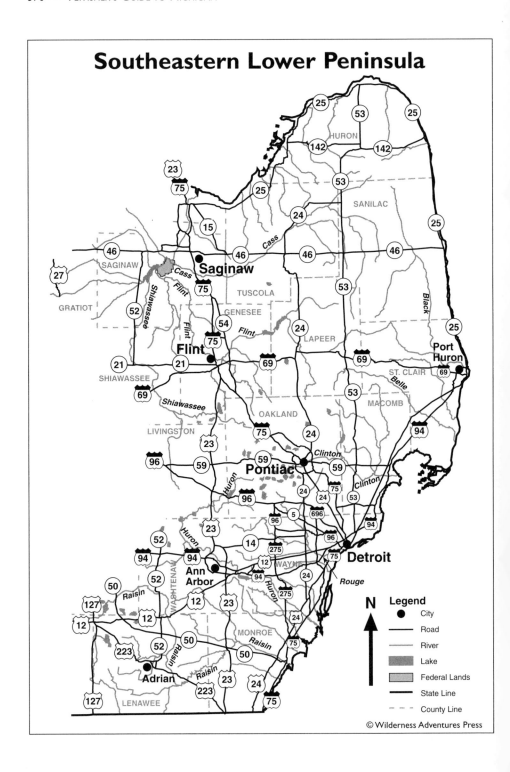

Southeastern Lower Peninsula

Southeastern Lower Peninsula

Because southeast Michigan is heavily populated, most anglers don't think of it as a place to go to cast a fly. It is true that much of this part of the state has been built up and paved, but there are still lots of open spaces and an excellent park system. The development of urban fisheries has been important to Michigan ever since the gasoline shortage. This may seem like a distant memory with the current surplus, but everything seems to go in cycles, and it will be great to have brought fish to the populated areas if fuel supplies get tight again. And visitors to the Detroit metro area on business can appreciate some nearby fishing opportunities.

South of Detroit, the Huron and Raisin Rivers flow directly into Lake Erie, while just to the north of the metro area the Clinton River meanders to Lake St. Clair. A number of smaller rivers drain Michigan's "Thumb" directly to Lake Huron and the St. Clair River, while the Cass River flows west and north to the Saginaw. In this region, the Flint and Shiawassee are two other major tributaries to the Saginaw River. The prime resident fish species is the smallmouth bass, with steelhead being the principal seasonal visitor to the rivers in southeast Michigan. Walleyes are resident in some rivers and make runs in these and others. Trout opportunities are limited to a few small tributaries of the large rivers.

There are a surprising number of lakes in southeast Michigan, and Oakland County, Michigan's second most populated, is blessed with hundreds of small lakes. Many of the small tributaries to Lake Huron in the Thumb are planted with steelhead and/or chinook at their mouths, creating shore and pier fishing opportunities.

River Raisin

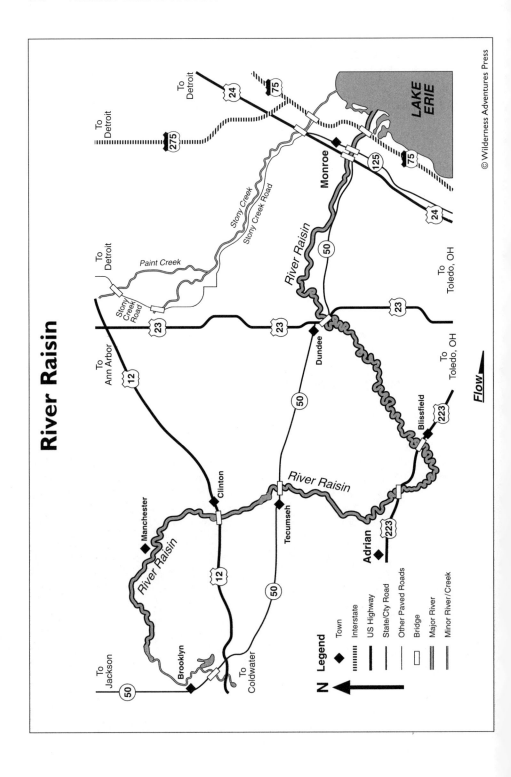

LAKE ERIE

To Detroit

To Detroit

To Detroit

To Detroit

To Ann Arbor

To Toledo, OH

To Toledo, OH

To Jackson

To Coldwater

Flow

© Wilderness Adventures Press

Monroe

Dundee

Blissfield

Clinton

Tecumseh

Manchester

Adrian

Brooklyn

River Raisin

Stony Creek

Stony Creek Road

Paint Creek

Stony Creek Road

N

Legend

◆ Town

Interstate

US Highway

State/Cty Road

Other Paved Roads

Bridge

Major River

Minor River/Creek

RIVER RAISIN

For some reason, two southeast streams have their names reversed: River Rouge and River Raisin. I believe they are the only two in the state so named. And I don't think the reason that this was done is due to the fact that the River Raisin reverses its flow at the mouth when there are strong winds from the east on Lake Erie.

The River Raisin begins very near the headwaters of the Grand River, south of Jackson. There are lakes in all of its headwater creeks, making the Raisin a warmwater stream from the start. Downstream from the town of Brooklyn, the stream is large enough to flyfish and contains an excellent population of smallmouth bass and northern pike. Except for several impoundments, the stream can be waded all the way down to Tecumseh. There are lots of bridges for access, and where the distance between bridges is more than 2 miles, floating is a good option. Logs and large rocks

A smallmouth bass comes to hand.

provide cover for bass and pike. Crayfish are abundant, and minnow-imitating streamers are also effective for taking fish.

Turbidity becomes a problem as the river continues downstream. Suspended fine clay and silt muddy the water up even during low flows. This is unfortunate because the lower river flows over bedrock and has excellent smallmouth bass habitat. Bass, along with some channel catfish and walleyes, are there, as bait anglers regularly prove, but there is rarely enough visibility for good flyfishing. Even the bass would do better if the water were clearer.

Just north of the Raisin, Stony Creek winds its way to Lake Erie, offering some fishing for smallmouth bass and northern pike. One of the region's two Paint Creeks is a tributary to this stream and offers some trout fishing. The problem is that trout are restricted to the upper creek where there is little room for casting, and stocking the stream has been curtailed lately. Some steelhead do stray into Stony Creek, probably from the large plant in the Huron River. I was once surprised by a lingering steelie while trout fishing on Paint Creek in midsummer. The 28-inch rainbow certainly dwarfed the 10- to 15-inch browns I was catching.

HURON RIVER

The Huron is one of the jewels of southeast Michigan. Local government units have recognized that this is a valuable natural resource close to millions of people and have created recreation areas (RA) and metroparks (MP) throughout its length. The stream is principally home to smallmouth and rock bass, with other warmwater species, such as northern pike, walleye, channel catfish, and panfish joining the mix. Steelhead provide action in the lower river, and a special trout fishery has been created for spring and early summer.

At its headwaters in Oakland County, much of the Huron either flows through lakes or is impounded. Downstream from Proud and Moss Lakes, the stream is large enough to be fished with a fly rod, and the bottom firms up for easy wading. A special early season trout fishery has been established between the outlet of Moss Lake and about 100 yards below Wixom Road. While almost all trout planted by the DNR in Michigan are fingerlings and yearlings that must grow to reach catchable size, an exception is made for the Huron. Since the river is too warm for year-round survival and there is a paucity of trout water in this part of the state, several thousand adult browns and rainbows are planted in the Huron each year.

Most of the trout are between 10 and 14 inches, but a number of larger brood stock browns and rainbows are often added to spice up the fishing. Of course, if your partner does not know about the possibility of a much larger fish, you might keep quiet and enjoy the reaction when he or she hooks a trout measured in pounds instead of inches. Each March the Huron is planted from Wixom Road upstream. This reach is entirely within the Proud Lake State Recreation Area. You can gain access to the river from Wixom Road or from trails in the recreation area. From April 1 to the last Saturday in April, angling is restricted to flies only, and all trout must be released. After this special

*An angler works a run
on the Huron River.*

season, regular rules apply and all methods may be used. Trout continue to be present until sometime in June, depending on the weather and how fast they are removed for the frying pan. Attractor patterns tend to work best for these hatchery fish.

Further description of this river makes it obvious that dam builders had a field day with this river. Where it is free-flowing, the Huron provides some fine fishing for smallmouth bass. There is a good population of rock bass, as well, and this predatory panfish can keep you busy if the smallies turn off. Below Kent Lake there is a good stretch of water down to a series of lakes at the county line. This stretch can be waded or floated, and public access is very good, since much of it flows through the Island Lake State Recreation Area and the Huron Meadows Metropark.

One of the Huron's longest free-flowing sections can be found below the chain of lakes and proceeding into Washtenaw County. The river is wide and has lots of rocky riffles between boulder-strewn pools. This is just the kind of habitat that smallmouth prefer, and the bass are there. Within the reach, there are about 6 miles of special no-kill water for smallmouth bass between the town of Dexter and the Delhi

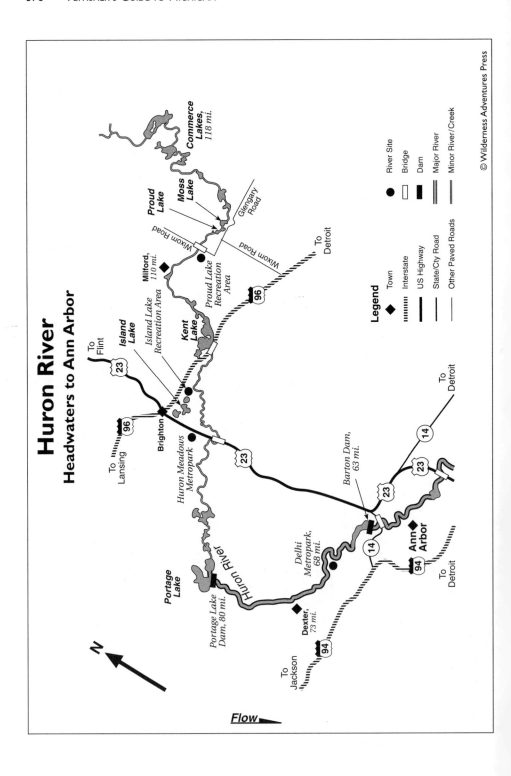

Huron River
Headwaters to Ann Arbor

Commerce Lakes, 118 mi.

Moss Lake

Proud Lake

Glengary Road

Wixom Road

Milford, 110 mi.

Proud Lake Recreation Area

Wixom Road

To Detroit

96

Island Lake

Island Lake Recreation Area

Kent Lake

To Flint

23

To Lansing

96

Brighton

Huron Meadows Metropark

23

To Detroit

14

Barton Dam, 63 mi.

23

23

Delhi Metropark, 68 mi.

Huron River

Portage Lake

14

Ann Arbor

94

To Detroit

Portage Lake Dam, 80 mi.

Dexter, 73 mi.

94

To Jackson

N

Flow

Legend

Town

Interstate

US Highway

State/Cty Road

Other Paved Roads

River Site

Bridge

Dam

Major River

Minor River/Creek

© Wilderness Adventures Press

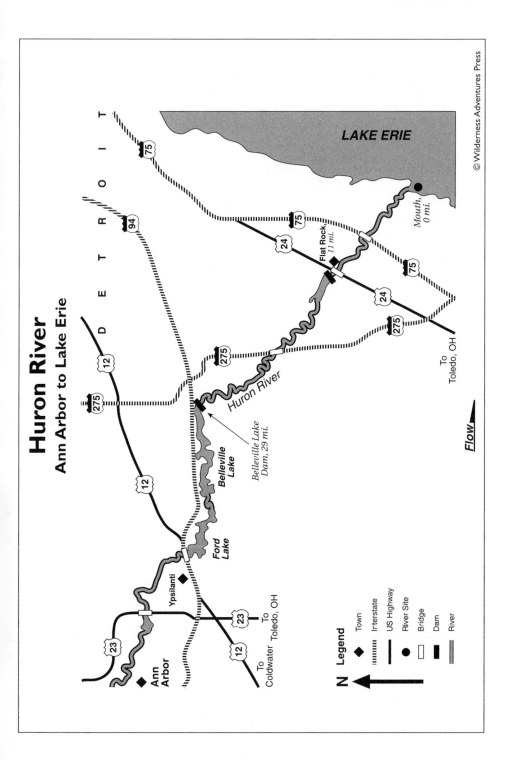

Huron River
Ann Arbor to Lake Erie

LAKE ERIE

DETROIT

Mouth, 0 mi.

Flat Rock, 11 mi.

Huron River

To Toledo, OH

Belleville Lake Dam, 29 mi.

Belleville Lake

Ford Lake

Ypsilanti

To Coldwater

To Toledo, OH

Ann Arbor

N

Legend
- ◆ Town
- ▬ Interstate
- ━ US Highway
- ● River Site
- ▭ Bridge
- ▮ Dam
- River

Flow

© Wilderness Adventures Press

A channel catfish
from the Huron River.

Metropark. The fishing is very good here, but it has been hard to determine if the no-kill regulation is helping since anglers frequently release smallmouth anyway.

This is great water for neophyte fly anglers to practice on before tackling tighter situations. And beginners get lots of positive feedback from the plentiful and eager smallies and rock bass. Muddlers, woolly buggers, and crayfish-imitating streamer patterns will all work well for these fish. Bass also come to the surface during hatches of large mayflies or for a swimming imitation of a frog, mouse, or wounded minnow. Large carp are present in the slower holes if you want to test your fish landing abilities, and the relatively clear water allows them to see your nymphs—red San Juan worms and red squirrel nymphs being especially effective.

From the Barton Impoundment in Ann Arbor down to Belleville Lake Dam, the Huron is mostly impounded. There is another stretch of good smallmouth water that runs below Belleville down to the shallow impoundment in Flat Rock. Below Flat Rock, the Huron becomes slow, deep, and unwadeable for the rest of its trip to Lake Erie.

The Huron gets a large plant of steelhead, which provide a good fishery from late fall into spring. Cold weather shuts the fishing down in the winter, but this is

Huron River walleye.

kind of the "warm spot" of Michigan, so the frozen periods are not quite as long. Though steelhead tend to stack up below the Flat Rock Dam, there is a ladder that allows them to move up to Belleville Lake. This provides lots more fishing room for the wading angler, because most of the reach below Belleville can be waded when the water is low and almost continuous parkland allows bank access when the water is higher. Egg flies as well as stonefly and mayfly nymphs are most commonly used here, but large gaudy marabou streamers may be a better bet, especially when there is some turbidity. The run usually gets going a bit earlier here than in the more northern streams, with the peak often coming in mid to late March.

Walleyes also run the Huron in early spring, but they usually do not ascend the fish ladder. Pearl and white Zonkers in sizes 4 and 6 are good bets for these Lake Erie fish, which can occasionally be in the double figure class. Other streamers in white and chartreuse colors also get the attention of spawning walleyes. The run's peak is likely to occur in late March or early April, so take your camera because you will have to release your fish.

Stream Facts: Huron River

Seasons
- Open all year.
- Bass must be released between January 1 and the Saturday before Memorial Day.
- Walleyes and northern pike must be released between March 15 and the last Saturday in April.

Special Regulations
- Catch and release for trout between April 1 and the last Saturday in April between the Moss Lake outlet and signs 100 yards below Wixom Road.
- Catch and release for smallmouth and largemouth bass all year between Mast Road bridge in Dexter and Delhi Road Bridge in Delhi Metropark.
- The size limit for steelhead between October 1 and last Saturday in April is 15 inches.

Fish
- Smallmouth and largemouth bass, northern pike, walleye, channel catfish, panfish, and carp, along with brown and rainbow trout in the spring and early summer above Wixom Road.
- Anadromous steelhead and walleye—fall through spring.

River Miles
- Lake Erie—0
- Flat Rock –11
- Belleville Lake dam—29
- Barton Dam—63
- Delhi Metropark—68
- Dexter—73
- Portage Lake Dam—80
- Milford—110
- Commerce Lake—118

River Characteristics
- This is a medium-sized river with slow to moderate gradient.
- It is one of the most heavily impounded rivers in the state, but where it is free flowing, the river usually has a firm sand and gravel bottom.

River Access
- Access to this river is excellent, with over a dozen metroparks and recreation areas on its banks.
- Access is also available at many bridges and at each landmark noted above with river miles.

HURON RIVER AND RIVER RAISIN MAJOR HATCHES

Insect	Jan	Feb	Mar	Apr	May	Jun	July	Aug	Sep	Oct	Nov	Dec	Time	Fly Patterns
Hendrickson				■	■								M/A	Hendrickson #12–14; Quill Gordon; Red Quill; Adams
Blue-winged Olive					■	■	■	■					A	Blue-winged Olive #18–20; Sparkle Dun Baetis; Iron Dun; Olive CDC Mayfly Dun
Net-building Caddis					■	■	■	■	■	■			M/A	Spotted Sedge #16–18; Eastern Elk Wing Caddis; Goddard Caddis
Sulphur Dun					■	■	■						A/E	Sulphur Dun #16; Pale Morning Dun; CDC Comparadun Yellow; Pale Evening Dun
Brown Drake					■	■							E	Brown Drake #10–12; Adams; CDC Brown Drake
Hexagenia						■	■						E	Hex #4–8; Great Olive-winged Drake; Spring's Wiggler; Hare's Ear
Trico						■	■	■	■	■			M	Tiny White Wing Black #24–28; Parachute Adams; CDC Trico; Spent Wing Trico
White Fly								■	■				E	White Fly #12–14; White Miller
Streamers		■	■	■	■	■	■	■	■	■	■	■	M/A/E	Woolly Buggers #6–12; Clouser's Minnow; Muddler Minnows; BC Craw; Matukas; Zonkers; Hellgrammites
Terrestrials						■	■	■	■				M/A/E	Woolly Worm #8–12; BC Spider; Letort Cricket; Joe's Hopper #6–10; Dave's Hopper; Dropper Hopper
Carp Nymphs					■	■	■	■	■				M/A/E	Red Squirrel Nymph #10–12; San Antonio Wiggler #8–10; Teeny Leech #6–8

HATCH TIME CODE: M = morning; A = afternoon; E = evening.

River Rouge

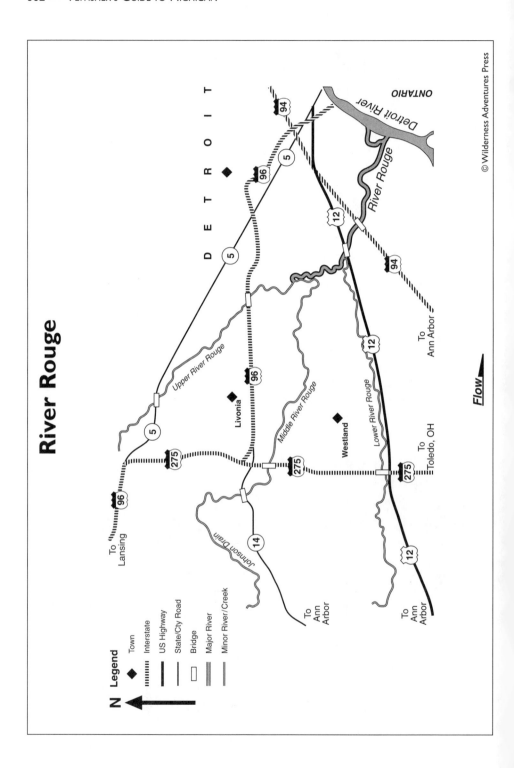

Legend

◆ Town

Interstate

US Highway

State/Cty Road

Bridge

Major River

Minor River/Creek

© Wilderness Adventures Press

River Rouge

The River Rouge is by far Michigan's most urban river. In terms of fishing, it is rarely mentioned and continues to carry the reputation of being very polluted. It has been confused a bit in the past with west Michigan's Rogue River, because writers have frequently misspelled it as the Rouge River. With the much more aesthetic and better fishing nearby in the Huron and Clinton Rivers, many would question its inclusion in this guide. A principal reason is that some may want to sample this river to see how its recovery is going and perhaps catch some game fish on a fly from this river that was once virtually devoid of fish. Another is that Johnson Drain, a tributary to the Rouge, offers the only chance for trout in Detroit's Wayne County.

CLINTON RIVER

For an urban river, the Clinton provides surprisingly good fishing opportunities for a variety of fish. It would be hard to find a stream that has benefited more than the Clinton from pollution control. The habitat has always been there, and the fish came back once the water quality improved.

The river begins in Oakland, close to the origin of the Huron River and, like the Huron, has many lakes in its headwaters. As it leaves the city of Pontiac, it is large enough to fish with a fly rod and float with a canoe. The fish that are present range from brown trout to panfish to northern pike. The good gradient and firm streambed make wading easy. Paint Creek, the best trout stream in southeast Michigan, joins the Clinton at the town of Rochester and helps keep the river cool. Despite the addition of a number of small tributaries, the Clinton can be waded until the Middle and

Walleye are being caught by more and more fly anglers.

Clinton River

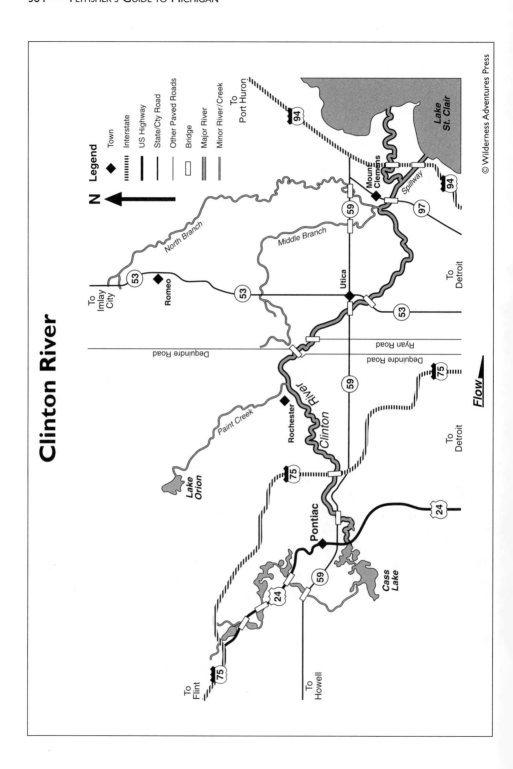

© Wilderness Adventures Press

North Branches join the mainstream just upstream from Mt. Clemens. From here to Lake St. Clair, the river is deep and slow and does not lend itself to flyfishing.

Except for a low head dam (Yates Dam) at Dequindre Road, below Pontiac the river is not impounded. Yates Dam stops walleyes and most of the steelhead that run the river. Some steelhead that are able to get past this obstacle when there is high water have successfully spawned in Paint Creek. Steelhead smolts are planted annually at Dequindre Road, so this is a focal point for fall and spring fishing for anadromous rainbows. There is a park here, and sometimes there are more spectators than there are anglers. The spring walleye run coincides with the steelhead run, so walleye also tend to concentrate here. The reach between here and Utica is the prime one for both anadromous and resident fish. It is classic water, with gravel riffles alternating with pools and lots of wood in the water for cover.

Interestingly, the mile of river between Dequindre and Ryan Roads is almost devoid of any sign of habitation except for a gun club, which is both good news and bad news. The bad news is that there are major Superfund contamination sites on each side of the river. The good news is that these are being remediated, and we don't ever have to worry about the Clinton River banks being developed in this reach. Wading or floating from bridge to bridge is a good way to cover all the water and is my favorite way to fish this section.

Paint Creek

Paint Creek is not a large stream, but most of it is open enough for flyfishing. The stream begins as the outlet of Lake Orion and joins Clinton River in the city of Rochester. A few years ago the DNR installed a deepwater draw out of Lake Orion that has helped cool down the stream and allow trout to thrive throughout its length. There is some natural reproduction, but yearling brown trout are planted each year. A couple of tiny tributaries contribute an occasional brook trout to the creek, and offspring of some of the steelhead that spawn in the creek will be present in the riffles. There is the chance to find a lingering adult steelhead during the first couple weeks of the season, and occasionally, some of the young steelhead don't smolt and become resident rainbows.

An abandoned railroad that parallels almost the entire length of the creek has been converted to a trail through the Rails-to-Trails Program. The result is super access to this stream, with one side of the stream almost always undeveloped. It is necessary to fish in backyards at times, but trout can be found there. My one complaint is that I wish homeowners would refrain from having to have lawn right down to the edge of the creek.

The stream is rich with a diverse population of insects. Creek chubs and crayfish are also present, so if there isn't a hatch, probe the undercuts and pools with streamers imitating these large food items and it's likely that you could hook up to some of the larger carryover trout.

Belle River

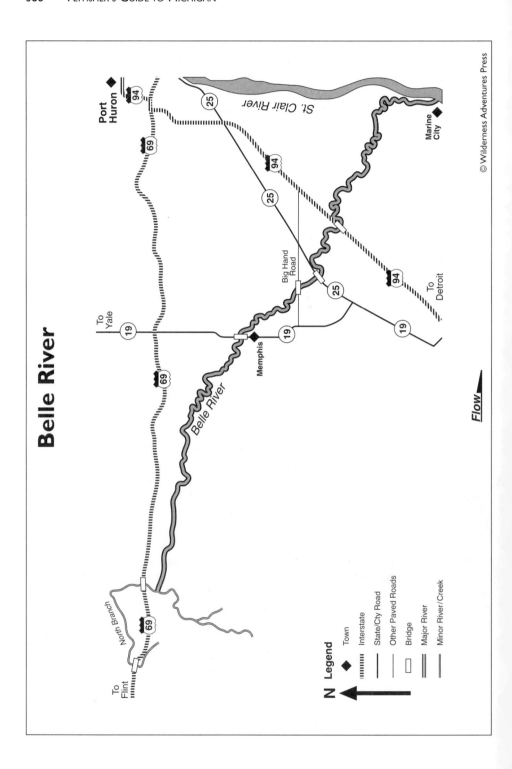

© Wilderness Adventures Press

North Branch of the Clinton

The North Branch of the Clinton is less urbanized than the mainstream. Most of it flows through farmland, with a number of golf courses built on its banks. Although smallmouth bass, northern pike, and rock bass are its main game fish, there are some trout in its headwaters. Unfortunately, the trout are tough to get at because of the creek's small size. Occasionally, trout move down into the mainstream in the spring.

While steelhead are not planted, some fish do stray into it each year. The North Branch clears faster after a rain, so it can be a backup stream if the main Clinton is too turbid. The reach downstream from Romeo is best for wielding a fly rod, both for resident warmwater fish and the chance for a steelhead or brown trout in the spring.

Belle River

The Belle River flows directly into the St. Clair River at Marine City. A small river that offers good fishing for smallmouth bass in the summer and steelhead in the spring, the Belle becomes fishable with flies downstream from Memphis. There is good access at numerous road crossings. Relative to its size, it receives a large steelhead plant at Big Hand Road, about 20 river miles up from its mouth. Gravel riffles are relatively scarce on this stream, so a good plan when steelhead fishing is to cover lots of water and concentrate your fishing when spawning gravel is located. Deep runs and holes just above or below riffles are prime spots.

A steelhead worth remembering.

Black River

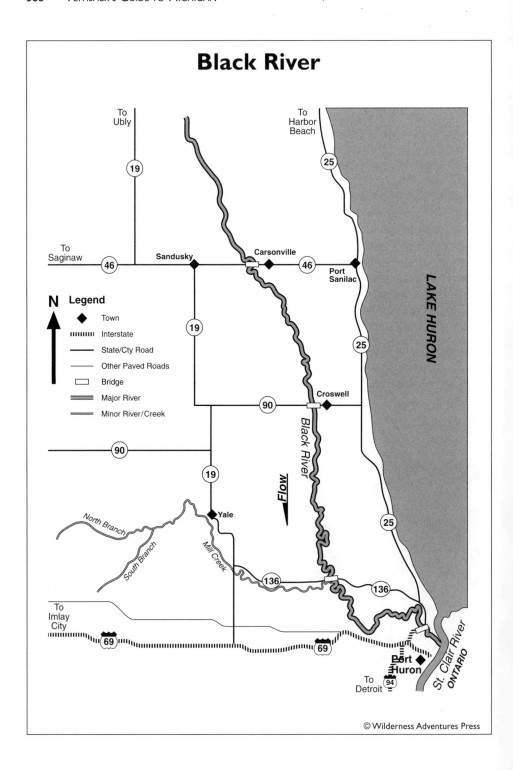

To Ubly

To Harbor Beach

19

25

To Saginaw

46

Sandusky

Carsonville

46

Port Sanilac

N

Legend

◆ Town

Interstate

State/Cty Road

Other Paved Roads

Bridge

Major River

Minor River/Creek

19

25

90

Croswell

90

Black River

Flow

19

25

North Branch

South Branch

Mill Creek

Yale

136

136

LAKE HURON

To Imlay City

69

69

Port Huron

To Detroit

94

St. Clair River

ONTARIO

© Wilderness Adventures Press

Black River

Still another Michigan Black River flows into the St. Clair River at Port Huron. Like many streams that drain the Thumb, this Black tends to be very turbid most of the time, making fishing opportunities limited. The reason it is included here is that its main tributary, Mill Creek, is a good smallmouth stream that gets a good run of steelhead in the spring. Steelhead are planted near the town of Yale, and fishing the sections below here from bridge to bridge is a great way to find and catch the silver visitors. There are bridges at almost every mile, and just as they do in the Belle River, steelhead are likely to be concentrated where you find good gravel. Because of the convenient road crossings, using the same tactics for smallmouth is a good plan. Quickly moving through the flatwater and then swinging streamers through the areas with good cover can produce hookups with the bronzebacks.

Both Mill Creek and Belle River are negotiable with kickboats, but you may have to walk around a few logjams. A friend regularly floats these small streams and efficiently finds the concentrations of steelhead.

CASS RIVER

The Cass is the largest river draining Michigan's Thumb. It is one of the major tributaries to the Saginaw River, joining the Shiawassee River just before it merges with the Tittabawassee to form the Saginaw. It begins as three fishable branches, but the prime fishing occurs after they have all merged at Cass City. While smallmouth bass are the main quarry in the Cass, there are also good numbers of northern pike, channel catfish, and walleyes.

*Channel catfish are slowly picking up in popularity with fly anglers—
this one took a crayfish streamer.*

Cass River
Headwaters to Caro

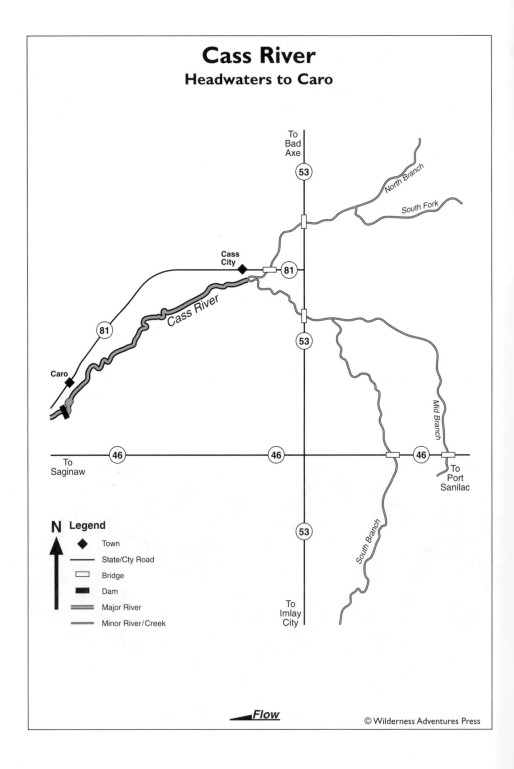

To
Bad
Axe

(53)

North Branch

South Fork

Cass
City

(81)

Cass River

(81)

(53)

Caro

Mid Branch

To
Saginaw

(46)

(46)

(46)

To
Port
Sanilac

N Legend

◆ Town

State/Cty Road

☐ Bridge

■ Dam

Major River

Minor River/Creek

(53)

South Branch

To
Imlay
City

Flow

© Wilderness Adventures Press

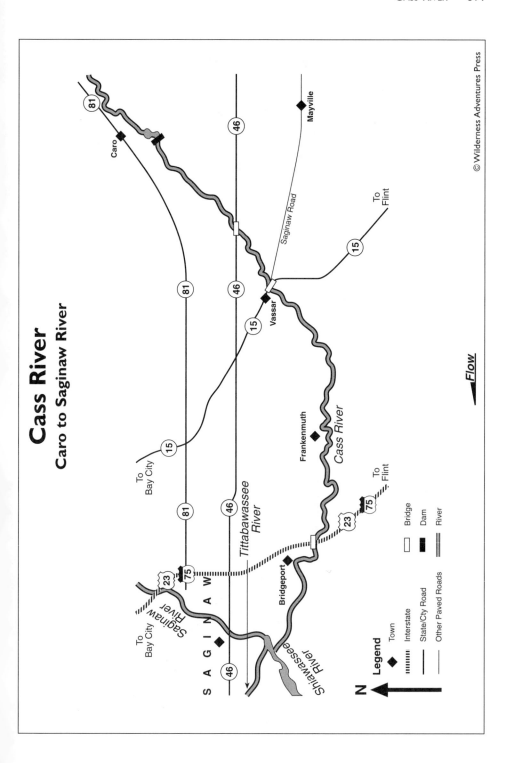

Cass River
Caro to Saginaw River

Flint River

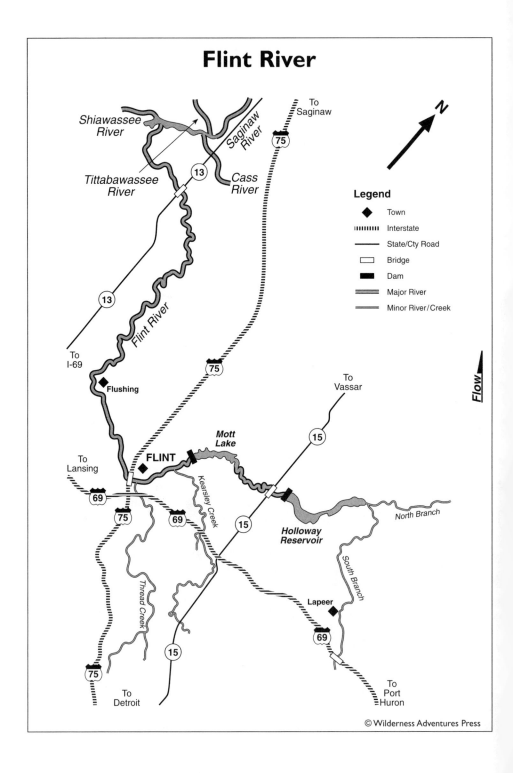

© Wilderness Adventures Press

The reach between Cass City and Vassar offers the best flyfishing opportunities. In the summer all of it can be waded except for a small impoundment at Caro. The flow is gentle, but there are surprising numbers of riffles. The wide, shallow, and rocky nature of the river is perfect for both smallmouth bass and the fly rodder. Access is mostly from bridges, but they are numerous and provide lots of choices. The river is also easily navigated with a canoe, and floating one of the stretches where the bridges are bit farther apart will get you into some lightly fished water.

One of the river's drawbacks is that it gets muddy after a good rainstorm. If the lower river is still too turbid for fishing after a rain, try moving upstream into the branches because it clears faster in those sections.

In addition to the resident walleyes that become established from fish stocked near Caro, there is also a run of walleyes from Saginaw Bay in the lower river. A few steelhead might also stray into the river at this time, so there is a chance to hook some large fish, but a break in spring rains is needed to clear the river in order to fish. There is a dam at Frankenmuth that blocks the migration, so the best fishing is found between the dam and Bridgeport. This reach is also a good one for large smallmouth in the summer.

FLINT RIVER

Paralleling the Cass River to the south, the similarly sized Flint River also joins the Shiawassee River nears its mouth. The Flint begins as two branches and soon after they join north of Lapeer, the river becomes impounded by Holloway Dam. Both branches have only modest numbers of northern pike and smallmouth bass, so unless you prefer to fish small water you would probably find better sport downstream.

The reach between the Holloway Dam and the backwaters of the next impoundment, Mott Lake, contains good numbers of smallmouth bass, walleyes, channel catfish, rock bass, and northern pike. In spring there is also a big run of crappies up to the dam that can provide great sport on small, white streamers. Largemouth bass also join the mix near the backwaters of Mott Lake. In addition to good numbers of fish, a plus for this stretch of the Flint is that 8-mile long Holloway Reservoir helps keep the river from getting too muddy when it rains.

As the Flint River winds through its namesake city, good fishing can be found at two city parks, Riverside and Whaley. A low head dam in Whaley Park blocks the upstream migration of walleye from Saginaw Bay, making this the place to try for trophy walleyes in early spring.

Downstream from Flint, the gradient picks up a bit and good smallmouth fishing can be experienced all the way to the Shiawassee. The river is wide and shallow for the most part, making wading and casting a piece of cake. Expect to find smallmouth and walleyes in the rocky areas and northern pike in the slow pools. Access is good at numerous road bridges, and there is a county park on the river in the town of Flushing.

Two tributaries of the Flint River, Kearsley and Thread Creeks, are planted with brown trout. The trout water is near the Genesee and Oakland County Line south of Flint, and access is found at road crossings. This is very tight flyfishing at best, but it does give you an opportunity to fish in trout-poor southeast Michigan.

SHIAWASSEE RIVER

The Shiawassee River begins on the watershed divide between the Saginaw and Grand River basins and travels mostly north to its junction with the Tittabawassee, forming the Saginaw River. While this river has great smallmouth bass habitat and the bass to go with it, angling pressure is generally light. Perhaps the reason is that the South Branch has a contamination problem relative to eating the fish.

Beginning as a series of mill ponds in northeastern Oakland County, the Shiawassee becomes large enough to flyfish downstream from Linden in southern Genesee County. From here to Byron the river, which is relatively slow, is home to mostly panfish and northern pike. The South Branch of the Shiawassee joins the mainstream at Byron, where the river widens and quickens.

In addition to having the fish consumption advisory on its finned inhabitants, the South Branch does not offer very good fishing, so it is best to concentrate on the

Prospecting on the Shiawassee River.

Doing battle with a smallmouth bass on the Shiawassee River.

mainstream. There continues to be an advisory on the main Shiawassee below the South Branch, but it mostly pertains to carp. Smallmouth and pike can be eaten occasionally. This "black cloud" hasn't affected the fish or habitat, and since fewer fish are kept, it may have actually improved.

Except for a couple of interruptions due to small impoundments, the Shiawassee continues to be prime habitat for smallmouth all the way to Chesaning. At Byron the river averages about 50 feet in width and gradually widens to slightly over 100 feet at Chesaning. Gravel riffles alternate with boulder- and cobble-lined pools. Smallmouth bass and rock bass are numerous, providing constant action. Compared to the Flint and Cass Rivers, the water is usually clear and much slower to muddy.

The clear water makes the Shiawassee easy to read, so that you can concentrate your casts where bass are most likely to be holding. Since much of the river flows over

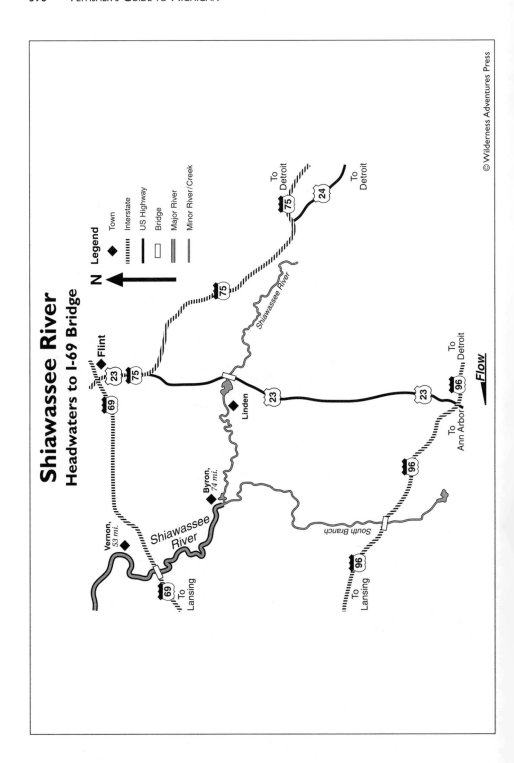

Shiawassee River
Headwaters to I-69 Bridge

© Wilderness Adventures Press

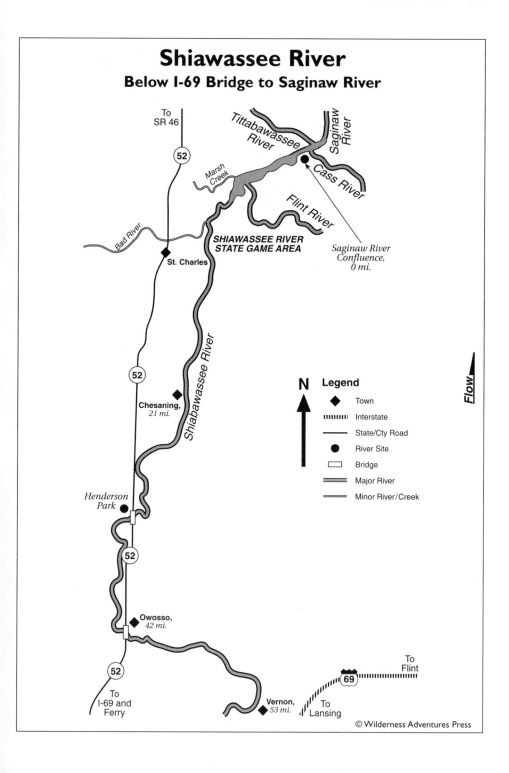

Shiawassee River
Below I-69 Bridge to Saginaw River

To
SR 46

52

Tittabawassee
River

Saginaw
River

Marsh
Creek

Cass River

Flint River

Bad River

SHIAWASSEE RIVER
STATE GAME AREA

St. Charles

Saginaw River
Confluence,
0 mi.

Shiabawassee River

52

Chesaning,
21 mi.

Henderson
Park

52

52

Owosso,
42 mi.

To
Flint

69

To
I-69 and
Ferry

Vernon,
53 mi.

To
Lansing

N

Flow

Legend

◆ Town

⠿⠿⠿ Interstate

—— State/Cty Road

● River Site

▭ Bridge

▬▬ Major River

══ Minor River/Creek

© Wilderness Adventures Press

shallow riffles, fish are quite concentrated during low summer flows. The bass share the slower deep holes in the river, with carp and northern pike found throughout the river. In the lower river below Chesaning, they are also joined by some walleye.

The combination of clear water and obvious deep holding water makes this river especially good for those who want to tangle with a carp on a fly rod. You can sight-fish for them and actually see the carp inhale your nymph. They may not be glamourous, but they sure will double over your 6-weight.

Numerous bridges provide access and allow flexibility on the length of river to wade or float. Henderson Park, about 5 miles north of Owosso, offers excellent access and fishing for smallmouth bass. Wading in an upstream direction is probably the better approach above Chesaning, while you can sneak up on fish when floating the lower river. In fact, a boat or canoe almost becomes necessary downstream from Chesaning because the river slows and eventually becomes deep and silt-bottomed when it enters the Shiawassee River State Game Area.

Bad River, another sluggish stream, joins the Shiawassee in the game area. Its claim to fame is a good population of northern pike and channel catfish, but the river is frequently too turbid to fish with flies. The best chance for fishable conditions on this stream is in late summer and fall during dry periods. There is good access at St. Charles, and a boat or canoe is needed because the soft stream bottom and depth make wading difficult.

Stream Facts: Shiawassee River

Seasons
- Open all year.
- Bass must be released between January 1 and the Saturday before Memorial Day.
- Walleyes and northern pike must be released between March 15 and last Saturday in April.

Special Regulations
- None

Fish
- Smallmouth and largemouth bass, northern pike, rock bass and other panfish, walleye, channel catfish.

River Miles
- Saginaw River—0
- Chesaning—21
- Owosso—42
- Corunna—45
- Vernon—53
- Byron—74

River Characteristics
- Most of the river between Byron and Chesaning is broad and shallow, with lots of gravel and rocks.
- Large pools are relatively scarce, and fish tend to be concentrated in them.

River Access
- Access is available at each landmark noted above with river miles.
- Many road crossings offer much additional access.

FLINT, CASS, AND SHIAWASSEE RIVERS MAJOR HATCHES

Insect	Jan	Feb	Mar	Apr	May	Jun	July	Aug	Sep	Oct	Nov	Dec	Time	Fly Patterns
Hendrickson				█	█								M/A	Hendrickson #12–14; Quill Gordon; Red Quill; Adams
Blue-winged Olive				█	█			█					A	Blue-winged Olive #18–20; Sparkle Dun Baetis; Iron Dun; Olive CDC Mayfly Dun
Net-building Caddis					█					█			M/A	Spotted Sedge #16–18; Eastern Elk Wing Caddis; Goddard Caddis
Sulphur Dun					█	█	█						A/E	Sulphur Dun #16; Pale Morning Dun; CDC Comparadun Yellow; Pale Evening Dun
Brown Drake						█							E	Brown Drake #10–12; Adams; CDC Brown Drake
Hexagenia						█	█						E	Hex #4–8; Great Olive-winged Drake; Spring's Wiggler; Hare's Ear
Trico						█	█	█	█	█			M	Tiny White Wing Black #24–28; Parachute Adams; CDC Trico; Spent Wing Trico
White Fly									█				E	White Fly #12–14; White Miller
Streamers	█	█	█	█	█	█	█	█	█	█	█	█	M/A/E	Woolly Buggers #6–12; Clouser's Minnow; Muddler Minnows; BC Craw; Matukas; Zonkers; Hellgrammites
Terrestrials						█	█	█	█				M/A/E	Woolly Worm #8–12; BC Spider; Letort Cricket; Joe's Hopper #6–10; Dave's Hopper; Dropper Hopper
Carp Nymphs			█	█	█	█	█	█	█	█			M/A/E	Red Squirrel Nymph #10–14; San Antonio Wiggler #8–10; Teeny Leech #6–8

HATCH TIME CODE: M = morning; A = afternoon; E = evening.

Southeastern Lower Peninsula Hub Cities

Ann Arbor
Population – 109,592

ACCOMMODATIONS
Bell Tower Hotel on U of M Campus, 300 South Thayer Street / 734-769-3010
Briarwood Inn, 3285 Boardwalk Street / 734-995-5200
Lamp Post Inn, 2424 East Stadium Boulevard / 734-971-8000
Red Arrow Motel, 5577 Plymouth Road / 734-662-9944

CAMPGROUNDS
The Sunshine Special, 6536 Scio Church Road / 734-665-5175
Camp Al Gon Quian, 350 South 5th Avenue / 734-663-0536
Daycroft, 100 Oakbrook Drive / 734-930-0333

RESTAURANTS
Angelo's Restaurant, 1100 Catherine Street / 734-761-8996
Ashley's Restaurant, 338 South State Street / 734-996-9191
Cloverleaf Restaurant, 201 East Liberty Street / 734-662-1266
Cooker Restaurant, 2000 Commonwealth Boulevard / 734-761-5858
Emerald City Restaurant, 4905 Washtenaw Avenue / 734-434-7978
Flim Flam Family Restaurant, 2707 Plymouth Road / 734-994-3036
Graham's Steakhouse, 610 Hilton Boulevard / 734-761-7800
Heidelberg Restaurant, 215 North Main Street / 734-663-7758
Inland Seafood House, 5827 Jackson Road / 734-747-9595

FLY SHOPS AND SPORTING GOODS
MacGregor's Outdoors, 803 North Main Street / 734-761-9200
Midwest Sport Shop, 10049 East Grand River, Suite 900 (Brighton 48116) / 810-227-3141

AUTO SERVICE
A 2 Auto, 745 South Wagner Road / 734-665-3255
Ann Arbor Shell, 3240 Washtenaw Avenue / 734-973-1350
Hahn's Service Center, 2280 West Liberty Street / 734-769-0170
Imperial Auto Service, 2344 Dexter Avenue / 734-761-3888
Joe's Auto Service, 1649 North Maple Road / 734-994-4757
Mallek's Service, 1500 Jackson Avenue / 734-668-6406
Ron's Garage, 1130 Rosewood Street / 734-662-8379

AIR SERVICE
Ann Arbor Airport, 801 Airport Drive / 734-994-2841

Wayne County Airport Administration, 231 Eureka Way (Romulus 48174) /
    734-942-3550

MEDICAL
Henry Ford Hospital and Medical Centers, 2755 Carpenter Road / 734-973-3090
St. Joseph Mercy Hospital Unit, 4972 East Clark Road / 734-434-9680
University of Michigan Medical Center / 734-763-5700

FOR MORE INFORMATION
Ann Arbor Area Chamber of Commerce
425 South Main Street
Ann Arbor, MI 48104
734-665-4433

Flint
Population – 140,761

ACCOMMODATIONS
Dort Motel, 3370 South Dort Hwy / 810-743-4100
Echo Inn, 2002 South Dort Hwy / 810-235-6621
Flint Motel, 5452 North Dort Hwy / 810-787-9261
Knights Court, 4380 West Pierson Road / 810-733-7570
Park Motel, 6060 North Saginaw Street / 810-789-0121

CAMPGROUNDS
Ballenger Park, Flushing & Dupont / 810-232-5332
Holts Mobile Home Court, 6576 North Dort Hwy / 810-787-5289
Memorial Park, 1026 Church Street / 810-767-4121
Seven Lakes State Park, 2220 Tinsman Road (Fenton 48430) / 810-634-7271

RESTAURANTS
Beech Tree An American Grill, 1519 West Bristol Road / 810-232-7811
Big John Steak & Onion, 5346 North Saginaw Street / 810-238-0571
Brown's Family Restaurant, 4031 Richfield Road / 810-736-1900
City Lights Restaurant, 432 North Saginaw Street / 810-232-8888
Country Kettle Restaurant, 2525 South Dort Hwy / 810-767-7471
Italia Gardens of Flint, 401 West Court Street / 810-233-4112
Ryan's Family Steak House, 4200 Miller Road / 810-732-8000

FLY SHOPS AND SPORTING GOODS
Golden Hackle Fly Shop, 329 Crescent Place (Flushing 48433) / 810-227-3141
Fishing Tackle Grab Bag, 5521 North State Road (Davidson 48423) / 810-653-4771
Hick's Tackle Shop, 5425 Clio Road / 810-785-9941
Gander Mountain, 6359 Gander Drive (Swartz Creek 48473) / 810-635-7800

AUTO SERVICE
All Automotive Repair, 2150 East Hemphill / 810-743-5620
American Auto Service, 1848 Tower Street / 810-767-8048
D & T Auto Repair, 5220 North Dort / 810-785-4071
Ewing's Auto Service Center, 4401 North Saginaw Street / 810-789-5504
Jerry's Service Garage, 711 Wager Avenue / 810-785-7661
Plowman's Auto Repair, 3220 Western Road / 810-736-1100

AIR SERVICE
Bishop International Airport, 3425 West Bristol Road / 810-235-0608

MEDICAL
Genesys Health System Health Park, 8423 Holly Road / 810-762-4710
McLaren Regional Medical Center, 401 South Ballenger Hwy / 810-342-2000

FOR MORE INFORMATION

Flint Chamber of Commerce
316 West Water Street
Flint, MI 48503
810-232-7101

Pontiac
Population – 71,166

Accommodations
Highlander Motel, 2201 Dixie Hwy / 248-338-4061
McGuire's Motor Inn, 120 South Telegraph Road / 248-682-5100
Sagamore Motel, 789 Woodward Avenue / 248-334-2592
Sherwood Motel, 2460 Dixie Hwy / 248-335-9417
Thrift Courts of America, 2201 Dixie Hwy / 248-338-4061

Campgrounds
Oakland County Parks, 1200 North Center / 248-625-6473
Dodge #4 State Park, 4250 Parkway Drive (Waterford 48328) / 248-666-1020

Restaurants
Chili Bowl Restaurant, 223 Oakland Avenue / 248-334-2267
Colangelo's Restaurant, 2 North Saginaw Street / 248-334-2275
Country Kitchen, 2041 Auburn Road / 248-338-2607
Jerry's Family Restaurant, 3330 West Huron / 248-682-8722
Joy Garden Restaurant, 2180 Dixie Hwy / 248-335-3080
Klancy's Restaurant, 709 South Opdyke Road / 248-334-0955
Ocean City Restaurant, 35 South Telegraph Road / 248-334-5320

Fly Shops and Sporting Goods
Paint Creek Outfitters, 203 East University (Rochester 48307) / 248-650-0442
Gander Mountain, 2230 Mall Drive East / 248-738-9600
The Hairy Hook, 4690 West Walton (Waterford 48328) / 248-618-9939

Auto Repair
Bud's Old Fashioned Service, 1076 Baldwin Avenue / 248-335-1035
Carter's Auto Repair, 1908 Wide Track Drive West / 248-332-2299
Dr. Dave's Auto Clinic, 619 Auburn Avenue / 248-334-4230
Jackson Auto Repair, 1025-1 Oakland Avenue # 2 / 248-334-0208
Marty's Auto Repair, 1001 Oakland Avenue / 248-332-2850
Perry Street Auto Service, 440 North Paddock Street / 248-338-2366

Air Service
Oakland-Pontiac International Airport, Highland Road, Waterford Twp.

Medical
Hospital Healthcare, 1473 Baldwin Avenue / 248-338-7575
North Oakland Medical Centers, 461 West Huron Street / 248-857-7200

For More Information
Pontiac Chamber of Commerce
30 North Saginaw Street
Pontiac, MI 48342
248-335-9600

Port Huron
Population—33,694

ACCOMMODATIONS
Alloways Motel, 5570 Lapeer Road / 810-984-3667
Darlington Motor Lodge, 4253 Lapeer Road / 810-987-2171
El Rancho Motel, 3756 Lapeer Road / 810-985-3228
Elmcourt Motel, 3600 Lapeer Road / 810-985-9545
Flamingo Motel, 3845 Lapeer Road / 810-984-3631
Pine Tree Motel, 3121 Lapeer Road / 810-987-2855
Serenade Motel, 2907 24th Street / 810-982-8529

CAMPGROUNDS
Burtchville Trailer Park, 7898 Lakeshore Road / 810-327-6131
Port Huron KOA, 5111 Lapeer Road / 810-987-4070
Port Huron Township Campground, 2301 Water Street / 810-982-6765
Lakeport State Park, 7605 Lakeshore Drive (Lakeport 48059) / 810-327-6224

RESTAURANTS
Armbruster's Restaurant, 1211 Griswold Street / 810-982-2255
Bridge Restaurant, 2127 11th Avenue / 810-982-4007
Fogcutter Restaurant, 511 Fort Street / 810-987-3300
Jeannie's Family Dining, 305 Bard Street / 810-984-1570
My Place Restaurant, 512 Quay Street / 810-982-2475
Rams Horn Restaurant, 3970 24th Avenue / 810-982-6600
Table Top Restaurant, 7116 Lakeshore Road / 810-385-4662

FLY SHOPS AND SPORTING GOODS
Pro Bait & Tackle, 2731 Pine Grove Avenue / 810-984-3232
Thompson's Bait & Tackle, 1222 Water Street / 810-982-2321
Trout's Choice, 4296 Peck Road / 810-985-7628

AUTO SERVICE
Agnew's Service, 936 Griswold Street / 810-982-1571
Bob's Truck & Auto Care, 2529 Walnut Street / 810-985-5339
Hall & Son Service Center, 3426 24th Street / 810-987-8257
Honest Engine Automotive Repair, 501 24th Street / 810-987-9614
Ingram's Service Center, 2803 Stone Street / 810-987-3396
McKinch's Garage, 1424 Stanton Street / 810-982-9051
Realistic Auto Service, 3970 Lapeer Road / 810-982-7232

MEDICAL
Huron Medical Center PC, 1214 Richardson Street / 810-982-5200
Mercy Hospital, 2601 Electric Avenue / 810-985-1500

FOR MORE INFORMATION
Chamber of Commerce of Greater Port Huron
920 Pine Grove Avenue
Port Huron, MI 48060
810-985-7101

Saginaw

Population – 69,512

ACCOMMODATIONS
Brockway House, 1631 Brockway Street / 517-792-0746
Carriage Inn, 3425 East Holland Road / 517-753-2461
Gratiot View Motel, 8435 Gratiot Road / 517-781-3030
Miller's Motel, 4853 Dixie Hwy / 517-777-5250
Montague Inn, 1581 South Washington Avenue / 517-752-3939
Northgate Motel, 6300 Bay Road / 517-790-9454

CAMPGROUNDS
Bridgeport Charter Township Bridge, 6206 Dixie Hwy / 517-777-4170
Grand Lakes Resort, 141 Harrow Lane / 517-799-6635
Thomas Township Parks, 355 North Miller Road / 517-776-6581

RESTAURANTS
Country Style, 5165 Bay Road / 517-249-8948
Ern's Seafood Restaurant, 3072 East Holland Road / 517-754-0800
Flashbacks Old Time Pub & Eatery, 3475 Bay Road / 517-249-4160
Houlihan's Ole Tyme Road House, 9620 Gratiot Road / 517-781-0160
Kings House Restaurant, 3649 Bay Road / 517-790-1072
Levi's Saloon, 6415 State Street / 517-790-3538
Render's Restaurant, 6383 Dixie Hwy / 517-777-7700

FLY SHOPS AND SPORTING GOODS
Country Anglers, 2030 South Thomas Road / 517-781-0997
Fly-Rite, 7421 South Beyer (Frankenmuth 48734) / 517-652-9869
John's Custom Flies, 12 West Wackerly Drive (Sanford 48657) / 517-687-9202
Frank's Bait and Tackle, 1206 North Huron Road (Linwood 48634) / 517-697-5341
Gander Mountain, 2270 Tittabawassee / 517-791-3500

AUTO SERVICE
Boensch Garage, 5045 East Washington Road / 517-755-7019
Bonner Service Center, 1519 Mackinaw Street / 517-791-1198
Dale's Automotive Service Center, 548 Shattuck Road / 517-752-9255
Ken's Auto Repair, 415 South Franklin Street / 517-753-5469
Schwarz Auto Repair & Service, 2470 Midland Road / 517-790-0196

AIR SERVICE
Tri-Cities International Airport

MEDICAL
Saginaw General Hospital, 1447 North Harrison Street / 517-771-4000
St. Mary's Medical Center, 830 South Jefferson Avenue / 517-776-8100

FOR MORE INFORMATION
Bay Area Chamber of Commerce
901 South Washington Avenue
Saginaw, MI 48601
517-752-7161

Adrian
Population – 22,097

ACCOMMODATIONS
Briaroaks Inn, 2980 North Adrian Hwy / 517-263-1659
Casey's Place, 1336 North Main Street / 517-265-6188
Pine Motel, 3895 South Adrian Hwy / 517-263-2444
Raisin River Inn, 1346 North Main Street / 517-265-3737
Sleepy Hollow Motel, 2457 East US 223 / 517-263-9274

CAMPGROUNDS
Monroe County KOA Kampground, US 23 at Summerfield Road (Petersburg 49270) / 517-856-4972

RESTAURANTS
Brass Lantern, 1853 West Maumee Street / 517-263-0411
Casey's Place, 1336 North Main Street / 517-265-6188
Dempsey's Restaurant, 4497 North Adrian Hwy / 517-263-8640
Fenby's Restaurant, 1002 South Main Street / 517-263-7424
Fortuna Restaurant, 2309 East US 223 / 517-263-2340
Jonathan's Restaurant, 1360 South Main Street / 517-265-8118
Ranch Steak & Sea Food, 720 South Main Street / 517-263-6880

FLY SHOPS AND SPORTING GOODS
Country Fields, 3975 South Adrian Hwy / 517-263-3134
RC Resale Bait Tackle, 1120 Treat Street / 517-264-0052

AUTO SERVICE
Big Al's Garage, 1430 Sutton Road / 517-263-4977
Bob's Car & Truck & Motor Repair, 4885 Tipton Hwy / 517-265-5400
D & E Auto Repair, 919 West Beecher Street / 517-265-9488
Lindsey Garage, 613 East Michigan Street / 517-264-0397
McKie's Amoco Service, 242 North Main Street / 517-263-6300
Ray's Auto Repair, 3378 East US 223 / 517-265-1553

AIR SERVICE
Detroit Metropolitan Airport

MEDICAL
Bixby Medical Center, 818 Riverside Avenue / 517-263-0711

FOR MORE INFORMATION
Lenawee County Chamber of Commerce
202 North Main St Suite A
Adrian, MI 49221
517-265-5141

Metro Detroit
Population – 2,000,000+

ACCOMMODATIONS
Blue Bird Motel & Kitchenettes, 21360 Telegraph Road (Southfield 48034) /
248-353-4699
Falcon Inn Motel, 25125 Michigan Avenue (Dearborn 48124) / 313-278-6540
Village Inn of Dearborn, 21725 Michigan Avenue (Dearborn 48124) /
313-565-8511
City Airport Motel, 10945 Gratiot Avenue (Detroit 48213) / 313-371-7700
La Renaissance Motel, 18850 Woodward Avenue (Detroit 48203) / 313-369-2811
River Place Grand Heritage Hotel, 1000 River Place Drive (Detroit 48207) /
313-259-9500
Plymouth Motel, 28021 Plymouth Road (Livonia 48150) / 313-427-2610
Terrace Inn, 30375 Plymouth Road (Livonia 48150) / 313-261-6800

CAMPGROUNDS
Green Valley Park, 57300 12 Mile Road (Northville 48167) / 248-437-4136
Haas Lake Park, 25800 Haas (Northville 48167) / 248-437-0900

RESTAURANTS
Cicero's Restaurant, 24299 Novi Road (Northville 48167) / 248-380-0011
Mackinnon's Restaurant, 126 East Main Street (Northville 48167) / 248-348-1991
Captain Hook's Fish & Chips, 19717 Schoenherr Street (Detroit 48205) /
313-839-8888
Docks Great Fish, 20240 Grand River Avenue (Detroit 48219) / 313-534-6046
Greek Express, 205 West Congress Street (Detroit 48226) / 313-963-1199
Chuck Muer's Big Fish, 700 Town Center Drive (Dearborn 48126) / 313-336-8558
Fairlane Park Place, 6356 Greenfield Road (Dearborn 48126) / 313-581-2344

FLY SHOPS AND SPORTING GOODS
Bueter's Outdoors Ltd, 120 East Main Street (Northville 48167) / 248-349-3677
Benchmark Fly Shop, 32715 Grand River (Farmington 48024) / 248-474-2088
Lakeside Fishing Shop, 34801 Grand River (Farmington 48024) / 248-473-2030
25110 Jefferson at 10 Mile (St. Clair Shores 48081) /
810-777-7003
Au Sable Outfitters, 17005 Kercheval (Grosse Pointe 48236) / 313-642-2000
Flymart Flyshop, 1002 North Main Street (Royal Oak 48067) / 800-573-6335
29229 Northestern Hwy (Southfield 48034) / 248-350-8484
31009 Jefferson Avenue (St. Clair Shores 48081) / 810-415-5650
Pro Angler Outdoors Inc., 28441 5 Mile Road (Livonia 48150) / 734-427-8863
The Sports Authority Dearborn, 5751 Mercury Drive (Dearborn 48126) /
313-336-6626

Bass Pro Shops Outdoor World, 4500 Baldwin Road (Auburn Hills 48326) /
    248-209-4200
Gander Mountain, 14100 Pardee Road (Taylor 48180) / 734-287-7420
            13975 Hall Road (Utica 48315) / 810-247-9900
Westbank Anglers Michigan, 6612 Telegraph Road (Bloomfield Plaza) /
    248-538-3474

AUTO SERVICE
Al's Auto Service, 3300 Holbrook Street (Detroit 48212) / 313-873-1960
Jerry's Auto Repair, 3366 Airport Hwy (Detroit 48226) / 313-382-3153
Alex Auto Service, 3316 Wyoming Street (Dearborn 48120) / 313-842-3808
Davis Auto Care, 807 Doheny Drive (Northville 48167) / 248-349-5115
Ben's Quality Service, 28945 Greenfield Road (Southfield 48076) / 248-559-1555
Southfield Auto Service, 23200 Telegraph Road (Southfield 48034) / 248-356-
    4120
Van Ess & Son Auto Repair, 28335 5 Mile (Livonia 48150) / 313-422-0320

AIR SERVICE
Detroit Metropolitan Airport

MEDICAL
Detroit Community Healthconnection, 10 Peterboro Street (Detroit 48201) /
    313-832-6300
Detroit Medical Center, 3901 Beaubien Street (Detroit 48201) / 313-745-5437
Oakwood Healthcare System, 18101 Oakwood Boulevard (Dearborn 48124) /
    313-593-5880
Detroit Medical Center, 4201 St. Antoine (Southfield 48037) / 248-827-2160
Grace Hospital, 6071 West Outer Drive (Southfield 48037) / 248-948-7990

FOR MORE INFORMATION
Greater Detroit Chamber
600 West Lafayette Boulevard
Detroit, MI 48226
313-964-4000

Fishing the Great Lakes

Imagine large trout and salmon, unlimited room to fight them, and no vegetation to grab your backcast. In spring and fall, the shorelines of the Great Lakes offer all of the above.

Tributary streams, both large and small, are the magnets that attract feeding trout and salmon because the water temperature is closer to their preferred range. In autumn tributaries are cooler than the big lakes, and in spring they warm up faster than the inland seas. In addition, chinook, pink, and coho salmon, and brown and lake trout are looking for a place to spawn in the fall. At times, steelhead also run in the fall, and they definitely seek their natal rivers in spring.

Baitfish are attracted to the inflows, as well, and they in turn attract predators. Smelt and then alewives also move to the beach and lower tributaries to spawn in the spring. Along with the above-mentioned species, splake and whitefish add to the variety of fish available close to shore.

Wave action typically creates a series of troughs and bars along the sandy shorelines of the Great Lakes. Commonly, water drops off into a trough that is 2 to 4 feet deep that becomes shallower and forms a bar that then drops into a second trough that is 4 to 6 feet deep. After coming up to the second bar, the bottom really drops off. Under low light conditions, such as dawn and dusk and heavily overcast days, trout feed in the first trough. Usually, however, the hot area is where stream currents meet

An egg-sucking leech brought this coho salmon in.

the second trough. Wading out to the first bar and then casting streamers to the outer trough is the best bet. Cast as parallel to the beach as possible while still getting the fly into the trough in order to swim the streamer in the trough as long as possible with your rod extended over the trough.

Most medium and large rivers have piers at their mouths. Usually, fly casting is not too practical from piers, but these structures do serve to concentrate fish that are patrolling the shoreline. Fishing the beach on the side the river is being pushed to is usually best, but there will be fish on both sides of the river mouth. Piers provide structure and cover for fish, so fishing where they meet the beach can be good. Especially along Lake Superior, a number of streams enter the lakes in rocky areas. These are prime spots for catching a big Great Lakes salmonid.

Streamers that imitate smelt, alewives, emerald shiners, or smolts are effective offerings. White Zonkers with mylar bodies are hard to beat. During spawning, egg flies that are very slowly moved just above the bottom are also killers.

In the southwestern Lower Peninsula, most of the tributaries are collected into good-sized rivers and join Lake Michigan through piers. There is usually public access to the beach on one or both sides of the piers on the Galien, St. Joseph, Black, Kalamazoo, Macatawa, and Grand Rivers. Small stream juncture possibilities exist in Warren Dunes State Park (Painterville Creek), Brandywine Creek south of South Haven, and the Pigeon River in Ottawa County.

The northwestern Lower Peninsula has many options, and you will often encounter anglers fishing bait and casting lures. While this means competition, it also can be a shortcut to finding concentrations of fish. From south to north the Muskegon, White, Pentwater, Pere Marquette, Manistee, Betsie, Jordan (Lake Charlevoix outlet), and Bear Rivers all have piers.

Many more rivers and creeks in this section of Michigan also empty into Lake Michigan, with some prime surf flyfishing opportunities. Again, from south to north, some of the best include: Flower Creek just south of the Ocean County line and Stony Creek in the center of Oceana County; Lincoln and Sauble Rivers just north of Ludington in Mason County; Platte River and Otter Creek north of Frankfort in Benzie County; Crystal River, Shalda Creek, Leelanau River, Boardman River, Mitchell Creek, and Elk River in and around Traverse City; and Big Sucker Creek in Wilderness State Park near the tip of the Lower Peninsula.

Swinging around to the Lake Huron side, the Cheboygan, Thunder Bay, and Au Sable Rivers flow through pier heads. In between, a number of smaller streams create their own mouth. The Black Mallard and Ocqueoc Rivers flow into Hammond Bay northeast of Rogers City. South of Alpena, the Devils and Black Rivers attract trout and salmon. Harrisville Harbor is planted with chinook, and you can reach these fish from the beach in September and October. A premier spot for surf fishing is the mouth of the East Branch of the Au Gres south of Tawas City. There is excellent public access, with a parking lot right at the river mouth. The Tawas River to the north and main Au Gres and Rifle to the south offer additional opportunities.

Fishing near the shore, this angler brought in a beautiful steelhead.

Continuing to the Upper Peninsula, the mouths of the Carp and Pine Rivers on northern Lake Huron are good choices. To the west along Lake Michigan, you can fish the beach at the Pointe Au Chenes, Brevoort, Cut, Millecoquins, Milakokia, and Manistique Rivers. The Bays de Noc are fed by numerous small rivers, along with several large ones, including the Fishdam, Sturgeon, Ogontz, Rapid, Tacoosh, Days, and Escanaba. Farther south in Green Bay, the Ford, Bark, and Cedar Rivers attract fish to their mouths in the spring and the fall.

The Lake Superior Coast is loaded with small streams carving their way into this huge freshwater sea. Some of the best are the Two Hearted and Hurricane Rivers in the eastern end of the Upper Peninsula. Around Marquette, try the mouths of Carp and Little Garlic Rivers. Moving west, the Huron, Silver, and Falls Rivers attract concentrations of trout and salmon. Some good choices in the Keweenaw Peninsula include the Tobacco, Eagle, and Salmon Trout Rivers. Sliding down toward Wisconsin, the number of streams rushing into Lake Superior number more than 100, but many of them are very small and can be intermittent. Some possibilities include the Misery, Firesteel, Iron, and Presque Isle Rivers, but if the mouths of these rivers don't pan out, there are plenty of nearby alternatives.

Lakes Michigan and Huron also have many other small creeks that attract trout and salmon to a lesser degree. However, if you hit them right and are one of the only anglers, it can be a bonanza. In general, spring fishing begins in March in the south and ends in May in the north. There is less latitudinal variation in the fall, with October and November being the prime months. Timing is very important in surf fishing, and a call ahead to the local bait shop or DNR field office should be made.

Another exciting possibility for fishing the Great Lakes with a fly rod occurs when steelhead and other species feed near the surface at vertical temperature breaks. These happen when the warming inshore water collides with the cold mass of mid-lake water. Currents at this interface cause insects and other food items to become concentrated. First, find the fish by trolling or visually sighting them and then drift through the feeding fish, casting from a big boat or from a kickboat that has been launched from the "mother ship." Obviously, a calm lake is needed to do this, but hooking a 10-pound silver steelhead near the surface in over 300 feet of water is mighty exciting. Jim Karr, a Lake Michigan charter boat captain, said that he was definitely interested in taking flyfishers out for this sport. For other captains, contact the Michigan Charterboat Association at 800-622-2971.

Stillwaters

With over 11,000 lakes as well as many additional ponds and gravel pits, a place to cast a fly is never more than a few minutes away in Michigan. Most of the lakes are home to warmwater fish, but there are trout lakes sprinkled throughout the state.

Flyfishing for bluegills and sunfish in May and June is almost a rite of spring in Michigan. Largemouth bass are also in the shallows at this time of year, providing shoreline sport throughout the summer in the evening and after dark. While foam-bodied, rubber-legged spiders in sizes 10 through 14 are the standard offering for bluegills, any buggy looking dry fly will catch these fish. The reason for the foam spider's popularity is probably its durability, because when fish are active, you can hook a lot of bluegills in an evening. Nymphs also catch these fish, and some anglers suspend a nymph below a spider, making doubles a common result.

Bass, both largemouth and smallmouth, also go for spiders and other poppers. Just move up in size from 4 through 8 for these predators. And adding to the variety, Michigan lakes also provide good fly rod sport for northern pike. Casting and actively retrieving streamers along weedbeds or other cover will catch them. Bass ambush streamers, as well. Remember that in lakes, just as in rivers, where there is a good crayfish population, there will also be a good bass population. A very effective way to use a crayfish pattern is to retrieve it erratically near rocks.

While there are not nearly as many trout lakes as there are warmwater lakes, they are plentifully scattered about the state. Some of the lakes are designated trout lakes and are open only during the normal trout season—the last Saturday in April through the end of September. Usually small in size, these lakes are concentrated in the Upper Peninsula. They are managed for trout only, and in most, trout can be reached in the summer with sinking lines and weighted nymphs and streamers. There are often special regulations on these lakes, so be sure to consult the "Michigan Fishing Guide." Possession and size limits are usually more restrictive, resulting in better fishing.

Many of the larger and deeper lakes also support trout. These are usually two-tier or two-story lakes that also contain warmwater species. Spring and fall are the prime times to flyfish for trout in these lakes. In summer, the cooler waters of the thermocline and hypolimnion (water lying below the thermocline that is noncirculating and remains perpetually cold) are not very reachable with fly tackle. This means that inlet streams are where trout can be found in these lakes, providing more ideal water temperature (warmer in the spring, cooler in the fall) and forage, and attracting spawning trout. Shoal areas with large rocks and other cover also hold good numbers of trout during the cool seasons. Lots of cover, coupled with an inlet stream having good flow, is almost a sure bet for some fine trout fishing.

WESTERN UPPER PENINSULA

In the Upper Peninsula, there are trout lakes in every county except Menominee. Beginning in Gogebic County in the far western end, some stillwater trout fishing opportunities include Castle, Cornelia, Little Duck, and Mishike Lakes, all of which are designated trout lakes. In addition, Finger and Imp Lakes in the southeastern part of the county are heavily planted with splake, and Beaton's Lake, a two-story fishery, receives an annual plant of rainbows and walleyes.

In eastern Ontonagon County, Trout Creek Pond, south of the town of the same name, is the only designated trout lake. However, splake are planted in Mirror Lake and brookies in Courtney Lake in the central part of the county. To the north, Houghton County is home to several brook trout lakes: Clear, Penegore, and Perrault. Lake On-Three and Emily Lake are planted with rainbows. There are no designated trout lakes in Keweenaw County, but there are brook trout in Manganese Lake, splake in Lake Fanny Hooe at the northern tip of the peninsula, and brown trout in Eliza Pond.

Baraga County is also without a designated trout lake, but brook trout are planted in Alberta Pond and Roland Lake. In the southeast corner of the county, Fence Lake, in the headwaters of the East Branch of the Fence River, receives a sizable stocking of rainbows.

In addition to having five blue ribbon trout streams, Iron County also contains many trout lakes. Sprinkled throughout the county are nine small lakes that are designated trout water: Fortune Pond, and Deadman's, Forest, Hannah, Kildeer, Madelyn, Skyline, Spree, and Timber Lakes. Timber Lake, a couple of miles east of Cooks Run, offers excellent flyfishing for brook trout. The limit on this lake is one trout, and the minimum size is 15 inches. There are another dozen lakes containing trout in Iron County, with Fire Lake receiving a large rainbow trout plant and Lake Ellen annually planted with splake.

Marquette County holds the heaviest concentration of trout lakes in Michigan. There are 16 designated trout lakes in the county and almost 20 additional lakes hosting trout populations. To the west and slightly north of Marquette, there are a number of small lakes that contain brook trout. These include Keyhole East, North Paul and South Paul, North Rockingchair and South Rockingchair, Clear, and Section 13 Lakes. Arfelin Lake is planted with browns, rainbows, and splake and Brocky Lake with rainbows, and both are somewhat larger in size than the brookie lakes. Silver Lake, an impoundment on the upper Dead River, is planted with splake. Though the lake is 3 miles long, the splake are very reachable from shore during spring and fall.

There are many small lakes in the southwest Marquette County, and some of the better trout lakes include Bedspring, Cranberry, Island, Just, Perch, Squaw, and Twin. Just Lake is especially good for brook trout. Although there are fewer lakes in the southeastern part of the county, there is quite a cluster around the town of Gwinn. Within 10 miles of this small town, good rainbow fishing can be found at Big Trout Lake, and brook trout fishing is available at Johnson, Kidney, Moccasin, and Swanzy Lakes and Silver Pond. Sporley and Crooked Lakes are planted with brown trout and splake.

Lying between Iron and Marquette Counties, which are blessed with an abundance of trout lakes, Dickinson County is surprisingly lacking in trout lakes. The only designated one is Kimberly Clark Pond, and splake are planted in Pickerel Lake in the northcentral part of the county.

EASTERN UPPER PENINSULA

The trout lakes in Delta County are concentrated in its northeast section. Bear, Carr, Norway, Square, and Killpecker Lakes, as well as Section 1 Pond, are designated trout lakes. Browns, rainbows, and brookies can be found in Bear Lake near the county line. To the north, Alger County is home to 10 designated trout lakes. Most of them are concentrated in an area south and southwest of Munising. Addis, Irwin, Trueman, Rock, and Hike Lakes, along with Cheryl's, Cole Creek, and Valley Spur Ponds, are all found within 20 miles of Munising.

Twilight and Ned's Lakes join this concentration of designated trout lakes just across the county line in Schoolcraft County. Lost and Dutch Fred Lakes and King's Pond are designated trout lakes found near the Fox River in the northeast corner of the county. For rainbow trout, give Banana, Bear, and Dodge Lakes a try in the south-

This largemouth bass resides in a Michigan pond.

ern half of Schoolcraft County. Twenty designated trout lakes and ponds are located in Luce County, with many of them near the Two Hearted River. Deer, Holland, Moon, Little Whorl, Sid, Trout, and Ward Lakes are designated trout lakes close to the famous river. Other nearby lakes containing trout include Bullhead, Camp 8, Perch, Pratt, Pretty, and Tank. Central Luce County holds another cluster of trout stillwaters, some with such interesting names as Brockies and Buckies Ponds, as well as Silver Creek and Spring Creek Ponds, Syphon, Wolverine, and Youngs Lakes.

Surprisingly, Mackinac County is very lacking in trout lakes. Its only designated trout lake is Millecoquin Pond, located in the western part of the county about 5 miles north of the much larger lake of the same name. Castle Rock Pond, just north of St. Ignace, is planted with rainbows each year. In Chippewa County, there are seven designated trout lakes and ponds, mostly located in the western half of the county. Naomikong Lake and Pond and Roxbury East and West Ponds are just a mile or two south of Lake Superior's Tahquamenon Bay. Highbanks Lake, east of Strongs, is a good rainbow lake, and there is a campground at Trout Creek Pond east of Trout Lake. Duke's Lake is the best bet for rainbows in the east side of the county and is just 3 miles southeast of Kinross.

NORTHWESTERN LOWER PENINSULA

There is only one designated trout lake in this section of Michigan, but the region is blessed with many large, oligotrophic lakes (lacking nutrients but highly oxygenated) teeming with trout. Long and narrow Walloon Lake is on the border between Emmet and Charlevoix Counties and is stocked with large numbers of brown and rainbow trout. Just to the west is Lake Charlevoix, a very large lake that contains lake trout along with browns and rainbows. It is fed by the Jordan and Boyne Rivers, which provide excellent spawning habitat for trout. There are a number of small creeks also flowing into Lake Charlevoix that attract trout in spring and fall. Splake are planted in Thumb Lake about 10 miles east of Boyne City.

The large and long Torch and Elk Lakes parallel the East Arm of Grand Traverse Bay. In addition to rainbow trout in each lake, there are browns in Elk Lake and landlocked Atlantic salmon in Torch Lake. Each lake has several small tributary creeks that attract trout in spring and fall. Four medium-sized lakes east of Kalkaska are planted with trout: Bear, Starvation, and Big Twin receive brown trout, while lake trout are planted in Big Blue Lake. Starvation Lake also receives yearling rainbows.

In the Traverse City area, try small lakes like Sand #1 and #2 along with Big Guernsey about 15 miles east of town. Sand Lake #2 is the region's only designated trout lake and is planted with brook trout. It is fly and artificial single point lures only, with a 15-inch and two-trout limit. Rainbows are the drawing card of Sand Lake #1, and browns are planted in Big Guernsey, which has a state forest campground on its shore. Brown trout are also the prime species in two much larger lakes southwest of Traverse City: Duck and Green. Lake trout are available in Green Lake. To the northwest are Lake Leelanau and Glen Lake, two very large two-story lakes with brown and lake trout as their principal coldwater species. Between these two giants, Lime Lake offers brown trout, as does tiny Solon Pond near the town of the same name.

Farther west, Crystal Lake, north of the town of Frankfort, is another very large, clear lake. Rainbow trout provide a fine shoal fishery in spring and fall, and in late fall you might even find a lake trout on the end of your tippet. Staying near Lake Michigan and moving south, we encounter Portage Lake, directly connected to Lake Michigan, that has resident brown as well as coho and chinook salmon passing through. Pine Lake, about 15 miles east of Manistee, is stocked with brown trout and has a campground. Another few miles to the south, Harper Lake also contains brown trout. Moving farther inland in Osceola County, there is a group of three trout lakes northeast of Big Rapids. Rainbow trout are present in Sunrise and Wells Lakes, while brown trout are planted in Center Lake. In the southern part of this region, there are two lakes in Newaygo County that are stocked with rainbows. Tiny Condon Lake is about 2 miles west of Bitely, and the much larger Crystal Lake is 5 miles southwest of White Cloud.

A bluegill caught on a Michigan lake.

NORTHEASTERN LOWER PENINSULA

Most of the designated trout lakes in the Lower Peninsula are located in this section of Michigan. In the north, Twin Lake #1 in northern Cheboygan County is planted with browns, with a 15-inch and two trout limit. Burt and Mullet are huge oligotrophic lakes fed by the Sturgeon and Pigeon Rivers, respectively. A number of small creeks also flow into each lake, attracting browns, rainbows, and lakers in fall and spring. To the east, try a small pond near Rogers City called Trout Creek Pond for brown trout. To the south in northern Otsego County, Pickerel is a good-sized designated trout lake featuring rainbows. In the southeast corner of Otsego County, less than 10 miles from Gaylord, there are four more trout lakes: Pencil and Big Chub are home to rainbows, while splake are planted in Heart Lake and browns in Bridge Lake.

There are no designated trout lakes in Montmorency County, but you can catch splake in Avalon Lake and rainbows in Long Lake, just north of Hillman. Splake are also

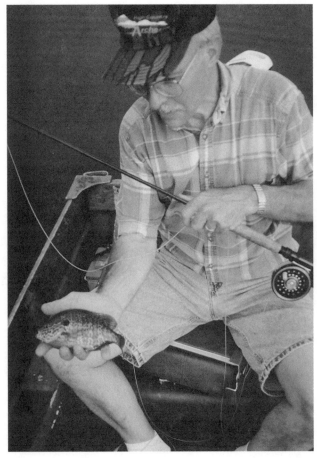

Lakes yield sunfish, along with many other species.

planted in Clear Lake, where there is also a state park, about 8 miles north of Atlanta. Southwest of Atlanta, Fifteen and McCormick Lakes are stocked with brown trout.

The next tier of counties is where the majority of designated trout lakes are found in the Lower Peninsula. In Crawford County, home of the Holy Waters of the Au Sable, there are five designated trout lakes. All are close to the river system, with Sandhill adjacent to the mainstream and Glory and Bright Lakes located north of Grayling near the East Branch. Kneff Lake is south of the mainstream, and Shupac Lake, east of Grayling, is near the North Branch just north of Lovells. Moving east, Loon and Crater Lakes are side by side about 10 miles south of Mio. Crater is the much smaller of the two and is a designated trout lake. Closer to Lake Huron, O'Brien, South Hoist, and Reid Lakes line up in the west central part of Alcona County. All three lakes are quite small, with Reid and O'Brien being designated trout lakes. All of the lakes in these three counties feature rainbows.

There are no designated trout lakes in Roscommon County, however, the state's best two-story lake lies in the northern part of the county. Higgins Lake has rainbows, browns, and lakers, and state parks are located on the north and south ends of this nearly 10,000-acre lake. In the abundant shoal areas, trout can be found cruising in fall and spring. In neighboring Ogemaw County, Grousehaven and Devoe Lakes, near the headwaters of the Rifle River east of Rose City, are planted with rainbows. Grousehaven also receives some yearling brown trout. Lake George, south of West Branch, receives a large plant of rainbows each year. To the east in Iosco County, Buck Creek Pond is a designated trout lake that is located 13 miles west of Oscoda.

In the center of the peninsula, Little Long Lake in Harrison is planted with brown trout. Staying in the center and moving south, Blanchard Pond in the town of the same name is a designated trout lake. Marl Lake is also in the Pine River watershed and provides fishing for rainbow trout. It is located 4 miles east of Edmore on M-46.

Most, but not all, trout lakes have been mentioned here. Conditions fluctuate on many of these lakes, so consulting with the DNR fisheries biologist for the watershed(s) is important. These biologists can also help you pick some of the best warmwater lakes in their respective areas for flyfishing.

SOUTHWESTERN LOWER PENINSULA

Although there are no designated trout lakes in southwestern Michigan, there are a number of two-story lakes containing trout. Considering that this is the banana, or should I say grape, belt of the state, this is surprising. North of Grand Rapids, near the Rogue River, Halfmoon, Marjella, and Lime Lakes are stocked with rainbow trout. Moving down to Allegan and Barry Counties, Pike Lake south of Allegan, Lake Sixteen north of Martin, and Deep Lake west of Hastings offer seasonal flyrodding for trout. The northern edge of Gull Lake extends into Barry County, and during fall and spring, the shoal area off the mouth of Prairieville Creek is the place to try for brown and rainbow trout. Atlantic salmon have also been planted in this lake in the past, so there is a chance to tangle with one of them.

A panfish coming in. (Photo by Pete Schmitz)

Much more of Gull Lake is found in Kalamazoo County, and you can also fish for trout at several parks in this county. Just south of Gull Lake, you can fish for rainbows in Three Lakes' West Lake. To the east, rainbow trout are planted in Lee Lake, about 10 miles south of Battle Creek. In Branch County to the south, there are three rainbow trout lakes to try. Cary Lake is about 5 miles southwest of Coldwater, while Lake Lavine and Gilead Lake are in the southwest corner of the county.

Circling back to the west, Corey Lake, 5 miles west of Three Rivers, receives a large stocking of rainbows. Crossing the county line into Cass County, four lakes hold rainbow trout: from north to south, they are Hemlock, Hardwood, Birch, and Shavehead Lakes. The latter two lakes are quite large and receive over 7,000 yearling rainbows each year. Moving into Berrien County in the corner of the state, you can fish for rainbows in Singer Lake near Baroda. To the north, there are a couple of choices in Van Buren County for rainbows: Cedar and Bankson Lakes, located close together in the southeast corner of the county. Completing a clockwise circle at the western edge of Kalamazoo County, Rupert Lake in the northwest corner and Little Paw Paw Lake at the headwaters of the East Branch of the Paw Paw River are both stocked with rainbows. I can indirectly attest to some healthy rainbows in Little Paw

Paw Lake, because I periodically encounter some of these acrobatic fish that have left the lake and moved down into the East Branch.

SOUTHEASTERN LOWER PENINSULA

Even though trout lakes are relatively few and far between in heavily populated southeastern Michigan, there are still some good opportunities. Starting along the Indiana border counties, there are two rainbow lakes south of Hillsdale in the county of the same name. Bear and Bird Lakes are stocked with large numbers of yearling trout relative to their size. Most of the lakes in Lenawee County are found in the northwest corner, where Allens and Deep Lakes are located. Though small, these lakes are planted annually with rainbows. Monroe County has no trout lakes, but to the north, Washtenaw County's Pickerel Lake, located in Pinckney State Game Area northwest of Dexter, offers trout fishing. I include here two Jackson County lakes stocked with rainbows that are actually in the Lake Michigan watershed but are closer geographically to the southeastern region: Swains Lake, 2 miles south of Concord, and Farewell Lake, east of Hanover.

In the next tier of counties, there are a lot more lakes, but relatively few of them are home to trout. In Livingston County, rainbow trout are planted in Appleton and Trout Lakes, located close to Brighton in the southeast corner of the county. Oakland County is loaded with lakes, and Maceday Lake is probably the best trout lake in southeastern Michigan. Very close to Pontiac, it is planted with rainbows and splake. Lake trout are also present in Maceday and are planted in Cass Lake, another large metro Pontiac lake. In the Thumb, there are relatively few lakes and none is suitable for trout.

Planning and Preparing for a Trip

Changing weather and water conditions are a given for Michigan. This book will help you select a time of the year for the kind of fishing you want to do, but it is important that you check conditions just before you come. Being flexible is the key to having a great time in this water wonderland. Weather that is too hot or too cold, too much wind, and water that is too high or low could alter your fishing plans, but it is very rare that some good fishing can't be found for those who are willing to change rivers, change to stillwaters, or change to a different species.

Below are suggestions on what to bring to insure that you will be prepared for most of the possibilities.

Rods

Always bring two rods for each type of fishing you plan to do. That is: two steelhead rods, two trout rods, two bass rods, etc. For those who are more specialized, two dry fly rods, two streamer rods, two nymph rods, etc. I have had rods broken and stolen over many years of fishing but have always had a spare to keep me going. A rod repair kit in your vest that contains an extra tip top, single foot guides, ferrule cement, and electrical tape adds more insurance.

Reels

A spare reel and spare spools with spare lines are all good ideas. Lots of spare leaders, from floating to various sink rates, are also important to have along. Tippet spools in various line weights for the flies you will be fishing, the size of the fish, and water clarity will keep you ready for the situation at hand.

Flies

Selection depends on your quarry and the expected hatches. It is important to have emergers as well as adults and immature forms. Unless you are a dry fly purist, streamers in crayfish, muddler, and woolly bugger patterns are a must.

Clothing

With Michigan temperatures ranging from subzero to the nineties, the time of year that you visit will dictate your clothing. Layering is the key — remember that you can take something off if it warms up, but you can't add layers if you don't have them. A lightweight, long-sleeved shirt in the summer will decrease the area exposed to the sun and mosquitoes. A billed cap or broad-brimmed hat is essential for shading your eyes as well as a pair of sunglasses.

Waders

Boot foot, 5mm neoprene waders are just the ticket for late fall through early spring. During spring and fall, you can switch to 3mm neoprene, and breathable waders are perfect for summer. Most Michigan anglers choose boot foot waders for all seasons, but stocking foot models with sturdy wading shoes can be better for rocky Lake Superior tributaries. A wading belt and staff are important accessories. Leave the hip boots at home, because even the small streams in Michigan have waist-deep water, and at other times, you will need to kneel to keep fish from detecting your presence. If you have room, take a spare pair of waders. Sun Set Super Patch for onstream repair and Aquaseal for permanent patching should be part of your gear. A rain jacket to complete your waterproofing is also a must.

Sunglasses

Polarized sunglasses are an absolute necessity. Those with amber or other light tints having high light transmittance are best most of the time in "cloudy" Michigan or on her well-shaded streams.

Net

Not easy to pack and you can probably borrow one but having one shortens the battle with large fish and increases successful landing and releasing.

Vest Checklist

Depending on the season, additional vest items to those noted above that should be considered include the following: Forceps or needle-nosed pliers, floatant, strike indicators, wetting agent and/or weighting material, hook file or stone, reel take-down tool and spare parts, insect repellent, sunscreen, point and shoot camera in reclosable plastic bag, line clipper and/or scissors, thermometer, penlight, compass, pocket scale and measuring tape, aspirin, and bandaids.

Baggage and Flying

If you are flying to Michigan, try to pack essential fishing gear in your carry-on bag. Always carry your rod case(s) on board, as well. The airlines might tell you they won't fit in the overhead bin, but then you can cabin check them and make sure they arrive with you.

Catch, Shoot, and Release

Most Michigan fish are delicious in the pan or on the grill, and there are relatively few situations where releasing your catch is mandatory. Some species, such as bluegill, perch, and other panfish, require regular harvesting to keep their numbers in check, while others, such as coho and chinook salmon are stocked for a put, grow, and take fishery. However, releasing some of your catch will help maintain and improve Michigan's fine sport fishery. In fact, when fishing for wild trout and steelhead or any large predator fish, releasing most or all of your catch is best.

Releasing a fish successfully begins with the catching: Never fight a fish to exhaustion. Use sturdy enough tackle to subdue your quarry in a relatively short amount of time. Pressuring the fish from the side with your rod rather than lifting it to the surface will tire it faster and enable you to quickly conquer large fish with relatively light tackle.

There's time to record this steelhead before releasing it.

Handle fish as little as possible. Small fish that can be controlled by grabbing the tippet can then be shaken free by grabbing the fly with forceps. A net greatly speeds the landing of large fish. Use it as a corral and leave the net bag in the water to minimize any abrasion damage or protective slime removal. If you must "beach" a large fish, never drag it up on dry land. Find a shallow area where the fish can be forced on its side while still having several inches of cushioning water.

Along with a net, a pair of forceps (or needle nose pliers for large fish) should be a mandatory part of every angler's equipment. Manually unhooking a fish can be hard on the fish and your fly, and, if the fish has sharp teeth like the trout and pike families, your fingers. Barbless hooks also help, but even they can be stubborn at times, and sometimes it's hard to pinch barbs down after a big fish has prematurely dislodged a weighted fly.

Usually, a fish is ready to take off after being unhooked, but if it needs some resuscitation, always take time to do this. The best way to do this is by gently cradling the fish as it faces into a slow current. If you are fishing in a lake, slowly move the fish forward until it recovers.

Releasing a brown trout, smallmouth bass, or steelhead of a lifetime can be tough to do, especially if you are fishing by yourself. The solution for letting a trophy fish swim away is to take a picture of it. A camera is always part of my gear, ready to capture a deer drinking at streamside, an eagle watching me as I fish, or a freshly caught beauty of a fish. If you plan to take pictures of your catch, always have everything ready before you lift a fish out of the water. Of course, if you are taking a picture of yourself with the timer, this will be automatic.

Releasing large trout, bass, and other game fish is one of the most satisfying things you can do. I mark many of the trout I release in the creeks that are close to my home, and it feels really great when I recapture a big brown. Lee Wulff was right on target when he said that game fish are too valuable to be caught only once.

Additional Fly Shops

This listing includes more shops that carry flyfishing supplies and equipment, from full service fly shops to stores with just the basics — arranged by city.

Acme
Orvis Streamside
6300 Us 31 N
616-938-5337

Ada
Thornapple Outfitters
1200 E Paris #4 49301
616-676-0177

Adrian
Country Fields
3975 S Adrian Highway
517-263-3134

RC Resale Bait Tackle
1120 Treat St
517-264-0052

Alpena
Buck's Bait & Tackle
8501 Us High 23 N

Ann Arbor
Macgregor's Outdoor, Inc
803 N Main St
313-761-9200

Auburn
Bass Pros Shops Outdoor World
4500 Baldwin Rd
248-209-4200

Baldwin
Baldwin Bait & Tackle, Inc.
3223 South M-37
231-745-3529

Ed's Sport Shop
712 N Michigan Ave
231-745-4974

Pere Marquette River Lodge
RR 1 Box 1290
231-745-3972

Streamside Woman
765 E Fifth St
231-745-9680

Battle Creek
Creekside Bait & Tackle
22551 Bedford Rd N
616-721-8990

Dickerson Sporting Goods
95 Sigel Ave
616-963-7429

Bay City
Hexagon Rod & Fly Shop
2973 Midland Rd
517-686-6212

Bellaire
Butchs Tackle And Marine
6235 Crystal Springs
616-377-6787

Belleville
South Street Tackle And Sporting
205 South Street
734-697-0990

Benton Harbor
Tackle Haven
741 Riverview Dr
616-925-0341

Benzonia
Backcast Fly Shop
1675 Benzie Hwy
231-882-5222

Bessemer
Big Sno Outfitters
309 E Lead St
906-663-4646

Birmingham
Wild Wings Gallery
155 S Bates
810-645-2266

Bloomfield Hills
Westbank Anglers Michigan
6612 Telegraph Road
248-538-3474

Brighton
Midwest Sport Shop
10049 E Grand River Ste 900
810-227-3141

Cadillac
Jd's Sport Shop
301 N Mitchell
231-775-8787

Pilgrim Village Fishing Shop
181 S. Lake Mitchell Drive
23-775 2401

Ron's Sporting Goods
1531 N Mitchell St
231-779-0750

Camden
Dick's Place
7100 W Territorial Rd
517-368-5283

Charlevoix
Bridge Street Bookshop
405 Bridge St.
616-547-7323

Clare
Jay's Sporting Goods
8800 S Clare Av
517-386-3475

Larry's Bait & Sport Shop
5449 Round Lake Rd
517-426-7205

Clarkston
Freeland Outfitters
10060 Big Lake Road

The Hairy Hook Co
6650 Wellesley Terrace
810-623-1702

Crystal Falls
DJ's Sport Shop & Marine
31 Superior Ave
906-875-3113

Davison
Fishing Tackle Grab Bag
5521 N State Rd
810-653-4771

Dearborn
The Sports Authority
5751 Mercury Dr
313-336-6626

Dundee
Cabela's
110 Cabela Blvd
734-529-4700

East Jordan
Jordan River Fly Shop
105 Main St
231-536-9925

East Tawas
Nordic Sports
218 W Bay St
517-362-2001

Edwardsburg
Lunker's
26296 East Us Highway 12
616-663-3745

Escanaba
Great Lakes Sports
6687 Us 2
906-789-9473

Land & Lakes Sports
845 N Lincoln Rd
906-786-5263

Farmington
Benchmark Fly Shop
32715 Grand River
248-474-2088

Lakeside Fishing Shop
34801 Grand River
248-473-2030

The Wooly Bugger
32715 Grand River Ave
313-477-8116

Ferndale
Geake & Sons Inc.
23510 Woodward
313-542-0498

Flint
Hick's Tackle Shop
5425 Clio Rd
810-785-9941

Flushing
Golden Hackle Fly Shop
329 Crescent Pl
810-659-0018

Frankenmuth
Fly-Rite
7421 S Beyer
517-652-9869

Gaylord
Alphorn Sports Shop
137 W Main St
517-732-5616

Gladstone
Bayshore Bait & Tackle
1323 Lakeshore Dr
906-428-2950

Grand Blanc
Angler's Den
E 5104 Cook Road
810-953-5530

Grand Haven
Anglers Edge
218 Washington
616-842-8588

Grand Rapids
Al & Bob's Sports
3100 S Division Ave
616-245-9156

Gander Mountain
2890 Acquest Ave Se
616-975-1000

Michigan Sporting Goods
3160 28th St
616-949-8510

Grayling
Cartwright & Danewell Provisioners
M-72 West
888-857-6500

Fly Factory, The Hatch Line
200 Ingram St.
517-348-5844

Gate's Ausable Lodge & Pro Shop
421 S Stephan Bridge Rd
517-348-8462

Hartman's Fly Shop
6794 E Country Road 612
517-348-9679

Rays Canoeing & The Fly Factory
200 Ingham St
517-348-5844

Skip's Sport Shop
5875 W M-72 Highway
517-348-7111

Greenwood
Pappy's Bait And Tackle
17092 Caberfae Hwy
616-894-4670

Grosse Pointe
Au Sable Outfitters
17005 Kercheval
313-642-2000

Hancock
Northwoods Trading Post
120 Quincy St
906-482-5210

Hastings
Al & Pete's Sport Shop
111 S Jefferson
616-945-4417

Bob's Guns And Tackle
2208 W. M-43 Hwy.
616-945-4106

Holland
American Tackle Outfitters
360 Douglass Ave
616-392-6688

Sportsman's Specialties
102 Walnut Ave
616-394-5858

Houghton
Dick's Favorite Sports
1700 W Memorial Dr
906-482-0412

Indian River
Studers Sporting Goods
3696 S. Straits Hwy
616-238-8125

Iron Mountain
Jim's Sport Shop
N Us Highway 2
906-774-4247

Northwoods Wilderness Outfitters
4088 Pine Mountain Rd
906-774-9009

Scott's Sporting Goods
1601 N Stephenson Ave
906-774-8520

Ironwood
Black Bear Sporting Goods
100 W Cloverland Dr
906-932-5253

Dunham's Discount Sports
1440 E Cloverland Dr
906-932-0990

Trek And Trail
1300 E Cloverland Dr
906-932-5858

Jonesville
The Book House, Inc.
208 W. Chicago St.
517-849-2117

Kalamazoo
Angling Outfitters
3207 Stadium Dr
616-372-0922

D & R Sports Center
8178 W Main St
616-372-2277

Kalkaska
Jack's Sport Shop
212 S Cedar St
231-258-8892

Lake Orion
Wings & Clay
2500 Kern Rd.

Lansing
Indian Country Sports
175 Front St
906-524-6518

BC Nymph Co.
302 S Waverly
517-321-3800

Four Seasons Bait And Tackle
1210 N Cedar
517-487-0050

Gander Mountain
430 Market Place Blvd
517-622-5700

Grand River Bait & Tackle
536 E Grand River
517-482-4461

Mid-Michigan Anglers
570 Riley St
517-485-5280

Linwood
Frank's Bait & Tackle
1206 N Huron Rd
517-697-5341

Frank's Great Outdoors
1212 M-13
517-697-5341

Livonia
Pro Angler Outdoors Inc.
28441 5 Mile Rd
734-427-8863

Lovells
Bill's Au Sable Rod & Fly Shop
Rt. 3 Box 3502
517-348-9777

Ludington
North Bayou Resort
4849 N Lakeshore Dr
231-845-5820

Pere Marquette Sport Center
214 West Ludington Ave
231-843-8676

Provisions Sport Shop
112 W Avenue
231-843-4150

Manistee
Fisherman's Center
263 Arthur St
231-723-7718

Northwind Sports
400 Parkdale Ave
231-723-2255

Manistique
Indian Lake Sports
Rr 1 Box 1354
906-341-5932

Marquette
Carpenter's Outdoor Outfitters
131 W. Washington St.
906-228-6380

Johnson Sport Shop
1212 N 3rd St
906-226-2062

Linquist's Outdoor Sports
131 W Washington
906-228-6380

Tom's Hunt And Fish
2162 Us Highway 41 W
906-228-8667

Melvindale
Vicking Tackle
17485 Dix Hwy
313-388-3040

Menominee
Acorns & Antlers Archery Ctr
2400 13th St
906-863-8026

Great Lakes Sports
2921 13th St
906-863-5797

Midland
Little Forks Outfitters
143 East Main St
517-832-4100

Milford
Read Between The Lines
341 N Main St
810-684-7285

Monroe
Cooks Sportland
6363 N. Monroe
734-242-0774

Munising
Curly's Hilltop
E9825 Country Rd Hwy 58
906-387-3056

Muskegon
Flies For Michigan
409 E Circle Dr
231-744-1524

Springs Sporting Goods
280 Ottawa St
231-722-7107

Newaygo
Parsley's Sport Shop
70 State St
231-652-6986

Newberry
Duke's Sport Shop
202 S Newberry Ave
906-293-8421

Hilltop Sport & Bait
2051 S Newberry Ave
906-293-8856

Rainbow Lodge
County Rd 423
906-658-3357

Northville
Beuter's Outdoor Ltd
120 E Main St
810-349-3677

Okemos
M Chance Flyfishing Specialties
5100 Marsh Rd B-4 Suite 3a
517-349-6696

Owosso
Emery-Pratt Co.
1966 West M 21

Petoskey
Whippoorwill Flyfishing Shop
305 E. Lake
231-348-7061

Plymouth
Wild Wings Gallery
388 S Main
313-455-3400

Pontiac
Gander Mountain
2230 Mall Drive E
248-738-9600

Port Huron
Pro Bait & Tackle
2731 Pine Grove Ave
810-984-3232

Thompson's Bait & Tackle
1222 Water St
810-982-2321

Trout's Choice
4296 Peck Rd
810-985-7628

Portage
Doc's Custom Fly Tackle
1804 Thrushwood
616-327-8917

Fishing Memories
8842 Portage Rd
616-329-1803

Gander Mountain
5348 S Westnedge Ave
616-388-9770

Rochester
Paint Creek Outfitters
203 E. University Dr
248-650-0440

South Bend Supply Co
203 E. University Dr
248-650-0440

Rockford
Michigan River Outfitters
2775 10 Mile Rd NE
616-866-6060

Rogers City
Adrian's Sport Shop
335 N Bradley Hwy
517-734-2303

Roscommon
Sports Barn
9475 N Cut Rd
517-821-9511

Royal Oak
Flymart Flyshop
1002 N Main St
248-584-2848

Saginaw
Country Anglers
2030 S Thomas Rd
517-781-0997

Gander Mountain
2270 Tittabawassee
517-791-3500

Saint Clair Shores
Flymart Flyshop
31009 Jefferson Ave
810-415-5650

Lakeside Fishing Shop
25510 Jefferson At 10 Mile
810-777-7003

Saint Ignace
Ace Hardware & Sporting Goods
7 South State St
906-643-7721

Sanford
John's Custom Flies
12 W Wackerly Dr
517-687-9202

Sault Sainte Marie
Hank's Sport Shop
3522 I-75 Business Spur
906-632-8741

Superior Sports
650 W Easterday
906-635-6220

Sodus
Church Tackle Co.
7075 Hillandale Rd
616-934-8528

Swartz Creek
Gander Mountain
6359 Gander Dr
810-635-7800

Tawas City
All Season Sporting Goods
1131 N Huron Rd
517-362-4512

Taylor
Gander Mountain
14100 Pardee Road
313-287-7420

Thompsonville
Aries Tackle
7567 Michigan Ave
231-378-4520

Traverse City
Austin & Nelson
104 S. Union St. Ste 211
616-933-4649

Can Am Angler
536 Washington
616-946-7477

Fieldsport Ltd
3313 W South Airport Rd
231-933-0767

Gander Mountain
3500 Marketplace Circle
231-929-5590

M.C. Sports
848 Us Highway 31 S
231-943-8280

Tackle Town
3680 S West Bay Shore Dr
231-941-5420

The Troutsman
4386 Us Highway 31 N
231-938-3474

Utica
Gander Mountain
13975 Hall Rd
810-247-9900

Waterford
Kellys Outfitters
7688 Highland Rd
313-666-1440

The Hairy Hook
4690 W Walton
248-618-9939

Wellston
Schmidt Outfitters
918 Seaman Rd
616-848-4191

West Branch
Bachelder Spool & Fly
1434 East State Rd
517-345-8678

J & P Sporting Goods
3275 West M-76
517-345-3744

Zettel's Sport Center
3091 W Houghton Ave
517-345-3159

Whitehall
Lakeland Outfitters
116 W Colby St
616-894-4670

Williamsburg
Streamside Orvis Shop
4400 Grand Traverse Village E-4
231-938-5337

Wolverine
Wolverine True Value & Quiet Sports
13386 Straits Hwy
231-525-8370

Important Phone Numbers

Department of Natural Resources Fisheries Division 517-373-1280
   Lake Superior Management Unit 906-293-5131
   Northern Lake Michigan Management Unit 906-875-6622
   Central Lake Michigan Management Unit 616-775-9727
   Southern Lake Michigan Management Unit 616-685-6851
   Northern Lake Huron Management Unit 517-732-3541
   Southern Lake Huron Management Unit 517-684-9141
   Lake Erie Management Unit 734-953-0241

Weekly Fishing Reports 517-373-0908

Fishing Hotline 800-275-3474

License Information 517-373-1204

DNR Law Enforcement Division 517-373-1230

Report All Poaching (RAP) Hotline 800-292-7800

Parks and Recreation Division 517-373-9900

State Campground Reservations 800-447-2757

Forest Management Division 517-373-1275

Tourist and Travel Information 888-784-7328

Michigan Game Fish

Michigan's abundant and diverse water resources are home to a large variety of native and introduced game fish. Most of these fish will readily take flies and can be reached with fly tackle for at least portions of the year.

BROOK TROUT

Although Michigan's native stream trout is the brookie, it was native only to the Upper Peninsula's streams. In the Lower Peninsula, the grayling filled this niche. Probably more miles of streams hold brook trout than any other species of trout, and the Upper Peninsula is still the stronghold for these fish.

A member of the char family, brook trout are colored so brilliantly, especially males near spawning time, they almost look like tropical aquarium fish. Because brookies are relatively slow growing and short-lived, most are less than 10 inches; any stream brook trout over 16 inches is a trophy. They do grow a bit larger in lakes, and if you hit a beaver dam just right, you might have a chance at a brookie pushing 20 inches.

Brook trout seem to prefer smaller streams where they compete fairly well with introduced browns and rainbows. In some of the larger rivers where brook trout are the primary prey, such as the Black River in northern lower Michigan, anglers are encouraged to keep the brown trout they catch. In fact, the DNR has purposely removed brown trout from this stream.

Brook trout are notorious for their gullibility and are often not very selective. Attractor patterns and flies larger than naturals are often the most effective. Remember, though, that big brookies didn't get that way by grabbing every angler's offering that drifted past them.

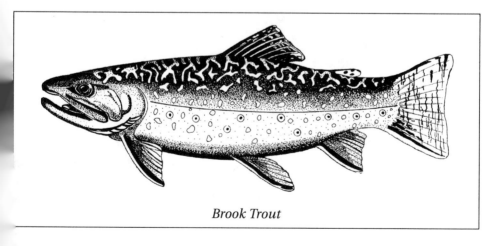

Brook Trout

BROWN TROUT

Michigan's Pere Marquette River was the first U.S. river to receive brown trout from Europe in the mid-1880s. Since then, it has certainly flourished in a large number of the state's trout streams. They are especially prominent in the Lower Peninsula.

Brown trout are true trout, with dark spots on an olive to brown background. They grow relatively fast in fertile waters and are long-lived when water quality is good. These fish are able to reach large size in relatively small waters. In most Michigan streams, browns range up to 22 inches, with good numbers of fish in the middle teens. Browns in the Great Lakes reach world record proportions, and some move up the rivers to spawn in the fall. If you catch a brown trout that is over 8 pounds in a river that is not blocked by dams, it is most likely a lake-run. When in doubt, check the spots. In most cases, stream resident trout have red ones, while lake-run browns never do.

Though brown trout are very wary, they rise well to good presentations of dry flies. Hatches of large, burrowing mayflies, such as the brown drake and *Hexagenia*, result in browns over 20 inches feeding on the surface at dusk and into the night. During the day, you can lure browns from wood and undercut bank hideouts with streamers imitating baitfish in the river or crayfish. Good-sized brown trout are especially fond of crayfish, so actively twitching a streamer that imitates them is a great way to "search the river" and draw browns out from cover.

Brown Trout

RAINBOW TROUT/STEELHEAD

Michigan's first rainbow trout introduction came from California's McCloud River. These trout were anadromous, and current lake-run rainbows or steelhead are descendants of these fish. Nonmigratory strains of rainbow trout, along with summer steelhead, have since been introduced. Most wild rainbows in Michigan streams become steelheads, but there are a few exceptions, with the resident rainbows in the Manistee's Pine River tributary the most notable. Rainbow trout have now been

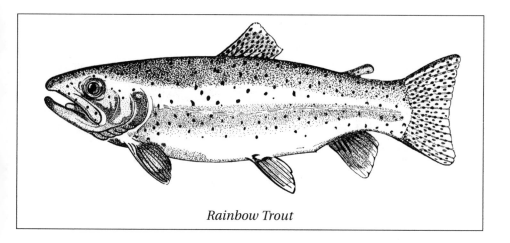

Rainbow Trout

declared a salmon by the fish taxonomists, but they will always be trout to me. They certainly seem to resemble a brown trout more closely than a chinook salmon, both physically and in their life history.

Steelhead run in just about every Michigan tributary to the Great Lakes. While some are stocked, many are wild. Steelhead average about 7 pounds and range from 2 to over 20. In early spring, these fish are on their spawning run, but they also enter rivers any month of the year. The angler's challenge is that rainbows don't actively feed on these runs. This means you must either invade their territory with a large marabou leech, woolly bugger, or other streamer or, taking advantage of their opportunistic feeding reflex, hit them on the nose with a nymph or egg fly.

Rainbows and steelhead put up exciting, aerial battles. Luckily, they don't often head for the logs on purpose, but they can find snags by accident as they randomly zip through the water. They tend to prefer faster water and use the current to their advantage when fighting the rod. Staying close to these trout is the key to landing them.

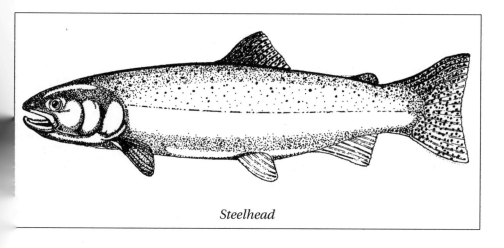

Steelhead

Lake Trout

LAKE TROUT AND SPLAKE

Lakers are Michigan's other native trout. Like brook trout, they are members of the char family, with light spots on a green to gray background. True to their name, these fish inhabit the Great Lakes and the deeper inland lakes. Even though they are slow growing, their long life span allows them to reach weights exceeding 50 pounds. Most of these weigh between 5 and 10 pounds, and any specimen over 20 pounds is a big one.

For most of the year they are not available to anglers using conventional fly tackle, but in late fall and early spring they cruise the shallows, and some enter rivers. Lake trout spawn in the fall, and when suitable spawning reefs in the lake are lacking, they sometimes move into rivers. The most dependable lake trout runs occur in the southern Lake Michigan tributaries. In the spring, some lake trout also enter tributaries while following smelt spawning migrations. Lake trout prefer water temperatures in the low 50s, and when this temperature occurs in the shallows, you can find lake trout there. They are almost exclusively fish eaters, so streamers matching forage fish draw the most strikes.

Sterile hybrids, splake are a cross between brook (speckled) and lake trout. They grow faster than lake trout and get larger than brook trout. When the water temperature is in the 50s, they cruise the shoreline in search of food. They are stocked both in the Great Lakes and inland lakes but are not found in streams.

ATLANTIC SALMON

Just to keep us confused, Atlantic salmon are really trout. These fish have been introduced at various times and various locations in Michigan with only modest success. Currently, strains of landlocked Atlantic salmon are stocked in the St. Mary's River and Torch Lake.

There is a very viable fishery for them in the St. Mary's, where they begin their run in late June and continue to be available throughout the summer. These fish

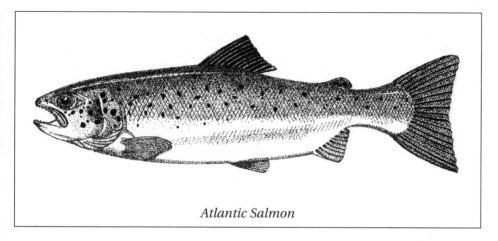

Atlantic Salmon

spawn in the fall and, like trout, do not die after spawning. Most of these fish weigh between 6 and 12 pounds, with one in the upper teens a really nice size.

The crystal clear water of the St. Mary's offers the chance to bring a fish to the surface in this very large river, but streamers and nymphs are likely to be more successful. Traditional Atlantic salmon flies work here, as do the patterns that are used for steelhead in May and June.

CHINOOK SALMON

Chinook, or king, salmon were successfully introduced to the Great Lakes by Michigan biologists in the late 1960s. These fish spawn in early fall, and the young smolt the following May and June. Thus, most Michigan rivers allow for some natural reproduction, and overall, wild fish now make up about 50 percent of the run.

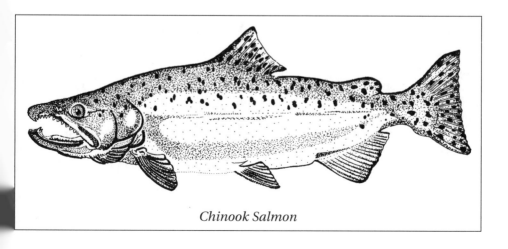

Chinook Salmon

444 — FLYFISHER'S GUIDE TO MICHIGAN

Chinook salmon live up to 6 years, but some precocious males (jacks) return to spawn after just one summer in the big lakes. My personal "inverse record" is a 7-inch sexually mature chinook, hardly a "king," and I certainly didn't need a 9-weight to land it. Most jack salmon are 2 and 3 years old and weigh from 4 to 12 pounds, while the largest portion of the run will be 4- and 5-year-olds weighing from 15 to 30 pounds.

Like all Pacific salmon, chinook die after spawning and their digestive tract starts to atrophy when they begin their river migration. In spite of this, they still strike flies out of a reflex feeding action, even though they can't swallow them. Invading their territory with gaudy streamers also elicits aggressive takes.

COHO SALMON

Coho, or silver, salmon were introduced to Lake Michigan a year earlier than chinook salmon. These fish did very well, producing a near world record and a 39-pound fish that was captured at the Little Manistee weir. Today the cohos, with much more competition for forage, are smaller but continue to add diversity to the anadromous fishery.

In Michigan, silver salmon begin running the rivers in mid-September and peak in October. They still add to the catch through December. These fish spend a year-and-a-half in the hatchery or river and a year-and-a-half in the Great Lakes. A fair number of jack males run after just one summer in the lakes, while these occasional fish will stay out for an extra year. Jacks weigh about 2 pounds, and adults range from 4 to 12 pounds.

Coho salmon are also accessible to surf and beach anglers in the early spring, with southern Lake Michigan the prime location. These fish are actively feeding and searching for the warmest water they can find. Streamers imitating alewives, smelt, and emerald shiners will catch them. On their spawning runs, salmon cannot feed, but they still grab egg flies and seem to be especially attracted to streamers that have a strong fluorescent red or orange component.

PINK SALMON

Pink salmon are definitely the "Rodney Dangerfield" game fish of Michigan. In spite of getting no respect and no help, they continue to flourish. They were introduced to Lake Superior in the 1950s when Ontario biologists tried to flush them down the drain. Obviously, all pink salmon are wild fish and are most commonly found in Lake Superior and northern Lake Huron tributaries.

Pink salmon have a two-year life cycle and typically weigh between 2 and 4 pounds as returning adults in the Great Lakes. The accidental stocking took place in an odd-numbered year, so odd-numbered years tend to have larger runs. However, enough salmon have stayed out for an extra year over the last 40 years to produce an almost equal even-year run. There was quite a stir about a possible world record pink salmon a few years ago, but it turned out to be a pink/chinook hybrid and was labeled a "pinook."

Pink salmon provide great sport on trout tackle. They run the rivers in September and can be present in large numbers. Nymphs and streamers in pink and purple hues seem to be most attractive to these fish. Egg patterns also produce hookups with pink salmon.

WHITEFISH

Unlike the West, Michigan doesn't have a whitefish that lives in its rivers, but there are two species in the Great Lakes. Lake and Menominee whitefish spend most of their lives in water too deep to be fished with fly tackle. In spring and fall, Menominee and, to a much lesser extent, lake whitefish move into the shallows near river mouths.

Single egg patterns are the most effective enticement, and it is important to use light tippets and limber rods. Most Menominee whitefish weigh less than a pound, and any fish over 2 pounds is a trophy. These are the walleye of the coldwater world, and most anglers who fish them are definitely planning on savoring their delicate flavor at the table.

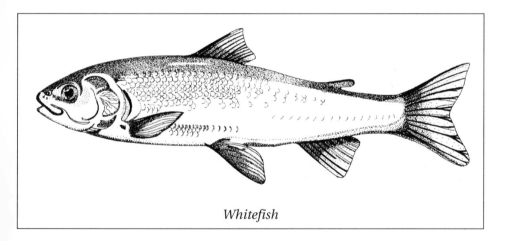

Whitefish

NORTHERN PIKE AND MUSKELLUNGE

Pike and muskie are categorized as cool water fish by fisheries biologists. Northerns are found throughout Michigan, while muskies are much more limited in distribution. Muskies are also pretty much limited to large lakes and rivers, while pike are found in most of the state's lakes and nontrout rivers and creeks. Sometimes, this water wolf also shows up in trout water where it is not very welcome.

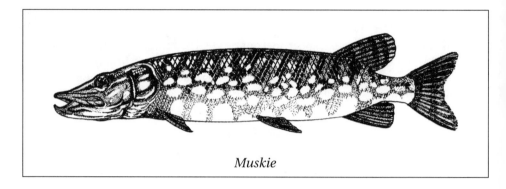

Muskie

Obviously, northern pike are much more available to the fly rodder than muskellunge. My only encounter with a muskie occurred when I was trout fishing in a creek that had a lake plated with tiger muskies—a cross between pike and muskie—in its headwaters. This fish moved out of the lake and obviously developed a preference for soft-rayed browns as opposed to spiny-rayed bluegills and perch. I am also happy to report that the muskie's trout-eating career ended that day.

Pike grow rapidly and provide the chance to catch a large fish in relatively small rivers and lakes. They usually range between 3 and 10 pounds in rivers, with fish over 10 pounds more common in lakes. A 20-pound fish is a trophy in either moving or still water. They are primarily fish eaters, so large streamers that imitate forage fish in the lake or stream you are fishing are the most effective. These fish ambush their prey and lurk wherever there is cover to hide them. This means you will want to be on the move and cover a fair amount river or shoreline/weedbeds in a lake.

WALLEYE

A member of the perch family, the walleye is considered a cool water fish. Michigan has developed a reputation as a top walleye state due to its fisheries in Saginaw Bay, Lake St. Clair, Lake Erie, the Bays de Noc, and the drowned river mouth lakes along Lake Michigan's shore. Concurrently—and with much less fanfare—there has been a big increase in numbers of river-dwelling walleyes where they can be caught with fly tackle.

River walleyes do not grow as fast as their lake brethren, but 5- to 8-pound fish are regularly caught. These fish prefer hard-bottomed reaches with lots of rocks and moderate current. If this sounds like smallmouth bass habitat to you, then you know your fish. It is also the reason that most of the river walleyes I catch are incidental bonus fish when fishing for smallies. You can increase your proportion of walleyes by fishing low light periods or moderately turbid water.

Walleyes are primarily fish eaters, but they also eat crayfish and large insects, such as hellgrammites and *Hexagenia* nymphs. Slowly fishing streamers or nymphs that imitate these food items entices walleyes to strike.

MICHIGAN GAME FISH — 447

SMALLMOUTH BASS

In my mind, smallmouth bass are the brown trout of warmwater rivers. They are both wary fish that like the same habitat. And crayfish seem to be the favorite food of the good-sized fish of either species. Often, as a Michigan trout stream becomes larger and therefore warmer, there is a transitional reach where both brown trout and smallmouth bass are found. I admit to being primarily a trout and steelhead nut, but those smallies sure do fight. Many times a "lunker brown" has turned into a 14-inch smallmouth in this transitional water.

Smallmouth bass in rivers mostly fall in the 8- to 16-inch range, but a 4- or 5-pound fish is possible. Just like trout, these fish grow larger in lakes. Rock- and log-laden pools below riffles are prime areas to find bronzebacks. Wide, relatively shallow rivers, which abound in Michigan, provide this kind of habitat.

It is hard to go wrong using a crayfish-imitating streamer for these fish. Smallmouth also eat minnows and aquatic insects. You can also catch them on the surface with large deer hair bugs. A 9-foot, 6-weight rod is the ideal compromise for casting large flies and enjoying the spirited fight of these beautifully marked bass.

Smallmouth Bass

LARGEMOUTH BASS

The biggest member of the sunfish family is a fine fly rod fish. Largemouth are primarily lake dwellers and are present in most of Michigan's lakes. Weedbeds and other heavy cover are where to find them when they move to the shallows.

Michigan's 14-inch size limit has helped increase the average size of bass and has also increased their numbers in most lakes. Most bass weigh between 1 and 4 pounds, but almost all lakes and ponds have trophy bass in the 5- to 8-pound range. These fish are true predators and seem willing to attack anything that moves. Try swimming

Largemouth Bass

streamers near weedbeds during the day and cork or foam-bodied poppers and spun hair bugs on the surface in the evening and after dark.

Because of where they live and the size/wind resistance of the flies, a heavier rod in the 8- to 9-weight range is best suited for largemouths. Even though largemouth don't fight nearly as hard as smallmouth, they are often hooked right in the weeds and need a stout rod and heavy leader to extract them.

PANFISH

Most of the fish in the sunfish family, along with yellow perch, are in the group called panfish. On light fly tackle, these fish are great fun. Bluegills, along with pumpkinseed and redear sunfish have small mouths and feed primarily on insects and other small invertebrates. Rock bass, crappies, perch, and green sunfish have proportionally larger mouths and eat other fish as well as insects. All of these fish are commonly found in lakes while rock bass and crappies are the most common river species.

Bluegills and sunfish frequently feed on the surface in late spring and early summer, and this is the most popular time to fish for them. A light trout rod and some small poppers or foam spiders are just the ticket for these warriors. Most of the fish will be between 6 and 9 inches, with a 10-inch bluegill that weighs a pound a real trophy. Rock bass are frequently found with their larger cousin the smallmouth and take the same flies, which can help to fill in the slow times when bigger fish are not hitting. Perch and crappies are not likely to provide surface action but can be fun to catch using small white marabou streamers.

CATFISH

Channel catfish are found in many Michigan rivers, especially in the state's southern half. In the larger rivers, they are joined by flathead catfish. Flatheads are strictly predators, while the channels are not nearly the scavenger they are made out to be. These fish grow large and offer the chance to catch fish weighing more than 10 pounds in the case of channel catfish, while flatheads can easily weigh more than 20.

Because of their relatively poor eyesight, the challenge in catching these fish on a fly is getting them to notice it. They readily hit lures, but I think vibration helps them find the hardware. Both species are found in the same habitat as smallmouth and walleyes. Large, marabou streamers pulsed very slowly or almost in place in the current offer the best chance for success. I've found that retrieving streamers very slowly for smallmouth results in some bonus catfish. Trying to target just catfish with flies is likely to result in very few hookups.

CARP

Carp are slowly gaining the reputation of being a fine fly rod adversary. This introduced species is found in all of Michigan's warmwater rivers and many lakes. Its size is always measured in pounds, and encounters with fish over 10 pounds are frequent in most waters.

Because carp feed near and on the bottom, they look for living organisms, such as insect nymphs and larvae. I am very impressed with their eyesight and thoroughly enjoy watching them inhale my red squirrel nymph. Red midge larva are a favorite food, so any nymph with lots of red is likely to be successful.

Surprisingly, carp are wary fish, so a careful approach is necessary to be successful. The need to use fairly light tippets adds to the challenge of landing these brutes. Even though don't move fast, they have lots of power and are difficult to turn when they head for the logs. Some lakes and Great Lakes' bays offer "flats" fishing for these freshwater bonefish. If you are used to catching 10-inch browns and brookies, they make a great change of pace while still using a trout rod.

Author's Fly Selections
JIM BEDFORD

The following lists are the flies that are in my arsenal when I ply my favorite rivers in Michigan. They are divided into the following categories: Trout, Warmwater, and Steelhead/Salmon. The fly box contents will be weighted toward the likely hatches, the species targeted, water conditions, and other factors. My specialty is actively swimming streamers and several of my favorite Michigan patterns will be described with tying instructions. Recipes for a pair of my favorite nymph patterns are also provided.

TROUT

DRY FLIES

Hendrickson	#12-14
Red Quill	#12-14
Adams	#12-16
Blue-winged Olive	#18-20
Sparkle Dun Baetis	#18-22
Sulphur Dun	#14-16
March Brown	#12-14
Gray Drake	#12-14
Brown Drake	#10-12
Parachute Adams	#10-14
Adult Hex	#04-08
CDC Trico	#24-28
Royal Wulff	#10-16
Black Ant	#16-18
Dave's Hopper	#06-10

NYMPHS & STREAMERS

Pheasant Tail	#12-16
Bead Head Pheasant Tail	#12-16
Cyclops	#06-10
Prince	#10-16
Bead Head Prince	#10-16
Spring's Wiggler	#04-08
March Madness (Hex Nymph)	#04-08
Muddler Minnow	#04-10
Bead Head Woolly Bugger	#04-10
Olive Matuka	#06-10
UB Crayfish Tubefly	#02-08

STEELHEAD/SALMON

Early Black Stonefly	#10-14
March Madness (Hex Nymph)	#04-08
Glo Bugs	#06-10
Popsicle	#04-08
Marabou Spey	#02-08
B. H. Red Cedar Spey	#02-08
NoBody Matuka Tubefly	#02-08
Egg Sucking Leech	#02-08

MY FAVORITE FLIES

NoBody Matuka Tubefly
Tubing- HMH Custom Tube Fly Blank (1" clear)
Thread- Fl. Red 3/0 Gudebrod
Wing- White Arctic Fox Fur
Hackle- Cream Saddle Hackle
Trailing Hook- Kamasan B982 #2-8
Thread- White 6/0 Gudebrod
Tail- White Arctic Fox Fur

Crayfish

UB Crayfish Tubefly
Tubing- HMH Custom Tube Fly Blanks (1" black)
Thread- Black 3/0 Gudebrod
Hackle- Black Saddle Hackle
Eyes- Black Hourglass (brass)
Head- Black Hares Blend Dubbing
Trailing Hook- Kamasan B982 #2-8
Antennae- (2) Olive Juicy Legs
Claws- (2) 1" pieces of medium Dark Olive Ultra Braid w/Olive Hares Blend Dubbing

March Madness

March Madness Hex Nymph
Hook- Tiemco #3761
Tail- Brown Marabou
Body- Sand Leech Yarn
Rib- Fine Copper Wire
Hackle- Brown Cock Saddle
Wing Case- Pheasant Tail
Head- Burnt Orange Dubbing
Eyes- Medium Mono Eyes
Thread- Tan 6/0

Spey

Bead Head Red Cedar Spey
Hook- TMC #7999
Bead- 3/16 Hot Bead
Thread- Bright Green 3/0 Gudebrod
Body- Pearl HT Braid
Hackle 1- Fl. Orange Marabou w/Gold G Flash
Hackle 2- Fl. Green Marabou
Note- another effective color combination is a solid white pattern with a fl. Red bead and pearl G Flash

You can purchase preceding three patterns at M. Chance Flyfishing Specialties, 5100 Marsh Road, Okemos, MI 48805, 517-349-6696 or on the web at www.tubeflies.com.

Cyclops
Hook- Tiemco #2457
Body- Green Sparkle Yarn
Head- 3/16" Brass Bead
Hackle- Pheasant Neck
Thread- Tan 6/0

The nymphs above can be obtained from the Instinct Rod and Fly Co., P.O. Box 3243, Grand Rapids, MI 49501, 616-774-4150, www.instinctrodandfly.com

Cyclops

Index

NOTES

WILDERNESS ADVENTURES GUIDE SERIES

If you would like to order additional copies of this book or our other Wilderness Adventures Press guidebooks, please fill out the order form below or call **1-800-925-3339** or **fax 800-390-7558.** Visit our website for a listing of over 2000 sporting books—the largest online: **www.wildadv.com**   **Mail To:**

Wilderness Adventures Press, Inc., 45 Buckskin Road • Belgrade, MT 59714

☐ **Please send me your quarterly catalog on hunting and fishing books.**

Ship to:

Name _____

Address _____

City _____ State _____ Zip _____

Home Phone_____ Work Phone_____

Payment: ☐ Check   ☐ Visa   ☐ Mastercard   ☐ Discover   ☐ American Express

Card Number _____ Expiration Date_____

Signature_____

Qty	Title of Book	Price	Total
	Flyfisher's Guide to Colorado	$26.95	
	Flyfisher's Guide to Idaho	$26.95	
	Flyfisher's Guide to Michigan	$26.95	
	Flyfisher's Guide to Montana	$26.95	
	Flyfisher's Guide to Northern California	$26.95	
	Flyfisher's Guide to Northern New England	$26.95	
	Flyfisher's Guide to Oregon	$26.95	
	Flyfisher's Guide to Pennsylvania	$26.95	
	Flyfisher's Guide to Washington	$26.95	
	Flyfisher's Guide to Minnesota	$26.95	
	Flyfisher's Guide to Utah	$26.95	
	Flyfisher's Guide to Texas	$26.95	
	Total Order + shipping & handling		

**Shipping and handling: $4.99 for first book,
$3.00 per additional book, up to $13.99 maximum**